Birnbaum's Walt Disney World®

Expert Advice from the Inside Source

Jill Safro EDITOR

Suzy Goytizolo SENIOR EDITOR

Keith Groshans ASSOCIATE ART DIRECTOR

Andrea Rotondo Hospidor CONTRIBUTING EDITOR

Linda Calderon EDITORIAL ASSISTANT

Alice Garrard CONTRIBUTING EDITOR

Alexandra Mayes Birnbaum CONSULTING EDITOR

Stephen Birnbaum FOUNDING EDITOR

DISNEY EDITIONS AND HEARST BUSINESS PUBLISHING, INC.

Table of

Getting Ready to Go

7

Here is all the practical information you need to organize a Walt Disney World visit, down to the smallest detail: when to go; how to get there; how to save money and work within a vacation budget; plus sample schedules, and hints for parents, travelers with disabilities, singles, and older visitors.

Transportation & Accommodations

43

Two big questions about Walt Disney World are where to stay and how to get around. Accommodations range from plush suites to modest campsites, with thousands of rooms, villas, even treehouses, in between. Our guide describes every Disney resort, along with some off-property options. And we explain the World's vast transportation system.

Magic Kingdom

89

The enchantment of Walt Disney World is most apparent in the wealth of attractions and amusements that fill this, the most famous entertainment zone of all. Our land-by-land guide describes all there is to see and do, where to shop, and how to avoid the crowds, plus plenty of other insider tips.

Epcot

119

A gleaming silver geosphere introduces Walt Disney World's wonderland of discovery—an ambitious exploration of the world of the future as well as the present. Future World and World Showcase offer every visitor the opportunity to be a global and cerebral voyager, without setting foot outside Florida. Here's how to make the most of this uniquely fascinating destination.

Disney-MGM Studios

151

Now's your chance to be part of Hollywood's golden years. Everything from the magic of animation to the excitement of daring stunts and special effects is waiting to be enjoyed. There are also opportunities to go behind the scenes and to create sound effects. We've developed strategies for seeing this Tinseltown, ensuring the most fun and the least time standing around.

Contents

Animal Kingdom

This latest addition to Disney's theme park lineup celebrates the circle of life and all the wonders of the animal world. Amid nature's soothing majesty, you'll experience a stirring African safari, dodge dastardly dinosaurs, and ride raging rapids. Our detailed coverage—which includes the park's newest land, Asia—guarantees a fun-filled trip to a place where humans are humbly reminded of their tenuous position in the food chain.

167

Everything Else in the World

Beyond the theme park boundaries lie countless acres full of just the sorts of wonders for which Walt Disney World is famous: state-of-the-art water parks, and a nighttime entertainment, shopping, and dining district among them. So if you want to ride down watery slides, dance the night away, shop at elegant boutiques, or even learn a few tricks of the trade by slipping behind the scenes, this chapter will help you find your way.

183

Sports

Walt Disney World has more tennis courts and golf greens than most posh resorts, plus plenty of places for boating, biking, horseback riding, swimming, and fishing. The rest of the sporting bases are covered by Disney's Wide World of Sports complex, a multi-sport facility that aims to please athlete and spectator alike. Here's how to combine these options with the rest of the fun at Walt Disney World.

205

Good Meals, Great Times

Restaurants around the Walt Disney World property run the gamut from simple snack shops to bastions of haute cuisine. Choices are nearly endless, so we've organized them into an area-by-area directory that lets you know where each restaurant is located and what specialties it offers, and a round-up of the dining spots we consider Birnbaum's Bests. We also tell you about the dinner shows, the best family fare, where to dine with Disney characters, and where to enjoy an after-dinner drink.

215

A WORD FROM THE EDITOR

For some of us, our first Walt Disney World experience dates back to 1971, the year this new "Disneyland in Florida" made its debut. At that time, the Magic Kingdom was the only theme park, and it could be explored easily in a few days. Early visitors will remember, too, that many of the attractions were still under construction. Nonetheless, for those who came, it was love at first sight, and we've returned again and again.

Never before has there been so much incentive to visit (and revisit) the memory-making capital of the world. We are both privileged and proud to provide readers with our extensively researched, insider look at some of the most cherished attractions on Earth.

The same sentiment applies to our exclusive coverage of recent additions, such as the exotic new resort, Disney's Animal Kingdom Lodge; the plush Wilderness Lodge Villas; and the high-flying new attraction, The Magic Carpets of Aladdin.

When Steve Birnbaum launched this guide back in 1981, he made it clear what was expected of anyone who worked on it. The book would be meticulously revised each year, leaving no attraction untested, no snack or meal untasted, no hotel untried. First-hand experiences like these, accumulated over the years, make this book the most authoritative guide to the World. Our expertise, however, was not achieved by being escorted through back doors of attractions (although we would have thoroughly enjoyed that). Instead, we've always waited in lines with everyone else, always hoping to have a Disney experience like that of any other guest. Happily, logistical pickles are few and far between, leaving us with ample time to investigate all the nooks and crannies of Walt's vast World.

After thirty fun-filled years, the World and the number of visitors have expanded—and so has our knowledge of the most popular vacation destination on the planet. On some occasions we've encountered sweltering weather and swelling crowds, times when even the happiest of families or best of friends turn into archenemies for a day. At times the lines seemed endless and, in a triumph of bad planning, we managed to take in just a few attractions before dinnertime. Had we known then what we know now, we could have spared ourselves some trying experiences. In one typical case, a staffer waited more than an hour to take a backstage tour at the Studios. Standing in line with a notebook, she was asked by another guest if there was a quiz at the end. When she explained what she was doing, he expressed surprise to learn that she was waiting with the rest of the masses. How better, she replied, to help people like you?

We've done our best to keep you from making any mistakes. We realize that even the most meticulous vacation planner needs detailed, accurate, and objective information to prepare an intelligent itinerary. Anyone who takes the time to read even the outlines of the pages that follow will find an emerging pattern that fits his or her special needs and tastes; for those unwilling to exert even that much effort, we've compiled specific daily itineraries to help you navigate the wonderful World of Disney.

This guidebook owes an enormous debt to the extraordinary people who manage and run Walt Disney World. Despite the designation "Official Guide," I want to stress that *the Walt Disney World staff members have exercised no veto power over the contents of this book.* What they *have* done is open their files and explain operations to us in the most generous way, so that we could prepare comprehensive appraisals to help visitors understand the complex workings of a very complex enterprise.

There have been times when the Disney folks were less than delighted with some of our opinions, yet these statements all remain in the guide. We've even sprinkled "Birnbaum's Bests" throughout the book, highlighting *our* favorite attractions and restaurants—the crowd-pleasers we believe stand head, shoulders, and ears above the rest.

You, the reader, benefit from the combination of our years of experience and our independent voice that, together with our access to accurate, up-to-date inside information from the Disney staff, makes this guide unique. We like to think it's indispensable, but we'll let you be the judge of that a few hundred pages from now.

The fact remains that this guide would never have become as useful as it is without the cooperation of Walt Disney World personnel at every level. Both in the park and behind the scenes, they've been the source of critical factual data. We hope we're not omitting any names in specifically thanking Chris Howd, Clark Galbreath, Sandy Hawkins (Entertainment); Craig Dezern, Rick Sylvain (Media Relations); Gene Duncan, Alain Boniec, Janice Hilliard (Photography); Tim Lewis (Disney Publishing); and Bo Boyd, Charlie Ridgway, Tina Rebstock, and Karen Haynes. To Linda Warren, Ken Potrock, Darlene Papalini, Laura Simpson, and Diane Hancock, who do so much to make our job easier, more thanks for their help. Special kudos to Kevin Banks and Darren Chiappetta, for the diligence with which they approached this project from beginning to end.

We'd also like to thank our favorite off-site Disney expert, Wendy Lefkon, who edited these guides for many years and is still instrumental in their publication as executive editor at Disney Editions. Hats off to editorial director Tom Passavant, for his discerning diplomacy and editorial expertise; Shari Hartford, for presiding over the press; Carolyn Ford Brunetto, for her creative contributions; and George Kimmerling and Sherie Holder, for their proofreading panache.

Of course, no list of acknowledgments would be complete without mentioning our founding editor, Steve Birnbaum, whose spirit, wisdom, and humor still infuse these pages, as well as Alexandra Mayes Birnbaum, who continues to be a guiding light—to say nothing of a careful reader of every word.

Finally, it's important to remember that every worthwhile travel guide is a living enterprise; the book you hold in your hands is our best effort at explaining how to enjoy Walt Disney World at this moment, but its text is in no way etched in stone. Walt Disney World is constantly changing and growing, and in each annual edition we refine and expand our material to serve your needs even better. For this year's edition, though, this must be the final word.

Have a great visit!

Don't Forget to Write

No contribution is of greater value to us in preparing the next edition of this book than your comments on what we have written and on your own experiences at Walt Disney World. Please share your insights with us by writing to:

The Editors, Official Disney Guides
Birnbaum's Walt Disney World 2001
1790 Broadway, Sixth Floor
New York, NY 10019

For Steve, who merely made all this possible

Other 2001 Birnbaum's Official Disney Guides

Disneyland
Walt Disney World For Kids, By Kids
Walt Disney World Without Kids

Getting Ready to Go

 8 **When to Go**

13 **How to Get There**

15 **Planning Ahead**

24 **Sample Schedules**

32 **Customized Travel Tips**

T he key to a fabulous vacation at Walt Disney World is advance planning. This remarkably varied complex is too vast and diverse to allow a spontaneous visit to be undertaken with much success—especially when you consider the rapid rate at which the World has expanded. That does not mean that even the most casual visitors can't have some significant fun, but they are bound to have regrets about things they missed because of time pressures or a simple lack of information. The main purpose of this guide is to eliminate that potential frustration.

What follows, then, is meant to provide a sensible scheme for planning a satisfying visit to Walt Disney World, one that will offer the most fun and the least amount of disappointment. But how do you know which of the countless activities will be the most enjoyable for you and your family? Do your homework—the best strategy is to make sure you have a clear idea of all that is available *before* you arrive in the Orlando area.

WHEN TO GO

When talk finally turns to the best time to make a trip to Walt Disney World, Christmas and Easter are often mentioned, as well as the traditional summer vacation period—especially if there are children in the family. But there is also good reason to avoid these periods, namely the tremendous crowds they attract. And when Disney World is crowded, it can be very crowded indeed. On the busiest days, visitors may wait as much as two hours to experience the more popular attractions. That's at least twice as long as during less busy times of the year.

Considering seasonal hours, weather, and the crowd patterns described in the charts that follow, optimal times to visit Walt Disney World are usually mid-January through early February, late April through late May, and September through December (except Thanksgiving and Christmas weeks).

HOT TIP The period between the end of Thanksgiving and the week before Christmas is one of the least crowded and most festive times of the year. It's a wonderful time to visit.

Note that during some of the less crowded times of the year—particularly during winter—some attractions are closed for renovations. In addition, water parks are often closed for refurbishment during cooler months. Call 407-939-4636 or check *www.disneyworld.com* for a current schedule, updated each season.

December is an especially festive time of year the world over, and Walt Disney World is no exception. All of the theme parks are decorated to the nines for the holiday season. The Magic Kingdom, Epcot, and the Disney-MGM Studios feature nightly tree-lighting ceremonies. Many other special events are held during this period, including Mickey's Very Merry Christmas Party in the Magic Kingdom (a separate admission ticket is required). The party brings a dusting of snow to Main Street from 8 P.M. to 1 A.M. for several days during the first three weeks of December. It also features holiday shows around the park, including Mickey's Very Merry Christmas Parade, plus a special finale of Fantasy in the Sky fireworks. Select performances from Mickey's Very Merry Christmas Party are also staged in the park during regular hours throughout the holiday season. Note that this event is extremely popular and usually sells out long ahead of time. Plan to purchase tickets in advance by calling 407-W-DISNEY (934-7639).

Epcot celebrates the season with Holidays Around the World, including the nightly Candlelight Processional, complete with 450-voice choir, 50-piece orchestra, and a reading of the story of Christmas by a celebrity narrator. Dinner packages are available for some World Showcase restaurants. (We recommend this package: It guarantees seating for dinner and preferred seating at the Candlelight Processional. Without the package, you should arrive at least one hour before showtime or risk being shut out of your preferred performance.) The Disney-MGM Studios features a display of about five million twinkling lights depicting holiday scenes. Special, complimentary eyeglasses add an extra touch of holiday cheer (they create a 3-D effect).

There are holiday decorations at each WDW hotel, too, including a Victorian Christmas at the Grand Floridian, a seaside party at the Yacht and Beach Club, a Southwestern Christmas at the Contemporary, and a Cajun holiday at Dixie Landings.

One way to take advantage of the festivities during this time of year is to book a Magical Holidays package, offered from late November through late December. Available for two to ten nights, most packages include unlimited admission to the theme parks and Pleasure Island. For reservations, contact a travel agent or call 407-W-DISNEY (934-7639) or the Walt Disney Travel Company at 800-828-0228. Note that special event tickets are also available separately. Call 407-934-7630 for information on how and when to purchase them.

Crowd Patterns

Day-to-Day Trends

Many visitors to Walt Disney World assume that weekends are the busiest days in the parks—and they generally are quite crowded. However, with the exception of certain holiday periods, each park tends to be the most crowded on its "surprise morning" (early-entry) days: Monday, Thursday, and Saturday at the Magic Kingdom; Tuesday and Friday at Epcot; and Wednesday and Sunday at the Disney-MGM Studios. Saturdays and Sundays are among the busier days at Disney's Animal Kingdom (it does not offer surprise mornings.)

When the time comes to plot an itinerary, it's helpful to know about crowd patterns beyond the four theme parks as well. As a rule, Downtown Disney (Pleasure Island, the Marketplace, and the West Side) and Disney's water parks host their largest throngs on weekends. Of course, in these circles, a bigger crowd can mean a better time.

Golfers should note that weekend tee times are typically in the highest demand, while Monday and Tuesday tee times are the easiest to come by.

Seasonal Shifts

The chart below indicates the density of crowds in the theme parks throughout the year. Though it's tough to generalize about a property as vast and ever-changing as Walt Disney World—special events and package deals can swell park attendance during a period typically marked by smaller crowds—the chart highlights historic trends.

"Least crowded" means that there may be lines, but most attractions can be visited without much waiting. "Average attendance" refers to times when there are lots of people around, but lines are manageable. "Most crowded" reflects times when lines at popular attractions can mean a wait of as much as two hours.

Least Crowded

- 2nd week of January through 1st week of February

- Week after Labor Day until Thanksgiving

- Week after Thanksgiving through week before Christmas

Average Attendance

- 1st week of January

- 2nd week of February until Presidents' week

- End of February through 2nd week of March

- Last week of April through May

- Thanksgiving week

Most Crowded

- Presidents' week

- 3rd week of March through 3rd week of April

- June through Labor Day

- Christmas through New Year's Day

Keeping WDW Hours

Since operating hours do fluctuate, we advise calling 407-WDW-INFO (939-4636) or visiting *www.disneyworld.com* for current schedules. The automated system is updated every three months or so.

THEME PARKS: Disney theme park hours vary seasonally. For more than a third of the year—in May, September, October, parts of November and December, and all of January—the Magic Kingdom is usually open from 9 A.M. to 7 P.M.; Epcot is open from 9 A.M. to 9 P.M. (Some parts of Future World open at 8:30 A.M., the rest opens at 9 A.M., World Showcase opens at 11 A.M.); the Disney-MGM Studios is open from 9 A.M. until about an hour after dusk; and Animal Kingdom is open from about 8 A.M. until about an hour after dusk.

The Magic Kingdom keeps later hours through summer and other busy periods. Epcot and the Disney-MGM Studios stay open until midnight during holiday periods (Thanksgiving, Christmas, and Easter). The parks are usually open until 1 A.M. or 2 A.M. on New Year's Eve. The Disney-MGM Studios often stays open until 11 P.M. in the summer, too. On select days, WDW resort guests can enter the Magic Kingdom, Epcot, or the Disney-MGM Studios up to 1½ hours before the official opening time. Note that only some attractions in a given park open early. For details about early-entry days, see "Park Primer" in each park chapter (pages 92, 122, 154, and 169).

DOWNTOWN DISNEY MARKETPLACE: Shops are usually open from 9:30 A.M. until 11 P.M. daily. Restaurant hours vary.

DOWNTOWN DISNEY PLEASURE ISLAND: Clubs are open from about 7 P.M. to 2 A.M. daily; shops, from 11 A.M. to 2 A.M.; and restaurants, from about 11:30 A.M. to midnight. Admission must be purchased after 7 P.M.

DOWNTOWN DISNEY WEST SIDE: At the AMC Theatres cineplex, movies are shown beginning at about 1 P.M. Restaurants are generally open from about 11:30 A.M. to 2 A.M. Shops are open from 10:30 A.M. to 11 P.M.

WATER PARKS: Although hours vary, the water parks are generally open from about 10 A.M. to 5 P.M., with extended hours in effect during summer months.

WDW WEATHER

	TEMPERATURE		RAINFALL
	AVERAGE		AVERAGE
	HIGH	LOW	(INCHES)
January	71	49	2.3
February	73	50	3.0
March	78	55	3.2
April	83	59	1.8
May	88	66	3.6
June	91	72	7.3
July	92	73	7.2
August	92	73	6.8
September	90	72	6.0
October	85	65	2.4
November	79	58	2.3
December	73	51	2.2

Holidays & Special Events

Special affairs are staged throughout the year, not only to mark holidays but also to celebrate other interests. The four theme parks and Downtown Disney host many happenings, from sporting events to festivals geared toward jazz, technology, and even soap operas. The dates listed below are subject to change without notice; call 407-WDW-INFO (939-4636) or check out *www.disneyworld.com* for additional information about specific events.

JANUARY

Walt Disney World Marathon (January 7): Some 15,000 entrants run through several theme parks, Disney's Wide World of Sports complex, and many other scenic areas of the World during this 26.2-mile race. Live bands, hot-air balloons, and Disney characters are on hand to inspire runners. There's also a 5K run for children. Special packages are available. Call 407-939-7810 for additional information.

FEBRUARY

Mardi Gras (February): Jazz bands, Creole food, and energetic street performers toast New Orleans' biggest party at Pleasure Island. At Epcot, visit World Showcase to see how other countries celebrate Mardi Gras. Nowhere is the atmosphere more festive than at Disney's Port Orleans resort, where the Mardi Gras mood is maintained year-round.

Black Heritage Celebration (February): Disney honors African-American achievers during Black History Month.

MARCH

Saint Patrick's Day (March 17): Everyone is Irish on Saint Patrick's Day—especially at Pleasure Ire-land. Epcot's United Kingdom pavilion marks the day with Irish dining and dancing, plus special appearances by a leprechaun or two. Don't forget to wear green while you celebrate the Emerald Isle.

APRIL

Epcot International Flower and Garden Festival (April 20–June 3): Epcot is blooming with elaborate gardens (including more than 30 million blossoms) and topiary displays, behind-the-scenes tours, gardening workshops, and guest speakers. Learn from the experts how to create a beautiful garden of your own.

Easter (April 15): An elaborate parade in the Magic Kingdom helps make this holiday celebration special. All of the Disney theme parks stay open late during the two weeks straddling the Easter holiday. Keep in mind that this is an extremely busy time to visit.

MAY

Star Wars Weekends (May): The Disney-MGM Studios celebrates the quartet of classic *Star Wars* films on weekends throughout the month.

JUNE

Black Music Month Celebration (June): Pleasure Island showcases gospel, rap, R & B, reggae, jazz, and more.

JULY

Fourth of July Celebration: Double-size fireworks over the Magic Kingdom, Epcot, and the Disney-MGM Studios make for an extremely colorful night. Pleasure Island kicks off the Independence Day festivities with fireworks at 12:01 A.M. on the evening of the Fourth (preceded by a lineup of special entertainment). River Country celebrates Independence Day all summer long with the All-American Water Party. This is a very busy time to visit.

SEPTEMBER

Official Disneyana Convention (September): A veritable heaven for Disney collectors. Packages, which include accommodations, are necessary for full admission to the auction, seminars, and behind-the-scenes tours.

Note: The 2001 convention may take place at Disneyland, in Anaheim, CA. For up-to-the-minute information, call 407-827-7600 or visit *www.officialdisneyana.com*.

Night of Joy (September): Two nights of celebration highlight contemporary Christian music. For dates and to purchase tickets, call 407-827-7200 or TicketMaster. Note that this very popular event attracts a bit of a rowdy crowd (of mostly teens and young adults).

OCTOBER

Teddy Bear & Doll Convention (October): Collectors flock to the Contemporary resort and Epcot to see world-renowned craftspeople's creations. Packages are required for full participation and include accommodations, theme park tickets, seminars and workshops, an auction, a limited-edition private sale, parties, and an awards ceremony. For information, call 407-827-7600.

National Car Rental Golf Classic (October 14–22): Top PGA Tour players compete alongside amateurs in this big tourney, played on the Palm and Magnolia courses. Special packages are available. For more information, call 407-824-2250.

Epcot International Food and Wine Festival (October 21–November 19): World Showcase celebrates the flavors of a variety of countries (even those not usually represented on the lagoon) through tastings ($1 to $3 per sample), demonstrations from top chefs, and wine and cooking seminars. It's an extremely satisfying way in which to wander World Showcase.

Halloween (October 28–31): The festivities vary from year to year. Past celebrations have included spooky window displays, performances by storytellers, and giveaways at Epcot's World Showcase.

Fort Wilderness Resort and Campground generally hosts a pumpkin-carving contest and a children's costume contest, followed by a screening of a scary movie.

Downtown Disney has hosted children's costume contests. (Shops dispensed candy to trick-or-treaters.) Grown-up ghouls have competed in a costume contest at the Hub Stage at Pleasure Island.

For specifics about what's on tap for this year's celebration, call 407-W-DISNEY as the calendar begins to approach October.

The Magic Kingdom will certainly play host to its usual Halloween spectacular: **Mickey's Not-So-Scary Halloween Party** (October 28–31). The special-ticket activities include a Halloween costume parade, dancing, appearances by Disney villains, trick-or-treating, and fireworks. This is an extremely popular Magic Kingdom event. Plan to purchase your tickets as far in advance as possible.

NOVEMBER

Festival of the Masters (November): This three-day fine arts show draws more than 200 top artists to Downtown Disney.

ABC Super Soap Weekend (November 10–11): A celebration of ABC daytime dramas is held at the Disney-MGM Studios. Guests can meet soap stars; collect autographs; compete in trivia contests; and see sets, props, and costumes. For more information, call 407-397-6808.

Pleasure Island Jazz Fest (November): Great jazz music is performed for one entire weekend throughout the island.

DECEMBER

Disney's Magical Holidays (December): Decorations and festivities abound in Walt Disney World's parks and resorts. The Magic Kingdom hosts **Mickey's Very Merry Christmas Party** on several nights during the first three weeks of December, complete with snow flurries on Main Street and hot cocoa. Entertainment for the special-ticket party includes **Mickey's Very Merry Christmas Parade** and a holiday edition of the fireworks; select performances are staged during regular hours throughout the holiday season.

Epcot's **Holidays Around the World** features "The Lights of Winter," and a Candlelight Processional, including a choral concert. The Candlelight Processional is free, but seating is limited and the event is popular. Arrive at least an hour before showtime or book a dinner package (which combines dinner at a World Showcase eatery with guaranteed seating at the Processional). For information call 407-939-3463.

The Osborne Family Spectacle of Lights brightens the Disney-MGM Studios with about five million lights on Residential Street. This popular free event is open after dark. Complimentary holographic glasses enhance the thrilling visual extravaganza.

Many vacation packages include admission to special-ticket parties. For more information on these events and the Magical Holidays packages, call the Walt Disney Travel Company at 800-828-0228. Note that, for some special events, it is also possible to purchase tickets separately.

New Year's Eve Celebration (December 31): There are extra-large fireworks displays over the Magic Kingdom, Epcot, and the Disney-MGM Studios. (The Magic Kingdom and Epcot are open until 2 A.M. and the Studios is open until 1 A.M. for the event.) Pleasure Island hosts a grand special-ticket bash. Many of the resorts, as well as the night spots at Downtown Disney West Side, also welcome the new year Disney-style.

HOW TO GET THERE

By Car

While most visitors to the Orlando area fly in, some prefer to drive. If you opt for a road trip, pack lots of CDs and tapes and figure on logging 350 to 400 miles a day—a reasonable distance that won't wear you down so much that you can't enjoy your trip.

Contact state tourist boards to inquire about the availability of free maps; for a Florida map and guide, call 888-735-2872. Other sources for maps are the *Rand McNally Road Atlas* and the *AAA North American Road Atlas*; both are sold in bookstores. Driving directions from most cities are also available on the Internet. One site to try is *www.mapquest.com*.

DID YOU KNOW...

It's perfectly legal to make a right turn at a red light on roads throughout the state of Florida.

Reputable automobile clubs offer help with breakdowns; towing; insurance that covers personal injury, accidents, arrest, bail bond, and lawyers' fees for defense of contested traffic cases; and travel-planning services, including free maps and route mapping. Services vary from one club to the next, and membership fees range widely, from $50 to $90 a year. (For more information, refer to page 14.)

From the Airport

By car: During rush hour, take the airport's South Exit to the Central Florida Greeneway (Route 417) to Route 536, which leads to Walt Disney World. The tolls run about $2.

For the shortest route to WDW, take the North Exit to Route 528 (Beeline Expressway), going west toward Tampa. Pick up I-4 west, and follow it to the appropriate WDW exit. The trip takes about half an hour, and tolls are $1.25. This route is heavily trafficked.

Shuttles: It's easy to get to WDW from Orlando International Airport without a car. Mears Motor Shuttle offers vans every 15 to 20 minutes around the clock, serving Disney resorts, Hotel Plaza Boulevard properties, and other hotels. On the return trip to the airport, Mears requires guests to be picked up at least 2 hours prior to their flight departure times. Reservations must be made 24 hours ahead.

The cost to most hotels is $14 one way, $27 round-trip per adult; $10 one way, $17 round-trip per child age 4 through 11; free for children under 4. Fares to International Drive properties are $2 to $4 lower. Call 407-423-5566 for information.

Car service: Florida Towncars offers service to Disney resorts for a flat rate of $75 round-trip (for up to five passengers). Call 407-277-5466 or 800-525-7246.

By Air

Each year, millions of visitors funnel through Orlando International Airport, where sleek monorail trains transport passengers to and from the central terminal, and a well-stocked Disney merchandise store portends what's to come.

When it comes to airfares, there is a trick to unearthing the most economical ones: Shop around. Call a travel agent, and keep these tips in mind:

• Watch your local newspapers for ads announcing short-term promotional fares. When a deal presents itself, grab it.

• The more flexible you can be in your dates and duration of stay, the more money you're likely to save.

• Take advantage of advance-purchase fares (lower rates that apply if a ticket is bought at least two to three weeks prior to departure).

• Keep in mind that the lowest airfares usually carry a penalty if you have to revise your flight schedule, and that certain discounted tickets are nonrefundable.

• When you call to make a reservation, inquire about any applicable fare restrictions, including an obligatory Saturday night stayover.

• Fly when most people don't: For vacation destinations, that usually means leaving the ground midweek.

• If a fare comes down after you've purchased a ticket, you can request a refund from the airline.

• Check out airline websites. Often they will e-mail you with information about special discounted fares.

By Train

Amtrak serves the Orlando area twice daily from New York City, with various stops made along the way. The trip takes

approximately 22 hours and costs from $150 to $408 round-trip, coach. (Book as early as possible for lower fares; discounts are often available, so be sure to ask.) If you're staying at Walt Disney World, plan to disembark at the station in Kissimmee instead of Orlando. It's closer and cab fares are cheaper. Rental cars are available by shuttle.

For reservations and information on this and other routes, call 800-USA-RAIL (872-7245), visit the Amtrak website at *www.amtrak.com*, or contact a travel agent.

By Bus

Relatively few vacationers travel to Walt Disney World by bus. But the bus can be economical, although the greater the distance involved, the more likely the lowest available airfare will be competitive.

Greyhound provides frequent direct service to Orlando and Kissimmee (the latter is closer to Walt Disney World). From either destination, you can take a taxi to your hotel, but first check to see if your hotel offers shuttle service.

For additional information, contact Greyhound at 800-231-2222.

PLANNING AHEAD
Logistics

Organizing a trip properly takes time, but most travelers find the increased enjoyment well worth the effort. The fact is, planning can become a pleasant sort of "armchair" exercise, and kids will enjoy their visit to Walt Disney World all the more if they, too, are involved in the process.

To assist in that effort, we immodestly recommend *Birnbaum's Walt Disney World For Kids, By Kids,* a colorful look at the World from a young person's perspective, written for readers ages 7 through 14. For adults traveling *sans* children, *Birnbaum's Walt Disney World Without Kids* is the definitive source.

Information Sources

For information about Walt Disney World, call 407-WDW-INFO (939-4636). Lots of current specifics, such as park hours, ticket prices, refurbishment schedules, and directions, are available through an automated system 24 hours a day. To speak with a representative, call weekdays 7 A.M. to 7 P.M. or weekends 7 A.M. to 8 P.M. For information by mail, write to Walt Disney World; Box 10000; Lake Buena Vista, FL 32830-1000.

Internet users can tap into updates about the World, get information on trip planning, reserve a room, order tickets, and get theme park hours and special events listings by entering *www.disneyworld.com.* Disney Cruise Line vacation packages may be booked at *www.disneycruise.com.*

For information and discounts on area attractions, restaurants, and hotels, contact the Official Visitor Information Center; 8723 International Dr., Suite 101; Orlando, FL 32819; 407-363-5871 or 800-551-0181. Another good website listing Orlando-area happenings is *www.go2orlando.com.*

For details about other Central Florida attractions, contact Visit Florida; Box 1100; Tallahassee, FL 32302; 888-735-2872 (to request a free visitors guide and map) or 850-224-6360; *www.flausa.com.*

Front-desk employees at Walt Disney World resorts may ask to see a photo ID upon check-in. Don't forget to pack one!

Disney Information Center: This full-service visitors center, located at the intersection of I-75 and S.R. 200 in Ocala, Florida, about 90 miles north of Orlando, can help WDW-bound vacationers plan their time, book (or confirm) hotel reservations, purchase park tickets, and even make priority seating arrangements. For departing guests who didn't buy enough Mouse ears, it also stocks character merchandise; 352-854-0770.

What to Pack

While there is hardly a dress code at Walt Disney World, casual clothing is the rule, with few exceptions. Most notably, jackets are required for men at Victoria & Albert's restaurant in the Grand Floridian resort. More generally, T-shirts and shorts are perfectly acceptable during the day. For evening, slacks, jeans, or Bermuda shorts are appropriate. Bathing suits are a must, along with the appropriate attire for any sport you want to pursue.

Lightweight sweaters are necessary even in summer—to wear indoors when the air-conditioning gets chilly. From November through March, warmer clothing is a must for evening. Pack for weather extremes so you'll be comfy should it become unseasonably warm or cool. Always bring plenty of sunscreen, and don't forget the bug spray. If possible, pack lightweight rain gear and a compact umbrella. The most important item of all? Comfortable walking shoes.

On-Site Resources: Those staying at Walt Disney World resorts should consider their hotel's Guest Services desk the primary resource. Resort guests also receive WDW information via their room's TV. Fort Wilderness campers are advised to stop at the Pioneer Hall Information and Ticket Window, call extension 2788, or touch 11 on a phone near any restroom.

Guests at the resorts on Hotel Plaza Boulevard can access a tourist-information TV program of their own. Some other area hotels also show a version of the orientation, usually aiming to provide an overview of all Central Florida attractions.

For Day Visitors: All day visitors—that is, those staying off Disney property or living in the Orlando area—receive a useful handout at the Auto Plazas (if you don't, just ask). When purchasing one-day admission to a given theme park, guests receive a complimentary guidemap to that park. Multi-day passholders may receive all four park guides upon request. Extra guidemaps are available at City Hall (in the Magic Kingdom) and at Guest Relations (in Epcot, the Disney-MGM Studios, and Disney's Animal Kingdom), as well as in many park shops and restaurants.

Package Pointers

The sheer number and diversity of packages offering vacations in Central Florida are enough to bewilder even the savviest traveler. Still, such plans are worth exploring. They offer the convenience of a vacation that's completely organized in advance, and one that will generally cost less than the sum of the same transportation, accommodations, and admission elements purchased separately. In addition, since most package providers purchase blocks of Disney rooms, they are an excellent source for securing a room on Disney property when the hotel of your choice is booked.

American Airlines Vacations (800-321-2121), Delta Vacations (800-872-7786), TWA Getaway Vacations (800-438-2929), US Airways Vacations (800-455-0123), American Express Travel (800-297-6898), and The Walt Disney Travel Company (800-828-0228 or *www.disneytravel.com*) offer packages

featuring Walt Disney World on-site hotels, as well as off-property accommodations. Many packages include the added attraction of low-cost air transportation. The American Automobile Association (800-564-6222) offers AAA Vacations and other travel packages, which include certain perks. For other possibilities, such as Kingdom Vacations or Go Go Tours, check the travel section of your local newspaper or consult a travel agent.

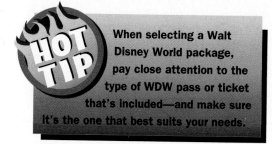

When selecting a Walt Disney World package, pay close attention to the type of WDW pass or ticket that's included—and make sure it's the one that best suits your needs.

The Walt Disney Travel Company's offerings run from value to deluxe lodging, with airfare, theme park admission, or rental car sometimes included. Certain packages allow you to add a meal plan or recreation options. Some WDW vacation plans are available year-round; others, such as Magical Holidays, Sunshine Getaway, and Fall Fantasy, are offered seasonally. Others are designed around a specific type of vacation—a golf getaway, a honeymoon—and include special elements, such as unlimited tee times or champagne upon arrival. Still others are tied to an annual Walt Disney World event, such as the Walt Disney World Marathon (see "Holidays & Special Events" on page 11 of this chapter). Finally, add-on escapes allow guests to combine a Walt Disney World vacation with a stay at the Disney resort at Vero Beach or a cruise to the Bahamas (see pages 69 and 78–79 in the *Transportation & Accommodations* chapter for more information about these options).

The value of a package depends on your specific needs. Before considering the options, use this book to help determine which of the myriad of accommodations, activities, and attractions at Walt Disney World most appeal to you. There's real value in some package elements, such as airport transfers and meal discounts. Several packages also include meals with the Disney characters, tennis lessons, golf greens fees, tennis court fees, boat rentals, and the like. Never choose a package that includes elements you don't want or won't have time to enjoy. While extras such as welcoming cocktails may sound appealing, their cash value is negligible. Also beware of any packages that tout as selling points certain services that are available to every Walt Disney World guest.

All About Theme Park Tickets

Disney defines a ticket as admission for one day only; admission media that are valid for longer periods are called passes. Passes are non-transferable. Prices and ticket options are subject to change. Call 407-WDW-INFO (939-4636) for current information.

Ticket and Multi-day Pass Options

One-Day Ticket: One-day tickets are valid for admission to one park only—the Magic Kingdom, Epcot, the Disney-MGM Studios, or Disney's Animal Kingdom. (The one day ticket does not allow for park-hopping.)

Park Hopper Pass: This pass can be used at all four theme parks—Magic Kingdom, Epcot, the Disney-MGM Studios, and Animal Kingdom—on the same day. It includes use of WDW transportation. Available for four or five days which need not be used consecutively. Unused days never expire.

At the end of your visit, make a note of the number of unused days on a multi-day pass. Write it on the pass itself.

Park Hopper Plus Pass: Available for five, six, or seven days, this pass is one of the more comprehensive options. It can be used at all four theme parks on the same day. Passholders are also given a number of "plus" options to choose from: admission to Blizzard Beach, Typhoon Lagoon, River Country, Disney's Wide World of Sports complex, or Pleasure Island. Five-Day Park Hopper Passes include

two plus options, Six-Day Park Hoppers include three plus options, and Seven-Day Hoppers include four plus options. Days and plus options need not be used consecutively and never expire. Includes use of Walt Disney World transportation.

DID YOU KNOW...

The phrase "E-ticket ride" is American slang for "the ultimate in thrills." It comes from the early days of Disney parks, back when tickets were used for each attraction. E-tickets were reserved for the most exciting rides of all.

Ultimate Park Hopper Pass: WDW resort guests can buy a multi-day pass geared to the length of their visit. It offers unlimited admission to the theme parks, water parks, Disney's Wide World of Sports complex, Pleasure Island, and DisneyQuest for the length of a guest's stay. *This pass expires on the evening of check-out.*

Theme Park Annual Pass: This pass offers unlimited admission to the four theme parks for a year. It can be used in more than one park on the same day (also known as park-hopping), and includes use of the Walt Disney World transportation system, as well as free parking anywhere on WDW property. Annual passes may only be purchased at the entrance to any of the theme parks. A photo ID must be presented for purchase by adults and may be required for future use of the pass. Annual passes are non-transferable.

Annual pass-bearers (including those who have the Premium Annual Pass described below) qualify for many WDW discounts and benefits, such as reduced rates at select Disney resorts at certain times of year. A special newsletter called the *Mickey Monitor* keeps passholders up-to-date regarding discount offers. The pass expires one year after it is purchased. A discounted "renewal rate" applies if the pass is renewed within one month of expiration. (The expired pass must be presented to receive the discounted renewal rate.) A pass may be renewed by mail or at the entrance to any theme park.

Premium Annual Pass: This pass has everything the Theme Park Annual Pass has to offer and more—namely, unlimited

E-Ride Nights

Imagine having the Magic Kingdom practically to yourself for an entire evening. It can happen if you're a WDW resort guest with a multi-day pass and ten dollars to spare. The E-Ride pass lets you stay in the Magic Kingdom *after* it closes to enjoy the park's best attractions time and time again. It's only available on select nights throughout the year, so ask about it when you check in.

admission to the water parks, Disney's Wide World of Sports complex, and Pleasure Island for a year. Premium Annual Passholders are eligible for the same discounts and benefits as Theme Park Annual Passholders; Premium Annual Passes may only be purchased at the entrance to any of the four theme parks. A photo ID must be presented for purchase by adults (kids need not show ID) and may be required for future use. Premium Annual Passes are non-transferable. These passes expire one year after purchase.

Deciding Factors

Choosing the Right Ticket: Only have a few days? Pick which parks you'd like to visit and purchase day passes. Single-day tickets are valid for admission to one park only, while most multi-day passes can be used at all parks on the same day. Will you have time to explore the rest of the World? Consider the Park Hopper Plus Pass. If you plan to concentrate on theme parks, buy a Four- or Five-Day Park Hopper Pass.

If you're not sure how many unused days remain on a park pass, stop by Guest Relations at any of the theme parks. They'll know.

Disney resort guests can get an Ultimate Park Hopper Pass, good practically everywhere for the entire trip. The downside? Unused days on the Ultimate Park Hopper Pass expire. The Park Hopper Plus has some limitations, but unused days and "plus" options never expire. Before you purchase the Ultimate Park Hopper Pass, create a day-by-day itinerary to determine if you'll have time (and energy) to make use of all it has to offer.

If you are planning a longer visit, or two trips within a year, we highly recommend an annual pass. In addition to unlimited admission to the theme parks, you'll get discounts on everything from dinner shows to room rates.

Note: Only one person per party need possess an annual pass to net a discount on a resort rate. This option is great for travelers with flexible vacation schedules, as the discounts do vary and are often announced just weeks before they go into effect.

Passes with Unused Days: Remaining days on any multi-day pass—with the exception of those on the Ultimate Park Hopper—may be used during a future visit to Walt Disney World. They never expire.

ADMISSION PRICES

ONE-DAY TICKET
Adult $48.76
Child* $39.22

PARK HOPPER PASS
Four Days
Adult $186.56
Child* $150.52

Five Days
Adult $218.36
Child* $177.02

PARK HOPPER PLUS PASS
Five Days
Adult $250.18
Child* $203.53

Six Days
Adult $281.99
Child* $230.03

Seven Days
Adult $313.79
Child* $256.54

ULTIMATE PARK HOPPER PASS

Length of Stay	Adult	Child*
2 days	$115.55	$92.24
3 days	$157.96	$126.76
4 days	$210.95	$168.56
5 days	$253.36	$203.53
6 days	$285.16	$230.03
7 days	$316.97	$256.54
8 days	$338.77	$283.05
9 days	$375.27	$298.94
10 days	$401.77	$314.85

THEME PARK ANNUAL PASS
Adult $343.44
Child* $291.50

Renewals
Adult $309.52
Child* $262.88

PREMIUM ANNUAL PASS
Adult $460.07
Child* $391.16

Renewals
Adult $414.48
Child* $351.95

Prices include sales tax and were correct at press time. Call 407-939-4636 to confirm.

*3 through 9 years of age; children under 3 free

For those of us who'd prefer not to waste time standing in line for theme park attractions, Disney's Fastpass is nothing short of a miracle. Basically, the system allows guests to forego the task of waiting in an actual line for a number of theme park attractions. How? Simply by walking up to the Fastpass booth (located near the entrance of participating attractions) and slipping their park pass into the Fastpass machine. In return, guests get a slip of paper with a time printed on it (in addition to the safe return of their park passes). That time, for example 12:20 P.M. to 1:20 P.M., represents the window in which guests are invited to return to the attraction and practically walk right on—without standing in a long line! Once you use your Fastpass to enter an attraction (or the time on it has passed), you can get a new Fastpass time for another attraction. It's also possible to get a Fastpass for a second attraction two hours after the first one is issued. For example, if one pass was issued at 12 P.M. you can get a Fastpass for another attraction at 2 P.M. Sound confusing? It won't be once you've tried it.

Disney's Fastpass service is free and available to everyone bearing a valid theme park pass. It should be available during peak times of the day and all peak seasons. We've placed the Fastpass logo (see above) beside the listing for all of the attractions that were participating at press time. However, since more attractions are scheduled for inclusion, check a park map for an up-to-the-minute listing of Fastpass attractions.

Note that all attractions continue to offer the option of standing in a traditional line. If you happen to enjoy the standing-in-line experience, by all means, go for it. Otherwise, take our advice: Fastpass is the way to go!

Purchasing Tickets and Passes

Admission media are sold at park entrances, WDW resorts, the resorts on Hotel Plaza Boulevard, Orlando International Airport, the Transportation and Ticket Center (TTC), and Downtown Disney Guest Services. Cash, traveler's checks, personal checks (with ID), American Express, Visa, MasterCard, Discover, Diner's Club, JCB Card, and The Disney Credit Card are accepted. Not all passes are available at each location, so be sure to check. Call 407-939-4636 to confirm.

We recommend buying passes in advance from a travel agent, or in one of these ways:

Passes by Phone: Multi-day passes can be purchased by phone; call 407-939-4636. There is a $3 handling fee. Allow two to three weeks for delivery.

Passes Online: Multi-day passes can be purchased through Walt Disney World's website (*www.disneyworld.com*). There is a $3 handling fee. Allow three weeks for delivery.

Passes at The Disney Store: Select multi-day theme park passes are available for purchase at The Disney Store.

Passes by Mail: (multi-day passes only) Allow three to four weeks for requests to be processed, and include a return address. Send a check or money order (for the exact amount plus $3 for handling), payable to Walt Disney World Company, to:

Walt Disney World
Box 10140
Lake Buena Vista, FL 32830-0030
Attention: Ticket Mail Order

Money-Saving Tips

While there's no denying that a Walt Disney World vacation can be a very expensive undertaking, it is possible to keep costs down. When budgeting for your trip, keep in mind that WDW prices are comparable to those in a large city. Here are a few tips to help you conserve cash.

LODGING

§ When it comes to saving money on accommodations, timing is truly the key. While off-season dates tend to vary, depending on the hotel, value season for most Walt Disney World resorts generally means January through mid-February, late August through late September, and early November through late December.

§ Consider how much time you will actually spend at your hotel, and don't pay for a place with perks you won't have time to enjoy. Hotels often allow kids to stay free in parents' rooms, but the cutoff age does vary. Budget chains are economical but usually offer few frills.

§ When considering the cost-effectiveness of off-property lodging, factor in the time, money, and inconvenience of commuting to and from attractions.

§ Realize, too, that the advantages of staying on-property (access to WDW transportation tops among them) also apply to those staying in the least expensive rooms in Disney's hotels. The most important addresses for budget-watching Disney fans, the three All-Star resorts, offer the lowest rates on Walt Disney World property. Rooms at Caribbean Beach, Dixie Landings, Port Orleans, and Coronado Springs are slightly higher priced. Also, note that the only difference between the least and most expensive rooms in a hotel is often the view. Consider how often you'll be looking out that window. See the *Transportation & Accommodations* chapter for more information.

FOOD

§ Visit the fancier dining establishments at lunchtime (if you so desire) rather than at dinner; the same entrées often cost less for the midday meal.

§ Sometimes certain Epcot eateries have early-bird dinner deals; it pays to ask.

§ Carry sandwich fixings and have lunches alfresco when possible (keeping in mind that outside food is not welcome inside Disney theme parks).

HOT TIP

Picnics are permitted in all of the water parks at Walt Disney World. (But not at any of the theme parks.)

§ Look for lodging with kitchen facilities: The savings on food, especially at breakfast time, may be more than the extra accommodations expense.

§ Refrigerators are available for about $10 a day at many Disney resorts.

§ A souvenir mug can be purchased at most resorts, good for refills during your stay at the resort. (Note that similar mugs are sold in the theme parks, but do not come with free refills.)

§ The Trail's End Buffet at Fort Wilderness has an inexpensive, yet very satisfying, all-you-can-eat country breakfast buffet.

www.disneyworld.com

So you've made the big decision to go to Disney World. What are you going to do now? Go to *www.disneyworld.com!* In addition to finding current theme park hours, special event information, Fastpass updates, color photos, and the lowdown on what's new, you can reserve a room at a Walt Disney World resort, purchase a vacation package, order Disney theme park admission passes, and much more.

Satisfying Substitutes

Fewer frills rarely mean less fun at Walt Disney World. Here are money-saving alternatives to two of Disney's higher-priced treats.

If you'd rather not spring for the Hoop-Dee-Doo Musical Revue dinner show (about $45 per adult, $32 per child, dinner included) then try the Diamond Horseshoe Saloon Revue for lunch (the show is included with Magic Kingdom admission; lunch options range from $5 to $10 per person). The jokes may not be quite as side-splitting, and the food is not of the all-you-can-eat variety, but the saloon-hall experience is certainly similar and the show is very appealing.

If the Grand Floridian ($314–$710 a night) doesn't quite fit into your budget, consider staying in a Mansion room at Dixie Landings ($129–$199 a night). Southern society replaces Victorian splendor, and the guestrooms aren't quite as spacious, but the understated elegance and air of sophistication make for a most satisfying stay.

DISCOUNTS

$ Membership in the Disney Club (formerly the Magic Kingdom Club) nets discounts on Disney vacation packages (including the Disney Cruise Line); park admission; car rentals; select theme park restaurant meals; select merchandise at Downtown Disney Marketplace, Pleasure Island, and in The Disney Store and The Disney Catalog; and more. Just ask if they offer the discount before making a purchase. Many companies offer free membership in the Disney Club as an employee benefit. Otherwise, the Gold Card costs $65 for a two-year family membership ($50 for seniors 55 and over and for Disney Company stockholders). Outside the United States, it's $85. For information, call 800-893-4763 or go to *www.disney.com*. Allow at least two weeks to receive membership materials. (*Specifics regarding Disney Club membership were correct at press time, but are subject to change.*)

Only one member of a party need have an annual pass to secure an annual pass room rate.

$ Theme Park Annual and Premium Annual Passholders receive so many discounts on meals, dinner shows, tours, room rates, and more that it may be worth purchasing an annual pass for longer visits or if you plan to take more than one trip within a year. Although the pass entitles the bearer to a slew of discounts, the potential for reduced room rates is by far the most valuable of them all. The lineup of Disney resorts that offer Annual Passholder rates varies from month to month (with occasional periods devoid of any special offers), and discounted rooms aren't always available for booking more than a month or so in advance (although we've been able to get reservations as far as a season ahead). It's best to be flexible with your travel dates. Call 407-560-PASS (560-7277) for specifics.

$ American Express cardholders can net discounts on everything from meals and merchandise to behind-the-scenes tours—when paid for with the American Express card, of course. For information, call 407-934-7639.

$ Discounts on Disney resort rates and theme park tickets are available to Florida residents, and other seasonal promotions occur. Call 407-WDW-INFO (939-4636) for details.

$ Several off-property hotels offer discounts to seniors and AAA or AARP members as well. AAA also offers members ten percent off some park passes.

$ Retail outlets, such as Filene's Basement and BJ's Wholesale Club, sell Walt Disney World vacation packages at a reduced rate.

$ To receive a complimentary copy of The Orlando Magicard (included in a free packet of Orlando information), call 800-643-9492. Cardholders receive discounts at Orlando-area hotels, restaurants, attractions, and shops, as well as on rental cars. Similar coupon offers can be found at the airport and Walt Disney World's Auto Plazas.

Making a Budget

A stay at Disney's kingdom need not cost a king's ransom. In fact, with a well-planned budget, money at Walt Disney World can stretch surprisingly far.

Vacation expenses tend to fall into five major categories: (1) transportation (which may include any combination of costs for airfare, airport transfers, train tickets, car rental, gas, parking, and taxi service; (2) lodging; (3) theme park tickets; (4) meals; and (5) miscellaneous (recreational activities, souvenirs, postcards, film, toiletries, and home expenses such as pet boarding, etc.).

When planning your budget, first consider what level of service suits your needs. Some people prefer to spend fewer days at Disney but stay at a deluxe hotel or dine at pricier restaurants, while others would rather make their money cover a longer vacation that includes a value-priced resort and less expensive meals. The choice is up to you. Once you've established your spending priorities, determine your price limit. Then make sure you don't exceed it when approximating your expenses—without a ballpark figure to work around, it's easy to get carried away.

Sample Budget

The following is an example of a low to moderately priced budget designed for a family of four (two adults and two kids planning to stay at WDW for five nights and six full days, with a spending limit of $3,250). Totals include tax.

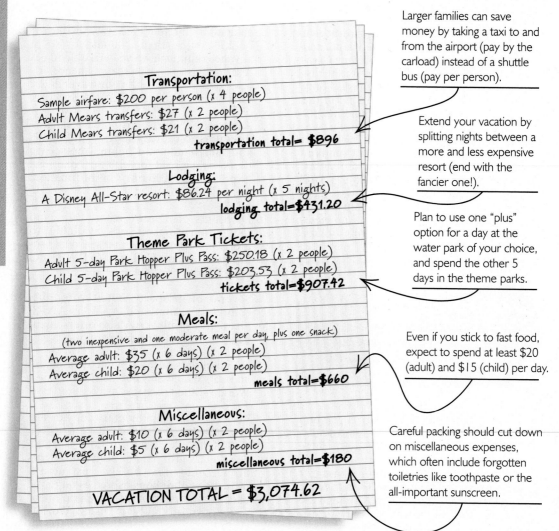

Transportation:
Sample airfare: $200 per person (x 4 people)
Adult Mears transfers: $27 (x 2 people)
Child Mears transfers: $21 (x 2 people)
transportation total= $896

Lodging:
A Disney All-Star resort: $86.24 per night (x 5 nights)
lodging total=$431.20

Theme Park Tickets:
Adult 5-day Park Hopper Plus Pass: $250.18 (x 2 people)
Child 5-day Park Hopper Plus Pass: $203.53 (x 2 people)
tickets total=$907.42

Meals:
(two inexpensive and one moderate meal per day, plus one snack)
Average adult: $35 (x 6 days) (x 2 people)
Average child: $20 (x 6 days) (x 2 people)
meals total=$660

Miscellaneous:
Average adult: $10 (x 6 days) (x 2 people)
Average child: $5 (x 6 days) (x 2 people)
miscellaneous total=$180

VACATION TOTAL = $3,074.62

Larger families can save money by taking a taxi to and from the airport (pay by the carload) instead of a shuttle bus (pay per person).

Extend your vacation by splitting nights between a more and less expensive resort (end with the fancier one!).

Plan to use one "plus" option for a day at the water park of your choice, and spend the other 5 days in the theme parks.

Even if you stick to fast food, expect to spend at least $20 (adult) and $15 (child) per day.

Careful packing should cut down on miscellaneous expenses, which often include forgotten toiletries like toothpaste or the all-important sunscreen.

Planning Your Itinerary
A Time Line

First Things First

- Make hotel and transportation arrangements as far ahead as possible. Note that many Disney hotels fill up more than six months in advance. Call 407-W-DISNEY (934-7639) to book a room at a Disney hotel; your confirmation should arrive within two weeks. Log it and other pertinent information in your Birnbaum Trip Planner at the end of this book. (Don't forget to bring the Trip Planner with you!)
- Create a day-by-day schedule, deciding which area of WDW to visit on each day of your vacation. This will help when it's time to make restaurant and recreation reservations.
- Dinner show reservations can be secured up to two years in advance. Consult page 243 for details and call 407-WDW-DINE (939-3463) for reservations.

6 Months

- Unless you purchased a package that includes theme park admission, it's time to order tickets. Refer to pages 17–19 for details and call 407-WDW-INFO (939-4636); passes should arrive within four weeks. Note that some passes are available at The Disney Store.

4 Months

- Choose dining spots from those listed in the *Good Meals, Great Times* chapter. Call 407-WDW-DINE to make priority seating arrangements (see page 248 for details). Add restaurant names, dining times, and priority seating numbers to your daily schedule.

3 Months

- Find out park hours for your stay, and add them to your day-by-day schedule. Closing times will be particularly helpful when making evening plans. Call 407-WDW-INFO (939-4636) or consult WDW's website (*www.disneyworld.com*).
- If you have purchased a golf package or will be staying at a WDW resort or a resort on Hotel Plaza Boulevard, you can book a tee time on one of WDW's golf courses now (see page 207 for details). Golf lessons can also be reserved at this time. Call 407-WDW-GOLF (939-4653) for reservations. Those not staying on WDW property can make reservations one month ahead.
- Fishing excursions (see pages 210–211) can be booked by calling 407-WDW-PLAY (939-7529).
- Tennis lessons and courts may be reserved by calling 407-WDW-PLAY. Turn to page 208 for more information.
- Parasailing and waterskiing excursions (for details, see pages 209–210) can be booked by calling 407-WDW-PLAY.
- If you'd like to add a behind-the-scenes tour to your vacation, now is the time to make a reservation. See page 203 for details and call 407-WDW-TOUR (939-8687).
- Some attractions may be closed for refurbishment during your visit. A new refurbishment schedule is released each season. Call 407-WDW-INFO.

1 Month

- Trail ride reservations can be made up to 30 days in advance. Call 407-WDW-PLAY.

2 Weeks

- Airline tickets and travel package vouchers should have arrived in the mail by now. Contact your travel agent or the travel company if they have not.

1 Week

- Reconfirm all reservations and priority seating arrangements. Finalize your day-by-day schedule, including all confirmation numbers. Make one copy for your suitcase and one to carry with you in the parks.

Step-By-Step Sample Schedules

Many visitors have a deep desire to cover each and every inch of Walt Disney World in the span of a few short days. While we hesitate to discourage these most ambitious of travelers, we feel the need to enlighten them: Walt Disney World is a staggeringly large place. In fact, it's as big as San Francisco, and jam-packed with about as many diversions as you'd expect from a city that size. One could spend two full weeks on Disney property and still not have time to do it all. The theme parks alone require every bit of four days just to see the major attractions.

What's the best strategy for organizing a Walt Disney World visit? Make a list of the parks, attractions, and activities you *most* want to see and use it to create an itinerary. Don't forget to allow time for swimming, boating, or relaxing in a hammock. This is, after all, a vacation.

Assuming you've narrowed your "must-do" list to the barely manageable, we recommend a stay of at least four to five days. This allows for a visit to each of the theme parks and some time to enjoy many of the recreational activities at your resort. Longer stays can include water parks, Downtown Disney, a dinner show, and more. When planning your days (which you should do before leaving home), be sure to take into account early-entry days at the theme parks and seasonal temperatures in Central Florida.

The following sample schedules assume that you eat breakfast at your resort (unless otherwise stated) and arrive up to 30 minutes before the official opening time. These schedules, though tirelessly tested and proven successful by Birnbaum's editors, are not written in stone. Use them as a guide, tailoring the itineraries to suit your family's individual tastes.

Note that we have not included specific instructions with regard to Fastpass in our sample itineraries. That's not because we don't love the service. In fact, we highly recommend using Fastpass, even if working it into a daily schedule is still an inexact science. As more and more attractions are added to the program, it gets easier and easier to breeze through the turnstiles in a highly organized manner. By all means, take advantage of the Fastpass opportunity every chance you get—not only will it make you feel like a VIP, but it will free up time in your schedule to do things you otherwise might not have gotten to.

Magic Kingdom One-Day Schedule

- Begin the day with a brisk stroll down Main Street, U.S.A. Cut through Adventureland on your way to Splash Mountain and Big Thunder Mountain Railroad. Backtrack to Pirates of the Caribbean, Jungle Cruise, The Magic Carpets of Aladdin, or The Enchanted Tiki Room—Under New Management.

- Access Frontierland via the path near the Tiki Room. Visit the Country Bears and Tom Sawyer Island. Consider lunching on the island (at Aunt Polly's), or the mainland at Pecos Bill Cafe or Columbia Harbour House.

- If time allows, squeeze in The Haunted Mansion before the afternoon parade comes through Liberty Square. Watch the parade and move on to Fantasyland. (But visit The Haunted Mansion first.)

- See as much of Fantasyland as possible, including It's a Small World, Peter Pan's Flight, and The Many Adventures of Winnie the Pooh.

- Cool off at Ariel's Grotto. If the wait to see the Little Mermaid is daunting, consider visiting other Disney characters at the nearby Fantasyland Character Festival or in Mickey's Toontown Fair. **Note:** *If you are staying at a monorail resort, consider taking an afternoon swim or nap at the hotel. When you re-enter the park, take the Walt Disney World Railroad to Mickey's Toontown Fair.*

- Explore Mickey's Toontown Fair. Take adventurous kids on The Barnstormer. As a calmer alternative, take a ride on the Walt Disney World Railroad. Afterward, tour the country homes of Mickey and Minnie Mouse. Mickey greets guests inside the Judge's Tent. The wait is usually shortest first thing in the morning or late in the day.

- Take a spin at the Mad Tea Party *before* dinner.

- If there's more than one performance of the evening parade scheduled, explore Tomorrowland during the earlier showing. Be sure to see Space Mountain, Buzz Lightyear's Space Ranger Spin, Alien Encounter, and the Tomorrowland Indy Speedway.

- View the fireworks from Main Street or the bridge to Tomorrowland.

- Browse the shops on Main Street before lining up for the parade.

- Watch the nighttime parade from Main Street, U.S.A.

- If there's time, revisit your favorite attraction (guests are admitted right up until closing time).

IF YOU HAVE YOUNG CHILDREN

Head directly to Fantasyland (walk right through Cinderella Castle) and ride Dumbo, Peter Pan, and Winnie the Pooh. Take Little Mermaid fans to meet Ariel in her grotto.

Go to Toontown Fair to meet Mickey in the Judge's Tent. Explore Toontown and stop at the teacups on the way to the Fantasyland Character Festival.

Check showtimes at Legend of the Lion King before riding the carousel and It's a Small World.

Line up for the afternoon parade about 30 minutes early. Or, skip the parade, finish up Fantasyland, and take a magic carpet ride in Adventureland.

LINE BUSTERS

Even when the park is packed, there are some attractions with shorter or faster-moving lines. Among them are: The Tomorrowland Transit Authority, The Timekeeper, Walt Disney World Railroad, The Enchanted Tiki Room—Under New Management, Pirates of the Caribbean, Country Bear Jamboree, It's a Small World, and Tom Sawyer Island.

Magic Kingdom Musts

Short on time? Here's a list of the attractions that put the magic in the Magic Kingdom:

Splash Mountain • **Big Thunder Mountain Railroad**
Pirates of the Caribbean • **The Haunted Mansion**
Peter Pan's Flight • **It's a Small World**
Buzz Lightyear's Space Ranger Spin • **Space Mountain**
The Many Adventures of Winnie the Pooh

Epcot One-Day Schedule

- Start the day by making a beeline for Future World's Test Track. (If the line is long, consider jumping on the "single riders" line. It moves much faster.) Follow it up with Wonders of Life, Universe of Energy, and The Living Seas pavilions.

- Stop for lunch at The Land's Sunshine Season Food Fair or Garden Grill, or the Coral Reef restaurant in nearby The Living Seas.

- After exploring The Land, be sure to see Honey, I Shrunk the Audience and Journey Into Your Imagination in the Imagination! pavilion. Save time to enjoy Image Works: Kodak "What If" Labs, a high-tech playground.

- If you're in the mood for some serious pin-trading (or shopping), stop by Pin Central in Innoventions Plaza. (Note that pin-trading can take place just about anywhere at any time. All Disney employees who are wearing pins are willing to trade.)

IF YOU HAVE YOUNG CHILDREN

Begin the day at the Wonders of Life pavilion, making sure to explore the Fitness Fairgrounds. Make your way over to The Living Seas before popping in at The Land. Be sure to hit Image Works in the Imagination! pavilion (but skip Honey, I Shrunk the Audience—it scares little ones silly).

At World Showcase, head to Mexico's boat ride, and, for braver tots, Norway's Maelstrom. Visit the Kidcot Funstop at each country.

LINE BUSTERS

If you need a break from long lines, go to: The Living Seas, *The Circle of Life* movie in The Land, Universe of Energy, or The American Adventure.

- See Spaceship Earth before hitting Innoventions. Be sure to explore the interactive area known as Global Neighborhood, located at the exit of the attraction.

- Make your way to World Showcase by early evening and start your circular tour of the world at Canada. Proceed counter-clockwise around the lagoon. Don't miss the *Impressions de France* movie in the France pavilion, the show in the American Adventure pavilion, and the Maelstrom attraction in Norway.

- After dinner, scope out a spot to watch IllumiNations: Reflections of Earth. (We enjoy the area near Japan, but there are excellent viewing locations all around the World Showcase lagoon.)

Timing Tip: If you have priority seating arrangements for dinner at World Showcase, give yourself 30 to 40 minutes to get there. Taking a *FriendShip* water taxi can shave a few minutes off your trip (although it isn't much faster than brisk walking).

Epcot Essentials

There is a lot to see and do at Disney's discovery park. Don't leave without investigating these outstanding attractions:

Universe of Energy • Honey, I Shrunk the Audience
Living with the Land • Test Track
Cranium Command • IllumiNations: Reflections of Earth
The American Adventure show • Impressions de France

HOT TIP

If you arrive at a theme park without having made priority seating arrangements, pick up a public phone and dial *88 (the call is free), head to Guest Relations, or stop by the eatery itself.

Disney-MGM Studios One-Day Schedule

- Some attractions open later in the morning: Consult a guidemap for exact times. Also, many shows here run on a schedule, so check for times throughout the day. Note that this park is not the easiest to navigate. You'll need a map to get your bearings in the region beyond the Chinese Theater.

- Daredevils should begin the day with a spin on the Rock 'n' Roller Coaster, followed by some eye-opening drops at The Twilight Zone Tower of Terror.

- If Beauty and the Beast is playing soon, grab a seat. Otherwise, plan to come back later and go to The Magic of Disney Animation, Voyage of The Little Mermaid, and Disney's Doug Live!

- Pause for lunch at the ABC Commissary, 50's Prime Time Cafe, Sci-Fi Dine-In Theater, or Hollywood & Vine.

- Line up 20 to 30 minutes early to watch the afternoon parade. (Note that if you skip the parade, it is an excellent time to see The Magic of Disney Animation or The Great Movie Ride.)

- Cool off by splashing near an open fire hydrant on New York Street.

- Be sure to see (and hear) Sounds Dangerous starring Drew Carey, followed by the Disney-MGM Studios Backlot Tour, Star Tours, Jim Henson's Muppet*Vision 3-D, and the Indiana Jones Epic Stunt Spectacular.

- Try to catch The Hunchback of Notre Dame—A Musical Adventure before the Honey, I Shrunk the Kids Movie Set Adventure, or Backstage Pass.

- If you haven't seen Beauty and the Beast—Live on Stage, go to the next available showing. Follow the show with dinner and then, if you haven't hit it yet, The Great Movie Ride.

- Keep an eye on the clock: You want to get a spot for Fantasmic! at least 60 minutes before showtime. Note that if you choose to skip Fantasmic!, plan to exit the park before the last show breaks.

IF YOU HAVE YOUNG CHILDREN

Begin with Voyage of The Little Mermaid, followed by the Muppets.

Have lunch at Toy Story Pizza Planet, then catch the parade. Afterward, romp in the Honey, I Shrunk the Kids Movie Set Adventure, get wet on New York Street, watch Disney's Doug Live!, catch Bear in the Big Blue House, and see Beauty and the Beast—Live on Stage.

Be sure to catch up with Disney characters on Mickey Avenue and New York Street.

LINE BUSTERS

When lines abound at the Disney-MGM Studios, we suggest the following: Indiana Jones Epic Stunt Spectacular (the theater accommodates 2,000 guests at a time), Honey, I Shrunk the Kids Movie Set Adventure, Disney-MGM Studios Backlot Tour (the line moves relatively quickly, and you get plenty of bang for your waiting buck), American Film Institute Showcase, and Toy Story Pizza Planet (as an arcade, it's not an attraction per se, but still a pleasant diversion).

Studios Standouts

If you're short on time, be sure to catch as many of the following four-star attractions at the Disney-MGM Studios as possible:

The Twilight Zone Tower of Terror

Rock 'n' Roller Coaster starring Aerosmith

Beauty and the Beast—Live on Stage • The Magic of Disney Animation

Jim Henson's Muppet*Vision 3-D • Star Tours • Disney's Doug Live!

Sounds Dangerous starring Drew Carey • Fantasmic!

Disney's Animal Kingdom One-Day Schedule

- Many shows here run on a schedule, so check for times throughout the day. Make a point of seeing Festival of the Lion King—it appeals to all ages.

IF YOU HAVE YOUNG CHILDREN

We recommend lingering a bit in The Oasis on your way into the park. Then, make a sharp left and head straight to Camp Minnie-Mickey. See Pocahontas and Her Forest Friends, mingle with some Disney characters, and watch Festival of the Lion King.

Stop by The Tree of Life to notice all of the animal carvings in its trunk. (Note that the show inside the tree, It's Tough to be a Bug!, is very intense, and may frighten young children.)

Eat lunch at Pizzafari or head to DinoLand U.S.A.'s Restaurantosaurus. Explore DinoLand, making sure to see The Boneyard playground, and the Cretaceous Trail.

In Asia, go to the Maharajah Jungle Trek. Ride Africa's Kilimanjaro Safaris and see the Pangani Forest Exploration Trail. Then take the Wildlife Express to Conservation Station.

LINE BUSTERS

When herds of guests mob Disney's Animal Kingdom attractions, there are a few places to escape the stampede: The Oasis, Pangani Forest Exploration Trail, Maharajah Jungle Trek, Safari Village Trails, The Boneyard playground, and Conservation Station. (You'll need to take the Wildlife Express to Conservation Station.)

- As you enter the park, pass through The Oasis and head toward DinoLand U.S.A. Ride Dinosaur (previously known as Countdown to Extinction) before eating breakfast with Donald Duck at Restaurantosaurus (advance priority seating is highly recommended) or getting breakfast rolls from the Dino Diner cart. Explore DinoLand before catching a performance of Tarzan Rocks! at the Theater in the Wild.

- In Asia, ride Kali River Rapids, dry off at the Maharajah Jungle Trek, and if it's playing soon, see Flights of Wonder at the Caravan Stage.

- Check a guidemap for the Festival of the Lion King schedule. Plan to arrive in Camp Minnie-Mickey at least 45 minutes before it starts (it's a wildly popular show). If possible, see Pocahontas and Her Forest Friends and mingle with Disney characters before seeing Festival of the Lion King.

- Stop at Tusker House or Pizzafari for lunch. Then jump aboard the Wildlife Express train to Conservation Station. Don't miss the Song of the Rainforest, a stirring "3-D" audio experience. Affection Section, a small, outdoor petting farm, allows for upclose encounters with cute, little critters.

- After experiencing Africa's Kilimanjaro Safaris, take a relaxing hike on the peaceful, animal-laden Pangani Forest Exploration Trail.

- Wander the Safari Village Trails that surround The Tree of Life, taking time to search for the many animals carved into the tree and its roots.

- Finish off the day with a screening of It's Tough to be a Bug! It is presented in a theater inside The Tree of Life.

Animal Kingdom Aces

An abbreviated visit to Disney's Animal Kingdom is enough to make anybody growl. The following attractions should help soothe the savage beast, er, guest:

Dinosaur • Kali River Rapids

Kilimanjaro Safaris • It's Tough to be a Bug!

Festival of the Lion King

Pangani Forest Exploration Trail

HOT TIP

Many attractions are in the steamy outdoors. Bring a refillable water bottle when you visit.

Half-Day Schedules

Magic Kingdom

MORNING AT THE MAGIC KINGDOM

- Where to begin—Tomorrowland or Frontierland? It's a big decision. Know that the area you postpone may have long lines by the time you get there. We'd start with Tomorrowland.
- Move rapidly from one attraction to the next—first to Space Mountain, then to Buzz Lightyear's Space Ranger Spin and Alien Encounter.
- Cut across Main Street and head for Pirates of the Caribbean, Splash Mountain, and Big Thunder Mountain Railroad.
- Grab lunch at Pecos Bill Cafe or Columbia Harbour House.
- Visit The Haunted Mansion and, if there's time before the parade, the Country Bear Jamboree.
- Watch the afternoon parade in Frontierland. Or skip the parade and see Fantasyland's Peter Pan's Flight, Winnie the Pooh, and It's a Small World.

> **HALF-DAY WITH YOUNG CHILDREN**
>
> Start at Mickey's Toontown Fair. (You can get there easily by boarding the Walt Disney World Railroad at Main Street Station.) Meet Mickey Mouse inside the Judge's Tent. After fully exploring Mickey's Toontown Fair, move on to Fantasyland. Soar on a magic carpet in Adventureland before calling it a day.

THE MAGIC KINGDOM AFTER LUNCH

- Start in Adventureland. Ride the Jungle Cruise and Pirates of the Caribbean.
- Head to Frontierland. Do Splash Mountain and Big Thunder Mountain Railroad. Then see the Country Bear Jamboree or stop by the Diamond Horseshoe Saloon Revue. Hop on the Walt Disney World Railroad to Mickey's Toontown Fair.
- Explore Toontown. If the wait to meet Mickey Mouse is more than 30 minutes, consider coming back in the late evening.
- Take a spin at the Mad Tea Party, and see the highlights of Fantasyland, including It's a Small World, Peter Pan, and Winnie the Pooh.
- Pop in at The Haunted Mansion before dinner.
- Now it's time for Tomorrowland. (If you have the energy, and the nighttime parade is running twice, plan to stay in Tomorrowland during the early run. See the parade later.) Go to Alien Encounter, Buzz Lightyear's Space Ranger Spin, and Space Mountain.
- Watch the nighttime parade.
- Shop on Main Street, U.S.A. while the exiting throngs file out.

Epcot

MORNING AT EPCOT

- Make a beeline for Test Track. Then head for Honey, I Shrunk the Audience (inside the Imagination! pavilion) and The Land.
- See Universe of Energy and the Wonders of Life before moving on to World Showcase (it opens at 11 A.M.). When hunger calls, stop for a light lunch. Visit the countries that interest you most, making sure to see the show inside the American Adventure and the boat ride in Norway.
- Finish up your Epcot visit by seeing Future World's Spaceship Earth.

> **HALF-DAY WITH YOUNG CHILDREN**
>
> Begin with a visit to Imagination!, taking time to fully explore the Image Works interactive play zone. After making the trip to The Living Seas, move on to the Wonders of Life, making sure to enjoy some hands-on fun at the Fitness Fairgrounds and catch a screening of Cranium Command.

EPCOT AFTER LUNCH

- If you don't have priority seating arrangements and would like to have dinner at a World Showcase restaurant, stop by Guest Relations to make them. If not, consider dining at the nearby BoardWalk resort (it's a short stroll or boat ride away). *(Continued on page 30)*

(Continued from page 29)

- Start at Spaceship Earth and see as much of Future World as possible before heading to World Showcase for dinner.
  - Spend the evening touring World Showcase. Keep an eye on the clock so you can secure a good spot around the Lagoon to watch the evening's presentation of IllumiNations. (The area by Italy is one of many prime viewing locations.)
  - Avoid the crush of exiting crowds by browsing in Mouse Gear in Future World.

Disney-MGM Studios

MORNING AT THE DISNEY-MGM STUDIOS

- Kick-start the day with Rock 'n' Roller Coaster, followed by a trip to The Twilight Zone Tower of Terror. From there, move to Jim Henson's Muppet*Vision 3-D and Star Tours.
  - See The Magic of Disney Animation, Beauty and the Beast—Live on Stage, and The Great Movie Ride.
  - Line up about 20–30 minutes early for the afternoon parade.

HALF-DAY WITH YOUNG CHILDREN

Start with Voyage of The Little Mermaid, followed by Bear in the Big Blue House—Live on Stage, Doug Live!, the Honey, I Shrunk the Audience Movie Set Adventure, Jim Henson's Muppet*Vision 3-D, and Beauty and the Beast—Live on Stage.

THE DISNEY-MGM STUDIOS AFTER LUNCH

- Begin with Twilight Zone Tower of Terror, Rock 'n' Roller Coaster, Beauty and the Beast—Live on Stage, and The Magic of Disney Animation.
- See Voyage of The Little Mermaid, The Great Movie Ride, Star Tours, Jim Henson's Muppet*Vision 3-D, and Disney-MGM Studios Backlot Tour.
- If there's time after dinner, see Doug Live!, Sounds Dangerous starring Drew Carey, and the Indiana Jones Epic Stunt Spectacular before securing a spot for Fantasmic!

Disney's Animal Kingdom

MORNING AT DISNEY'S ANIMAL KINGDOM

- Pass quickly through The Oasis, and go directly to Dinosaur in DinoLand U.S.A. Then head to Asia for Kali River Rapids and the Maharajah Jungle Trek.
- Experience the Kilimanjaro Safaris and the Pangani Forest Exploration Trail in Africa.
- Check a guidemap for the next performance of Festival of the Lion King and arrive at least 45 minutes early.
- Approach The Tree of Life, taking time to notice the animals carved into its trunk and roots. Then see It's Tough to be a Bug! inside the tree.

HALF-DAY WITH YOUNG CHILDREN

Spend some time scoping out animal life in The Oasis before heading to Camp Minnie-Mickey. See the Pocahontas and Her Forest Friends show, as well as the Festival of the Lion King. Meet a few Disney characters before visiting DinoLand U.S.A. Explore The Boneyard and Cretaceous Trail. If time allows, take the Wildlife Express to Conservation Station, where kids can bond with live animals in the Affection Section.

DISNEY'S ANIMAL KINGDOM AFTER LUNCH

- Check a guidemap for the next performance of Festival of the Lion King. Arrive 45 minutes before showtime. Say hello to Disney characters in Camp Minnie-Mickey.
- If there is entertainment scheduled, stick around Safari Village to enjoy it. Otherwise, head to Africa for the Kilimanjaro Safaris ride. Walk along the Pangani Forest Exploration Trail and take the train to Conservation Station.
- In Asia, ride Kali River Rapids and do the Maharajah Jungle Trek.

- After dinner, wander the Safari Village Trails and see It's Tough to be a Bug!
- Head to DinoLand, U.S.A., where you'll dodge dinosaurs on the thrilling Dinosaur attraction and catch a performance of Tarzan Rocks!

Making the Most of Longer Visits

Longer stays allow the chance to sample some of the World's myriad other offerings. Spend another day in the one park you most enjoyed. Lounge by the pool, play tennis or golf, or bike. Go shopping at Downtown Disney. Cool off at one of Disney's innovative water parks. Have lunch at a WDW resort and try a special dinner at Victoria & Albert's in the Grand Floridian, or at California Grill in the Contemporary. Check out the clubs at Pleasure Island or Downtown Disney West Side, or spend the evening at the BoardWalk. Take golf or tennis lessons. Go fishing, water-skiing, or horseback riding. Visit a spa. Participate in a behind-the-scenes program. Play a round of miniature golf. See a game at Disney's Wide World of Sports complex. For even more ideas, see our *Sports*, *Everything Else in the World*, and *Good Meals, Great Times* chapters.

How to Save a Rainy Day

Florida rain showers come and go with such regularity that you could set your watch by them, especially during summer months. They're usually brief, though torrential. Of course, there are times that gray clouds linger longer. Here are some ways to make the most of a soggy day:

- Head for DisneyQuest, a huge interactive play zone at Downtown Disney West Side. It'll keep the whole family entertained (and dry) for hours.
- See a movie on one of AMC Theatres' 24 screens at Downtown Disney.
- Consider taking in an indoor event at Disney's Wide World of Sports complex. For information, call 407-363-6600.
- Don your rain gear and go to Epcot. The pavilions in Future World house a bounty of sheltered diversions. (Ponchos are sold throughout Walt Disney World for about $5 each.)

CUSTOMIZED TRAVEL TIPS
Traveling with Children

Tell youngsters that a Walt Disney World vacation is in the works and the response is apt to be overwhelming. Our guide, *Birnbaum's Walt Disney World For Kids, By Kids*, written for children ages 7 through 14, can be a useful resource for getting them involved in the planning from the outset. Filled with information about the World from a kid's perspective, it can be used as a reference before and during the trip, and as a souvenir after.

Walt Disney World ranks among the easiest spots on earth for families with children. Keep in mind, however, that kids under seven must be accompanied by an adult to enter the theme parks; kids under ten must be accompanied at the water parks. With teens, however, it is enough to establish a meeting place and time inside the Magic Kingdom, Epcot, Disney-MGM Studios, or Animal Kingdom.

Resort Fun: All Walt Disney World resorts have at least one room stuffed with video games. Most of the hotels have playgrounds.

Child Care: The Polynesian, Grand Floridian, Contemporary, Animal Kingdom Lodge, Wilderness Lodge, Yacht and Beach Club, BoardWalk, Swan, and Dolphin have children's activity centers. In-room child care can be summoned to all WDW resorts; contact the Guest Services desk. There is also a center known as KinderCare, which accepts kids ages one through four. For details and availability, phone 407-827-5444.

Strollers: Available for rent for $6 (plus a $1 refundable deposit) at stroller and wheelchair rental shops at each of the theme parks. (Strollers are not available at the water parks.) Double strollers cost $13 plus a $1 deposit. Present the receipt when returning the stroller to get a Disney Dollar back.

Keep in mind that strollers are not permitted inside the attractions (they can be parked near each attraction entrance). If a stroller disappears while you're in an attraction, a replacement may be obtained. Ask a park worker for the nearest replacement location. Guests have to pay only once a day for a stroller. If you rent one in the morning and plan to spend the afternoon at another park, just present your receipt for a stroller there.

Baby Care Centers: Located in all theme parks, these centers are helpful to parents with young children. There are rooms with rocking chairs and love seats for nursing mothers, and cheery feeding rooms. Baby Care Centers have facilities for changing infants, preparing formula, and warming bottles. Disposable diapers, bottles, formula, pacifiers, juices, and baby food are among the supplies for sale. Changing areas are available in most women's and some men's restrooms as well.

Lost Children: All Disney employees know what to do if a child starts to call for his or her parents. This is a welcome thought on those rare instances when a child suddenly disappears or fails to show up on schedule. If this happens, stop in at the Baby Care Center or City Hall in the Magic Kingdom; at Guest Relations or the Baby Care Center in Epcot; at Guest Relations at the Disney-MGM Studios; or at Guest Relations, just inside the park entrance, in Animal Kingdom. A new computerized system allows for a detailed description of the child and his or her status, helping to minimize delays in reuniting families. There are no paging systems in the parks, but in serious emergencies an all-points bulletin can be put out among Disney employees. The Guest Relations staff of each theme park can also help.

Parental Perk

Families with small children should know about the "rider switch" policy at the theme parks. At attractions with age or height restrictions, a parent who waits with a young child while the other parent rides the attraction can go right on when the first parent comes off. Be sure to ask the attendant.

Traveling Without Children

Walt Disney World has become a popular destination for adults without children, appealing to singles, young couples, and empty nesters alike. Disney has responded to the demand with an expanded entertainment complex and sophisticated dining for grown-ups without kids in tow.

- Consider perusing *Birnbaum's Walt Disney World Without Kids*, our adult-oriented companion guide to this book.
- Crowds can be extremely heavy during traditional school break times. Schedule your visits for off-peak seasons.

Older Travelers

Walt Disney World may be a cinch for a five-year-old to maneuver, but it can sometimes be overwhelming for older travelers. The theme parks can be disorienting because of the crisscrossing pathways. And the heat, particularly in summer, can be hard to take. But with the proper planning and precautions, it's just as delightful for older visitors as for kids.

- Try to eat early or late to avoid the mealtime crowds. In the Magic Kingdom, select restaurants such as Cinderella's Royal Table in Cinderella Castle. Or take the monorail to the peaceful Polynesian, Contemporary, or Grand Floridian resorts, where pleasant dining options abound (check ahead to find out which restaurants serve lunch). In Epcot, the Coral Reef restaurant and Le Cellier Steakhouse are especially pleasant spots. At the Disney-MGM Studios, the Hollywood Brown Derby offers a relaxing sit-down meal.

Lost Adults

Occasionally, traveling companions get separated in the crush of the crowds, or someone may fail to show up at a meeting spot. When this happens, it's good to know that messages can be left for fellow travelers at Guest Relations in any of the four theme parks.

- The Florida sun tends to be brutal year-round—always wear sunscreen.
- Don't underestimate distances at Epcot or Animal Kingdom; you may need to walk more than three miles in a day. If that's daunting, consider renting a wheelchair. (Epcot's *FriendShip* boats on the lagoon can also ease the burden on weary feet.)
- Pace yourself. It's smart to head back to your hotel for a swim or a nap in the afternoon and then return to the parks later on. The hotels connected by monorail are particularly convenient for this.
- Many Orlando-area hotels and attractions offer discounts to seniors and AARP members. Contact the Official Visitor Information Center (407-363-5872) for details.

Young Singles

While it's not exactly a happening singles scene, Walt Disney World is a lot of fun to visit with friends.

- Downtown Disney's clubs and restaurants can prove to be fertile meeting places. The BoardWalk is another lively destination. Sports fans find the ESPN Club most inviting.
- The lounges at WDW hotels are relaxed and welcoming. The same atmosphere prevails at the Tune-In Lounge in the 50's Prime Time Cafe at the Disney-MGM Studios, and at the Rose & Crown Pub (in the United Kingdom pavilion) and the Matsu No Ma lounge (Japan) in Epcot's World Showcase.

Solo Travelers

Those who travel alone for the freedom and fun of it can have as memorable a time here as they would anywhere else.

- Solo travelers with time on their hands should consider signing up for a behind-the-scenes tour.
- Many of the finer restaurants now have counters to sit at—perfect for lone diners.
- Need a tennis partner? Check out the player matching program at Disney's Racquet Club (407-824-3578).
- Other recreational opportunities for unencumbered travelers include parasailing (at the Contemporary resort), horseback riding (at Fort Wilderness), taking a spin in a racecar (at the Richard Petty Driving Experience), and watching a pro baseball game (at Disney's Wide World of Sports). Call 407-WDW-PLAY (939-7529) for information.
- **A Note for Budget Watchers:** Rates at all Walt Disney World resorts, the resorts on Hotel Plaza Boulevard, and most other area accommodations are the same whether one or two persons occupy a room.

Tips for International Travelers

Visitors from outside the U.S. need not feel like strangers in a strange land when they arrive at Walt Disney World—even if they speak a language other than English. Information is readily available in many languages. These tips may also help:

• International Welcome Centers are open in the theme parks during regular park hours.

• Free theme park maps can be found in different languages at the entrance to all parks, as well as at Guest Relations and the International Welcome Center in each park.

• Several Disney resorts offer services for their International guests. Ask about them when you inquire about reservations.

• When making priority seating arrangements through 407-WDW-DINE (939-3463) ask to speak with a foreign language host.

• Most Disney restaurants offer menus in various languages. Some have picture menus, too.

• Foreign currency exchange is available at Guest Relations in the theme parks. Travelers' checks can be purchased at the Contemporary, Epcot's American Express traveler's desk, and the SunTrust bank by Downtown Disney.

• A Disney World resort room key will act as a charge card—purchases made at WDW can be billed to a credit card number (reducing the amount of currency to be exchanged).

• Many Disney employees are fluent in more than one language. Flags on their name tags symbolize which languages they speak.

• Guided tours of theme parks are offered in several languages. Ask at Guest Relations or the International Welcome Center for details.

• A tape-recorded walking tour is available for the Magic Kingdom and Epcot in a selection of languages. The device can be rented for a small fee (with a $100 refundable deposit) at the park's International Welcome Center.

• Guests traveling long distances and through time zones should conserve their energy. It might be wise to relax by the hotel's pool on the day of arrival, instead of trying to fit in a full day at a theme park—it's never beneficial to start a vacation exhausted!

• Phone cards good for international calls can be purchased at several Walt Disney World shops. Look for a yellow star on the theme park map to locate one of the stores.

Tips for Teens

When it comes to teens at Disney World, *The Little Mermaid*'s Ariel has plenty of company. Of course, be they of the fish or human variety, teenage guests have special needs all their own. Here are some tips, courtesy of Amy Newcomer, Birnbaum's WDW teen expert:

• Bring a Walkman. It's perfect for the trip to WDW and for sitting poolside at your resort. But you don't have to bring every CD you own. Just bring a few favorites.

• Have some of your own money on hand. If it's your hard-earned cash, you won't spend it as fast as you would Mom and Dad's!

• Pack a hat. Why? It's much easier to throw a hat on then taking time to do your hair.

• There are lots of great restaurants for teens: Rainforest Cafe has a lot of action going on. Planet Hollywood does, too. It's fun to look at all the movie memorabilia. One of

the best restaurants is 50's Prime Time Cafe at the Disney-MGM Studios. It's great to see your parent get yelled at by the "Mom" and "Dad" waiters! It's also fun to sit in a car and eat at Sci-Fi Dine-In Theater.

• Try to get along with your brothers and sisters—even if it isn't always easy. Don't bug them to do the things you want to do all the time. Offer to do things they want to do, too.

• One of the coolest things for teens to do is an "E-Ride Night" at the Magic Kingdom. It lets you stay in the park after hours and ride all the best rides with basically no wait! Another good thing to do at night is shop, especially at Downtown Disney.

• *Attention parents!* Try to include your teens in planning your trip. If they get a say during planning, they'll be happier when they arrive at Walt Disney World. Also, don't make them get up every morning at 6 A.M. Try to give them a day or two to wake up late and lounge around the pool or a water park.

Travelers with Disabilities

Walt Disney World tends to get high marks from travelers with disabilities because of the attention paid to their special needs. Here is an overview of the services provided.

GETTING AROUND: Special parking is available for guests at all four theme parks; ask for directions at the Auto Plazas upon entering. From the Transportation and Ticket Center (TTC), the Magic Kingdom is accessible by ferry or by monorail (for those using wheelchairs, the former is preferable, since the monorail ramp has a steep slant). Note that all WDW monorail stations are accessible to wheelchairs. Valet parking is available at Downtown Disney and is free to guests with disabilities.

Wheelchairs: Wheelchairs can be rented in all theme parks; they cost $6 per day, with a $1 refundable deposit. In the Magic Kingdom, they are available at the Stroller and Wheelchair Rental on the right side of the souvenir area, just inside the turnstiles. Epcot's rental area is inside the main turnstiles on the left, and near the International Gateway entrance. Oscar's Super Service rents wheelchairs at Disney-MGM Studios. At Animal Kingdom, wheelchairs are available at Garden Gate Gifts near The Oasis.

Electric Convenience Vehicles (ECVs) are available for rent in every park. They cost $30 plus a $10 refundable deposit, per park per day. They usually sell out early.

There are designated areas for guests in wheelchairs to view the fireworks at Epcot, and to view the parades in the Magic Kingdom and the Disney-MGM Studios. Check a park guidemap for locations.

Accessibility: It's easy to get around the theme parks by wheelchair. Most attractions are accessible to guests who can be lifted from chairs with assistance from a member of their party, and many can accommodate guests who must remain in wheelchairs at all times. Consult the *Guidebook for Guests with Disabilities* (see box) for details about attraction access, or check with the ride host or hostess. At the water parks, life jackets are available for travelers with disabilities.

All WDW hotels have accommodations for guests with disabilities, including roll-in showers. For assistance in selecting one that best fits your requirements, ask for the Special Requests Department when you call Central Reservations (407-934-7639).

RESOURCES: At Walt Disney World, much has been done to ensure that travelers with disabilities have a fun, hassle-free visit.

Visual Disabilities: Guests with visual disabilities can obtain a tape recorder and a cassette that describes each theme park, as well as a Braille guidebook. Each requires a $25 refundable deposit.

Hearing Disabilities: Pay phones equipped with Text Typewriters (TTYs) are available throughout Walt Disney World. For more information, call 407-827-4636. Sign language interpretation is available for some shows. Call at least two weeks ahead for arrangements.

Listening devices that amplify attraction sound tracks are available at City Hall in the Magic Kingdom and at Guest Relations in Epcot, Animal Kingdom, and the Disney-MGM Studios. A $25 refundable deposit is required. Sites with assistive listening systems are listed on park guidemaps.

Ask about the availability of reflective and video captioning devices. The former project show dialogue onto panels positioned in front of a guest; the latter activate captioning on video monitors. Theme park guidemaps indicate at which attractions these devices can be used. Also, written scripts are available at most shows and attraction for use by guests with hearing disabilities. Contact a park employee for assistance.

Note: Service animals are permitted in all the parks.

Booking the Trip: The following organizations and travel agencies specialize in assisting physically challenged travelers:
- The Society for the Advancement of Travel for the Handicapped (347 Fifth Ave., Suite 610; New York, NY 10016; 212-447-7284). Send a check or money order for $5 to receive a listing of member agents.
- Accessible Journeys; Ridley Park, PA (610-521-0339 or 800-846-4537)
- Flying Wheels Travel; Owatonna, MN (507-451-5005 or 800-535-6790)
- Travel by Touch (for the visually impaired); Los Angeles, CA (310-473-0653 or 888-868-2455)

Theme Park Resource

The *Guidebook for Guests with Disabilities* provides details on the accessibility and services available in all WDW theme parks. It's available at wheelchair rental locations, Guest Relations, and ticket booths. To get this information in advance, visit WDW's website (*www.disneyworld.com*) or write to Walt Disney World Guest Communications; Box 10000; Lake Buena Vista, FL 32830.

WDW Weddings & Honeymoons

Walt Disney World is the most popular honeymoon destination in the country. The resorts offer some romantic stretches of white-sand beaches for evening strolls, fine restaurants for candlelight dinners, and a host of activities to rival almost any European or Hawaiian destination. Add to that the fantasy of the Magic Kingdom, the wonder of Epcot, the glamour of the Disney-MGM Studios, and the majesty of Animal Kingdom, plus Downtown Disney and BoardWalk nightlife, water parks, and the Disney Cruise Line, and it's not very hard to see why Walt Disney World is number one with newlyweds. Because honeymooners have been flocking to the WDW resorts for many years, a variety of packages cater specifically to newly married couples. For information, call toll-free: 877-566-0969. (You don't have to buy a package to get special treatment; just let the reservationist know you're on your honeymoon.)

For years, the folks at Walt Disney World received requests from couples who wanted to marry at a WDW theme park. Today, couples can tie the knot in evening ceremonies at some parks during seasons when they close early. (The area in front of Cinderella Castle is one of Walt Disney World's wedding hot spots, as are several Epcot sites.) Morning ceremonies are offered at Epcot's World Showcase.

The Yacht and Beach Club, BoardWalk, Polynesian, and Wilderness Lodge resorts also host their share of weddings. The Wedding Pavilion, near the Grand Floridian Resort and Spa, offers a Victorian-style indoor setting with a prime view of Cinderella Castle. A combination of stained glass, sage green and soft pink florals, and benches with heart-shaped cutouts (seating around 250) creates the romantic ambience. Couples can fill their wedding albums with photos taken at Picture Point, under a trellis of climbing white roses, with the faraway castle prominently in the background. Private ceremonies can also be performed at this scenic spot.

Weddings range from elegant affairs, without a hint of Disneyana, to ceremonies in which the bride arrives in Cinderella's coach and Mickey and Minnie are among the guests at the reception.

At Franck's Bridal Studio, WDW specialists work with couples to customize each wedding. Unique merchandise is available for purchase. Among the services offered are cakes, photography, hairstyling, flower arranging, and musical entertainment. Specialists can help secure accommodations, rehearsal dinners, bachelor parties, and more. For information about planning a Walt Disney World wedding, call 407-828-3400; for honeymoon packages, call 877-566-0969.

The newest option for lovebirds is the Walt Disney World engagement package. Here, prospective spouses can pop the question amid classic Disney splendor. Packages start at $295. For additional information or to book a Disney engagement package, call 407-824-5130.

FINGERTIP REFERENCE GUIDE

BARBERS AND SALONS

The most amusing place to get a haircut is the Magic Kingdom's old-fashioned Harmony Barber Shop. It's tucked away at the end of the cobblestone cul-de-sac just off the west side of Main Street.

Haircuts, coloring, manicures, and other services are available at the following resorts: the salon in the Contemporary (407-824-3411), the Periwig Salon at the Yacht and Beach Club (407-934-3260), Ivy Trellis at the Grand Floridian (407-824-3000, ext. 2581), the Niki Bryan shop at the Swan and Dolphin (407-934-4250), and the Casa de Belleza at Coronado Springs (407-939-3965).

BUSINESS SERVICES

Disney provides a range of services for those who simply must mix business with pleasure. Photocopiers, fax machines (also found at Guest Relations in the theme parks), pocket pagers, and FedEx materials are available at Guest Services at any Walt Disney World resort. In addition, the Contemporary, Grand Floridian, Animal Kingdom Lodge, Yacht and Beach Club, Disney Institute, and Coronado Springs resorts each provide secretarial services, computers, printers, and Internet access for a fee. A Vista-United videoconferencing center (407-827-2000) is located near Downtown Disney.

CAMERA NEEDS

Photo spots around the theme parks can help you capture the best shots. To photograph fireworks, your camera must have a manually adjustable shutter speed and aperture (it helps to have a tripod, too). Use color negative film (ISO 400). Set the aperture at f/8 and the shutter speed at B. Hold the lens open for three to five seconds at each burst; cover between bursts.

Flash photography is not permitted inside any Walt Disney World attraction. Film and disposable cameras are available at many shops throughout the World. The best selection can be found at the camera shops in each park. Also, when capturing moments with Disney characters on videotape, refrain from using camera lights. (The lights are too bright for the characters' sensitive eyes.)

Minor Repairs: If your camera isn't working, take it to Town Square Exposition Hall in the Magic Kingdom; the Camera Center near Spaceship Earth, Cameras and Film at the Imagination! pavilion, or World Traveler at International Gateway in Epcot; The Darkroom on Hollywood Boulevard in the Disney-MGM Studios; or Garden Gate Gifts near The Oasis in Animal Kingdom.

Film Processing: Processing is available at the theme parks, all WDW resorts, and Downtown Disney wherever a Photo Express sign is displayed. Film is developed on site.

CAR CARE

Several Exxon gas stations with convenience stores are on the property, all of which are open 24 hours a day. One is on Buena Vista Drive across from Pleasure Island; another is on Floridian Way near the Magic Kingdom Auto Plaza. The third, near the BoardWalk resort on Buena Vista Drive, also has a car wash.

Breakdowns sometimes occur, but they don't spell disaster. All WDW roads are patrolled constantly by security vehicles equipped with radios that can be used to call for help. If you need a tow, contact security (407-824-4777). If your car needs servicing but does not need to be towed, call the AAA Car Care Center (407-824-0976). Located in the Magic Kingdom Auto Plaza, the AAA Car Care Center offers full mechanical services and free towing on property, Monday through Saturday. For off-property car care needs, rely on Riker's Wreckers (407-352-0842 for towing; 407-238-9800 for repairs), or AAA (if you're a member).

DRINKING LAWS

In Florida, the legal drinking age is 21. There are many bars and lounges all over Walt Disney World; minors are permitted to accompany their parents but are prohibited from sitting or standing at the bar. No alcohol is served in the Magic Kingdom, but alcoholic beverages are sold at restaurants and bars in Epcot, the Disney-MGM Studios, Animal Kingdom, and Downtown Disney.

Alcohol is sold in at least one shop at most WDW resorts. Liquor may be purchased from room service at the Polynesian, Animal Kingdom Lodge, Contemporary, Grand Floridian, Yacht and Beach Club, BoardWalk, Swan, and Dolphin resorts; beer and wine are usually available for delivery at other resorts.

LOCKERS

Attended lockers can be found in the following theme park locations: underneath Main Street Railroad Station in the Magic Kingdom, on the west side of Spaceship Earth in Epcot, next to Oscar's Super Service inside the main entrance at the Disney-MGM Studios, and just inside the entrance and to the left at Animal Kingdom. Lockers are also available at the Transportation and Ticket Center (TTC). Items too big to fit can be checked with the locker attendant at the Magic Kingdom, at Package Pickup in Epcot, and at Guest Relations at the Disney-MGM Studios and Animal Kingdom. Cost is $5 per day (including a $2 refundable deposit) for unlimited use. Be sure to save your rental receipt; it can be used again that day for a locker in any of the four theme parks.

LOST & FOUND

The extensive indexing system maintained by Walt Disney World's Lost and Found department is impressive, especially when a prized possession turns up missing, whether it's false teeth or a camera. (Both have been lost in the past; the dentures were never claimed.)

If you lose (or find) something, report it at any one of these Lost and Found locations: the Transportation and Ticket Center (TTC), City Hall in the Magic Kingdom, the Guest Relations lobby in Innoventions East at Epcot, Oscar's Super Service just inside the Disney-MGM Studios, Guest Relations near the Animal Kingdom entrance, or Guest Services at any WDW resort. At Fort Wilderness, dial 7-2726 from a comfort station telephone; from outside the campground, phone 407-824-2726; and from Downtown Disney, phone 407-828-3058.

Items lost in a theme park can be claimed on the day of the loss at the park's Lost and Found, and thereafter at the Transportation and Ticket Center (TTC) Lost and Found station. To report lost items after your visit, call 407-824-4245. Hats, strollers, sunglasses, and WDW merchandise are kept for one month; everything else is kept three months.

MAIL

Postage stamps can be purchased at all WDW resorts; at City Hall in the Magic Kingdom; at most shops near the lockers in Epcot, the Disney-MGM Studios, and Animal Kingdom; and at Guest Services in the Downtown Disney Marketplace.

The old-fashioned mailboxes in the theme parks are not official U.S. post boxes, but letters can be mailed from them. Postmarks read "Lake Buena Vista," not "Walt Disney World."

A post office at the Shoppes at Lake Buena Vista shopping center (opposite Summerfield Suites) is open from 9 A.M. to 4 P.M. weekdays and 9 A.M. to noon on Saturday. In Orlando, there's a post office at 10450 Turkey Lake Road, near the Official Visitor Information Center. Call 800-275-8777 for information.

Mail may be addressed to guests care of their hotel. The address for all WDW resorts is Walt Disney World; Box 10000; Lake Buena Vista, FL 32830.

MEDICAL MATTERS

Travelers with chronic health problems should carry copies of prescriptions and get names of local doctors from hometown physicians. However, Walt Disney World is equipped to deal with many types of medical emergencies. In the Magic Kingdom, next to the Crystal Palace, there's a First Aid Center staffed by a registered nurse; there is another at Epcot in the Odyssey Center complex. At the Disney-MGM Studios, the First Aid Center is in the Guest Relations building at the main entrance, accessible from both inside and outside the park. The Animal Kingdom First Aid Center is in Safari Village near the back side of Creature Comforts.

WDW resort guests and those staying at other area hotels have access to services providing nonemergency medical care. Centra Care Walk-In Medical Care, owned and operated by Florida Hospital, has two locations near Walt Disney World. Both are adjacent to pharmacies, and one has X-ray facilities. For information, call 407-238-2000.

One of the facilities, at 12500 South Apopka-Vineland Road, is open 8 A.M. to midnight weekdays, 8 A.M. to 8 P.M. weekends. The other, at 12139 South Apopka-Vineland Road, is open 9 A.M. to 9 P.M. during the week, 10 A.M. to 10 P.M. weekends. Call 407-239-6463 to be connected to a Centra Care facility.

Courtesy transportation is available from most area hotels to Centra Care clinics, and there is a no-tipping policy. Waits in walk-in clinics can be lengthy, but Centra Care drivers call ahead to learn which has the shorter wait. For patients who prefer to have the doctor come to them, Centra Care offers 24-hour in-room visits (407-238-2000), as does Doctors On Call Service. A house-call only medical service, Doctors On Call can be reached at 407-399-DOCS (399-3627).

The most common maladies reported by Disney guests? Sunburn, colds, fevers, earaches, and injuries from falls.

For emergencies dial 911, or call nearby Sandlake Hospital (407-351-8550) or Celebration Health (407-303-4000).

For Diabetics: Walt Disney World resorts provide refrigeration services for insulin. All villa accommodations have their own refrigerators, and small refrigerators are available at other resorts for about $10 a night.

Prescriptions: For a referral to a pharmacy or to find out how to have medications delivered, call Centra Care (407-239-7777).

MONEY

Cash, traveler's checks, personal checks, American Express, MasterCard, Visa, Discover Card, Diner's Club, JCB Card, and The Disney Credit Card are accepted as payment for most charges at Disney. Checks must bear

your name and address, be drawn on a U.S. bank, and be accompanied by proper ID—a valid driver's license and a major credit card. Note that some snack stands only accept cash.

A Disney resort guest perk: Leave a credit card imprint at check-in and the hotel IDs may be used to cover purchases in shops, lounge and restaurant charges, and recreational fees incurred inside Walt Disney World. A bill will be sent home for all charges made past check-out time.

ATMs: Automated Teller Machines are scattered throughout Walt Disney World. Theme park locations include the Magic Kingdom (under the train station on Main Street, U.S.A., in Adventureland near The Enchanted Tiki Room, and in the Tomorrowland arcade), Epcot (near the main entrance, on the pathway between Future World and World Showcase, and in Germany), the Disney-MGM Studios (at the entrance and inside Toy Story Pizza Planet), and Animal Kingdom (at the entrance), plus the TTC. All WDW resorts have ATMs in the lobby; the Fort Wilderness ATM is outside Pioneer Hall. Three can be found in Downtown Disney: near the Rock N Roll Beach Club at Pleasure Island, next to Guest Services in the Marketplace, and by the West Side's Forty Thirst Street. Most bank cards and credit cards are accepted; the fee ranges from $2 to $2.50.

Banking: SunTrust, located across from Downtown Disney Marketplace, offers a variety of services. Guests can get cash advances on MasterCard and Visa credit cards; receive incoming wire transfers (for a $30 fee); and cash, replace, or purchase American Express traveler's checks. This branch is open from 9 A.M. to 4 P.M. weekdays, until 6 P.M. Thursdays (407-237-4786, 800-432-4760, or 800-786-8787). The drive-thru is open until 6 P.M. Monday through Friday.

Disney Dollars: Money bearing the image of Mickey, Goofy, or Minnie is available for purchase at City Hall (Magic Kingdom) and Guest Relations (Epcot, the Disney-MGM Studios, and Animal Kingdom) in $1, $5, and $10 denominations. (The exchange rate is always a buck for a buck.) Disney Dollars are accepted as cash throughout the World.

Traveler's Checks: Even the most careful of vacationers occasionally loses a wallet, and traveler's checks can take the sting out of that loss. Look for promotions by banks at home in the months preceding a vacation to see if one of the major brands—American Express, MasterCard, Visa, Citibank, and Bank of America—is available free. Stash the receipt bearing the check numbers in a place separate from the checks themselves, along with a piece of identification such as a duplicate driver's license or a spare credit card to speed the refund process should your checks get lost.

To purchase, cash, or replace American Express traveler's checks, go to the SunTrust bank across from the Downtown Disney Marketplace (an American Express referral number is required for check replacement; call 800-221-7282) or one of the American Express travel offices (in Epcot or the Contemporary resort). AAA members can visit the AAA Travel Center in the Magic Kingdom for traveler's check assistance.

Foreign Currency Exchange: Up to $50 per person in foreign currency may be exchanged daily at Guest Relations in the theme parks, and up to $500 at the Guest Services desk at WDW resorts. Foreign currency exchange is also available at the SunTrust bank across from Downtown Disney and in the Gooding's grocery store at the Crossroads shopping center near Hotel Plaza Boulevard.

PETS

No pets (other than service dogs) are allowed in the theme parks, or the WDW resorts, except at certain campsites at Fort Wilderness (request a pet site for $3 extra per day). Travelers who bring pets along can lodge them in one of the five air-conditioned Pet Care Kennels: near the Transportation and Ticket Center (TTC), to the left of the Epcot Entrance Plaza, at the entrance to Disney-MGM Studios, at the Disney's Animal Kingdom entrance, and at the Fort Wilderness campground entrance, next to a field where owners can take their pets out for a run. During busy seasons, it is best to arrive before the 9 A.M. rush hour. Note that kennels close one hour after the closest theme park closes. In the event of an emergency, kennel workers will contact a veterinarian on your pet's behalf.

Animals such as bears, cougars, and ocelots have all been accommodated by the kennels, and exotic pets may be accepted—if a bit reluctantly. However, owners must put more unusual animals into the kennels' cages, and rabbits, birds, turtles, hamsters, nonpoisonous snakes, and other animals unsuited (because of their size) to cat- and dog-size cages must have their own escape-proof accommodations.

Guests may board pets overnight in any of the kennels on property. While there are no staffers on duty overnight, it just takes a phone call to gain access to your pet after hours (guests receive the number when they check their pet in). Cost is $11, including Friskies dry food (WDW resort guests pay $9 per night to leave pets overnight); a day stay is $6, with one feeding. Guests who board pets overnight must walk them at least three times a day, as animals are not otherwise let out of their cages. Pets will be fed special food, if provided. For information, call 407-824-6568. Reservations are not accepted.

Be sure to bring along your pet's certificate of vaccinations, since Florida law requires proof of immunization for animals involved in biting incidents. It's always a good idea to pack your pet's favorite blanket, pillow, or toy, too. And never leave pets in your car. It is extremely dangerous for the animal and is against the law.

Outside Walt Disney World: A few hotels in the Orlando area, including the Quality Inn Plaza (for $5 per day), permit pets to stay with guests. Call the Orlando/Orange County Convention & Visitors Bureau (407-363-5871 or 800-551-0181; the latter is a recording).

POCKET PAGERS

Two types of devices are available to signal a telephone call or message. They can be rented at nearly all WDW hotels; inquire at the front desk.

RELIGIOUS SERVICES

A number of religious services are held at WDW and in the surrounding area.

Protestant: 9 A.M. on Sunday at Luau Cove at the Polynesian resort.

Muslim: Prayer takes place five times a day at Jama Masijid; 11543 Ruby Lake Rd. Call 407-238-2700 for more information.

Catholic: 8 A.M. and 10:15 A.M. on Sunday at Luau Cove at the Polynesian resort. For more information, check with Guest Services at any WDW hotel, or call 407-939-4636. The closest Catholic church off the property is Mary, Queen of the Universe Shrine, 2½ miles north of Lake Buena Vista, at 8300 Vineland Ave. This enormous church seats 2,000 people and has beautiful gardens, fountains, and a large gift shop, which is open daily. Call 407-239-6600 for mass times.

Jewish: Reform services are held at the Congregation of Liberal Judaism (928 Malone Dr., Orlando; 407-645-0444), near Winter

Park about 20 miles from Walt Disney World. Conservative services are held at Temple Ohalei Rivka, also known as the Southwest Orlando Jewish Congregation (11200 Apopka-Vineland Rd.; 407-239-5444), approximately three miles from Downtown Disney.

SHOPPING FOR NECESSITIES

Almost any everyday item can be purchased right on the property. At least one shop in every WDW resort stocks toiletries. In addition, a number of over-the-counter health aids, plus many other useful items, can be purchased at the Emporium on Main Street in the Magic Kingdom; they're kept behind

DID YOU KNOW...

When it comes to fashion, Walt Disney World is the biggest clothes horse of them all. There are more than 2.5 million garments in its corporate closet, making it the largest working wardrobe in the world.

the counter, so ask for what you want. Aspirin and sunscreen are also available at Island Supply in Adventureland, and Mickey's Star Traders in Tomorrowland. In Epcot, sundries are sold in at least one shop in each World Showcase pavilion and at all Future World stores. At the Disney-MGM Studios, stop by the Crossroads of the World and Movieland Memorabilia shops. At Animal Kingdom, you can pick up bare necessities at Island Mercantile.

SMOKING

A strict, new Walt Disney World smoking regulation took effect in 2000. It prohibits smoking in the four theme parks, with the exception of specifically designated areas. Smoking is also prohibited at all WDW-owned restaurants, with the exception of some outdoor seating areas. However, most clubs (except the Adventurers Club and Comedy Warehouse at Pleasure Island), as well as many resort lounges, allow smoking in some spots. The same goes for water parks, miniature golf courses, and Disney's Wide World of Sports Complex. Tobacco products are not sold in any of the theme parks. Guests may purchase tobacco products at the WDW resorts and at Downtown Disney.

All Walt Disney World resorts have rooms designated for smokers and nonsmokers alike. Be sure to request the room-type of your choice as you check into your resort.

TELEPHONE CALLS

It takes more than the traditional seven digits to make a local call in this neck of the woods. Every time a local call is placed in Central Florida, callers must dial the area code and the seven-digit number. The rule applies to calls made within the same area code as well as for those that connect with other area codes. For local calls, it is not necessary to dial a 1 before the ten-digit number.

Local calls made from payphones cost 35 cents a piece. Rates charged by local resorts tend to vary quite a bit (for local and long distance calls alike). Be sure to inquire about phone rates and fees before you make any calls beyond your resort.

TIPPING

Tips are no less valued at Walt Disney World resorts than at any other hotel—$1 per bag is appropriate for lugging luggage; $1 to $2 per night for housekeeping services. Gratuities of 15 to 18 percent (excluding tax) are customary at full-service restaurants. (If service is exceptional or otherwise, adjust the tip accordingly.) Gratuity is included in the room service bill at WDW resorts and some off-property hotels. Check before you tip twice. Note that a ten percent gratuity is automatically included at the Pepper Market food court in Disney's Coronado Springs resort (despite the self-serve set-up).

Give cab drivers a 15 percent tip for good service. Baggage handlers at the train station and airport expect about $1 per bag.

WEATHER

Call Walt Disney World Weather Information (407-824-4104), or check The Weather Channel website (*www.weather.com*).

Magical Milestones

Even frequent visitors have trouble keeping up with all the changes at Walt Disney World. The time line below will help you determine which major attractions have opened since your last visit.

left margin: GETTING READY TO GO

1971	Magic Kingdom
1972	Carousel of Progress
1973	Pirates of the Caribbean, Tom Sawyer Island
1974	Star Jets (now Astro Orbiter)
1975	Space Mountain, WEDway PeopleMover (now Tomorrowland Transit Authority)
1976	River Country
1980	Big Thunder Mountain Railroad
1982	Epcot
1983	Journey into Imagination pavilion (now Imagination!)
1984	Morocco pavilion
1986	The Living Seas
1988	Wonders of Life, Norway, Mickey's Birthdayland
1989	Disney-MGM Studios, Mickey's Starland (replaced Birthdayland), Body Wars and Cranium Command, Typhoon Lagoon, Pleasure Island
1990	Star Tours, Honey, I Shrunk the Kids Movie Set Adventure
1991	SpectroMagic, Jim Henson's Muppet*Vision 3-D

1992	Splash Mountain, Voyage of The Little Mermaid
1993	New productions of The Hall of Presidents and Carousel of Progress
1994	Legend of the Lion King, The Timekeeper, Innoventions (replaced Communicore), Honey, I Shrunk the Audience (replaced Captain EO), Food Rocks (replaced Kitchen Kabaret), The Circle of Life, The Twilight Zone Tower of Terror, Blizzard Beach
1995	Alien Encounter
1996	Mickey's Toontown Fair (replaced Starland), Ellen's Energy Adventure, Backstage Pass, Disney's The Hunchback of Notre Dame—A Musical Adventure, Fantasia Gardens, Celebration, BoardWalk
1997	Disney's Wide World of Sports complex, Downtown Disney West Side
1998	Disney's Animal Kingdom, Buzz Lightyear's Space Ranger Spin, Enchanted Tiki Room—Under New Management, Fantasmic!, DisneyQuest, Disney Cruise Line
1999	Kali River Rapids, Maharajah Jungle Trek, Test Track, Rock 'n' Roller Coaster starring Aerosmith, The Many Adventures of Winnie the Pooh, Cirque du Soleil, Journey Into Your Imagination, Sounds Dangerous starring Drew Carey

WHAT'S NEW?

To spotlight attractions making their debut, some listings are marked with a special stamp, shown here. Look for it throughout the book. Here are a few highlights:

- **Disney's Animal Kingdom Lodge** (page 76)
- **Disney's Wilderness Lodge Villas** (page 59)
- **Image Works: Kodak "What If" Labs** (page 129)
- **The Magic Carpets of Aladdin** (page 97)

Transportation & Accommodations

44 Getting Oriented

45 Walt Disney World Transportation

48 WDW Resorts

52 Rates at WDW Properties

80 Resorts on Hotel Plaza Boulevard

84 Off-Property Accommodations

The popularity of Walt Disney World has made the region around Orlando one of the world's major tourism and commercial centers, and transportation facilities, from a state-of-the-art airport to an efficient network of highways, bring visitors to the area by the millions.

There's no doubt that getting to and around the Walt Disney World region can be very confusing. The only more perplexing dilemma may be choosing the best accommodations for your family from among the huge assortment of hotels and motels.

The accommodations operated by Walt Disney World itself range from futuristic high-rise towers to treehouses buried deep in piney woods. In between are resorts that evoke striking images of Africa, the South Pacific, historic Florida, the Pacific Northwest, the Caribbean, New England, early Atlantic City, Louisiana, the Southwest, Mexico, and the sports, movie, and music worlds, plus rustic cabins in a sprawling, beautifully maintained campground. And that list doesn't include the many villas that provide extraordinary space and luxury, or the studios and homes with one, two, and three bedrooms that can be purchased through a special vacation-ownership system. What follows should help travelers sort out all the lodging options on Walt Disney World property, as well as shed light on the broad range of possibilities that exist outside the WDW gates.

GETTING ORIENTED

rlando, the Central Florida city of more than one million residents, is the municipality with which Walt Disney World is most closely associated. Walt Disney World, however, is in a far smaller community called Lake Buena Vista, 15 miles from Orlando's business center. A number of hotels and restaurants are located in Lake Buena Vista, though there are many more in Orlando.

ORLANDO-AREA HIGHWAYS: The most important Orlando traffic artery is I-4, which runs diagonally through the area from southwest up to northeast, cutting through the southern half of Walt Disney World. It then angles on toward Orlando and Winter Park, ending near Daytona Beach at I-95, which runs north and south along the coast.

All the city's other important highways intersect I-4, and each has a name as well as a number. From south to north, they include U.S. 192 (a.k.a. Irlo Bronson Memorial Highway), which takes an east-west course that crosses the WDW entrance road and leads into downtown Kissimmee on the east; S.R. 528 (a.k.a. the Beeline Expressway), which shoots eastward from I-4; S.R. 435 (a.k.a. Kirkman Road), which runs north and south and intersects International Drive, where many motels catering to WDW visitors are located; U.S. 17-92-441 (a.k.a. the Orange Blossom Trail), which runs north and south, paralleling Kirkman Road on the east; and S.R. 50 (a.k.a. Colonial Drive), which runs east and west.

WALT DISNEY WORLD EXITS: The 47-square-mile tract that is Walt Disney World is roughly rectangular. I-4 runs through its southern half from southwest to northeast. The major WDW destinations are most efficiently reached by taking the I-4 exits suggested below; off the highway, clear signage makes it easy for visitors to get anywhere in the World. Keep in mind that special events will often require rerouting of traffic patterns, so it's best to follow signs as directed.

- **Exit 27**, marked "S.R. 535/Lake Buena Vista," is the route taken to the resorts on Hotel Plaza Boulevard and the Crossroads of Lake Buena Vista shopping center.

- **Exit 26B**, marked "Epcot/Downtown Disney" leads to Epcot, Typhoon Lagoon, Downtown Disney, Lake Buena Vista golf course, the Disney Institute, Bonnet Creek Golf Club, the BoardWalk, Caribbean Beach, Swan, Dolphin, Yacht and Beach Club, Port Orleans, Dixie Landings, and Old Key West resorts. It is also a good alternate route to the Disney-MGM Studios.

- **Exit 25**, marked "192/Magic Kingdom," leads to the Magic Kingdom, Disney-MGM Studios, Disney's Animal Kingdom, Blizzard Beach, Fort Wilderness, River Country, Palm and Magnolia golf courses, Disney's Wide World of Sports complex, and Disney's Animal Kingdom Lodge, All-Star Music, Sports, and Movies, Coronado Springs, Contemporary, Polynesian, Grand Floridian, and Wilderness Lodge resorts.

HOT TIP Parking spaces are cleverly labeled throughout Walt Disney World. Yet, many drivers still misplace their vehicles. Avoid being "dopey": Always write down the location!

WALT DISNEY WORLD TRANSPORTATION

Walt Disney World transportation is extensive, with boats, buses, and the monorail all doing their part to shuttle guests around. Visitors staying at WDW hotels should receive a detailed brochure about transportation options at check-in. (If you don't, just ask.) For transportation information, call 407-WDW-INFO (939-4636).

The system's central hub is called the Transportation and Ticket Center (TTC), located near the Magic Kingdom. Monorail, bus, and ferry service connect the TTC to points throughout the World. Day visitors must park here before taking a monorail or ferry to the Magic Kingdom. (Most Disney resort guests can bypass the TTC via direct buses.)

The monorail runs along a circular route near the Magic Kingdom, stopping at the TTC, Polynesian, Grand Floridian, Contemporary, and Magic Kingdom. A separate extension of the monorail system connects the TTC to Epcot. Bus service is the cornerstone of the WDW transportation system. It is efficient, if occasionally confusing. With a few exceptions, buses arrive every 15 to 20 minutes, from one hour before park opening until about an hour after closing; bus stops are clearly marked. Travel times vary, depending on the route.

Although Disney resort guests receive complimentary transportation to all sites on-property, that transportation is not always direct. *Build in extra time for travel*, especially if you have made priority seating arrangements at a restaurant. Also, know that traveling between resorts can be time-consuming and usually requires at least one transfer.

Should You Rent A Car?

If you plan to spend all of your time on WDW turf, you can spare yourself the expense. Shuttle service from the airport to all area hotels is available around the clock, and taxis are in good supply. Within the World, an exhaustive (sometimes exhausting) network of transportation brings guests from point to point. Most area hotels offer their own bus service to and from Disney theme parks (inquire in advance about schedules and costs, if any).

However, for those planning to visit Orlando-area restaurants and any attractions outside Walt Disney World, a rental car is a must. Also, certain routes are more convenient by car. It's easiest to rent from one of the companies at the airport: National (800-227-7368), Avis (800-331-1212), Budget (800-527-0700), or Dollar (800-800-4000). Other rental agencies provide shuttles from the airport, so it may be worth the extra time if you get a good deal. For day trips, consider National at the Magic Kingdom Auto Plaza (407-824-3470) or one of the rental agencies that have desks at the resorts on Hotel Plaza Boulevard, or simply inquire about car rental at the front desk of your resort.

From several Walt Disney World locales, water launches usher guests to the Magic Kingdom, Epcot, the Disney-MGM Studios, Downtown Disney, or between resorts. Boats generally depart every 20 to 30 minutes.

TRANSPORTATION ID REQUIREMENTS: Guests wishing to use the Walt Disney World transportation system may be asked to present proof of their riding privileges. Accepted IDs afford different degrees of access. WDW resort ID cards, Park Hopper Passes, Park Hopper Plus Passes, Ultimate Park Hopper Passes, and Annual Passes allow guests unlimited use of all Disney buses, monorails, and boats. Valid one-day theme park tickets permit guests to use all monorails and the ferries running between the TTC and the Magic Kingdom, but do not allow use of buses.

TAXI SERVICE: Cabs are available for about $1.50 per mile. Stick with the yellow cabs or other authorized cab services. Avoid independent cabs whenever possible—many charge outrageous rates. Disney employees can direct you to authorized taxis. If you plan to travel between resorts that aren't joined by water taxi or monorail, and time is of the essence, we recommend taking a taxi.

THE MONORAIL: The Walt Disney World monorail system, frequently referred to as the "highway in the sky," is an extremely efficient (and to many, downright exciting) way to travel. There are two main loops, which converge at the Transportation and

DID YOU KNOW...

The Walt Disney World monorail system—a 14.7-mile highway in the sky—has carried more than a billion passengers since 1971.

Ticket Center (TTC) stop. One loop connects the Contemporary, Polynesian, and Grand Floridian resorts with the Magic Kingdom and the TTC. The other loop links Epcot with the TTC, making the monorail a park hopper's dream come true. Note that guests staying in the aforementioned resorts

Transportation Tips

• If you are staying at a Disney resort, request a complimentary Walt Disney World transportation guidemap at check-in.
• Most buses are equipped with wheelchair lifts. Such buses have a blue emblem on the windshield and rear door.
• When using the WDW transportation system to travel between your resort and a theme park or from one park to another, allow an extra 30 minutes to get to your destination.
• The interval between the arrivals of most Disney buses is about 20 minutes.
• Be forewarned: It takes a long time to travel by bus from resort to resort. Plan on a trip of up to 90 minutes.
• Monorails usually run until two hours after the latest theme park closing time. (One hour after Magic Kingdom E-Ride Nights.)
• Note that there is no direct transportation between Disney's BoardWalk and other resorts. You must first travel to Downtown Disney, and transfer to the appropriate bus.
• *Never* attempt to vacate a theme park just as a park closes. Instead, plan to linger a bit in a shopping area, or grab a seat and watch the crowds crawl toward their respective buses, boats, cars, and monorails.
• It is not uncommon, especially at park opening and closing times, for guests to be asked to stand on the bus or monorail.
• Keep in mind that the most obvious mode of transportation may not be the quickest. For example, it is much faster to walk to the Magic Kingdom from the Contemporary resort than it is to take the monorail or boat.
• It's possible to rent a car from any Disney resort. For details, inquire at Guest Relations, or contact the front desk.
• WDW resort guests who arrive with a car receive a complimentary parking permit upon check-in. The permit, good for the length of your stay, allows you to park anywhere on property (including at other resorts), for free.

have a private track on the Magic Kingdom loop, making for a hastier exit at closing time. All Disney resort guests are entitled to unlimited use of the monorail (with a valid resort ID), as are day visitors with a valid transportation ID. Monorails run from 7 A.M. until about two hours after park closing.

Timing Tip: It takes about 3 to 4 minutes to get from one stop to the next on the Magic Kingdom monorail loop, making for a grand circle total of about 15 to 20 minutes.

ACCOMMODATIONS

With hundreds of resorts in the Orlando area to choose from, the challenge of picking a hotel may seem insurmountable. Our advice is to approach the matter in stages and make no hasty decisions.

Weigh the Options: First decide whether to stay on or off Disney property. We recommend staying at a Disney resort because the conveniences and perks offered to resort guests are significant (see page 48) and a Disney stay means the show never ends. That said, there are two major factors that tend to lure guests off property: budget and schedule.

Travelers on a tight budget will find some off-property options that are quite reasonable. Remember, however, that Disney offers rooms as low as $77 per night, so choose off-property accommodations only if the difference in price is substantial.

Guests who will spend only part of their trip exploring Walt Disney World may also prefer an off-property hotel—one that's closer to the other attractions on their itinerary. Note that WDW resort guests who plan to venture beyond Disney boundaries will find it economical to rent a car for the day (see page 45).

Does an off-property hotel seem to suit your needs? Don't reserve that room just yet. There's one final aspect to consider—the Disney atmosphere. Every Disney resort offers a full battery of whimsical diversions and a never-ending supply of festive ambience. From shower soaps bearing the tri-circle imprint of Mickey's head to wake-up calls by the Mouse himself, every detail sings of Disney. And to many devotees these touches are worth it.

Deciding Factors: Once the on- or off-property decision has been made, it's time to look at the specific hotels. The biggest differences among accommodations, at both Disney-owned and independent resorts, seem to be in the size of the rooms and bathrooms, attention to decor, level of service, variety of dining options, recreational facilities, landscaping, location, and, of course, cost.

Consider how much time you plan to spend in the room, whether you'll need to return to the hotel during the day, or if you'll have time to use the facilities (golf courses, tennis courts, etc.) and room amenities that are included in the price. Parties with five or more members have an additional concern: how best to accommodate their group. It may be less expensive (and more private and spacious) to reserve adjoining, value-priced rooms instead of one larger luxury room or villa.

Ask the Right Questions: Once a hotel that meets all basic criteria is selected, it's best to do one last round of research, so there will be no surprises at check-in.

For example, ask about any possible hidden costs, like shuttle service to and from Walt Disney World (which can be more than $20 per person, round-trip) or taxes that may not be included in the quoted price.

Though most off-property hotels offer transportation to WDW, the frequency and number of buses vary significantly. Find out the exact schedule and the stops made. If you miss the first bus, how long will you have to wait for the next bus traveling to your destination? In certain cases, it may be hours.

Some hotels advertise a misleading proximity to Walt Disney World. Remember that WDW is 47 square miles, so while a hotel may be only a short distance from the Disney border, the commute to the theme parks could still be considerable. Get the specifics.

Guests traveling with children should check the age at which children staying in the same room with adults will be billed as extra adults. (At Disney resorts, the age is 17.)

Safety is an issue that many people overlook while on vacation. Inquire about the hotel's layout: Will you enter the room from the building's interior or exterior? Is there a central building or many smaller villas? How long and well lit is the walk from the bus stop to the rooms? These factors are important to all visitors, but especially to the elderly or young single guests traveling in small groups.

Reserve a Room: Found the perfect hotel? Now book it before someone else does, and don't forget to ask about any special discounts or seasonal promotions.

WALT DISNEY WORLD RESORTS

Walt Disney World hotels fall into two categories: Disney-owned and non-Disney-owned resorts. Of the 27 WDW properties, the Swan and Dolphin, and the resorts on Hotel Plaza Boulevard do not belong to Disney. Expect services and benefits in the non-Disney resorts to be slightly modified (see pages 65 and 80).

On-Property Perks: Disney resorts offer guests early admission to the Magic Kingdom, Epcot, and the Disney-MGM Studios on designated days; unlimited use of the WDW transportation system; the convenience of charging most purchases to your hotel bill; free delivery of packages to the resort; the ability to reserve golf tee times up to 90 days in advance; and access to a well-informed Guest Services staff.

Room Amenities: All Disney rooms have alarm clocks; toiletries; safes; voice mail; TVs with local and national channels, including the Disney Channel and ESPN, as well as WDW event information. There are hair dryers, irons (with boards), and coffeemakers in many rooms. These extras are always available upon request. Laundry facilities, dry cleaning, and room service are provided propertywide.

Resort Primer

Payment Methods: Hotel bills and room deposits may be paid by credit card (American Express, Visa, MasterCard, Diner's Club, Discover, JCB, or The Disney Credit Card), traveler's check, cashier's check, money order, cash, or personal check. Checks must bear the guest's name and address, be drawn on a U.S. bank, and be accompanied by proper ID (a valid driver's license or a government-issued passport).

Room Deposit Requirements: A deposit equal to one night's lodging (or campsite rental) is required *within 14 days* of the time that a reservation is made. Reservations are automatically canceled if deposits are not received by the 14-day deadline. (Reservations booked less than 30 days prior to arrival will receive special instructions for deposits.)

When booking by phone, guests can pay the deposit by giving an American Express or Disney Card account number. Those who wish to use another payment method may do so by mailing it in along with the payment stub that comes with the reservation confirmation.

Cancelation Policy: Deposits will be fully refunded if the reservation is canceled at least *5 days* before the scheduled arrival.

Additional Charges: When more than two adults (age 17 and up) occupy a standard room, the added per-day fee for each extra adult is $2 at Fort Wilderness campsites; $5 at Fort Wilderness Cabins; $10 at the All-Star resorts; $15 at Caribbean Beach, Port Orleans, Dixie Landings, and Coronado Springs; and $25 at all other WDW resorts. Note that in some resorts, an additional bed may be required to sleep an extra adult. If so, the cost for the bed is $15.

Check-In and Check-Out: The early check-out time (11 A.M. at all WDW lodgings) and the late check-in times (1 P.M. at the campsites, 3 P.M. in most hotels, 4 P.M. at The Villas at the Disney Institute, Board-Walk Villas, The Villas at Wilderness Lodge,

HOT TIP Nonsmoking rooms and rooms equipped for guests with disabilities are available at all WDW resorts.

All-Star resorts, and Old Key West) often come as a surprise. The late check-in hour need not be an inconvenience. Guests who arrive before check-in time can preregister, store luggage at Guest Services (without fee) and head to the parks or relax by the pool.

WDW ID Cards: Issued on arrival at Disney resorts, the cards (which double as room keys) entitle guests to unlimited use of WDW transportation (through the last day of your stay), and charge privileges (provided you leave a credit card imprint with the hotel) to cover purchases in shops, lounges, and restaurants, as well as recreational fees incurred anywhere in the World.

Note: Any charges incurred on a hotel ID after check-out will be reflected in a revised bill, which will be sent to you by Disney. Swan and Dolphin guests may not use their IDs to charge meals at restaurants outside the two hotels. Other restrictions may apply. Read the cards carefully when checking in.

WALT DISNEY WORLD RESORT FINDER

Name & Location	Setting/Theme	Favored By	Romantic Hideaways	Kids Adore	Dining Tip	Resort Category & Amenities
Animal Kingdom Lodge Animal Kingdom area (page 76)	African wildlife preserve	Animal lovers—nearly every room affords an upclose view of wandering wildlife; Art afficionados—authentic African artwork abounds	Private balconies by moonlight; Sunset lounge overlooking the savanna	The kopje, a rocky outcropping from which to spy on critters; Story time beside the lobby fireplace; Rustic bunkbeds (on request)	Sample the exotic eats and atmosphere of Boma while savoring the sights of the savanna	Full-service restaurants, fast food spots, room service
BoardWalk* Epcot area (page 68)	Turn-of-the-century Atlantic City	Night owls—the entertainment options are numerous and right in the backyard; Epcot-lovers, who will appreciate the short commute; Disney Vacation Club members	Moonlight strolls along the boardwalk; A special fireworks cruise	The Keister Coaster, a 200-foot water slide at the main pool; The face-painting booth on the boardwalk at night	Snack on salt water taffy, cotton candy, or old-fashioned sticky buns while strolling along the boards	Bellman luggage service
Contemporary Magic Kingdom area (page 54)	Retro-futuristic	Families—the monorail whisks through it and the Magic Kingdom is a short walk away; Professionals, who can take advantage of the hotel's many business services	The rooftop look-out, which helps make up for the resort's otherwise less-than-romantic atmosphere and decor	One of the best Disney resort arcades; The party held every 45 minutes at Chef Mickey's fabulously fun character meals	For a fireworks seating at California Grill, make arrangements through 407-WDW-DINE well in advance	Valet parking
Grand Floridian Magic Kingdom area (page 57)	Victorian seaside resort	Honeymooners, who will love spending much of their vacation basking in the resort's unebbing romantic atmosphere; Magic Kingdom and monorail fans	Manicured rose gardens; Honeymoon suites; The Grand Lobby for a cocktail while an orchestra performs on the balcony	Child-size robes can be sent to the guest rooms; The complimentary activities, like face painting and storytelling	Have a spot of traditional afternoon tea, accompanied by a scone, at the Garden View Lounge	Swimming pools
Polynesian Magic Kingdom area (page 55)	South Pacific	Romantics—the white-sand beaches and lush, tropical setting will make you swoon; Vacationers looking for a hotel with a real resort feel; Magic Kingdom and monorail fans	Hammocks or beach coves for two; Sunset Pointe	The weekend torch-lighting ceremony in the Great Ceremonial Hall; The slide- and waterfall-endowed pool	The Polynesian Luau is favored by many for its knock-out entertainment, though the menu elicits few raves	Beach access‡

Additional Resort Category & Amenities (DELUXE):
- Full-service restaurants, fast food spots, room service
- Bellman luggage service
- Valet parking
- Swimming pools
- Beach access‡
- On-site recreation, such as boat rentals‡
- On-site kid's activities
- Most rooms sleep 5 guests
- Monorail, bus, or boat transport to all parks

($189–$1,995)

‡Except Disney's Animal Kingdom Lodge

❤ This resort hosts character meals.   * BoardWalk, Wilderness Lodge, and Fort Wilderness also have Home Away From Home accommodations.

WALT DISNEY WORLD RESORT FINDER

Name & Location	Setting/ Theme	Favored By	Romantic Hideaways	Kids Adore	Dining Tip	Resort Category & Amenities
						DELUXE
Swan & Dolphin Epcot area (page 65)	Maritime whimsy	Conventioneers—the services are excellent Guests who want many of the Disney perks but not necessarily the Disney hotel Serious swimmers—the only WDW resort lap pool is here	The Lobby Court cigar bar at the Dolphin The small beach tucked behind the main pool at the Swan	The swan-shaped pedal boats The giant swan and dolphin statues perched atop their respective resorts	Save room for Dolphin Fountain's Banana Fo-Fana Split or a seven-scoop doozy called the Dolphin Splash	Full-service restaurants, fast food spots, room service Bellman luggage service Valet parking Swimming pools Beach access‡ On-site recreation, such as boat rentals‡ On-site kid's activities Most rooms sleep 5 guests Monorail, bus, or boat transport to all parks ($189–$1,995) ‡Except Disney's Animal Kingdom Lodge
Wilderness Lodge* Magic Kingdom area (page 59)	America's grandest national parks	Sweethearts—love is always in the air at this resort Winter visitors—the warm, cozy atmosphere is even more inviting when the many fireplaces are roaring Disney Vacation Club members	Steamy, bubbling "hot springs" whirlpools The cozy alcoves hidden on each floor of the main building	Totem poles, an erupting geyser, and countless Hidden Mickeys—there's even a free tour to help guests find them	Sample the Wild King salmon, an Artist Point signature dish Savor morning coffee from a fireside rocking chair	
Yacht & Beach Club Epcot area (page 64)	Martha's Vineyard and Nantucket Island	Ambitious guests—those who plan to see and do everything Disney has to offer will like the central location Everyone—the deluxe atmosphere and amenities appeal to all	The Yacht Club's peaceful gazebo Secluded whirlpools The beach, perfect for twilight strolls	Stormalong Bay—the sand-bottomed 3-acre pool, with water jets, a series of water slides, and a shipwreck to play on	Cape May Cafe's bountiful nighttime clam bake has many a surf-and-turf fan lining up for more	
						HOME AWAY FROM HOME
Disney's Old Key West Downtown Disney area (page 73)	Key West	Guests looking for a homey, village atmosphere Disney Vacation Club members	Private whirlpool tubs—they come with all resort rooms except the studios	The weekly Tiny Tot Tea Parties and Un-Birthday Parties with snacks, games, and treats, held at Community Hall	Order the delicious Key lime pie at Olivia's Cafe. It's sold by the slice or by the pie	Kitchens, restaurants, pizza delivery Luggage service Swimming pools On-site recreation, such as boat rentals Front-door parking Rooms sleep 4–12 guests Bus or boat transport to all parks ($209–$1,700)
Villas at the Disney Institute Downtown Disney area (page 72)	Sleepy village	Sports aficionados—the resort's tennis courts and swimming pools, plus nearby golf courses provide ample opportunity for sporting pursuits Guests for whom bliss is summed up in one word: spa	The beautifully maintained gardens	Living like the Swiss Family Robinson (with much plusher digs) at the Treehouse Villas	Take the boatride to nearby Downtown Disney where an eclectic selection of eateries awaits	

Amenities & price ranges by category

	MODERATE ($129–$199)	VALUE ($77–$104)	CAMPGROUND ($34–$279)
Amenities	Restaurant, food court, limited room service; Bellman luggage service; Swimming pools with slides; On-site recreation, such as bikes and boat rentals; Rooms sleep 4 guests; Bus transport to all parks	Food court, pizza delivery; Hourly luggage service; Swimming pools; Bus transport to all parks	Recipient of perfect ratings from *Woodall's* and *Trailer Life* magazine; Bus transport to all parks

Resort comparison

Resort	Theme	Best suited for	Most romantic / special spot	Don't miss	Money-saving / insider tip
Caribbean Beach — Epcot area (page 62)	Tropical islands	Families—while all Disney resorts have kid appeal, the colorful design, themed pool and beach setting make this hotel ideal for families with kids of any age	Aruba beach—the hotel's longest, most secluded strip of sand	The fortress pool and Parrot Cay Island; The coconut postcards sold at the Calypso shop (real coconuts!)	Try a food court kids meal—it's served in a sand bucket with a shovel (and keep an ear out for the talking trash cans!)
Coronado Springs — Animal Kingdom area (page 77)	Mexico and Southwest USA	Conventioneers, which means more business services (and a health club), higher food prices, and slightly less family entertainment than at the other moderate resorts	The waterfront in the peaceful Casitas area; The gazebo-style boat rental dock at twilight	The Dig Site, which encompasses the resort's playground and main pool with its Mayan temple water slide	Carry-out items at the Pepper Market food court are spared the ten percent gratuity charge
Dixie Landings — Downtown Disney area (page 71)	Antebellum South	Love-birds on a budget—the decor is similar to many of Disney's deluxe hotels, as is the romance factor, but the price is considerably less	Any room in Magnolia Bend's stately mansions; The Cotton Co-op, with its handsome leather couches, fireplace, and lively piano player	The pool, fishing hole, and extensive playground at Ol' Man Island; The resort's 30-foot working waterwheel	Consider Cotton Co-op's hearty appetizers for light or late-night dining
Port Orleans — Downtown Disney area (page 70)	New Orleans' French Quarter	Peace seekers. This Disney resort is much smaller than the others in its price category. Guests feel immediately at home and relaxed	The Sassagoula River Cruise, which transports guests by moonlight to Dixie Landings or the docks of Downtown Disney	A spin in a pedal boat past Beaux Tie Island; Doubloon Lagoon—a magnificent, sea serpent-themed family pool	Toast the evening at Scat Cat's Club with a cup of Mardi Gras punch or a little French Quarter TNT
All-Star Movies, Music & Sports — Animal Kingdom area (page 75)	Comic book	Penny-savers of all ages. These three resorts offer fun theming and bold decor, plus all the Disney perks, at a notably lower price than at other Disney resorts	All-Star Music's Jazz and Broadway areas (note that Music tends to attract more couples without children than the other two themes)	Awe-inspiring, super-size icons—the movie and sports themes score the highest points; Extra-large arcades	Buy an All-Star refillable mug for unlimited refills during your stay (it makes for a nice souvenir, too)
Fort Wilderness Resort and Campground* — Magic Kingdom area (page 61)	Rustic woods	Motor home mavens—Disney's hook-ups are considered top-notch. Families, who appreciate the kitchen and extra space of the cabins, which fit six	The Fort Wilderness beach at night, perfect for viewing the Electrical Water Pageant on Bay Lake	Pony rides, hayrides, a blacksmith shop, petting farm, and River Country right next door	Join the nightly campfire circle and roast marsh-mallows with Chip and Dale

♥ This resort hosts character meals.

* BoardWalk, Wilderness Lodge, and Fort Wilderness also have Home Away From Home accommodations.

TRANSPORTATION & ACCOMMODATIONS

	Value	Regular	Peak*
DELUXE			
Animal Kingdom Lodge			
Rooms (sleep 4 to 5)	$199–$335	$230–$375	$275–$435
Rooms–Concierge (5)	$380	$435	$510
Suites (4 to 10)		Call 407-934-7639 for prices	
BoardWalk Inn			
Rooms (5)	$279–$340	$309–$375	$364–$435
Rooms–Concierge (5 to 6)	$405–$485	$460–$535	$520–$580
Suites (4 to 6)		Call 407-934-7639 for prices	
Contemporary			
Rooms–Garden Buildings (5)	$224–$260	$244–$285	$284–$330
Rooms–Tower (5)	$320–$375	$355–$410	$410–$470
Rooms–Concierge (4)	$455	$510	$565
Suites (4 to 8)		Call 407-934-7639 for prices	
Grand Floridian Resort & Spa			
Rooms (5)	$314–$380	$359–$425	$414–$495
Rooms–Concierge (5)	$435–$565	$490–$630	$560–$710
Suites (4 to 10)		Call 407-934-7639 for prices	
Polynesian			
Rooms (5)	$289–$365	$324–$405	$379–$465
Rooms–Concierge (5)	$365–$445	$405–$490	$465–$560
Suites (4 to 6)		Call 407-934-7639 for prices	
Swan & Dolphin (For reservations, call 800-227-1500)			
Rooms (5)	$310–$375	not applicable	$350–$445
Rooms–Club Level (5)	$460	not applicable	$490
Suites (5 to 10)		Call 800-227-1500 for prices	
Wilderness Lodge			
Rooms (4)	$189–$240	$219–$270	$265–$315
Suites (4 to 6)		Call 407-934-7639 for prices	
Yacht & Beach Club			
Rooms (5)	$279–$325	$309–$365	$364–$425
Rooms–Concierge** (5)	$405–$445	$460–$500	$520–$560
Suites (5 to 10)		Call 407-934-7639 for prices	

**Yacht Club only

HOME AWAY FROM HOME			
Disney's BoardWalk Villas Resort			
Studios (5)	$279	$309	$364
1-BR Villas (4)	$375	$415	$480
2-BR Villas (8)	$520	$670	$884
Grand Villas (12)	$1,275	$1,440	$1,595
Disney's Old Key West Resort			
Studios (4)	$244	$269	$309
1-BR Vacation Homes (4)	$330	$365	$420
2-BR Vacation Homes (8)	$459	$525	$635
3-BR Grand Villas (12)	$955	$1,050	$1,170
Fort Wilderness			
Cabins (6)	$219	$254	$279
The Villas at Wilderness Lodge			
Studios (4)	$264	$294	$349
1-BR Villas (4)	$360	$400	$465
2-BR Villas (8)	$509	$625	$755

WORLD PROPERTIES

	Value	Regular	Peak*
HOME AWAY FROM HOME			
The Villas at the Disney Institute			
Bungalows (sleep 4)	$209	$239	$259
1-BR Townhouses (4)	$254	$274	$294
2-BR Townhouses (6)	$359	$394	$414
Treehouse Villas (6)	$379	$404	$424
Fairway Villas (6 to 8)	$419	$454	$474
Grand Vista Homes (6 to 8)	$1,100–$1,350	$1,200–$1,450	$1,300–$1,550
MODERATE			
Caribbean Beach			
Rooms (4)	$129–$144	$149–$164	$174–$199
Coronado Springs			
Rooms (4)	$129–$144	$149–$164	$174–$199
Suites (4 to 6)	Call 407-934-7639 for prices		
Dixie Landings			
Rooms (4)	$129–$144	$149–$164	$174–$199
Port Orleans			
Rooms (4)	$129–$144	$149–$164	$174–$199
VALUE			
All-Star Movies, All-Star Music, and All-Star Sports			
Rooms (4)	$77	$99	$104
CAMPGROUND			
Fort Wilderness Campsites			
Sites w/partial hookup (10)	$34	$47	$55
Sites w/full hookup (10)	$39	$57	$65
Preferred Sites (10)	$47	$62	$70

Check-in time: 3 P.M. except at The Villas at the Disney Institute, BoardWalk Villas, The Villas at Wilderness Lodge, All-Star resorts, and Old Key West, where check-in is at 4 P.M. and at Fort Wilderness Resort and Campground, where it's 1 P.M. **Check-out time:** 11 A.M. for Fort Wilderness and all hotels.

2001 Value rates apply: January 1 to February 14, August 26 to September 26, and November 4 to December 20 for all Value and Moderate resorts, Wilderness Lodge, Animal Kingdom Lodge, and Fort Wilderness Cabins; January 1 to February 14 and August 5 to December 20 for the Campground; January 1–15 and May 1 to December 22 for Swan and Dolphin; January 1 to February 14, July 4 to September 26, and November 4 to December 20 for all other WDW properties. **2001 Regular rates apply:** April 29 to August 25 and September 27 to November 3 for all Value and Moderate resorts, Wilderness Lodge, Animal Kingdom Lodge, and Fort Wilderness Cabins; April 29 to August 4 for the Campground; April 29 to July 3 and September 27 to November 3 for all other WDW properties (except Swan and Dolphin). **2001 Peak rates apply:** February 15 to April 28 for all WDW properties; and January 16 to April 30 and December 23–31 for Swan and Dolphin. **2001 Holiday rates apply:** December 21–31.

Room capacity: Numbers in parentheses reflect maximum occupancy based on existing beds. A trundle bed (for one) can be rented at some properties for $15 a day. Cribs can be requested for free in most resorts. Rates include up to two adults. There is an additional charge for each extra adult in a room.

CALL 407-934-7639 FOR RESERVATIONS

Notes: The prices provided here were correct at press time, but rates do change, so be sure to double-check with the hotels before setting your final budget. Charge is for single or double occupancy.

*During holiday season, rates are higher. Call for information.

TRANSPORTATION & ACCOMMODATIONS

Magic Kingdom Area

Contemporary

Watching the monorail trains disappear into this hotel's enormous 15-story A-frame tower never fails to amaze first-timers. The sleek trains look like long spaceships docking as they slide inside. (Note that the monorail platform here is now accessible by elevator as well as escalators.)

Passengers, for their part, are impressed by the cavernous lobby, with its tiers of balconies and, at its center, the soaring 90-foot-high, floor-to-ceiling tile mural depicting Native American children, stylized flowers, birds, and other scenes from the Southwest. (Look carefully and you may be able to spot the five-legged goat.)

This imposing structure has 1,030 rooms in its tower and the garden buildings that flank it on either side. There are six shops, three restaurants, three snack bars, two lounges, a marina, a beach, a health club, and more. The pool area incorporates two whirlpools, a water slide, and water jets. The lively Food and Fun Center—a vast area with an exceptional arcade and a snack bar—is open 24 hours a day. The large convention center offers access to business services. Perhaps the resort's most notable feature is its 15th-floor observation deck. From here guests can enjoy a bird's-eye view of the Magic Kingdom.

A concierge package is available for guests who stay in the hotel's 14th-floor suites. Amenities include express check-in and check-out, complimentary continental breakfast, hors d'oeuvres and refreshments in the evening, and nightly turndown service. The Tower Club also provides guests with special concierge privileges. To contact the Contemporary, call 407-824-1000.

ROOMS: Bold colors and wild patterns drive the quirky decor of these recently refurbished rooms, evenly apportioned among the tower and two garden buildings. Rooms located in the tower boast private balconies and views of Bay Lake or the Magic Kingdom. Most rooms can accommodate five guests (plus one child under three). Typical units have a day bed and two queen-size beds; some rooms have a king-size bed and a daybed. Connecting rooms may be requested. Bathrooms in the Contemporary resort are spacious and well laid out. A variety of suites, consisting of a living room and one or two bedrooms, can accommodate 4 to 8 people.

WHERE TO EAT: In addition to the many restaurants and snack spots, 24-hour room service provides a wide range of offerings.

California Grill: On the 15th floor. The specialty is California fare, including pizza baked in wood-burning ovens, grilled meats, seafood, and market vegetables. An added treat: the spectacular view of the Magic Kingdom fireworks and sensational sunsets.

Chef Mickey's: Located on the fourth-floor concourse. Mickey and his friends host daily buffets. Breakfast features Mickey Mouse pancakes as well as more traditional items. It's a thoroughly rewarding breakfast experience. Dinner offers carved meats, prime rib, nightly specials, peel-and-eat shrimp, and a variety of entrées, plus a sundae and dessert bar.

Concourse Steakhouse: On the fourth-floor concourse. A full breakfast; burgers, salads, and sandwiches for lunch; steak, seafood, and pasta for dinner.

Food and Fun Center: On the first floor. Serves light fare 24 hours a day.

WHERE TO DRINK: The Magic Kingdom's no-alcohol policy doesn't trickle over to its nearest neighbor.

California Grill Lounge: On the resort's 15th floor, adjoining the California Grill. Prime views provide a dramatic backdrop for sipping California wines and other drinks, and nibbling on appetizers.

Contemporary Grounds: A lobby coffee bar, near the escalators. Serves cappuccino, espresso, lattes, and other gourmet coffees, as well as biscotti.

Outer Rim: On the fourth-floor concourse, overlooking Bay Lake. Serves appetizers, cocktails, and specialty drinks.

Sand Bar: This poolside spot offers drinks, fruit plates, and light snacks from the grill.

WHAT TO DO: Volleyball nets are set up on the beach and a basketball court is nearby. Waterskiing, parasailing, and fishing excursions may be arranged (see *Sports* for details).

Boating: Sailboats (including Sunfish and Hobie Waves), canopy boats, Water Mouse and jet boats may be rented at the marina.

Children's Program: The Mouseketeer Clubhouse is open from 4:30 P.M. to midnight for kids ages 4 through 12 (four-hour maximum stay). Cost is $5 per hour per child. Reservations are necessary; call 407-824-1000, ext. 3038.

Health Club: The Olympiad health club has modern Cybex equipment, stair climbers, bicycles, a sauna, lockers, and massage (by appointment).

Parasailing: Supervised excursions are offered at the marina. Cost is about $75 per person, or $115 for two to ride tandem. Reservations are necessary; call 407-WDW-PLAY.

Salon: Contemporary Resort Salon on the third floor of the tower provides haircuts, facials, manicures, and other services.

Shopping: The fourth-floor concourse is home to first-class shops. Fantasia sells character merchandise, including plush animals, and clothing for both children and adults. Contemporary Woman offers quality clothing (and plenty of bathing suits) in all price ranges, and the adjoining Contemporary Man stocks casual clothes and resortwear. The adjacent Kingdom Jewels Ltd. specializes in jewelry. Bayview Gifts carries souvenirs and fresh flowers. Concourse Sundries & Spirits has newspapers, magazines, books, snacks, and liquor—just what's needed for a cocktail party on the terrace.

Swimming: In addition to a round quiet pool, the free-form pool features a 17-foot-high curving slide. Two large whirlpools have been added. Water jets shoot unexpectedly while smaller fountains spout randomly, delighting older and younger kids alike.

Tennis: Disney's Racquet Club, Walt Disney World's premier tennis center, is located near the north wing. It features six state-of-the-art hydrogrid clay courts. Private lessons are available (see *Sports* for details). The shop here has tennis equipment, clothing, and shoes. Racquet restringing is also available.

Video Arcade: On the first floor, the Food and Fun Center boasts everything from Skee-Ball to air hockey, and all the favorites of the pinball-and-electronic-games-playing set. It's one of the best gamerooms at WDW.

Waterskiing and Wakeboarding: Ski boats complete with skilled instructors may be rented at the marina.

TRANSPORTATION: The Contemporary resort is connected to the Transportation and Ticket Center (TTC) and the Magic Kingdom by monorail. From the TTC, Epcot can be reached via monorail, and Typhoon Lagoon and Downtown Disney can be reached by bus. Buses also go to the Disney-MGM Studios, Animal Kingdom, and Blizzard Beach. Watercraft travel from the marina to Fort Wilderness, Wilderness Lodge, and River Country.

Polynesian

The Polynesian resort is as close an approximation of the real thing as Walt Disney World's designers could create. The vegetation is lush, and the architecture summons the tropics. The mood is set by a three-story garden that occupies most of the lobby. Water cascades over craggy volcanic rocks, while coconut palms tower over about 75 different species of tropical and subtropical plants.

The structure that contains this mass of greenery, the Great Ceremonial House, is the central building in the Polynesian complex. The front desk, shops, and most of the restaurants are located here. Flanking the Great Ceremonial House on either side are 11 two- and three-story village longhouses named for various Pacific islands. These structures house the resort's 847 rooms. The monorail stops at this hotel, making it an especially convenient place to stay; in fact, it's just a short ride to the Magic Kingdom.

DID YOU KNOW...

The white sand on the beaches near the Polynesian and Grand Floridian resorts and along the Seven Seas Lagoon actually came from the bottom of Bay Lake, located behind the Contemporary resort.

The Polynesian's concierge service offers such amenities as express check-in and checkout, continental breakfast, cookies and soft drinks every afternoon, hors d'oeuvres and desserts every evening, and access to a lounge with a prime fireworks view. Concierge rooms and suites are located in the Tonga and Hawaii buildings. The telephone number for the Polynesian is 407-824-2000.

ROOMS: Many of the rooms, which were all completely refurbished in 1998, have balconies, and most have a view of the gardens, Seven Seas Lagoon, or one of the resort's swimming pools; rooms in the Tokelau, Tahiti, and Rapa Nui buildings are the largest. Most rooms have two queen-size beds and a daybed, and can accommodate five guests (plus a child under age three). Connecting or adjoining rooms may be requested. The resort's suites—located exclusively in the Tonga building—can accommodate four to six guests. Some have a king-size bed in the bedroom and one queen-size bed in the parlor.

WHERE TO EAT: A variety of specialties are available from room service between 6:30 A.M. and midnight. Also, some interesting eating spots are located here.

Captain Cook's Snack Company: On the lobby level of the Great Ceremonial House. This is a good spot for continental breakfast. Snacks are available 24 hours a day.

Kona Cafe: On the second floor of the Great Ceremonial House. This family restaurant serves lunch and dinner with a decidedly Asian flair, while the breakfast menu is filled with more traditional American selections. An expansive coffee bar provides the perfect capper to any meal.

'Ohana: On the second floor of the Great Ceremonial House. 'Ohana serves family-style dinners roasted in the World's largest fire pit. Minnie hosts a character breakfast every morning.

WHERE TO DRINK: The Polynesian theme has inspired a whole raft of deceptively potent potables. As might be expected, both the drink offerings and the settings in which they are served are as tropical as they come.

Barefoot Bar: Adjoining the Swimming Pool Lagoon, and open seasonally.

Tambu: There's a tropical air about this lounge adjoining 'Ohana. The bar serves appetizers and exotic specialty drinks.

WHAT TO DO: A wide range of activities is available at the Polynesian resort, including a scenic jogging path. Fishing excursions can also be arranged (see the *Sports* chapter for details).

Boating: Several types of sailboats (including catamarans), Water Mouse boats, canopy boats, and pontoon boats are available for rent at the marina.

Children's Program: The Never Land Club is a supervised evening activity program for children ages 4 through 12. The program operates between 5 P.M. and midnight, with a kids' buffet from 6 P.M. to 8 P.M. The cost is $8 per hour. Reservations are necessary; call 407-939-3463.

Playground: The playground near the Swimming Pool Lagoon features equipment for climbing, swinging, and sliding.

Shopping: News from Civilization, on the first floor of the Great Ceremonial House, is the locale for hotel and Polynesian items, as well as newspapers, magazines, film, sun care products, and gifts. Robinson Crusoe, Esq., sells casual sportswear and swimwear for men; the Polynesian Princess stocks brightly colored resort fashions, bathing suits, and accessories for women. Upstairs, Trader Jack's sells a

Shades of Green

This 228-room resort is situated near the Grand Floridian but is not linked with the monorail system. Shades of Green is a recreational retreat for active and retired military personnel and their families, members of the reserves and the National Guard, and Department of Defense employees.

The resort features two tennis courts, two pools, a small health club, restaurant, bar and lounge, gift shop, arcade, laundry facilities, and free transportation around WDW.

Room rates are based on military or civilian grade. Select multi-day tickets are offered at a discount. The property's three golf courses—the Palm, the Magnolia, and Oak Trail—are open to all WDW guests (see *Sports* for details). All other activities are for hotel guests and their families only. The telephone number for Shades of Green is 407-824-3400. To make reservations, call 407-824-3600.

variety of Walt Disney World souvenirs, toys, fashions, and other items; the Grog Hut has food, liquor, wine, beer, soft drinks, salty snacks, and other fixings for an impromptu room party.

Swimming: There are two main pools here: the elliptical East Pool, in the shadow of the Tokelau, Hawaii, Tuvalu, Niue, and Tahiti buildings, and the larger free-form Swimming Pool Lagoon, found closer to the marina and main beach. The latter is framed by a large cluster of boulders that form a water slide much beloved by youngsters; to get to the ladder they must duck underneath a waterfall. Toddlers have their own shallow wading pool.

Video Arcade: Moana Mickey's Arcade has a large assortment of video games. It is located on the eastern edge of the property near the Tokelau guest building.

TRANSPORTATION: The Polynesian resort is on the monorail line to the Magic Kingdom and the Transportation and Ticket Center (TTC). From the TTC, Epcot is accessible by another monorail, and Typhoon Lagoon and Downtown Disney can be reached by bus. Buses go to the Disney-MGM Studios, Animal Kingdom, and Blizzard Beach. Launches leave from the Polynesian dock for the Magic Kingdom and the Grand Floridian.

Grand Floridian Resort & Spa

At the turn of the century, Standard Oil magnate Henry M. Flagler saw the realization of his dream: The railroad he had built to "civilize" Florida had spawned along its right-of-way an empire of grand hotels, lavish estates, prominent families, and opulent lifestyles. High society blossomed in winter, as the likes of John D. Rockefeller and Teddy Roosevelt checked into the Royal Poinciana in Palm Beach, enjoying the sea breezes from the oceanside suites.

The hotel later burned to the ground, and Florida's golden era faded with the Depression. But nearly a century after Flagler first made Florida a fashionable resort destination, Walt Disney World opened a grand hotel—a 900-room Victorian structure with gabled roofs and carved moldings—on 40 acres of Seven Seas Lagoon shorefront, between the Magic Kingdom and the Polynesian.

Like its late-19th-century predecessors, the Grand Floridian resort boasts abundant verandas, ceiling fans, intricate latticework and balustrades, turrets, towers, and red-shingle roofs. And yet, it offers all the advantages of modern living—including monorail service. With five restaurants, two lounges, five shops, and an arcade, plus a child care facility, convention center, swimming pool, marina, and full-service health club and spa, the Grand Floridian is not only a grand hotel but a complete resort.

The main building houses the Grand Lobby, a palatial space soaring five stories to a ceiling of stained-glass domes and glittering chandeliers. Palms and an aviary decorate the sitting area; an open-cage elevator carries guests to the shops and restaurants on the second floor. The turn-of-the-century theme is everywhere, from the costumes worn by the employees to the shop displays, restaurants, and room decor. The telephone number for the Grand Floridian resort is 407-824-3000.

ROOMS: The recently refurbished rooms are decorated as they might have been a century ago—with printed wall coverings, marble-topped sinks, ceiling fans, and Victorian woodwork. Amenities include hair dryers, bathrobes, mini-bars, nightly turndown service, and daily newspaper delivery.

The main building houses concierge rooms and suites; lodge buildings, each four and five stories high, contain standard rooms, slightly smaller "attic" chambers, and suites. Most rooms measure about 400 square feet and include two queen-size beds, plus a daybed, to accommodate up to five people. Many rooms have terraces. Suites include a parlor, plus

DID YOU KNOW...

Movie buffs may find the Grand Floridian strangely familiar. Its design is based, in part, on that of the Hotel Del Coronado in California. Scenes from the classic film *Some Like It Hot* were shot there.

one, two, or three bedrooms; there are king-size or queen-size beds in the bedrooms. Most of the 15 honeymoon rooms, located on the second, third, fourth, and fifth floors, enjoy wonderful views. In the main building, access to the upper three concierge-suite levels is restricted by private elevator.

On the third floor, the concierge desks offer such services as reservations and information. The fourth floor features a quiet seating area where continental breakfast and evening refreshments are served. Concierge service is also available in lodge building 6.

WHERE TO EAT: Most restaurants and lounges are located on the first two floors of the main building. Room service offers a wide assortment of items 24 hours a day.

Cítricos: The largest of the hotel's restaurants is also the newest. It features market-fresh cuisine from the South of France. Open for dinner. Some seating affords excellent views of the nightly fireworks presentation at the Magic Kingdom.

Gasparilla Grill & Games: This 24-hour snack bar offers light items for all-day dining and snacking, plus a selection of video games.

Grand Floridian Cafe: Its peaches-and-cream color scheme and veranda-like feel make this a great place for a quick, sit-down breakfast. Lunch and dinner are also served.

Narcoossee's: This casual restaurant and bar has a romantic shoreline location. The ever-changing menu includes such staples as roast lamb chops and seafood. The partially open kitchen is the focal point of the restaurant. Guests can sip cocktails on the veranda.

1900 Park Fare: A buffet restaurant decorated with carousel horses, plants, and Big Bertha—the carnival organ. Characters host breakfast and dinner daily.

Victoria & Albert's: Disney's finest eatery, it is named after the former queen and prince consort of England. Elegant meals are served to no more than 60 guests; service is impeccable. Jackets are required for men and priority seating is a must.

WHERE TO DRINK: Guests will find the refined lounges here to be especially nice escapes. Cocktail service is provided in the lobby from 4 P.M. to 11 P.M. daily. Cítricos and Narcoossee's both have lounges, complete with scenic views of the Magic Kingdom.

Garden View: This pretty spot on the first floor offers a view of the hotel's lush, landscaped garden and pool area. Afternoon tea is served (as are finger sandwiches and small desserts).

Mizner's: Named after the eccentric, wildly prolific architect who defined much of the flavor of Palm Beach County, this bar is on the second floor.

Summerhouse: The place for pool and beachside refreshments, this spot features a variety of snacks and beverages.

WHAT TO DO: The Grand Floridian offers all the recreational facilities of a beach resort. Fishing excursions can be arranged (refer to the *Sports* chapter for details). Volleyball equipment is available.

Boating: Sailboats, canopy boats, pontoon boats, and Water Mouse boats are available for rent at Captain's Shipyard Marina. The *Grand 1* yacht (complete with a captain and first mate) can be rented for $275 an hour.

Children's Programs: The Mouseketeer Club is a supervised program for kids ages 4 through 12. It's open from 4:30 P.M. to midnight; the cost is $8 per hour for each child. There is a four-hour maximum. Reservations are required; call 407-824-2985. Kids ages 3 to 10 may also embark on a special Pirate Cruise and search for treasure near the Magic Kingdom. The 90-minute trip costs $20 per child. For information and to make reservations call 407-WDW-DINE (939-3463).

Health Club: The health club boasts modern exercise equipment, plus saunas, whirlpools, and steam rooms.

Playground: Adjacent to the Mouseketeer Clubhouse, the play area includes swings and climbing equipment.

Salon: The Ivy Trellis salon offers a full line of hair care services.

Shopping: On the first floor of the main building is Summer Lace, a women's apparel shop, and Sandy Cove, which stocks gifts and sundries. One level up is the M. Mouse Mercantile character shop, a Bally leather-goods store, and Commander Porter's, a men's shop.

Spa: The spa offers more than a dozen treatment rooms for massage, herbal wraps, and aromatherapy. There are some spa programs for kids.

Swimming: In addition to a sizeable pool, there is a whirlpool and a white-sand beach.

Tennis: There are two clay courts for play. Reservations are suggested; call 407-WDW-PLAY (939-7529).

Video Arcade: Gasparilla Grill & Games is located on the first floor of the main building.

TRANSPORTATION: The Grand Floridian is connected to the Transportation and Ticket Center (TTC) and the Magic Kingdom by monorail. From the TTC, Epcot is accessible by another monorail, and Typhoon Lagoon and Downtown Disney can be reached by bus. Buses travel to the Disney-MGM Studios, Animal Kingdom, and Blizzard Beach. Water launches go to the Magic Kingdom and the Polynesian.

Wilderness Lodge & Villas

This resort recalls the spirit of the early American West and the feeling of the National Park Service lodges built during the early 1900s. These grand structures architecturally unified the elements of the unspoiled wilderness parks, kept harmony with nature, and incorporated the culture of Native Americans. The Wilderness Lodge artfully recaptures this rustic charm.

The resort is located between the Contemporary and Fort Wilderness on Bay Lake. The lobby, which is shared by the lodge and villas, is in an eight-story, log-structured building. Massive bundled log columns support a series of trusses, while two Pacific Northwest totem poles soar 55 feet into the air. Four levels of corridors surround the lobby, providing access to guestrooms, sitting nooks, and terraces. The resort is not accessible by monorail. The telephone number for the Wilderness Lodge and Villas is 407-824-3200.

ROOMS: Most of the 728 guestrooms have two queen-size beds, a table and chairs, and a balcony. Some have a queen-size bed and a bunk bed. The bathrooms have separate vanity areas with double sinks. The wallpaper has a Native American-motif border, and the colorful bedspreads and plaid curtains add to the decor. Images of wildlife complete the theme. Suite rooms include an iron (with board), hair dryer, and newspaper delivery.

The 181 deluxe villas, opening in early 2001, are housed in a five-story tower adjoining Disney's Wilderness Lodge. The style of the villas building was inspired by the grandeur of Rocky Mountain geyser country. This tribute to turn-of-the-twentieth-century design represents a wave of expansion by the Disney Vacation Club. (The villas are available to all guests when not occupied by Vacation Club members.)

Each studio has a queen-size bed and a double sleeper sofa, plus a kitchenette with microwave, coffeemaker, and refrigerator. Larger (one- and two-bedroom) villas sleep four to eight, and have dining areas, kitchens, laundry facilities, master baths with whirlpool tubs, and VCRs. They include king-side beds in the master bedroom, living rooms with queen sleeper sofas, and two queen-size beds (or one bed and a sleeper sofa) in extra bedrooms. All rooms come with an iron (and board) and hair dryer. Rooms in the Wilderness Lodge have daily newspaper delivery.

WHERE TO EAT: The Northwest theme is carried out with flair in the hotel's eateries. Room service runs from 7 A.M. to 11 A.M.; dinner is available from 4 P.M. to midnight.

Artist Point: Decorated with art representing painters who first chronicled the Northwest landscape, this fine dining spot features salmon, game, steak, seafood, and wines from the Pacific Northwest. Winnie the Pooh and friends host breakfast daily.

Roaring Fork: Fast food is available here.

Whispering Canyon Cafe: A casual, family-style restaurant with all-day dining.

WHERE TO DRINK: Two spots are available for a relaxing break.

Territory: This lounge honors the survey parties who led the move westward. In addition to specialty drinks, microbrewed beer, and espresso, a light lunch is served.

Trout Pass: The poolside bar features a variety of specialty drinks and snacks.

WHAT TO DO: The resort offers many recreational activities. Teton Boat & Bike Rental is in the Colonel's Cabin by the lake. Volleyball equipment is available.

Coming Attraction

What do you get when you mix a hundred years of American pop culture with a sprawling new resort? Disney's Pop Century resort! Rising from the ground near the Disney-MGM Studios, the first phase of this "value" resort should open in late 2002. Focusing on the last five decades of the twentieth century, it will feature larger-than-life icons (think All-Star resorts), bringing the fifties through the nineties whimsically to life. Be on the lookout for everything from giant jukeboxes and bowling pins to yo-yos, peace signs, and cell phones. (Phase two of the resort, celebrating the first half of the century will follow soon after.)

Reservations for Disney's Pop Century resort will be accepted starting in early 2001; call 407-934-7639.

Free daily tours offer insight into the architecture of the Wilderness Lodge. Ask about them at Guest Services.

Fishing excursions may be arranged (see *Sports* for details). Or consider taking a free guided tour of the lodge.

Biking: Bikes can be rented for scenic rides around the resort. A three-quarter-mile path leads to Fort Wilderness and River Country.

Birthday parties: Children's birthday parties can be arranged by calling 407-939-7529. Each two-hour party includes lunch on the beach of the Wilderness Lodge, cake, decorations, prizes, and more. The cost is $20 per child. Hayrides, pony rides, and Water Mouse boat rides can be included for an additional charge.

Boating: A variety of watercraft, including Water Mouse boats, canopy boats, sailboats, and pontoon boats, can be rented for a trip around Bay Lake.

Children's Program: The Cubs Den is a supervised dining and entertainment club for kids ages 4 through 12. Supervised activities, including Disney movies and western-themed arts and crafts, occupy kids from 4:30 P.M. to midnight. Cost is $5 per hour per child. Dinner is $8 extra. Call 407-939-3463 for reservations, which are required.

Health Club: The only thing rustic about Sturdy Branches, this new health club, is the structure it's housed in. It features Cybex equipment, stair climbers, bicycles, a sauna, and more. (Opening in early 2001.)

Iron Spike Room: A fireplace and railroad memorabilia add atmosphere to this relaxing room, equipped with comfy seating, tables, and games. (Opening in the villas in early 2001.)

Shopping: Wilderness Lodge Mercantile stocks necessities and sundries as well as a line of clothing with the Wilderness Lodge logo and Disney character merchandise.

Swimming: The main pool looks as if it were carved from the rockscape. A beach, a kiddie pool, two whirlpools, and a geyser complete the design. Fire Rock Geyser erupts on the hour from early morning until 10 P.M. The Hidden Spring pool near the Villas provides a quieter alternative. (Opening in early 2001.)

Video Arcade: The Roaring Fork Arcade features about 30 games to keep kids busy.

TRANSPORTATION: Boats go to the Magic Kingdom, Contemporary, and Fort Wilderness. Buses go to Epcot, the Disney-MGM Studios, Animal Kingdom, Blizzard Beach, and the Transportation and Ticket Center (TTC). From the TTC, transfer to buses for Typhoon Lagoon and Downtown Disney.

Fort Wilderness Resort & Campground

The very existence of this canal-crossed expanse—with more than 700 acres of cypress and pine—always surprises visitors who come to Walt Disney World expecting to find nothing more than theme parks.

Tucked among the campsites are hundreds of air-conditioned Wilderness Cabins for rent, complete with housekeeping service. The cost is comparable to that of some of the more expensive rooms at Disney resorts. The phone number for the Fort Wilderness resort and campground is 407-824-2900.

CAMPSITES: Fort Wilderness has 784 traditional sites. They feature electricity hookups (30/50-amp), water, sanitary disposal, and cable television. (Note that the pet loops are not wired for cable.) Partial-hookup campsites supply electricity and water hookups only. All campsites feature a paved driveway pad, picnic table, and charcoal grill. Most loops have at least one air-conditioned comfort station equipped with restrooms, private showers, an ice machine, phones, and a laundry room. A site allows for occupancy by up to ten. Each site has room for one car (in addition to the camping vehicle). Other cars can be parked in the main lot.

The various campground areas are designated by numbers. The 100–500 loops are closest to the beach, the Settlement Trading Post, and Pioneer Hall. The 1500–2000 loops are farthest away from the beach and many other Fort Wilderness activities, but they are quieter and more private. Pets are welcome at certain campsites for a nightly charge of $3.

WILDERNESS CABINS: These woodland dwellings offer a rustic escape. The interiors of the six-person log-cabin-like buildings are decorated with wilderness accents. Each one is shaded by a pine canopy. Cabins include two TVs, a VCR, full bath, hair dryer, iron, a deck, picnic table, and charcoal grill.

Note: No extra camping equipment is permitted; all guests must be accommodated in a the cabin. (For prices, see pages 52–53.)

WHERE TO EAT: There are a couple of options, but most people cook here. Groceries and supplies are available at the Meadow Trading Post and the Settlement Trading Post (8 A.M. to 10 P.M. in winter, to 11 P.M. in summer). Gooding's supermarket is located at the Crossroads of Lake Buena Vista.

Trail's End Buffet: This log-walled spot in Pioneer Hall serves home-style fare three meals a day. Pizza is an option from 9:30 P.M. to 11 P.M. nightly. Beer and wine are available.

WHERE TO DRINK: Cocktails are served at Crockett's Tavern in Pioneer Hall.

FAMILY ENTERTAINMENT AFTER DARK: The Hoop-Dee-Doo Musical Revue is presented three times a night. Reservations should be made well in advance; call 407-939-3463. There's also a nightly campfire program held near the Meadow Trading Post. (For details, see *Everything Else in the World* and *Good Meals, Great Times*.)

WHAT TO DO: There's a plethora of activities to choose from, including pools, tennis courts, bikes to rent, trails to hike, horses to ride, even a museum to visit. There are two arcades, too: one in Pioneer Hall and another in the Meadow Trading Post.

All Fort Wilderness activities are described in detail in the *Everything Else in the World* and *Sports* chapters.

TRANSPORTATION: Buses circulating at 20-30 minute intervals provide transportation within the campground, while buses and watercraft connect Fort Wilderness to the rest of the World. The Magic Kingdom, the Contemporary, and the Wilderness Lodge are most efficiently reached via watercraft that depart regularly from the marina. Buses make the trip from the Settlement Depot to Blizzard Beach. To get to other WDW points, take a bus from the Fort Wilderness visitor parking lot to the Transportation and Ticket Center (TTC). Here, change to a monorail for Epcot or take another bus for the Disney-MGM Studios, Animal Kingdom, Typhoon Lagoon, and Downtown Disney.

Electric golf carts and bikes can be rented at the Bike Barn as alternative means of getting around within the campground. Call 407-824-2742 for reservations.

Caribbean Beach

This bright, colorful hotel is set on 200 acres southeast of Epcot and near the Disney-MGM Studios. It is composed of five brightly colored "villages" surrounding a 45-acre lake called Barefoot Bay. Each village is identified with a different Caribbean island—Martinique, Barbados, Trinidad, Aruba, and Jamaica—and features pastel walls, white railings, and vividly colored metal roofs. There are 2,112 rooms in all, making Caribbean Beach one of the largest hotels in the United States.

The villages consist of a cluster of two-story buildings, a swimming pool, a guest laundry, and a lakefront stretch of white-sand beach. Guests check in at the Custom House, a reception building that immediately projects the feeling of a tropical resort. Decor, furnishings, and staff costumes all reflect the Caribbean theme. Old Port Royale, a complex located near the center of the property, evokes images of an island market. Stone walls, pirates' cannons, and tropical birds and flowers add to the atmosphere. The area houses the resort's food court, restaurant and lounge, arcade, and two shops.

The port opens onto a lakeside recreation area that includes a pool with waterfalls and a slide; the main beach; the Barefoot Bay Boat Yard and Bike Works, where boats and bicycles may be rented; a 1.4-mile promenade around the lake that's perfect for biking, walking, or jogging; and Parrot Cay Island, an area in the middle of Barefoot Bay. It should come as no surprise that children love it here. The telephone number for the Caribbean Beach resort is 407-934-3400.

ROOMS: Rooms are located in two-story buildings in each island village. A typical 340-square-foot room has two double beds and can sleep up to four. The rooms here are a bit larger than standard rooms at Disney's other moderately priced resorts, and the bathrooms are amply sized. Rooms are decorated in tones softer than the colors found on the exterior. Each room has a coffeemaker. A note for the budget-conscious: All rooms here are identical in terms of size and comfort, and the only difference between the most and least expensive is the view.

WHERE TO EAT: A full-service eatery called Captain's Tavern and a food court are located in Old Port Royale. Limited room service (pizza, chicken in a basket, and sandwiches) is available from 4 P.M. to midnight.

Bridgetown Broiler: Spit-roasted chicken and home-style meals are menu highlights.

Captain's Tavern: The menu at this Old Port Royale restaurant includes prime rib, baked chicken, and a catch of the day. Wine, beer, and cocktails are served.

Cinnamon Bay Bakery: Freshly baked rolls, croissants, and pastries are available in addition to ice cream and other treats.

Kingston Pasta Shop: Skads of savory pasta dishes are served.

Montego's Market Deli: Soups, salads, and cold sandwiches are offered.

Port Royale Hamburger Shop: Hot sandwiches and burgers are on the menu.

Royale Pizza Shop: Pizza is available by the slice or the pie, along with a variety of hot and cold pasta dishes.

WHERE TO DRINK: The tropical Caribbean theme is carried out in the specialty drinks found at **Banana Cabana**. Light snacks are also available at this poolside spot.

WHAT TO DO: There are many recreational opportunities here. The 1.4-mile promenade around the lake is perfect for walking, biking, or a morning jog.

Biking: Bikes can be rented at the Barefoot Bay Boat Yard and Bike Works.

Boating: Sailboats, Water Mouse boats, canopy boats, canoes, pontoon boats, and pedal boats are available for rent at the Barefoot Bay Boat Yard and Bike Works for use on the resort's scenic 45-acre lake.

Playgrounds: Playgrounds are located on Parrot Cay Island, as well as on the Barbados, Jamaica, and Trinidad beaches.

Shopping: At Old Port Royale, there's the Calypso Straw Market, which carries items with the Caribbean Beach resort logo and a variety of island-themed goods. Calypso Trading Post stocks a large selection of character merchandise and sundries.

Swimming: Each village has its own pool, and the main pool has a waterfall and a slide in a Caribbean-themed setting, conjuring up images of pirates and their swashbuckling adventures on the high seas.

Video Arcade: Goombay Games at Old Port Royale offers a selection of amusements.

TRANSPORTATION: Buses go to the Magic Kingdom, Epcot, the Disney-MGM Studios, Animal Kingdom, and Blizzard Beach. Other bus routes lead to Downtown Disney and Typhoon Lagoon.

Meetings & Conventions

Convention centers at Walt Disney World range in size from 20,000 to over 200,000 square feet. The Dolphin's center, featuring an exhibit hall and an executive boardroom, is the largest; the Swan provides additional space. The Contemporary has three ballrooms and a spacious pre-function area with lots of natural light. The convention center at the Yacht and Beach Club is reminiscent of a grand turn-of-the-century New England town meeting hall. The Grand Floridian Resort and Spa has a lavish center with silk brocade walls. The BoardWalk offers a smaller conference area with a lakeside gazebo for outdoor events. And Coronado Springs, the first moderately priced Disney resort to offer convention facilities, boasts the largest hotel ballroom in the U.S.

Among the unique services available to Disney conventioneers is the use of Disney characters and performers for events. Special events can even be held in the parks. Resort business centers have clerical staffs and computers, in addition to faxing and photocopying equipment. (These services are available to all resort guests.)

Those interested in scheduling a convention should call 407-828-3200. Organizers are advised to book their events six months in advance, especially for large groups. Keep in mind that the busiest convention times are January, May, September, and October.

Yacht & Beach Club

The New England seaside exists at Walt Disney World in the form of the Yacht and Beach Club. Situated just west of Epcot, the resorts, designed by noted architect Robert A. M. Stern, are set around a 25-acre lake. The adjacent properties share most facilities—including a convention center offering access to business services—and transportation options.

The Yacht Club's design evokes images of the New England seashore hotels of the 1880s. Guests enter the five-story beige clapboard building along a wooden-planked bridge. Hardwood floors, millwork, and brass enhance the nautical theme. A lighthouse on the pier serves as a beacon to welcome guests back to the hotel from WDW attractions. To reach the Yacht Club by telephone, call 407-934-7000.

Distance from the ocean is irrelevant over at the sand-and surf-focused Beach Club resort, approached along an entrance drive flanked by oak trees. A patterned walkway leads past a croquet court to beachside cabanas on the white-sand shore. Guests are met by hosts and hostesses dressed in colorful beach resort costumes of the 1870s. The telephone number for the Beach Club resort is 407-934-8000.

ROOMS: The rooms at the Yacht Club are spacious and decorated in a nautical motif. The Beach Club's rooms are also amply sized and, naturally, reflect a beach motif. In each room the furniture is white, and the headboard design on the one king-size bed or two queen-size beds incorporates small ship's wheels. Some rooms have daybeds. Most of the suites have a king-size bed as well as two sleeper sofas. In the large bathrooms there is a separate vanity with double sinks and mirrors trimmed with brass. Each room has a ceiling fan, iron (with board), hair dryer, newspaper delivery, mini-bar, wall-mounted

makeup mirror, a small table (complete with a checker-board top), and two chairs. Chess and checkers sets can be provided. Concierge rooms are available.

WHERE TO EAT: The themes of yachting and the sea play an important role in the restaurants that are found at their respective resorts. A wide variety of menu items is available from room service 24 hours a day.

Beaches & Cream Soda Shop: A classic American soda fountain where shakes, malts, and sundaes are the prime lures. (The shop is located between the two resorts.)

Cape May Cafe: An indoor clambake is held here at the Beach Club each night. The varied buffet features several types of clams and mussels, plus pasta and chicken. Lobster is available for an extra charge. A character breakfast is presented daily.

Hurricane Hanna's Grill: Burgers, hot dogs, sausages, and other snacks are served at this spot on the shores of Stormalong Bay. A full bar is also located here, and poolside beverage service is available.

Yacht Club Galley: The buffet breakfast is bountiful. Breakfast, lunch, and dinner are available from an à la carte menu.

Yachtsman Steakhouse: Select cuts of aged beef are the specialty of the house. Fresh seafood and poultry are also offered.

WHERE TO DRINK: The lounges in both resorts offer a variety of specialty drinks in relaxing seaside settings.

Ale and Compass: This Yacht Club lobby lounge, featuring specialty coffees and drinks, provides a nice respite after a long day.

Crew's Cup: The place to try a wide assortment of beers shipped in from the world's seaports before dining at Yachtsman Steakhouse next door.

Martha's Vineyard: This lounge at the Beach Club offers selections from American and international vineyards, served in sample sizes and by the glass or bottle.

Rip Tide: The Beach Club lobby lounge features a variety of California wines, wine coolers, and frosty concoctions.

WHAT TO DO: There is enough to do here to fill an entire vacation. A sand volleyball court and a croquet court may be found on the Beach Club side of the property. Equipment for both pursuits is available at no cost at the Ship Shape health club. The Fantasia Gardens Miniature Golf complex is close at hand, and guided two-hour fishing excursions can be arranged (see *Sports* for details). Free 45-minute garden tours are available throughout the week. And last but not least, the BoardWalk entertainment district is just a short trip around the lake.

Boating: Hydro Bikes, and pedal, canopy, pontoon, and Water Mouse boats are available for rent at the Bayside Marina.

Children's Program: The Sandcastle Club, for children ages 4 through 12, is available from 4:30 P.M. to midnight. Cost is $5 per hour for each child. Reservations are required; call 407-939-3463. Toys, videos, games, and computers are on hand to keep children entertained. Dinner is available for about $8.

Health Club: The Ship Shape health club features Nautilus and cardiovascular machines, sauna, whirlpool, steam room, and massage (by appointment). The health club is open to all WDW resort guests over the age of 13.

Playground: A small play area with a slide and climbing apparatus is located by the pool.

Salon: The Periwig salon for men and women is located in the central area.

Shopping: At the Yacht Club, Fittings & Fairings Clothes and Notions is an all-purpose shop offering nautical fashions, character merchandise, and sundries. At the Beach Club, Atlantic Wear and Wardrobe Emporium features a similar selection of goods (albeit with a beach theme).

Swimming: Between the marina and the beach is the centerpiece of the dual resort—Stormalong Bay, a three-acre pool that's really a mini water park. There is a lagoon expressly for relaxed bathing, and another with currents, jets, and sand-bottomed areas. Several whirlpools are scattered throughout the area. Adjacent to the main pool is a shipwreck, where guests can enjoy a water slide. There is one unguarded, quiet pool and a whirlpool at the far end of each hotel.

Tennis: There are two lighted tennis courts on the Beach Club side of the property. Rental equipment is available at the Ship Shape health club.

Video Arcade: Lafferty Place Arcade, located in the central area, has about 60 video games and pinball machines.

TRANSPORTATION: Guests travel to Epcot and the Disney-MGM Studios via ferry boats or walkways. Buses go to the Magic Kingdom, Animal Kingdom, Downtown Disney, Typhoon Lagoon, and Blizzard Beach.

Swan & Dolphin

These massive sister resorts, situated on the shores of Crescent Lake, can easily be distinguished by the 46-foot swan and 56-foot dolphin statues that top them. The waterfalls, lush rows of palm trees, and beachfront location all reflect the tropical Florida landscape that was their inspiration. Both hotels were designed by noted architect Michael Graves as prime examples of "entertainment architecture." The rolling turquoise waves on the colored facade of the Swan's 12-story main building and two 7-story wings are clearly evidence of this design, as is the Dolphin's exterior mural, which features a playful banana-leaf pattern. The soaring 27-story triangular tower at the center of the Dolphin, is flanked by four 9-story guestroom wings.

The resorts share extensive convention facilities, many recreational options, and a host of restaurants. The Swan and Dolphin are operated by Westin and Sheraton, respectively, but are treated as Walt Disney World resorts; guests here enjoy most WDW resort benefits. One notable difference involves room-key charging privileges: Guests cannot use their room keys to charge purchases on Walt Disney World property, with the exception of within the resorts themselves. The phone number for the Swan is 407-934-3000; for the Dolphin, it's 407-934-4000. Reservations can be made by calling 800-227-1500 or by visiting *www.swandolphin.com.*

Be aware that there is an automatic $5 room charge assessed per day to cover services such as newspaper delivery, local telephone calls (30 minutes per day), coffee, use of the health club, etc. If you prefer to skip such amenities and the daily fee, make your intentions known at check-in. Valet parking costs $8 per day. Free self-parking is also available.

ROOMS: The corridors outside the Swan guestrooms feature patterned carpets and murals on the walls that extend the wave theme from its exterior design. Inside, the rooms are decorated in shades of coral and turquoise, and they feature such whimsical touches as lamps in the shape of birds and pineapples painted on the dressers. Each has one king-size or two queen-size beds; safes and refrigerators are among the amenities. There are 45 concierge rooms on the 11th and 12th floors, and 64 suites.

The 1,509 rooms at the Dolphin, including 136 suites, are decorated in a light-hearted fashion, with lamps in the shape of pineapples and colorful bedspreads and curtains. All feature two double beds or a king-size bed, as well as refrigerators, vanity dressing areas, irons and ironing boards, and coffeemakers. Concierge rooms are located in the main building. There are rooms equipped for guests with disabilities, and nonsmoking rooms are available at both resorts. Unlike at most Walt Disney World resorts, the guestrooms here do not have ceiling fans.

WHERE TO EAT: In addition to many restaurant choices, 24-hour room service provides an extensive all-day dining menu.

Cabana Bar & Grill: This full-service poolside spot near the Dolphin serves burgers, sandwiches, yogurt, and fruit. The full bar serves specialty drinks.

Coral Cafe: Buffets, as well as à la carte selections, are served during breakfast, lunch, and dinner in a casual setting at the Dolphin. Sunday breakfast is a Disney character affair.

Dolphin Fountain: Homemade ice cream is the specialty here. Huge sundaes, shakes, malts, and burgers are also offered.

Garden Grove Cafe: This Swan eatery features a greenhouse atmosphere, and serves breakfast and lunch daily. At dinner, the restaurant transforms into Gulliver's Grill. A buffet breakfast with the characters is held on Saturday, while a character dinner takes place several nights a week.

Shula's Steak House: The newest entry to the lineup of Dolphin eateries, Shula's is an upscale celebration of two American favorites: steak and football.

Juan & Only's: Southwestern food is served at this Dolphin hot spot. The atmosphere is festive, filled with the warm hues and rich fabrics of the Southwest.

Palio: A fine Italian eatery, located at the Swan, featuring veal specialties, homemade pasta, and brick-oven pizza. There are daily specials and live entertainment.

Splash Grill: A poolside cafe near the Swan serving lunch and snacks. A full-service bar is also located here.

Tubbi's: A cafeteria with a little flair. The checkerboard design makes this a pleasant place for a quick meal at the Dolphin resort. The 24-hour convenience store here sells snacks and sundries.

WHERE TO DRINK: With two full-service resorts to choose from, it's easy to find a nice cocktail spot.

Copa Banana: The tropical atmosphere makes this a lively place for a drink. Deejay music, a dance floor, and a large-screen TV provide the entertainment at this Dolphin fun spot.

Lobby Court: This spot at the Swan offers a respite from the hubbub. Enjoy gourmet coffees with fresh pastries in the morning, and wine and specialty drinks at night in a European-style bistro setting.

Kimonos: The Asian decor makes this Swan lounge an inviting place for sake, sushi, and other Japanese specialties.

Only's Bar & Jail: Patrons at the companion lounge to the Dolphin's Juan & Only's restaurant can enjoy the warm atmosphere here while sampling margaritas and other festive spirits.

Shula's Steak House Lounge: Settle into a comfy chair, light up a stogie, and sip a cocktail in this cozy lounge adjacent to Shula's dining room.

WHAT TO DO: The Swan and Dolphin share a multitude of recreation options. Volleyball nets and hammocks are set up on the beach.

Special Room Requests

Central Reservations accepts requests for rooms with particular views or in certain locations. Agents will do their best to accommodate such requests, but cannot guarantee they will be able to fulfill every wish. Call 407-W-DISNEY (934-7639).

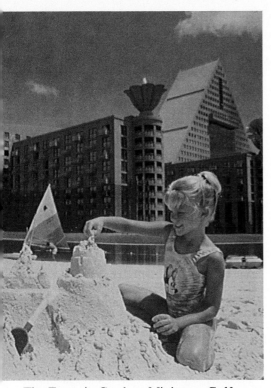

The Fantasia Gardens Miniature Golf complex and BoardWalk are nearby (the close proximity to BoardWalk and Epcot is a tremendous plus.)

Boating: Pedal boats and Hydro Bikes are available for rent on the white-sand beach between the Swan and Dolphin.

Children's Program: Camp Dolphin, welcomes children 4 through 12 and offers supervised activities from 1:30 P.M. to 4 P.M. The cost is $12 per child per hour. The Dinner Club (within Camp Dolphin) is open from 6 P.M. to 11 P.M. It costs $45 for the first child, $30 for the second child, and $20 for each additional child.

Health Clubs: A branch of Body By Jake (named for famous fitness guru Jake Steinfeld) is near the pool area at the Dolphin. State-of-the-art equipment is available, as are personal trainers. There are aerobics classes (including water aerobics), a sauna, steam room, large whirlpool, and massage therapists. There's also a smaller health club with basic exercise equipment near Splash Grill at the Swan.

Playground: A play area with a slide, swings, wooden chain bridge, sandbox, and several jungle gyms is located next to the grotto pool.

Salon: The Niki Bryan shop at the Dolphin resort provides a full battery of salon services, including hairstyling, manicures, and pedicures.

Shopping: Disney Cabanas, located in the lobby of the Swan, features men's and women's fashions, a line of character merchandise, and sundries. Four specialty shops are located at the Dolphin. A large selection of Cartier and other brand-name watches can be found at Brittany Jewels. Indulgences allows chocolate lovers the chance to sample some tasty concoctions. Statements of Fashion offers resortwear for men and women. Daisy's Garden is the place to find character goods at the Dolphin.

Swimming: A large rectangular pool near the Dolphin is perfect for swimming laps, a lovely themed grotto pool with a slide lies between the Swan and Dolphin, a small rectangular pool is situated near the Swan, and several whirlpools are scattered around the area.

Tennis: Four hard-surface tennis courts are located behind the pool area closest to the Dolphin resort. They are lighted for night play and are open 24 hours a day.

Video Arcades: A room full of video games is located near Tubbi's. Another can be found adjacent to the pool.

TRANSPORTATION: Guests travel to Epcot and the Disney-MGM Studios via ferry boats or walkways. Buses go directly to the Magic Kingdom, Animal Kingdom, Downtown Disney, Typhoon Lagoon, and Blizzard Beach.

A Room with a View

There's a lot to be said for throwing back the curtains and gazing at a breathtaking view, provided you have the time to appreciate it and that your view is within your price range. The following is a breakdown of different "views" you may select from at the various WDW resorts. Refer to it before booking accommodations—it will help you determine the best view for your budget.

Although the categories vary, depending on the resort type, the "standard view" is always the lowest rate available. Call 407-W-DISNEY (934-7639) for rate information.

- **Value Resorts**
  Standard View = Parking lot, pool, garden, and everything else

- **Moderate Resorts**
  Standard View = Parking lot or landscaping
  Water View = Pool, marina, lake, river

- **Deluxe Resorts**
  Standard View = Parking lot
  Garden View = Landscaping
  Water View = Pool, lake, or other water
  Lagoon View = Seven Seas Lagoon
  Savanna View = Animal pastures (at Animal Kingdom Lodge)

BoardWalk Inn & Villas

The enchantment of a bygone era is recaptured in the BoardWalk. The resort combines a waterside entertainment complex with deluxe hotel accommodations and vacation villas. Dining, recreation, shopping, and entertainment venues line the boardwalk, and twinkling lights trim the buildings. The ambience continues throughout, with intricately detailed architecture featuring sherbet-colored facades, flagged turrets, and striped awnings, all reminiscent of the turn of the twentieth century. The BoardWalk resort is adjacent to Epcot's International Gateway and connected to it via walkway. The phone number for BoardWalk is 407-939-5100.

ROOMS: Accommodations here evoke the charm of early eastern seaboard inns. Most have private balconies or patios. The Board-Walk Inn has 372 deluxe hotel rooms decorated with cherry-wood furniture, boardwalk postcard-print curtains, and light green accents. Guestrooms at the Inn sleep up to five, and feature two queen-size beds (or one king-size bed) and a child's daybed. Romantic two-story garden suites each have a private garden enclosed by a white picket fence. They sleep four, and feature a living room on the first floor and a king-size bed in the bedroom loft. The Inn also has concierge suites.

The 520 vacation villas are collectively called Disney's BoardWalk Villas. These are Disney Vacation Club villas, available when not occupied by members. Each studio has a queen-size bed and double sleeper sofa, plus a kitchenette with microwave, coffeemaker, and small refrigerator. Larger (one-, two-, and three-bedroom) villas sleep 4 to 12 people, and feature dining areas, fully equipped kitchens, laundry facilities, master baths with whirlpool tubs, and VCRs. They also include king-size beds in the master bedroom, living

rooms with queen sleeper sofas, and two queen-size beds (or one plus a double sleeper sofa) in any additional bedrooms. Rooms at the BoardWalk Inn include free newspaper delivery. All rooms have an iron (with board) and a hair dryer.

WHERE TO EAT: This resort has a wealth of dining and snacking options. A variety of vendors along the boardwalk tempt with hot dogs, crêpes on a stick, gourmet coffee, and more. For those looking to eat in, 24-hour room service is available.

Big River Grille & Brewing Works: This working brewpub features a full menu, complemented by fresh specialty ales. View the on-site brewmaster through floor-to-ceiling glass walls.

BoardWalk Bakery: A popular stop that offers fresh baked goods, sandwiches, espresso, and cappuccino. Huge display windows allow passersby to watch bakers at work. Bun rises are held here every morning. Note that the line moves slowly.

ESPN Club: A serious sports bar for serious sports fans, it provides interactive sports video entertainment and all-day dining.

Flying Fish Cafe: This restaurant has a show kitchen, and its dinner menu emphasizes seafood, steak, and fresh seasonal items.

Seashore Sweets': An old-fashioned sweetshop serves candies, saltwater taffy, ice cream, frozen yogurt, and specialty coffees.

Spoodles: Mediterranean cuisine is the focus of this establishment geared toward families; the appetizers are meant for sharing.

WHERE TO DRINK: Guests of this resort have a multitude of options right in their backyard, with the BoardWalk's clubs and lounges on hand.

Atlantic Dance: Dance, twist, and swing to classic tunes at this waterfront dance club. Live bands perform on select nights; deejays take care of business on others. You must be 18 to enter. The cover charge is generally $5, but may change for special events.

Belle Vue Room: Listen to old-time tunes on antique radios and play board games in this cocktail lounge near the lobby. Appetizers are served.

Jellyrolls: Dueling pianos provide live entertainment in a casual warehouse atmosphere. The cover charge is generally about $5 nightly. You must be 21 to enter.

Leaping Horse Libations: The carousel-themed pool bar at Luna Park serves a variety of cocktails, as well as tuna sandwiches, salads, hot dogs, fruit, and ice cream.

WHAT TO DO: The three-quarter-mile pathway encircling Crescent Lake (en route to Epcot) provides a ready venue for walkers and joggers. BoardWalk guests may rent boats from a neighboring resort's marina.

The Fantasia Gardens Miniature Golf complex is nearby. At the resort itself, Ferris W. Eahlers Community Hall rents out equipment for many recreational pursuits, including croquet, shuffleboard, table tennis, pole fishing, badminton—even books and videos. Fishing excursions can be arranged.

Biking: Community Hall offers a variety of bicycles for rental. In addition, surreys (canopied quadracycles for four) can be rented along the boardwalk.

Children's Program: The Harbor Club provides supervised activities for children ages 4 through 12 from 4:30 P.M. to 11:45 P.M. Cost is $5 per child per hour; dinner is available for an additional charge. Call 407-939-3463 for necessary reservations.

Health Club: Muscles & Bustles health club offers steam rooms, tanning, Cybex machines, and circuit-training equipment, as well as massages (by appointment). Additional fees apply.

Midway Games: This area on the Board-Walk's WildWood Landing features games of luck and skill similar to those found along traditional boardwalks.

Playground: An amusement park-themed play area offers kids a pool to clown around in and other fun activities.

Surrey Ride: A trip around Crescent Lake in a pedal-powered surrey is available for a fee.

Shopping: Dundy's Sundries in the lobby is the source for film and basic necessities. Character Carnival on the boardwalk features children's apparel as well as a large selection of Disney character merchandise. Screen Door General Store stocks groceries, dry goods, snacks, and beverages. Thimbles & Threads, located on the boardwalk, carries resortwear, swimwear, and accessories for men and women. Wyland Galleries features marine and environmental art and collectibles.

Swimming: The BoardWalk's swimming area, Luna Park, features a large pool with a 200-foot water slide, "Keister Coaster," patterned after a wooden roller coaster. A family of elephants is found posed throughout the area; their trunks act as a shower for adults on the pool deck or children in the wading pool. The resort's two quiet pools are heated. There are three whirlpools, one in each pool area.

Tennis: Two lighted soft-surface tennis courts are available for play.

Video Arcades: Side Show Games Arcade has a selection of video games, and a sports-themed arcade called The Yard Arcade entertains at the ESPN Club.

TRANSPORTATION: Guests travel to Epcot and the Disney-MGM Studios via ferry boats or walkways. Buses transport guests to the Magic Kingdom, Animal Kingdom, Typhoon Lagoon, Blizzard Beach, and Downtown Disney.

Disney Vacation Club

Imagine a club that grants members the convenience of flexible vacations from year to year, with the ability to choose when and where to visit, how long to stay, and the type of accommodations. It starts with the purchase of a real estate interest in a Disney Vacation Club property. For a one-time price and annual dues, members garner vacation stays that can be enjoyed at Disney's Old Key West Resort, Disney's BoardWalk Villas Resort, and The Villas at Disney's Wilderness Lodge at Walt Disney World; Disney's Vero Beach Resort in Florida; and Disney's Hilton Head Island Resort in South Carolina—plus access to additional destinations around the globe. Through "Member Getaways" members can also elect to stay at their choice of nearly 300 resorts worldwide, including most Disney resorts and the Disney Cruise Line.

Disney's Vero Beach Resort is a two-hour drive from Walt Disney World. It has villa-type accommodations comparable to those at Disney's Old Key West Resort—with lush surroundings, beach, and lots of local sights. The proximity makes it easy to tack a beach vacation onto a WDW visit.

Disney Vacation Club information centers can be found at each of the Walt Disney World hotels and theme parks. For more information, call 800-500-3990, or visit *www.dvcmagic.com*.

Port Orleans

This 1,008-room resort invites comparisons to the historic French Quarter of New Orleans. Starting at the entrance gate, with its wrought-iron portal and overgrown landscape, the appeal of the Delta City surrounds arriving guests. The entry drive leads to the heart of the city, which is Port Orleans Square. The central building, The Mint, was based on an original turn-of-the-century mint where farmers would go to trade their harvest for "dixes." A dix was a ten-dollar bill, and when the farmers said they were going to get their dixes, they probably didn't know they had coined a phrase. The Mint houses the hotel's check-in facilities, a shop, food court, arcade, and restaurant. It has a vaulted ceiling, and the check-in desks are designed as old-fashioned bank-teller windows. The musical notes in the mural are the notes to "When the Saints Go Marching In." The telephone number for Port Orleans is 407-934-5000.

ROOMS: The guestrooms are located in seven 3-story buildings (with elevators). Each room has two double beds; some king-size beds are available. The rooms are a bit smaller than the standard rooms at the more expensive Disney hotels, but they are comfortable for a family of four. The photographs on the walls were donated by Disney employees, and the captions explain their history.

The buildings are painted cream, pink, blue, purple, and yellow, and feature wrought-iron railings of varying designs. About half of the rooms have doors that connect to a neighboring room. Connecting rooms can be requested but can't be guaranteed. The least expensive rooms overlook gardens or parking areas and the most expensive rooms offer water views.

WHERE TO EAT: Options here include one restaurant with table service and a food court with counter-service stands. Also, the Sassagoula Pizza Express delivers pizza, chicken wings, and ice cream from 4 P.M. to midnight.

Bonfamille's Cafe: The name of this table-service eatery comes from the Disney movie *The Aristocats*. Steak, seafood, and Creole cooking highlight the dinner menu. Breakfast is also served.

Sassagoula Floatworks & Food Factory: A variety of specialty foods is available in this food court, including gumbo, chicken with red beans and rice, fresh beignets, and other traditional Creole dishes. Burgers, pizza, ice cream, and baked goods are also on the menu.

WHERE TO DRINK: The New Orleans theme is carried through in the hotel's watering holes.

Mardi Grogs: The poolside bar serves specialty drinks, popcorn, hot dogs, and ice cream during pool hours.

Scat Cat's Club: A traditional bar featuring nightly entertainment and a light menu of hors d'oeuvres.

WHAT TO DO: A special pool is the highlight of the recreational opportunities here.

Biking: Bicycles are available for rent at Port Orleans Landing.

Boating: Pedal boats, kayaks, canoes, rowboats, canopy boats, and pontoon boats are available for rent at Port Orleans Landing.

Playground: A small play area with slides is located across from the food court.

Shopping: Jackson Square Gifts & Desires, located at Port Orleans Square, features Disney character merchandise, clothing bearing the Port Orleans logo, and sundries.

Swimming: Doubloon Lagoon is a pool built around a sea serpent. The water slide is actually the serpent's tongue. A shower at the pool has an alligator's head, and there is a large clamshell where an alligator band serves as the centerpiece of a fountain. There is a whirlpool nearby. Port Orleans guests may also swim at Ol' Man Island at Dixie Landings.

Video Arcade: South Quarter Games is located at Port Orleans Square. It features state-of-the-art video and arcade games.

TRANSPORTATION: Buses go to the Magic Kingdom, Transportation and Ticket Center (TTC), Epcot, Animal Kingdom, the Disney-MGM Studios, Typhoon Lagoon, Blizzard Beach, and Downtown Disney. The Sassagoula River Cruise makes the trip to Dixie Landings and Downtown Disney.

Dixie Landings

The city feel of Port Orleans gives way to the rural South upriver at Dixie Landings. The resort is divided into "parishes." Closest to the "city," guestrooms are found in Mansion homes; farther upriver are the Bayou rooms, with a more rustic feel. The guest registration area is located in a building designed to resemble a steamship. When guests check in, they are booking passage on the steamboat. The food court, restaurant, lounge, and shop are all located in the same building. The telephone number for Dixie Landings is 407-934-6000.

ROOMS: The 2,048 Mansion and Bayou guestrooms are of the same size, and each room features two double beds (some king-size beds are available); 963 of the Bayou rooms have trundle beds (designed to sleep one child) as well. There is an additional fee of $15 per night for a trundle bed. The Magnolia Bend Mansion rooms, appointed with tapestries and cherry furniture, are situated in sprawling, elegant manor homes with stately columns and grand staircases. The Alligator Bayou rooms are in rustic, weathered-wood buildings that are tucked among trees and bushes native to the area. Note that although all buildings have two to three floors, only the Magnolia Bend Mansions have elevators.

The Bayou rooms surround Ol' Man Island, a 3½-acre recreational area with a pool, playground, and fishing hole. Decorative touches in the rooms include wood and tin armoires and pedestal sinks with brass fittings. The beds have hickory bedposts. The rooms are a bit smaller than standard rooms at the more expensive Disney hotels, but they are comfortable for a family of four.

WHERE TO EAT: In addition to a restaurant and food court, the hotel offers limited room service via Sassagoula Pizza Express, which delivers from 4 P.M. until midnight.

Boatwright's Dining Hall: This 200-seat table-service eatery, next to Colonel's Cotton Mill, serves Cajun specialties and traditional American fare for dinner. Breakfast is also served.

Colonel's Cotton Mill: This food court resembles an old-fashioned cotton mill with a 30-foot working waterwheel that powers the real cotton press inside.

The five counter-service stands here offer all sorts of choices. Basic selections are available for breakfast. **Acadian Pizza 'n' Pasta** has pasta dishes, pizza, and calzone. **Blue Bayou Burgers and Chicken** offers fried and grilled chicken and an assortment of burgers. **Cajun Broiler** serves spit-roasted chicken and barbecued ribs. **Riverside Market and Deli** is a convenience store that stocks snack foods, soda, salads, sandwiches, beer, and wine.

Southern Trace Bakery serves pastries, pies, and sticky buns. Soft drinks can be refilled at no extra charge on a meal-by-meal basis.

WHERE TO DRINK: Two lounges possess an enticing degree of charm.

Cotton Co-Op: Situated in a room designed as a cotton exchange, this lounge features specialty drinks, some light hors d'oeuvres, and live entertainment.

Muddy Rivers: The poolside bar serves specialty and traditional drinks, plus hot dogs, popcorn, and ice cream during pool hours.

WHAT TO DO: Many of the resort activities are at Ol' Man Island, a 3½-acre recreation center featuring a pool, whirlpool, wading pool, playground, and fishing hole stocked with a variety of fish for catch and release.

Biking: Bicycles of all types can be rented at the Dixie Levee.

Boating: Pedal boats, canoes, rowboats, canopy boats, and pontoon boats are available for rent at the Dixie Levee.

Fishing: Two-hour guided fishing excursions are available (see *Sports*), and guests may fish on their own at the Ol' Fishin' Hole.

Playground: An elaborate play area is located on Ol' Man Island next to the pool.

Shopping: Fulton's General Store in the Dixie Landings building stocks Disney character merchandise, clothing with the Dixie Landings logo, and sundries.

Swimming: In addition to the main pool and kiddie pool at Ol' Man Island, there are five pools set among the parishes of the resort. Guests may also swim at Port Orleans.

Video Arcade: The Medicine Show Arcade, located in the Dixie Landings building, features a small selection of games.

TRANSPORTATION: Buses go to the Magic Kingdom, Epcot, the Disney-MGM Studios, Animal Kingdom, Typhoon Lagoon, Blizzard Beach, and Downtown Disney. Port Orleans and Downtown Disney can also be reached aboard the Sassagoula River Cruise.

The Villas at the Disney Institute

The area near the Downtown Disney Marketplace and the Lake Buena Vista golf course is dotted with villa-type accommodations, most fitted out with fully equipped kitchens and other extras and amenities. Some may cost more than individual guestrooms at conventional Disney hotels, but they accommodate more people as well. For families of more than five (who might otherwise need an extra room), this is the most economical way to stay on-property. Many guests stretch their budget by preparing some meals in their villa.

The villas are spacious and secluded—albeit decorated on the dull side, at least as Disney accommodations go. The pace is relaxed and the atmosphere is low-key (except at the Townhouses near Downtown Disney Pleasure Island, which can be lively until late in the evening). Note that Downtown Disney is within walking distance. The telephone number for The Villas at the Disney Institute is 407-827-1100.

TYPES OF ACCOMMODATIONS: There are five major types of villas. All have either full kitchens or wet bars with small refrigerators. Check-in and check-out for all guests take place at the Welcome Center near the Bungalows and the Fairway Villas. Note that the Fairway Villas can accommodate guests with disabilities.

One-Bedroom Bungalows: The 316 Bungalows are situated slightly northeast of the Townhouses. The smallest one-bedroom units are roughly L-shaped, with a sitting area (equipped with daybed, wet bar, refrigerator, microwave, and coffeemaker) that's removed from the sleeping area, with its two queen-size beds. The layout provides families with a bit more privacy and space than they would get in the standard rooms at the WDW hotels. (The single disadvantage: small bathrooms.) All have a balcony or a patio.

One- and Two-Bedroom Townhouses: These accommodations are about a five-minute walk from Downtown Disney. They are simple in feeling and decor; living rooms have cathedral ceilings.

A one-bedroom unit can accommodate up to four; there's a queen-size bed in the loft bedroom and a queen-size sleeper sofa in the living room. A two-bedroom unit, which can accommodate six, features a queen-size bed in the master bedroom, two twin-size beds in the loft bedroom, and a queen-size sleeper sofa in the living room.

Fairway Villas: These cedar-sided, slant-roofed units, located near the first, second, eighth, and ninth fairways of the Lake Buena Vista golf course, are among the World's most spacious, with cathedral ceilings, rough-hewn walls, large windows, contemporary-styled furniture, and an overall feeling that there's a lot of elbow room. There is a queen-size bed in one bedroom, two double beds in the other, and either a pull-out bed or a double sleeper sofa in the living room. Each villa can sleep eight, plus there's room for a crib.

Treehouse Villas: Guests who lodge in one of these octagonal houses-on-stilts, scattered along a barbell-shaped roadway, go to sleep to a cacophony of crickets and wake up to a chorus of birds. You're literally in the woods, alongside some of the winding Walt Disney World canals, and you feel a million miles from the rest of the World. Upstairs are the small (but modern) kitchen, the living room (where a television set is located), two bedrooms (each with a queen-size bed), and two bathrooms; the entire floor is surrounded by a deck. Downstairs, there's a bedroom with a double bed and TV, and a utility room equipped with a washer and dryer. The roadways—shady, flat, and generally untrafficked—are great for jogging.

Grand Vista Homes: Four homes—each with two or three bedrooms and a fully equipped kitchen—are available for rent. Each features a master bedroom with a king-size bed, and most of the other bedrooms have two queen-size beds (some have two twins). Bed turndown service, daily newspaper delivery, and furnishings are all first-class. The use of golf carts and bicycles is included. (For complete price information, refer to the "Rates at Walt Disney World Properties" chart starting on page 52.)

WHERE TO EAT: At press time, major changes were in store for the eateries at the Disney Institute. Call 407-WDW-DINE (939-3463) for up-to-the-minute information regarding their status. Note that there are many dining options at Downtown Disney (see *Good Meals, Great Times*) and the resorts on Hotel Plaza Boulevard.

Groceries: In these parts, in-room grocery delivery is available and many guests cook their own meals. Dabblers, located in the Welcome Center, has a limited selection of groceries. The Gourmet Pantry at the Downtown Disney Marketplace stocks staples of all sorts. Purchases can be delivered to your villa; if you won't be there to receive them, arrangements can be made for the delivery person to be let in so that perishables can be stashed in the refrigerator. It's also possible to order by phone; call 407-827-4147 for Disney Institute grocery delivery, or 407-828-3886 for the Gourmet Pantry. A Gooding's supermarket is located at the Crossroads of Lake Buena Vista shopping center nearby.

WHERE TO DRINK: At Downtown Disney Marketplace you will find Rainforest Cafe and Cap'n Jack's Restaurant quite convenient. The clubs at Downtown Disney Pleasure Island and West Side are a bit further away, but worth the trip (for information, refer to *Everything Else in the World*).

WHAT TO DO: In addition to boating, pole fishing, and shopping at the Downtown Disney Marketplace (discussed in detail in *Sports* and *Everything Else in the World*), you can also enjoy many activities around the villas themselves. Two sand volleyball courts are situated among the villas. Note that the enrichment programs previously offered by the Disney Institute are no longer available. (For more information, refer to page 200 in the *Everything Else in the World* chapter.)

Biking: The rustic pathways and meandering roads around the villas can make for an enjoyable hour of pedaling. Bicycles can be rented at Recreation Rental Center.

Boating: Canoes and pedal boats may be rented at the Recreation Rental Center.

Golf: Fairways of the Lake Buena Vista course based here nudge right up to the Fairway and Treehouse Villas. Practice greens and a driving range are available, along with top-quality rental clubs and shoes. (For fees and starting information, see the *Sports* chapter.)

Health Club: The large Spa and Fitness Center features a gymnasium and Cybex equipment. A full-service spa is located in the center (use of facilities is included with the purchase of spa treatments).

Playground: A play area is located near the Fairway Villas.

Shopping: Dabblers in the Welcome Center offers a mix of merchandise, including groceries, sundries, and more Disney character items.

Swimming: There are six pools and several whirlpools dotted about the grounds.

Tennis: There are four lighted clay courts which can be booked by any guest with a fitness center pass.

TRANSPORTATION: Buses go to the Magic Kingdom, Epcot, the Disney-MGM Studios, Animal Kingdom, Blizzard Beach, Typhoon Lagoon, and Downtown Disney. They circulate through the villa areas, making pickups at bus stops located along the roadways.

Another option: transport to the Downtown Disney Marketplace via an electric golf cart or bike. Both are rented at the Recreation Center.

Disney's Old Key West Resort

Escape to the spirit of the Florida Keys. Disney's Old Key West Resort is the flagship Disney Vacation Club property (see the box on page 69 for details), but villas not occupied by members are available for nightly rental. It has the laid-back feel of a resort community and all the amenities that go with resort life. The homey accommodations have lots of space and the convenience of kitchen facilities, making the resort especially comfortable for longer stays. The villas are designed in a Key West theme, with soothing color schemes of seafoam green and mauve. The telephone number for Disney's Old Key West resort is 407-827-7700.

VILLAS: There are studios and villas with one, two, or three bedrooms. A studio consists of a large room with two queen-size beds, a table and chairs, and a small refrigerator, coffeemaker, microwave, and sink. The bathrooms are spacious. Each of the

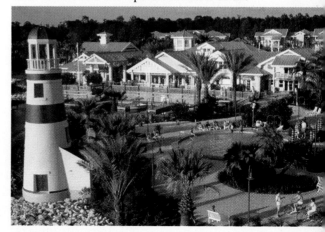

one-bedroom villas has a king-size bed in the master bedroom and a queen-size sleeper sofa in the living room; the master bath has a whirlpool tub, sink, and shower.

The two-bedroom villa features a king-size bed in the master bedroom, two queen-size beds in the second bedroom, a living room with a queen-size sleeper sofa and a VCR, a dining room, and a spacious kitchen with a refrigerator, dishwasher, toaster, and coffeemaker, plus dishes, silverware, cooking utensils, and more.

The master bathroom is divided into two separate rooms with an extra-large whirlpool tub and a sink in one and an oversize shower, sink and vanity, and toilet in the other. There's a porch or balcony off the living room and bedroom, and ceiling fans in each room. The configuration of the two-story, three-bedroom Grand Villas is similar to that of the two-bedroom models, but adds a third bedroom with two double beds. As for capacity, the studios and one-bedroom villas sleep 4 people, the two-bedroom villas sleep 8 guests, and two-story three-bedroom villas accommodate 12.

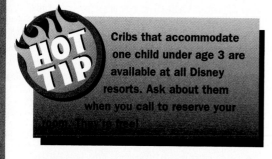

HOT TIP Cribs that accommodate one child under age 3 are available at all Disney resorts. Ask about them when you call to reserve your room. They're free!

WHERE TO EAT: In addition to the restaurant and snack bar here, there are grills and picnic tables available for enjoying meals outdoors. Pizza delivery is available from nearby Dixie Landings between the hours of 4 P.M. and 12 A.M. The eateries of Downtown Disney are easily accessed by boat.

Good's Food to Go: The perfect place to pick up fixin's for a continental breakfast, this place also offers burgers, conch fritters, salads, sandwiches, and simple snacks.

Olivia's Cafe: This casual full-service restaurant serves Key West favorites, plus more traditional items, for breakfast, lunch, and dinner. Menus change seasonally. A Winnie the Pooh-themed character breakfast is held on Monday, Wednesday, and Sunday mornings.

WHERE TO DRINK: The watering holes at Old Key West are as laid-back and inviting as they come.

Gurgling Suitcase: Near the main pool area, this bar serves specialty drinks, cocktails, wine, beer, and soft drinks. Sit at outdoor tables or on stools inside.

Turtle Shack: In the recreation area located off Turtle Pond Road, this poolside spot serves pizza, salads, sandwiches, and snacks. Open seasonally.

WHAT TO DO: At Conch Flats Community Hall, table tennis, board games, playing cards, a large-screen TV, video rentals, and planned activities are offered. Basketball, shuffleboard, and volleyball courts are located throughout the resort, and equipment is available at Hank's Rent 'N Return.

Biking: A variety of bicycles may be rented from Hank's.

Boating: Pedal boats, rowboats, and pontoon boats are available for rent at Hank's Rent 'N Return.

Health Club: The R.E.S.T. health club features Nautilus and cardiovascular machines, a sauna, and massage (by appointment).

Playground: A kids' play area is located by each of the resort's swimming pools.

Shopping: Conch Flats General Store has groceries, books, magazines, sun care products, sundries, and character merchandise.

Swimming: The sprawling main pool, with a large whirlpool nearby, is located behind the Hospitality House. The children's pool and play area resembles a giant sandcastle. Additional pools are found around the resort.

Tennis: There are two lighted tennis courts located near the main pool. A third court, in a more removed area, is not equipped for night play.

Video Arcade: The Electric Eel Arcade is in the Hospitality House. The Flying Fish arcade, by the Turtle Shack snack bar.

TRANSPORTATION: Buses go to the Magic Kingdom, Epcot, the Disney-MGM Studios, Animal Kingdom, Blizzard Beach, Typhoon Lagoon, and Downtown Disney. Water launches also make the trip between the resort and Downtown Disney.

Animal Kingdom Area

All-Star Movies, Music & Sports

The All-Star resorts are the most brightly and boldly themed at Walt Disney World. Each resort has 1,920 rooms housed in ten buildings devoted to five Disney movies, types of music, and sports, respectively.

Sports fans will find themselves in a world of baseball, football, tennis, surfing, or basketball at the All-Star Sports resort. Brightly colored, larger-than-life football helmets, surfboards, tennis balls, basketball hoops, and baseball bats adorn the buildings.

At the All-Star Music resort, Broadway, country, jazz, rock, and calypso are the themes. A walk-through, neon-lit jukebox, a three-story pair of cowboy boots, and a Broadway theater marquee are among the giant icons.

The All-Star Movies resort celebrates five classic Disney films: *Toy Story*, *The Mighty Ducks*, *Fantasia*, *101 Dalmatians*, and *The Love Bug*. Buildings are adorned with such icons as 40-foot dalmatians and wildly oversize versions of Buzz Lightyear and Woody.

As value resorts, the All-Star properties offer few frills, but the service and whimsical atmosphere are pure Disney.

Guests check in at Cinema Hall for All-Star Movies, Melody Hall for All-Star Music, or Stadium Hall for All-Star Sports. Each has a food court, arcade, shop, and Guest Services. To reach All-Star Movies, call 407-939-7000; to phone All-Star Music, call 407-939-6000; to contact All-Star Sports, call 407-939-5000.

ROOMS: The guestrooms, measuring 260 square feet, are rather small compared with those at Port Orleans and Dixie Landings, which are 314 square feet. Each room has two double beds (with the exception of rooms

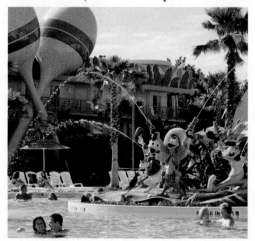

designed for travelers with disabilities, which have one king-size bed), a vanity area with a sink, a separate bathroom, a small dresser, and a small table with chairs.

WHERE TO EAT: Three food courts: **World Premiere** in Cinema Hall, **Intermission** in Melody Hall, and **End Zone** in Stadium Hall. Each features a bakery, convenience market, and several stands geared to barbecue, pizza and pasta, and burgers. Each food court has a seating area with a beverage bar.

For entertainment, the End Zone offers Disney movies during the day and showcases big games on its big-screen TV. The All-Star resorts all deliver pizza, salads, beer, and wine to rooms from 4 P.M. to midnight.

WHERE TO DRINK: There are no lounges at the All-Star resorts; however, the **Silver Screen Spirits**, **Singing Spirits**, and **Team Spirits** pool bars serve drinks throughout the day and evening. The bars are in the main pool areas.

WHAT TO DO: Guests may swim in any of the All-Star pools. All-Star guests may rent boating equipment at any WDW resorts.

Playground: A playground is located in each hotel's courtyard area.

Shopping: Maestro Mickey's in Melody Hall, Sport Goofy's Gifts and Sundries in Stadium Hall, and Donald's Double Feature in Cinema Hall all have magazines, books, character merchandise, and sundries.

Swimming: Each hotel has two pools and one kiddie pool. The main pool at All-Star Movies has a *Fantasia* theme. (Look for Sorcerer Mickey.) The smaller Duck Pond Pool is based on *The Mighty Ducks*. At the All-Star Music resort, the Calypso Pool is in the form of a giant guitar, while the Piano Pool resembles a grand piano. At All-Star Sports, Surfboard Bay has a soothing ocean motif. The smaller Grand Slam Pool pays tribute to our national pastime—it's shaped like a baseball diamond (Goofy is on the mound).

Video Arcades: Each of the All-Star resorts boasts one video arcade.

TRANSPORTATION: Buses make pickups at Cinema Hall, Melody Hall, and Stadium Hall for trips to each of the four theme parks, Blizzard Beach, Typhoon Lagoon, and Downtown Disney. Each resort has its own bus line.

A word about All-Star resort transportation: The bus service at these "value" resorts tends to be slightly *more efficient* than the service at other locations. The combination of fewer stops and connections is a nice bonus for guests staying here.

Disney's Animal Kingdom Lodge

At first glance, Walt Disney World's newest resort, Disney's Animal Kingdom Lodge, evokes images of a sleepy, little thatched-roof game lodge in the wilds of southern Africa. Upon closer examination, however, it's clear that the only things sleepy or little

about this place are the small creatures that live in its shadow. Those animals, along with their more sizeable cousins, inhabit the 33 acres of meticulously re-created African savanna, which practically surround this 1,293 room resort. In all, more than 100 birds and hoofed animals, including zebras, giraffes, and wildebeest, call Disney's newest wildlife reserve home. With the freedom to wander within a dozen or so yards of the lodge itself, these critters allow guests to go on safari without leaving their balconies.

The resort, located about a mile from Disney's Animal Kingdom park, is expected to open in Spring 2001. The lobby is a tremendous, high-ceilinged room, richly appointed—as is the rest of the property—with colorful African artwork and artifacts. The biggest draw here is neither the large mud fireplace nor the rope bridge spanning this cavernous chamber, but the four-story observation window overlooking the savanna. It's just one of many oversize portals through which to gaze upon meandering wildlife.

Like the African game lodges on which it is based, Disney's Animal Kingdom Lodge was constructed using a semicircular design. From overhead, it looks a bit like a horseshoe. This allows for maximum animal-viewing potential. Indeed, 90 percent of the resort's guestrooms have direct views of the savanna areas. The telephone number for Disney's Animal Kingdom Lodge is 407-938-3000.

ROOMS: The 1,293 standard and deluxe rooms, all finished in traditional tapestries and vibrant colors, feature handcrafted dark wood furniture (no two pieces are exactly alike), sand-colored walls, and earth-tone patterned carpets. Deluxe rooms are a bit more spacious

than their standard counterparts. Most rooms have two queen beds (some king-size beds are available), plus a daybed to accommodate up to five people; bunk beds are available in many rooms. All rooms have balconies. Suites include a parlor, plus one, two, or three bedrooms; there are king-size or queen-size beds in the bedrooms. Bathrooms have a separate vanity area with double sink. All rooms include an iron (with board), hair dryer, and newspaper delivery. Like at real African game lodges, some beds come draped with mosquito netting. Unlike in Africa, however, the nets here are purely decorative!

WHERE TO EAT: In addition to its restaurants, the hotel has 24-hour room service.

Boma—Flavors of Africa: Boma is modeled after a bustling, African marketplace. This sprawling, family restaurant boasts many different types of cuisine, in what chefs describe as a "global fusion" style. The cuisine is a blend of French, Malaysian, Indian, Chinese, and English. Meals are prepared in an onstage kitchen.

Jiko—The Cooking Place: The colors of sunset are the backdrop for this sublime eatery with an African flare.

The Mara: A spacious fast food restaurant serving such crowd-pleasers as pizza, burgers, and chicken fingers.

WHERE TO DRINK: The lounges here are rustic and inviting. Some even offer the opportunity to sip cocktails while observing animals on the savanna.

Capetown Lounge and Wine Bar: Adjacent to Jiko—The Cooking Place, this spot features wines imported from South Africa.

Uzima Springs: The resort's poolside bar serves specialty and traditional drinks during regular pool hours.

Victoria Falls: Set alongside a soothing waterfall, this mezzanine-level lounge features coffee, tea, South African wines, and assorted cocktails.

WHAT TO DO: Spying on wildlife is the main event in these parts. However, if you can manage to pry yourself away from those hoofed exhibitionists for a bit, there are plenty of other diversions available. Note that guests staying at Disney's Animal Kingdom Lodge are welcome to partake in activities offered at other Walt Disney World resorts.

Children's Programs: The Simba's Clubhouse play area, for kids ages 4 through 12, is open in the evenings starting at 4:30 P.M. Reservations are required. Kids may also learn about the wildlife surrounding the resort through nature-themed activities. For more information or to make reservations, call 407-938-3000.

Health Club: The Zahanati health club boasts state-of-the-art exercise equipment, a sauna, and whirlpool, plus spa services, including massage (by appointment).

Playground: The Bana playground is located near the pool.

Shopping: Zawadi Marketplace stocks Africa-themed gifts, Disney character merchandise, clothing with the Animal Kingdom Lodge logo, and sundries.

Swimming: The resort has just one swimming pool, but it is huge. More impressive than its size, however, is the view from the pool deck. In addition to a kiddie pool, there are two whirlpools nearby.

Video Arcade: Pumbaa's Fun & Games features a selection of video games.

TRANSPORTATION: Buses go to the Magic Kingdom, Epcot, the Disney-MGM Studios, Animal Kingdom, Typhoon Lagoon, Blizzard Beach, and Downtown Disney.

Coronado Springs

This resort reveals its Southwestern U.S.-Mexican theme in such elements as a tiled stucco lobby with a fountain, and a pyramid with water tumbling down from it that appears to have created the Mayan ruin-themed pool. The hotel's 1,921 rooms are found in three guest areas that stretch around Lago Dorado, a 15-acre lake. (It can take five minutes or more to walk to the farthest rooms.) The food court, restaurant, and lounge are all near the lobby. A convention center offers access to business services. The telephone number for Coronado Springs is 407-939-1000.

ROOMS: Standard rooms are smaller than those at Disney's deluxe hotels, but adequate for a family of four; each has two double beds (some king-size beds are available). In-room amenities include a coffeemaker, hair dryer, and modem port. Decor varies in each section but is characterized by yellow, blue, and scarlet accents. In the Casitas area, where most of the suites are located, terra-cotta guest buildings occupy a citylike landscape. In the pueblo-style Ranchos, scattered along a dry streambed, rooms have a rustic feel. Cabanas, located along the rocky palm-lined beach, reflect the casual feel of their namesake. Walkways link guestroom areas with recreational facilities.

WHERE TO EAT: In addition to a full-service restaurant and food court, limited room service is available for breakfast and dinner.

Maya Grill: Open for breakfast and dinner, this spot offers seafood, steak, lamb, and pork cooked over an open-pit wood-fired grill.

Pepper Market: High ceilings make this nontraditional food court feel like an open-air market. The fare includes tacos, tostadas, pizza, pasta, and omelettes made to order. Note that there is an automatic ten percent gratuity for dining in the Pepper Market.

WHERE TO DRINK: There are two places to wet your whistle at Coronado Springs.

Francisco's: This colorful lounge provides cocktails and evening entertainment and is located in the main building.

Siesta's: In the Dig Site area, this poolside bar lets swimmers and archaeologists enjoy a variety of cocktails and light snacks.

WHAT TO DO: There is an array of water sports in which to participate, as well as volleyball, and a short nature trail. (For more information, see *Sports*.)

Biking: Bikes may be rented at La Marina.

Boating: A variety of boating equipment is available for rent at La Marina.

Health Club: La Vida health club offers a full range of fitness equipment.

Playground: The Explorer's Playground is part of the Dig Site play area and includes a huge sandbox, complete with Mayan carvings waiting to be excavated.

Salon: The Casa de Belleza salon, located near La Vida health club, offers a large variety of spa services.

Shopping: Panchitos Gifts & Sundries is where to find items with a Southwestern flavor, Disney merchandise, film, and necessities.

Swimming: The main pool can be found in the Dig Site area. It surrounds a Mayan pyramid and features a towering water slide. There is a 22-person whirlpool and a kiddie pool nearby. Each of the guestroom areas features an unguarded quiet pool.

Video Arcades: The Jumping Bean Arcade is found in the main building, and the Iguana Arcade is in the Dig Site area.

TRANSPORTATION: Buses take guests to the Magic Kingdom, Epcot, the Disney-MGM Studios, Animal Kingdom, Typhoon Lagoon, Blizzard Beach, BoardWalk, and Downtown Disney.

Disney Cruise Line

In the summer of 1999, the *Disney Wonder* joined its sister ship, the *Disney Magic*, in the ranks of the world's finest oceangoing vessels. Although the onboard experience is essentially the same on both ships, some restaurant names and theming differ.

A Disney Cruise Line seven-day land-and-sea-vacation begins with a three- or four-day stay at a WDW resort. After that, guests (except those at the Swan and Dolphin) retain the same room keys for their staterooms aboard the *Disney Wonder*. There is no second check-in on the ship. Staterooms closely match the category of the resort accommodations, from moderate to deluxe. Guests may also opt for a seven-day sea-only trip. This package does not include a stay at a WDW resort. All seven-day cruises take place on the *Disney Magic*.

When transfers are purchased, guests travel via private motor coach to Port Canaveral, the departure point for all cruises. They then board a 1,750-passenger ship for their journey. From the innovative ship design to entertainment options, families, teens, and adults without kids all have their own comfort zones—without ever having to say goodbye to Mickey. (In addition to the Mouse, the usual cast of characters is on board.) One itinerary includes a stop at Nassau in the Bahamas. Another takes passengers to Freeport. The seven-day, Caribbean cruise option takes guests to the U.S. Virgin Islands. Each voyage ends with a day at Disney's private island, Castaway Cay. ID is required to enter the Bahamas—a passport or birth certificate will do.

The ships' classic exteriors recall the majesty of early ocean liners. For example, *Disney Magic* guests enter a three-story atrium, where traditional definitions of elegance expand to include a bronze statue of Mickey as helmsman and subtle cutout Disney character silhouettes along the grand staircase. There's even a 15-foot, topsy-turvy statue of a "goofy" painter hanging off the *Disney Magic*'s stern.

Vacations can be booked through a travel agent or by calling 800-511-1333 or visiting *www.disneycruise.com*.

ROOMS: All 875 staterooms aboard both ships are a cut above the standard cruising cabin. On average, staterooms offer about 25 percent more space, most have a bath and a half, and 73 percent are outside rooms with ocean vistas—many with verandas. All feature telephones with "land lines," televisions, hair dryers, and safes. There are rooms equipped for guests with disabilities. All rooms are nonsmoking.

There are 12 stateroom categories that correspond to Walt Disney World resorts with comparable room rates. The seven-day land-and-sea-vacations start at $829 for adults per person, double occupancy. (Packages for kids start at $349.) The seven-day land-sea package price includes Walt Disney World accommodations, admission to the theme and water parks, shipboard meals, cruise and port charges, and more. Depending on availability, guests may opt for a three- or four-day sea-only vacation. The seven-day sea-only packages start at $829 for adults, per person, double occupancy. Packages for kids start at $399.

WHERE TO EAT: There are three themed dining rooms (and one adults-only alternative), in addition to 24-hour room service, on each ship; guests dine in each of the three main rooms, enjoying a different culinary experience each night.

Note: The restaurants, clubs, and activities described below focus on the *Disney Magic*. However, their counterparts on the *Disney Wonder* deliver comparable experiences.

Animator's Palate: Here the restaurant and the food are works of art. As in the movie *The Wizard of Oz*, everything begins in black and white—from the floors to the waiters' attire. As the meal progresses, color creeps into the picture. When dessert arrives, the room is awash in brilliant hues.

Lumière's: Continental food, chandeliers, and *Beauty and the Beast* trompe l'oeil effects characterize this casually elegant dining room. An abundance of roses completes the theme.

Palo: A dining room reserved for adults, Palo is a romantic restaurant perched atop the vessel. Chefs prepare Italian cuisine in an exhibition kitchen. Reservations are required.

Parrot Cay: In a colorful Caribbean setting complete with Sebastian wall sconces, this restaurant features tasty tropical cuisine.

Topsider Buffet: An indoor-outdoor cafe serving breakfast, lunch, snacks, and a buffet dinner for kids.

WHERE TO DRINK: Among the options are a variety of lounges, including an ESPN Club sports bar, and a number of other watering holes. Beat Street, like Pleasure Island, is an adults-only cluster of nighttime entertainment venues.

Offbeat: An anything goes, improvisational comedy club.

Rockin' Bar D: A dance club with a live band and deejay.

Sessions: An intimate piano bar lounge.

WHAT TO DO: Recreational areas on each ship, as well as at its ports of call, are strategically located to attract families, teens, and adults to different areas, with nearly an entire deck devoted to kids. A cruise director keeps guests apprised of the options.

Adult Activities: Adults-only activities range from wine tasting to special guest lectures. There is an adults-only pool onboard and a secluded beach for grown-ups at Castaway Cay.

Biking: Bikes are available for rent at Castaway Cay.

Buena Vista Theater: A 270-seat cinema, this theater features a variety of first-run movies and classic Disney films.

Children's Programs: A huge area dedicated exclusively to kids offers supervised, age-specific programs for kids ages 3 through 12 from 9 A.M. until 1 A.M. The Oceaneer Club provides engaging activities for the 3- through 8-year-old set. The Oceaneer Lab, designed for children 9 through 12, is a science-based interactive play area. This amusement center keeps older kids entertained for hours at a time.

Deck Parties: Guests can dance to live music, sip cocktails, and nibble snacks at informal, yet swinging shindigs at sea.

Shopping: In addition to the colorful shipboard shops—Mickey's Mates, Treasure Ketch, Shutters, and ESPN Locker Room—guests can indulge their shopping fantasies while exploring the various ports of call.

Studio Sea: At this family lounge, guests participate in live entertainment, such as cabaret acts and a family game show, in a setting that looks like a television studio.

Swimming: There are several whirlpools and three swimming pools on each ship: a family pool, a sports-activity pool, and an adults-only pool. Guests may also swim off the sandy shores and lagoon of Castaway Cay.

Teen Entertainment: In a coffee bar called Common Ground, teens (and teens only) can hang out, watch movies, and listen to music. There are also teen-oriented activities on the sports deck, as well as on Castaway Cay.

Vista Spa and Salon: Guests get in ship-shape at this modern facility, which offers exercise equipment and spa treatments, educational and enrichment programs, sauna, steam room, whirlpool, and massage. The salon offers many services, including haircuts, manicures, and pedicures (for an extra fee). Note that spa appointments fill up fast—book yours as soon as possible once aboard the ship.

Volleyball: Guests can play water volleyball in the ship's pool and sand volleyball at Castaway Cay.

Walt Disney Theater: A tribute to the grand theatrical palaces of long ago. Guests see an original musical production each night.

Anchors Aweigh!

Every Disney Cruise Line trip includes a visit to Castaway Cay (pronounced *key*). Disney has maintained the island's natural beauty while providing a host of outdoor activities, including snorkeling, biking, and hiking. The island has a beach for families, and a mile-long stretch of secluded sand—complete with massage cabanas—for adults seeking less action and more privacy.

As guests awaken at the island, they find their ship docked at Castaway Cay's private pier. The pier allows for easy access to and from the ship.

Castaway Cay, a 1,000-acre tropical island, is in the Bahamas, east of Fort Lauderdale. Trams are available for guests who wish to explore the island. All of the architecture, including a bar, restaurant, market, and even a post office, is in true Bahamian style.

Resorts on Hotel Plaza Boulevard

These seven hotels—Best Western Lake Buena Vista, Courtyard by Marriott, DoubleTree Guest Suites, Grosvenor, Hilton, Royal Plaza, and Wyndham Palace Resort and Spa—though inside WDW boundaries, are neither owned nor operated by Disney. However, many have been here since the park opened, in 1971, or soon thereafter (sometimes under different names), accommodating Mickey enthusiasts from the beginning. The hotels are not themed, but the three largest (the Hilton, Wyndham Palace, and Grosvenor) do have meals hosted by Disney characters.

Often referred to as the Downtown Disney Resort Area Hotels, they line mile-long Hotel Plaza Boulevard. The Hilton, Wyndham Palace, and Grosvenor are across the street from the Marketplace, with its shops, restaurants, and nightlife. The other four properties are a 10- to 25-minute stroll away. They are also close to the Crossroads of Lake Buena Vista shopping center, home to inexpensive eateries and a 24-hour grocery. Privileges of staying in one of these hotels include:

• Guests are entitled to purchase "E-Ride" passes to the Magic Kingdom. (They are sold in on-site Disney-run gift shops.)

• Car rental on the premises (at all but the Best Western Lake Buena Vista resort)

• Free bus service to the four theme parks, with limited service to Downtown Disney, Typhoon Lagoon, and Blizzard Beach. The buses, which are not part of the Disney transportation network, make two trips every hour; be sure to allow extra time for bus travel. One bus serves the Hilton and Wyndham Palace; another, the other hotels (it takes ten minutes to stop at all five). Buses stop in the middle of the parking lots at some theme parks.

• Flexibility to book tickets for both on- and off-WDW-property attractions

• Preferred access to Disney golf courses

• Free Disney Channel and ESPN for in-room viewing

• Twenty percent discount on Downtown Disney Pleasure Island admission when you present a receipt showing that you have eaten dinner at one of the hotels' restaurants on the same evening

• Preferred seating at Planet Hollywood before 5 P.M.

Note that guests staying in the resorts on Hotel Plaza Boulevard do have to pay for parking at Disney parks and other Walt Disney World attractions, and they cannot charge purchases made at WDW shops and restaurants with a resort ID or have purchases shipped to their rooms free of charge.

To book a room, call the individual hotel's toll-free number or WDW Central Reservations at 407-W-DISNEY (934-7639). The resorts on Hotel Plaza Boulevard are included in several Walt Disney Travel Company packages. Internet users can get information via *www.downtowndisneyhotels.com.*

All of the hotels offer nonsmoking rooms and accommodations for travelers with disabilities. To get to the hotels from the airport, take Exit 27 off I-4.

BEST WESTERN LAKE BUENA VISTA:

This mostly leisure-oriented, 18-story hotel is surrounded by pines and has an entry lined with oaks draped in Spanish moss. Besides new room furnishings, its new windows ensure a quiet stay. Each of the 325 spacious rooms and suites have either one king-size bed and a queen sofa bed or two queen-size beds, as well a balcony (floors 7 through 18 provide a panoramic Walt Disney World view). Rooms also come with voice mail, free coffee and tea, a safe, hair dryer, and iron with board. Baths have one sink and plenty of counter space. Small refrigerators may be rented for $5 a day, large ones for $10. All the rooms with Walt Disney World views are nonsmoking.

Each of the four suites occupies a corner of the 18th floor and features a wet bar, two phones, two TVs, a whirlpool tub, and an impressive glassed-in porch with skylights and a ceiling fan; they offer fine views of the other resorts on Hotel Plaza Boulevard and, from the nonsmoking rooms, the (distant) fireworks at Disney theme parks.

The hotel also has an arcade, heated pool, kiddie pool, playground, sundries shop, and laundry facilities. Other amenities include

room service and overnight film processing. Traders restaurant serves breakfast and dinner; the Parakeet Cafe offers breakfast, lunch, and dinner, as well as snacks and pizza.

The hotel's new lobby and restaurant area feature a Pizza Hut, cocktail lounge, and a game room. Rates range from $89 to $169 for guestrooms; $199 to $399 for suites. Best Western Lake Buena Vista Resort; 2000 Hotel Plaza Blvd.; Box 22205; Lake Buena Vista, FL 32830; 407-828-2424 or 800-348-3765; *www.orlandoresorthotel.com.*

COURTYARD BY MARRIOTT:

The 323 guestrooms, some of the most spacious on Hotel Plaza Boulevard, are situated in a 14-story tower and a 6-story annex. They feature two double beds in most rooms, sitting areas, modem ports, voice mail, movies and Nintendo (for a fee), coffeemakers with china

mugs, irons (with boards), and safes. The bathrooms are a little small, but they feature double vanities and hair dryers.

Tables topped with colorful umbrellas, the 2 Go breakfast bar, and the Tipsy Parrot lounge fill the inviting atrium lobby. The Courtyard Cafe & Grille is a full-service restaurant with a breakfast buffet; the Village Deli serves snacks and sandwiches, TCBY yogurt, and Pizza Hut pizza. Room

service is available. There are three small heated pools, including one for young children; a whirlpool; playground; arcade; small exercise room; and guest laundry. The pool bar is open seasonally. Rates range from $99 to $219 year-round. Courtyard by Marriott; Box 22204; 1805 Hotel Plaza Blvd.; Lake Buena Vista, FL 32830; 407-828-8888 or 800-223-9930; *www.courtyard.com.*

DOUBLETREE GUEST SUITES:

This 229-unit property has a stellar staff, homey atmosphere, low-slung facade reminiscent of WDW's Contemporary hotel, bright colors and whimsical patterns throughout, and an aviary in the lobby, where a child's check-in desk adjoins the one for grown-ups. Kids get a bag of goodies, and everyone gets cookies. The only all-suite hotel at Walt Disney World, it has roomy (625 square feet) units, each with a living room and sleeper sofa, dressing area, and separate bedroom. The one-bedroom suites sleep up to six people; there are five two-bedroom suites as well. Most bedrooms have two double beds; a few kings are available.

The decor features vibrant blues, greens, and oranges, with plaid chairs and sofas. Lamp bases resemble chess pieces, and even the picture frames are colorful. (More subdued surroundings are available.) Room amenities include two TVs, pay-per-view movies, wet bar, refrigerator, coffeemaker, microwave oven, hair dryer, and safe ($2.50 daily charge). The bathroom has a full vanity area and a small TV.

Recreational facilities include a large heated pool and a whirlpool in a landscaped area with two hammocks, as well as a fitness room, sand volleyball court, two lighted tennis courts, and small playground. The children's playroom has a big-screen television, toys, games, free popcorn, and seasonal activities. Streamers restaurant features American classics and a breakfast buffet; it's also the source for more of those tasty cookies. Streamers Market sells snack items and groceries.

Rates range from $129 to $299. DoubleTree Guest Suites; 2305 Hotel Plaza Blvd.; Lake Buena Vista, FL 32830; 407-934-1000 or 800-222-8733; *www.doubletreeguestsuites.com*.

GROSVENOR:

GROSVENOR: This hotel (pronounced *GROVE-nor*) attracts many international guests. The 626 rooms are located in a 19-story tower and two wings framing two large, formal courtyards with griffin centerpieces. Each room has voice mail, a coffeemaker, and a VCR; movie rentals are available. Most rooms have two double beds, though some 35 king rooms are available; 65 rooms also have daybeds and can sleep up to five people. Bathrooms are small but stocked with toiletries.

Extensive recreational facilities—the property's major appeal—include an exercise room, two lighted tennis courts, shuffleboard, basketball, volleyball, two heated pools, children's pool, large play area, and arcade. Changing rooms with showers accommodate guests who check in or out early. Baskervilles restaurant incorporates a replica of Sherlock Holmes' office (a highlight), and serves breakfast and dinner buffets; Disney characters come for breakfast on Tuesday and Thursday; Murder Watch Mystery Theatre takes place on Saturday at 6 P.M. and 9 P.M.

Crumpets Cafe, open 24 hours a day, serves continental breakfast, snacks, and light fare. Crickets lounge has occasional entertainment, but Moriarty's pub is more inviting. Rates range from $99 to $165 for two guests, year-round; suites are $345 to $480. Grosvenor; 1850 Hotel Plaza Blvd.; Lake Buena Vista, FL 32830; 407-828-4444 or 800-624-4109; *www.grosvenorresort.com*.

HILTON: This hotel, with a colorful facade and palm-lined drive, gets high marks for its 23 well-groomed acres, laid-back ambience, impressive pool area, and upscale shops. The 814 rooms, all of which recently underwent extensive refurbishment, have mini-bars, phones with voice mail, and computer hookups.

Among the resort's seven restaurants and lounges, casual Finn's Grill offers dinners of seafood and steaks (Saturday night features a seafood buffet with cooked-to-order pasta), wines by the glass, themed evenings, and creatively presented bread; Cape Cod–themed Covington Mill serves breakfast (with characters in attendance on Sunday), lunch, and dinner; Rum Largo

Poolside Cafe serves hamburgers, sandwiches, salads, and tropical drinks alfresco. Mainstreet Market, open until midnight, is part gourmet deli, part country store. For light meals, snacks, or cocktails, drop by John T's. After-dinner drinks, specialty coffees, beer, and wines by the glass are served at Mugs Coffee Bar.

Recreational facilities include a couple of whirlpools, two heated swimming pools, a kiddie pool, fitness room, and large gameroom. The Vacation Station Kids' Hotel, designed for children ages 4 through 12, has beds, a video room, play area, and scheduled activities supervised by a trained staff. The cost is $6 for the first child, with a $1 discount for each additional child. Rates range from $160 to $345; suites are $359 to $1,500. Hilton; 1751 Hotel Plaza Blvd.; Lake Buena Vista, FL 32830; 407-827-4000 or 800-782-4414; *www.hilton-wdwv.com*.

ROYAL PLAZA: A pineapple motif, a symbol of hospitality, permeates this hotel, which has been transformed over the past couple of years. The 394 guest units, including 22 suites, are divided between a 17-story main tower, with a glass-enclosed elevator scaling the facade and two-story lanai wings with standard and superior rooms, and gated patios or small balconies. Each hotel guestroom has a sitting area set off by shuttered partitions, a desk, dresser, double armoire with closet space, oversize bathtub, safe, and mini-bar. Baths have marble

counters and corner tubs (whirlpools on the concierge level); baths in the spacious rooms with king-size beds have a separate glass-enclosed shower. All rooms are decorated in shades of coral, teal, and green; they have either two double beds or a king-size bed, ceiling fans, sofabeds, VCRs, hair dryers, safes, mini-bars, and free coffee and tea.

Recreational facilities include a large heated pool, a whirlpool, a large fitness room (for guests 16 and older), gamerooms for adults and kids, and four lighted tennis courts. The hotel also has video rentals, a business center, and a lending library.

The Giraffe Grill offers all meals, including an impressively ample breakfast buffet; the Marketessen is open until 2 A.M. Depending on the season and the view, room rates range from $109 to $179 for up to five in a room; suites, $209 to $699. Royal Plaza; Box 22203; 1905 Hotel Plaza Blvd.; Lake Buena Vista, FL 32830; 407-828-2828 or 800-248-7890; *www.royalplaza.com.*

WYNDHAM PALACE RESORT & SPA: The tallest resort at Walt Disney World and the largest of the resorts on Hotel Plaza Boulevard (it's actually at the intersection of Hotel Plaza Boulevard and Buena Vista Drive) is a cluster of towers set on 27 acres beside Lake Buena Vista. Each of the 1,014 rooms has a ceiling fan, two phones (with voice mail, speakerphone, and computer

hookup), two queen beds or a king, a coffeemaker, and weekend newspaper delivery. Most rooms have a balcony or patio. There are also concierge accommodations, one- and two-bedroom suites (with coffeemakers, microwaves, refrigerators, mini-bars, and living rooms with queen sofas), and two-story penthouses. Safes are available for a charge.

The resort's European-style spa features myriad treatments and services, a full-service salon, fitness center, and private lap pool with a resistance jet stream. Recreation Island accommodates two swimming pools, a kiddie pool, whirlpool, sauna, three lighted tennis courts, sand volleyball court, and children's playground. Kids' Klub is a year-round recreational program for children 4 through 12.

The hotel also provides 24-hour room service, and it has boutiques and a guest laundry. Dining spots include the lakeside Watercress Cafe, which serves all meals, with breakfast and dinner buffets available (characters are in attendance Sunday morning); the Watercress Pastry Shop, open 24 hours for baked goods and sandwiches; Arthur's 27, upscale but austere; The Outback restaurant (not part of the national chain) for seafood and steak; and the Courtyard Mini-Market, serving snacks and smoothies in a tranquil outdoor setting.

The Laughing Kookaburra Good Time Bar, nicknamed "The Kook," has live entertainment and dancing. Noise from the restaurants can flow through the atriums and penetrate the solid oak doors, so if silence is golden, stay in the 27-story tower or the Palace Island Suites complex. The Top of the Palace lounge provides the perfect perch to gaze at the sunset or fireworks over a glass of fine wine. For the allergy prone, 65 EverGreen Rooms provide filtered air and water. Rates for rooms range from $129 to $269 per night (no charge for kids under 18); suites are $229 to $529. Rollaways cost $15 per night; cribs are free. Wyndham Palace Resort & Spa; 1900 Buena Vista Dr.; Lake Buena Vista, FL 32830; 407-827-2727 or 800-327-2990; *www.wyndham.com.*

PHOTO BY ALICE GARRARD

OFF-PROPERTY ACCOMMODATIONS In Lake Buena Vista

A full lineup of accommodations, from laid-back to luxurious, abuts the crossroads at I-4 and S.R. 535 in the heart of Lake Buena Vista. Most offer free transportation to the four main Disney parks. All of the following properties have nonsmoking rooms and accommodations for guests with disabilities, unless otherwise indicated.

HOLIDAY INN SUNSPREE–LAKE BUENA VISTA: Pretty and pink, this 507-unit hotel is located about 2 miles from the Downtown Disney Marketplace. Its 231 Kidsuites provide privacy for adults and kids; the latter get a soundproof, themed room within a room. Among the 15 options: Kid Space, Dinoland, Bug Catcher's Bunk House, an igloo, and a space capsule—each complete with two to four bunk beds, TV, VCR, Nintendo, and cassette player. Some Teensuites, designed to appeal to older kids, have movie, music, and sports theming; full-size twin bunk beds; a desk; and a vanity with a makeup mirror. King Family Rooms are similar to Teensuites, only roomier and semiprivate, with six-foot-high partitions and one set of bunk beds.

All rooms have a kitchenette with a refrigerator, microwave, coffeemaker (free coffee daily), large bath, hair dryer, safe, and VCR. All standard rooms have two queen-size beds, although some king-size beds and sleeper sofas are available. Camp Holiday, an activity program for children 3 through 12 and a real bargain, is open 8 A.M. to midnight at no charge. Parents can rent a beeper for $5 so they can be reached at any time.

Kids may register at their own check-in desk, and can get a free bedtime tuck-in from Max, the hotel's mascot, on request. Children under 13 eat all meals for free (ordered from a special child's menu) when accompanied by a paying grown-up. Max and his friends make appearances at breakfast and dinner.

Recreational facilities include a heated pool, kiddie pool, two whirlpools, a basketball court, playground, fitness center, and the CyberArcade (a rather impressive one at that). Maxine's Food Emporium food court serves a buffet breakfast and dinner, and features outlets of national fast-food chains. Pinky's Convenience Court has microwavable and refrigerated items. Free scheduled transportation to the four Disney theme parks is provided. Rates run $88 to $129, depending on the season; add an additional $39 to $49 for Kidsuites or $24 to $29 for King Family Rooms. Guests 50 and over can join the Senior Fun Club for special discounts. Holiday Inn SunSpree–Lake Buena Vista; 13351 S.R. 535; Lake Buena Vista, FL 32821; 407-239-4500 or 800-366-6299; *www.kidsuites.com.*

HYATT REGENCY GRAND CYPRESS AND VILLAS OF GRAND CYPRESS: Less than a mile from the hotels that line Hotel Plaza Boulevard, and just three miles from Epcot, the Grand Cypress resort covers 1,500 acres that incorporate the luxurious Hyatt Regency hotel, and the more secluded Villas of Grand Cypress (the two properties are 1½ miles apart, separated by 45 holes of Jack Nicklaus-designed golf and connected by a shuttle that operates continuously from 6 A.M. to 2 A.M.), wood trails, and a 21-acre lake.

Flush with plants and artwork, the Hyatt Regency Grand Cypress has a dramatic 18-story atrium lobby and 750 Florida-inspired guestrooms and suites with wicker furniture; ceiling fans; shutters; hues of rose and mint green; lake, garden, or pool views; cable TV; and 24-hour room service.

The hotel has four bars and five restaurants, including Hemingway's, which serves fresh seafood and steak; Cascade, featuring numerous healthy entrées and terrific Key lime pie; the White Horse Saloon, known for its steak and live entertainment; and La Coquina, where the lavish Sunday brunch is legendary.

The Villas of Grand Cypress provide Mediterranean-style accommodations and are particularly popular with groups. Each club suite features a spacious bedroom with a separate sitting area, large luxury bath with separate shower and tub, and sundeck, patio, or veranda. The villas are even larger, with a substantial living room, dining room, and fully equipped kitchen. At the Villas enclave there are three dining possibilities to choose from—the Black Swan restaurant, in the clubhouse; the casual Fairways; and the Poolside Snack Shop. (The Hyatt is still your best dining bet.)

The Hyatt Regency's crowning glory is a half-acre, 800,000-gallon free-form swimming pool with 12 waterfalls, 2 water slides, and 3 whirlpools. A health club, a gameroom, and the On the Rocks bar are tucked under a grotto. There is also a pool with a whirlpool at the Villas, rental boats on Lake Windsong, a tennis complex with 12 courts, 2 racquetball courts, beach volleyball, fire pit, playground, 4.7-mile jogging and biking path, a pair of equestrian trails, pro shop, and tack shop.

The resort's superb North South course features two Scottish-style shared greens, grassy dunes, elevated tees, and a greens fee that will set you back $150 ($110 in the summer). The Grand Cypress Academy of Golf, Equestrian Center, and Racquet Club offer classes and still more activities. Camp Hyatt welcomes kids age 3 and older. Complimentary shuttle service to the four Disney theme parks departs hourly from the Hyatt.

Rates at the Hyatt Regency range from $205 to $540; suites start at $695. Rates at the Villas range from $295 to $440 for a club suite, $395 to $540 for a one-bedroom villa, and $570 to $860 for a two-bedroom villa. Hyatt Regency Grand Cypress; One Grand Cypress Blvd.; Orlando, FL 32836; 407-239-1234 or 800-554-9288. Villas of Grand Cypress; One N. Jacaranda; Orlando, FL 32836; 407-239-4700 or 800-554-9288; *www.hyattgrandcypress.com.*

PERRIHOUSE BED & BREAKFAST INN:
This ranch-style house in a quiet, country setting is less than two miles from Walt Disney World. The accommodations (eight nonsmoking rooms off a cedar-paneled central library and a separate farm house) are well-appointed, though a bit cluttered. Each of the five king and three family rooms has a private entry, TV, telephone (local calls are on the house), robes, and honor bar. Complimentary fruit, tea, coffee, and juice are always available. Guests have their own refrigerator and laundry ($4 charge for the latter), and they can use the whirlpool, small swimming pool, and kitchen 24 hours a day.

Hosts Nick and Angi Perretti maintain a welcome board in the kitchen that lists current guests by first names and hometowns;

their small hallway gallery is filled with mementos of (and from) past visitors. The library has couches, books, a bird-sighting journal, games, and gift items. This peaceful place, filled with the songs of birds and crickets, celebrates its tenth anniversary this year.

PerriHouse room rates start at $99 and include a continental breakfast buffet. Three-, five-, and seven-day packages are available. PerriHouse Bed & Breakfast Inn; 10417 Centurion Court; Box 22005; Lake Buena Vista, FL 32830; 407-876-4830 or 800-780-4830; *www.perrihouse.com.*

SUMMERFIELD AND SIERRA SUITES LAKE BUENA VISTA:
A half mile from the Crossroads of Lake Buena Vista, the popular Summerfield all-suite hotel has 150 units (most of which feature two separate bedrooms with a king-size bed in the master bedroom) each with a private bath, living room, three televisions, VCR, and good-size, fully equipped kitchen with full-size refrigerator.

The living rooms and bedrooms feature new furnishings, including mattresses, and tropical colors, complete with vivid pink walls. An arcade, guest laundry, and convenience store are on property. The staff will even do your grocery shopping for you if you provide them with a list early in the day. Nearby restaurants offer takeout. The pool is in an enclosed courtyard. Complimentary shuttle service to the Disney parks is provided by the Lake Buena Vista location only.

Rates range from $119 to $249 for a one-bedroom unit (for up to four guests), $159 to $289 for a two-bedroom unit (for up to six guests), and $179 to $319 for a two-bedroom trio (for up to eight guests). Prices include a continental breakfast buffet.

The hotel chain's Sierra Suites studio apartments, located nearby, are priced $30 to $70 lower than the Summerfield Suites, with weekly rates available. Breakfast is not served at the Sierra, nor is transportation to the WDW parks provided. The 125 Sierra units have modern decor with Southwest touches, two queen beds (some kings are available), Harlequin-print rugs, pale yellow walls, modern artwork, hair dryers, irons and ironing boards, good-size bathrooms with separate vanities, beanbag chairs that kids love, kitchens equipped with everything except an oven (the stoves have two burners), and safes ($1 a day). The property has a heated pool, exercise room, gameroom, laundry, video rental, and pleasant courtyard with two gas grills.

Summerfield Suites by Wyndham; 8480 International Dr.; Orlando, FL 32819; 407-352-2400 or 800-830-4964. Sierra Suites Lake Buena Vista; 8100 Palm Parkway; Orlando, FL 32836; 407-239-4300 or 800-830-4964. For either hotel: *www.summerfield-orlando.com.*

In Orlando

Some of Orlando's top hotels are on International Drive, or I-Drive, as it is known locally. This famous thoroughfare has two distinct sectors: the more orderly south end, which stretches from Sea World, past the Orange County Convention Center and local restaurants, to Sand Lake Road. From here north, it morphs into a strip crammed with T-shirt shops and outlet stores.

Old-fashioned I-Ride trolleys travel back and forth along a three-mile stretch of I-Drive daily from 7 A.M. to midnight, from Sea World to the Belz factory outlet stores, stopping every two blocks. The fare is only 75 cents per ride (25 cents for seniors 65 and older); children 12 and under ride free with a paying adult. A one-day pass costs $2; three days, $3; five days, $5; and seven days, $7. Exact change is required (407-248-9590).

The following hotels, all located at the southern end of I-Drive, offer nonsmoking rooms and accommodations for guests with disabilities, unless otherwise indicated.

ROSEN PLAZA: This 810-room hotel attracts guests with its lively ambience, large outdoor heated pool, spacious accommodations, and convenient location next door to the convention center. Each of the rooms has pale-wood furniture, teal carpeting, and painted headboards; amenities include voice mail, Nintendo, a safe, iron and board, hair dryer, separate vanity area, and movies. The property also has a whirlpool, three restaurants, arcade, guest laundry, concierge, gift shop, baby-sitting service, car rental, and business center.

Jack's Place, named after the owner's late dad, a talented caricaturist, specializes in steak, seafood, and memorable desserts. Cafe Matisse serves outstanding buffet and à la carte meals, Rossini's Pizza has calzones and chicken wings, and Lite Bite is a 24-hour bakery-deli. Backstage, the hotel's nightclub, stays open until 2 A.M.; it features a deejay, large-screen television, daily happy hour, and no cover charge. Shuttle service to Walt Disney World costs $10 round-trip. Reservations are necessary.

Rates for up to four people range from $189 to $209 for doubles, although special-value rates are almost always available; suites are $275 to $868. No charge for children under 18. Rosen Plaza; 9700 International Dr.; Orlando, FL 32819; 407-996-9700 or 800-627-8258; *www.clarionplaza.com.*

COUNTRY HEARTH INN: This is the kind of place you'd expect to find in Savannah, not Orlando. Rocking chairs line the porch, and a patterned tin ceiling, hardwood floors,

and half a dozen chandeliers grace the lobby. The Country Parlor restaurant serves a complimentary continental breakfast, à la carte dinner, and Sunday brunch with live music.

The beautifully maintained property is across the street from the convention center (though you'd hardly know it), and while it does attract conventioneers, it also maintains a loyal following among vacationers, wedding parties, and locals. Each of the 150 guestrooms has French doors, pine furniture, colorful drapes and bedspreads, a veranda, cable TV, refrigerator, safe, and coffeemaker. Most guestrooms have two queen-size beds; handicapped rooms have one queen bed and a sofa bed. There is plenty of hanging space, but it is not enclosed. Movie rental is available.

A good-size (but unheated) pool is set in a large landscaped courtyard with a gazebo as its centerpiece. The inn offers room service and has a popular cocktail lounge, the Front Porch. Shuttle service to the four Disney theme parks is $11 round-trip. Rates range from $79 to $149. Country Hearth Inn; 9861 International Dr.; Orlando, FL 32819; 407-352-0008 or 800-447-1890; *www.countryhearth.com.*

THE DOUBLETREE CASTLE: When the owner of The Castle discovered he and his daughter couldn't spend the night in Cinderella Castle in Disney World, he created his own version. The resulting turreted nine-story hotel has 216 rooms, including six junior suites, each with a large mirror reminiscent of a court jester's cap, creative decor, hair dryer, refrigerator, electronic safe, iron, coffeemaker, makeup mirror, tiled bath, and soundproof windows. Most rooms have two queen beds, but a few kings are available. The turret rooms are more spacious. Each junior suite has a king bed with either a sofabed or a Murphy bed, microwave, refrigerator, three telephones, and a Sony PlayStation.

Medieval music and sounds of nature are piped throughout the property, even into the guestrooms and out to the striking circular pool, with its playful fountain centerpiece and nearby whirlpool. Casual Cafe TuTu Tango and upscale Vito's Italian Chop House are on-site, along with a poolside bar and lobby lounge. A court jester entertains kids every day at breakfast (the room is small, so get there early). Complimentary coffee and tea are provided daily.

Guests also enjoy a gameroom, fitness room, large shop with gift items inspired by Merlin, and free passes to the nearby YMCA Aquatic Center, which has two Olympic-size pools. The whimsical ninth-floor Moon and Stars Terraces provide views of the Epcot fireworks. Complimentary shuttle service to the four WDW theme parks is provided.

Rates range from $99 to $195, depending on the season; junior suites are $20 to $30 more (kids under 18 stay free in their parents' room); always ask if special rates are available. A $2 daily charge covers the use of the room safe and fees for phone calls. The DoubleTree Castle; 8629 International Drive; Orlando, FL 32819; 407-345-1511 or 800-952-2785; www.doubletreecastle.com.

PEABODY ORLANDO: The sister property to the famed Peabody in Memphis, this 27-story, 891-room hotel is I-Drive's most luxurious establishment. It's also home to the famous Peabody ducks, which waddle into the lobby daily at 11 A.M., lounge in the marble fountain, and waddle back at 5 P.M. (To parade with them, just check with the hotel's Duck Master.) Each of the guestrooms has a hair dryer, two telephones, and two TVs (including one in the bathroom). Facilities include a heated pool, four lighted tennis courts (lessons available), tennis and golf pro shops, arcade, and health club with personal trainers. Baby-sitting is available.

Dux (where no duck is served) is the hotel's premier restaurant. Capriccio showcases northern Italian cuisine and mesquite-grilled specialties in an exhibition kitchen, and offers a champagne brunch on Sunday; the fifties-style B-Line Diner serves entrées, sandwiches, and homemade confections 24 hours a day. Afternoon tea is offered Monday through Friday in the Dux foyer. The hotel has four bars, including the elegant Mallard.

The Peabody's Double-Ducker bus provides shuttle service to the four Walt Disney World theme parks for guests and the public for $6 round-trip. Room rates are $330 to $420, or a reasonable $125 for guests 50 and older; $550 to $1,500 for suites. Peabody Orlando; 9801 International Dr.; Orlando, FL 32819; 407-352-4000 or 800-732-2639; www.peabody-orlando.com.

QUALITY INN PLAZA: A sister property to the more upscale Clarion Plaza, it marries an excellent location with low room rates. The 1,020 rooms fill seven four-, six-, and ten-story buildings surrounding a large courtyard landscaped with hibiscus, shrubs, pines, and three freshwater pools. The rooms face the pool or I-4 and have tropical decor, two double beds (rooms for guests with disabilities

Driving to the WDW theme parks from the southern end of International Drive (I-Drive) usually takes about 30 minutes, but plan on an extra 20 minutes during rush hour times and when large conventions are in town.

have one king bed or a double with a twin), TV, refrigerator, microwave, and coffee-maker. Hair dryers and irons are available. There are two gamerooms, laundry, gift shop, and mini market/deli.

Kids 11 and under eat free with a paying adult at the Plaza Gardens, open for breakfast and dinner buffets daily. Fast food is available at Lite Bite, open 24 hours. Zebra's Sports Bar has darts, a juke box, and live entertainment four nights a week. Shuttle service to the four Disney theme parks costs $10 round-trip. Rates range from $36 to $89; rollaways are $9. Quality Inn Plaza; 9000 International Dr.; Orlando, FL 32819; 407-996-8588, or 800-999-8585; www.qualityinn-orlando.com.

WYNFIELD INN WESTWOOD: Right off I-Drive, the Wynfield offers landscaped grounds and two swimming pools (one heated) with adjacent wading pools that particularly appeal to families. Shutters give the three-story motel the look of an inn, and each of the 300 rooms features two double beds, voice mail, and a separate vanity. A $2.50 daily fee covers local calls and an in-room safe. Request a poolside room to avoid expressway noise. Other amenities include a poolside bar, sandy picnic area, and arcade. There is no place to eat on the premises, but the Village Inn is next door. Free shuttle service to three Disney (and three other) theme parks is provided. Rates range from $69 to $109. Wynfield Inn Westwood; 6263 Westwood Blvd.; Orlando, FL 32821; 407-345-8000 or 800-346-1551; www.wynfield.com.

In Kissimmee

U.S. 192, also known as Irlo Bronson Memorial Highway, intersects S.R. 535 and I-4 in Kissimmee, and the hotels and motels at this juncture are closer to Disney's theme parks than the flashier accommodations along Orlando's better known International Drive. The area itself is less interesting, but it does represent a notable bargain for budget travelers. Many rooms go for $90 or less a night, and as low as $30 off-season.

The following properties all offer non-smoking rooms and accommodations for guests with disabilities. They are within a couple of miles of Walt Disney World, a large drugstore, 24-hour grocery, discount shopping mall, one-hour dry cleaner, numerous eateries, and Celebration, the incorporated town that Disney founded in 1996 (see page 204).

DOUBLETREE GUEST SUITES ORLANDO MAINGATE: This secluded, wooded enclave has 150 bi-level one-, two-, and three-bedroom villas that sleep four, six, or eight people. Each unit feels like a small apartment, with a tiled entry, patio, two baths, two TVs, living/dining area with an atrium ceiling, full kitchen, ceiling fans, and good lighting throughout, plus a sitting area with desk and sofa bed. An iron with board, clothes basket, toiletries, and daily maid service are provided.

The complex has a small dining room (serving breakfast, lunch, and dinner), bar, fitness room, two lighted tennis courts, basketball court, market, large fenced-in swimming pool, kids' pool and playground, whirlpool, and guest laundry. A mini-golf course is next door. Complimentary transportation to the four Disney theme parks is provided by the hotel.

Rates for the one- and two-bedroom villas range from $119 to $189; for the three-bedroom units, they are $159 to $229. Double-Tree Guest Suites Orlando Maingate; 4787 W. Irlo Bronson Memorial Hwy. (at road marker 12); Kissimmee, FL 34746; 407-397-0555 or 800-222-8733; *www.orlandofamilyhotel.com.*

Last-Minute Lodging

If you arrive in the area without lodging, go to the Official Visitor Information Center, at 8723 International Dr., Suite 101 (407-363-5872), and ask what's available in the "black book" that day. You have to show up in person, but it can save you time and money in the long run.

HOWARD JOHNSON MAINGATE EAST: The world's largest Howard Johnson has other notable attributes: It's privately owned and carefully tended, and boasts an inviting lobby, guest services desk, enormous gift shop, up-to-date arcade, two heated pools, whirlpool, fenced-in playground, guest laundry, and 24-hour security. Set back from the street, its 567 rooms, in 8 two- and three-story buildings with blue trim, are quiet, spacious, and decorated in mauve and burgundy. Entry is via key cards; the safe costs $1.50 a day. Most rooms have two double beds, though some have king beds. Deluxe doubles feature a microwave, refrigerator, and poolside location. One-bedroom suites (with a king-size bed, or a queen and a sleeper sofa, and new curtains and spreads) and efficiency units with fully equipped kitchens are also available.

Guests enjoy pay-per-view movies and Nintendo. The hotel, which has no restaurant, serves free hot beverages in the lobby. It is flanked by IHOP (which has a "kids eat free" program) and the Waffle House; the town of Celebration, with more dining options, is a half mile away. The hotel provides scheduled transportation to the Magic Kingdom each morning and picks up from there and from Epcot in the afternoon. Rates range from $75 to $115; suites are $20 extra; efficiency units, $10 extra. Howard Johnson Maingate East; 6051 W. Irlo Bronson Memorial Hwy. (between road markers 8 and 9); Kissimmee, FL 34747; 407-396-1748 or 800-288-4678; *www.hojomge.com.*

ORLANDO/KISSIMMEE RESORT HOSTEL: In a renovated motel on 2.5 acres beside Lake Cecile and a real find for budget travelers, this "resort hostel" provides spacious private rooms for families and couples, each with telephone, television, private bathroom, and closet. Dormitory rooms accommodate up to six people; bunk-bed sheets are complimentary.

Other amenities include a kitchen, modern laundry, common room, TV room, outdoor pool, volleyball court, barbecue area with picnic tables, and free pedal boats. Evening activities take place regularly. A pharmacy and grocery store are across the street; local buses bound for Walt Disney World and the airport stop two doors away.

Private rooms at the hostel run from $35 to $81; dormitory rates are $16 to $20. Hostelling International Orlando/Kissimmee Resort Hostel; 4840 W. Irlo Bronson Memorial Hwy. (between road markers 11 and 12); Kissimmee, FL 34746; 407-396-8282 or 800-909-4776; *www.hiayh.org.*

Magic Kingdom

91 Getting Oriented

92 Park Primer

94 Attractions

111 Shopping

115 Entertainment

118 Hot Tips

The Magic Kingdom is the most enchanting part of the World. Few who have visited it are disappointed, and even the most blasé travelers manage a smile. The sight of the soaring spires of Cinderella Castle, the gleaming woodwork of the Main Street shops, and the crescendo of music that follows the parades never fail to have their effect. Even when the crowds are large and the weather is hot, a visitor who has toured this wonderland dozens of times can still look around and think how satisfying this place is for the spirit.

What makes the Magic Kingdom timeless is its combination of the classic and the futuristic. Both childhood favorites and space-age creatures have a home here. Every "land" has a theme, carried through from the costumes worn by the hosts and hostesses and the food served in the restaurants to the merchandise sold in the shops, and even the design of the trash cans. Thousands of details contribute to the overall effect, and recognizing these touches makes any visit more enjoyable.

But the delight most guests experience upon first glimpse of the Magic Kingdom can disappear when disorientation sets in. There are so many bends to every pathway, so many sights and sounds clamoring for attention, it's too easy to wander aimlessly and miss the best the Magic Kingdom has to offer. So we earnestly suggest that you study this chapter before your visit.

LIBERTY SQUARE

◼ The Hall of Presidents
◼ The Haunted Mansion
◼ Liberty Belle Riverboat

FANTASYLAND

19 Cinderella's Golden Carrousel
20 Dumbo the Flying Elephant
21 It's a Small World
22 Mad Tea Party
23 The Many Adventures of Winnie the Pooh
24 Peter Pan's Flight
25 Legend of the Lion King
26 Snow White's Scary Adventures
27 Ariel's Grotto

MICKEY'S TOONTOWN FAIR

28 Donald's Boat
29 Mickey's Country House
30 Minnie's Country House
31 Toontown Hall of Fame
32 The Barnstormer
33 Walt Disney World Railroad Station

TOMORROWLAND

34 Astro Orbiter
35 Buzz Lightyear's Space Ranger Spin
36 The ExtraTERRORestrial Alien Encounter
37 Tomorrowland Indy Speedway
38 Space Mountain
39 The Timekeeper
40 Walt Disney's Carousel of Progress
41 Tomorrowland Transit Authority

MAIN STREET, U.S.A.

1 Main Street Vehicles
2 Walt Disney World Railroad
3 Main Street Exposition Hall

ADVENTURELAND

4 Jungle Cruise
5 Pirates of the Caribbean
6 Swiss Family Treehouse
7 The Enchanted Tiki Room– Under New Management
8 The Magic Carpets of Aladdin

FRONTIERLAND

9 Big Thunder Mountain Railroad
10 Country Bear Jamboree
11 Frontierland Shootin' Arcade
12 Splash Mountain
13 Tom Sawyer Island
14 Diamond Horseshoe Saloon Revue
15 Walt Disney World Railroad Station

·········· Parade Route

Mickey's Toontown Fair

Fantasyland

Frontierland

Adventureland

Main Street, U.S.A.

Tomorrowland

DISNEY RESORT BUS FACILITY

▼ FERRYBOAT LANDING

▼ BOAT LAUNCH

MONORAIL STATION

N ←

When you visit Walt Disney World's original theme park, it's vital to know the lay of the lands. The Magic Kingdom has seven "lands"—Main Street, U.S.A.; Adventureland; Frontierland; Liberty Square; Fantasyland; Mickey's Toontown Fair; and Tomorrowland. Main Street begins at Town Square, located just inside the park gates, and runs directly to Cinderella Castle. The area in front of the castle is known as the Central Plaza or, more aptly, the Hub. Bridges over the several narrow waterways here serve as passages to each of the lands.

As you enter the park, the first bridge on your left goes to Adventureland; the next, to Liberty Square and Frontierland. On your right, the first bridge heads to Tomorrowland, the second to Fantasyland and Mickey's Toontown Fair. The end points of the pathways leading to the lands are linked by a street that is roughly circular, so that the layout of the Magic Kingdom resembles a wheel. All attractions, restaurants, and shops are found along the wheel's rim and spokes.

Free guidemaps are available just inside the turnstiles, at City Hall in Town Square, and at many shops throughout the park. Be sure to pick one up as soon as possible. You'll find it an invaluable navigational and scheduling resource.

HOW TO GET THERE

Take Exit 25 off I-4. Continue about four miles to the Auto Plaza and park; walk or take a tram to the main entrance complex, known as the Transportation and Ticket Center (TTC). Choose a seven-minute ferry ride or a slightly shorter trip by monorail for the last leg of an anticipation-filled journey.

By WDW Transportation: From the Grand Floridian, Contemporary, and Polynesian: monorail (Contemporary also has a convenient walkway). From Epcot: monorail to the TTC, then transfer to the Magic Kingdom monorail or ferry. From the Disney-MGM Studios, Animal Kingdom, Downtown Disney, and the resorts on Hotel Plaza Boulevard: buses to the TTC, then transfer to ferry or monorail. From Fort Wilderness and the Wilderness Lodge: boat. From all other Walt Disney World resorts: buses.

PARKING

All-day parking at the Magic Kingdom is $6 for day visitors (free to WDW resort guests with presentation of resort ID). Simply bear left shortly after passing through the Auto Plaza; attendants will direct you into one of a dozen lots, all named after Disney characters. Minnie, Sleepy, and Dopey are within walking distance of the TTC; other lots are served by trams. Be sure to note the section and aisle in which you park. Also, know that the parking ticket allows for re-entry to the parking area throughout the day.

HOURS

The Magic Kingdom is generally open from 9 A.M. to 7 P.M. However, during busy seasons, it is open later than usual. It's best to plan on reaching the park entrance at least half an hour before the posted opening time.

HOT TIP

Mondays tend to be the most crowded days at the Magic Kingdom.

Another way to avoid the morning crush is to put off your visit until 1 P.M. or later. Call 407-939-4636 for up-to-the-minute schedules.

GETTING AROUND

Walt Disney World Railroad steam trains make a 20-minute loop of the park, stopping to pick up and drop off passengers at stations on the edge of Main Street, Frontierland, and Mickey's Toontown Fair. Horseless carriages, a fire engine, and horse-drawn trolleys take turns offering one-way trips down Main Street.

PARK PRIMER

BABY FACILITIES

The best place in the Magic Kingdom to take care of little ones' needs is the Baby Care Center. This cheery center, equipped with changing tables and facilities for nursing mothers, is located at the Hub end of Main Street next to the Crystal Palace restaurant. Disposable diapers are kept behind the counter at many Magic Kingdom shops; just ask. All restrooms are equipped with changing facilities.

CAMERA NEEDS

The Camera Center in the Town Square Exposition Hall proffers disposable cameras as well as film and batteries. Two-hour film processing is available here and wherever you see a Photo Express sign. Film is also sold in most Magic Kingdom shops.

DISABILITY INFORMATION

Most Magic Kingdom shops and restaurants, and many attractions, are accessible to guests in wheelchairs. Additional services are available for guests with visual or hearing disabilities. The *Guidebook for Guests with Disabilities* provides a detailed overview of all services available, including transportation, parking, and attraction access. For more information, refer to the "Travelers with Disabilities" section of the *Getting Ready to Go* chapter.

EARLY-ENTRY DAYS

On Monday, Thursday, and Saturday, guests staying at Walt Disney World resorts may enter the Magic Kingdom up to 1½ hours before the official opening time to head for Space Mountain and Fantasyland attractions. Early-entry days and attractions are subject to change.

The theme parks are the busiest on their respective early-entry days. WDW resort guests should "hop" to another park once the general public is admitted. Day guests should avoid early-entry days at all costs.

FERRY VS. MONORAIL

For guests arriving by car or bus, it's necessary to decide whether to travel to the Magic Kingdom by ferry or monorail. The monorail makes the trip from the Transportation and Ticket Center (TTC) in about five minutes, while the ferry takes about seven. During busy seasons, the ferry will often get you there faster (long lines can form at the monorail and most people don't make the short walk to the ferry landing). Vacationers who use wheelchairs should note that while the monorail platforms are accessible, the ramp leading to the boarding area is a bit steep.

FIRST AID

A registered nurse tends to minor medical problems at the First Aid Center, located near the Crystal Palace restaurant at the Hub end of Main Street.

INFORMATION

City Hall, just inside the park entrance, serves as the Magic Kingdom's information headquarters. Guest Relations representatives can answer questions. Park guidemaps, updated weekly (including details about entertainment, as well as character greeting times and locations), are available here, and all kinds of arrangements can be made, including priority seating for restaurants. Should you have problems with your park pass or a question about the number of unused days remaining on a pass, City Hall is the place to go.

LOCKERS

Attended lockers are located at Station Break, underneath the Main Street Railroad Station just inside the park entrance. Lockers are also available at the Transportation and

Ticket Center (TTC). Cost is $5 per day (including a $2 refundable deposit) for unlimited use. Oversize items can be checked at the Station Break desk.

LOST & FOUND

On the day of your visit, report lost articles at City Hall or at the TTC. Recovered items can also be claimed at these locations. After your visit, call 407-824-4245.

LOST CHILDREN

Report lost children at City Hall or the Baby Care Center, or alert a Disney employee to the problem.

MONEY MATTERS

The Magic Kingdom has three ATMs: under Main Street's train station, near the Diamond Horseshoe Saloon in Frontierland, and at the Tomorrowland Light & Power Co. arcade (near Space Mountain). Most foreign currency can be exchanged at City Hall.

Credit cards (American Express, Visa, MasterCard, JCB, Discover Card, Diner's Club, and The Disney Credit Card) are accepted as payment for admission, merchandise, and meals at all full-service restaurants and fast-food locations. Traveler's checks and WDW resort ID cards are also accepted. Some food carts accept cash only.

Disney Dollars are available at City Hall in $1, $5, and $10 denominations. They are accepted for dining and merchandise throughout Walt Disney World and can be exchanged at any time for U.S. currency.

PACKAGE PICKUP

Individual shops can arrange for large or heavy purchases to be transported to a location next to Main Street's Emporium for pickup after noon and until two hours before the Magic Kingdom closes. The service is free. (Disney resort guests may have packages delivered to their rooms at no extra charge.)

SAME-DAY RE-ENTRY

Be sure to have your hand stamped and to retain your ticket upon exiting the park if you plan to return later the same day.

STROLLERS & WHEELCHAIRS

Stroller and Wheelchair Rental, on the right, inside the Magic Kingdom entrance, offers one-day rentals of strollers, wheelchairs, and Electric Convenience Vehicles (ECVs). The cost for strollers and wheelchairs is $6, plus a $1 refundable deposit; $30 for ECVs, with a $10 refundable deposit. Quantities are limited. Remember to keep your rental receipt; it can be used on the same day to obtain a replacement stroller or wheelchair at Epcot, the Disney-MGM Studios, Animal Kingdom, or here at the Magic Kingdom.

TIP BOARDS

Located at the end of Main Street, U.S.A., closest to Cinderella Castle and in Tomorrowland; Tip Boards are an excellent source of information on waiting times for attractions, as well as showtimes and other entertainment information. Check the boards throughout the day.

Admission Prices

ONE-DAY TICKET

(Restricted to use only in the Magic Kingdom. Prices include sales tax and are subject to change.)

Adult...$48.76
Child*...$39.22

*3 through 9 years of age; children under 3 free

MAIN STREET, U.S.A.

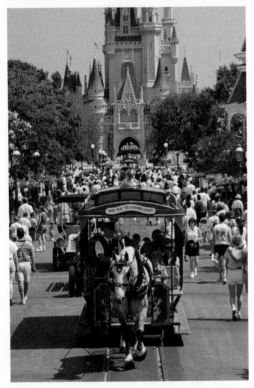

Most of the structures along the thoroughfare are given over to shops, and each one is different. Some emporiums are big and bustling, others are relatively quiet and orderly; some are spacious and airy, others are cozy and dark. Inside and out, maintenance and housekeeping are superb.

HOT TIP Plan to do your shopping in the early afternoon, rather than at day's end when the Main Street shops are normally jammed.

White-suited sanitation workers patrol the street to pick up litter and quickly shovel up any droppings from the horses that pull the trolley cars from Town Square to the Hub. As in the rest of the Magic Kingdom, the pavement here is washed down every night with fire hoses. There's one crew of maintenance workers whose sole job is to change the little white lights around the roofs; another crew devotes itself to keeping the woodwork painted. As soon as these people have worked their way as far as the Hub, they start all over again at Town Square. The greenish, horse-shaped cast-iron hitching posts are repainted 20 times a year on average—and totally scraped down each time.

The "attractions" along Main Street, U.S.A., are relatively minor compared to the really big deals such as Tomorrowland's Space Mountain, Frontierland's Splash Mountain, or The Haunted Mansion in Liberty Square. But each and every shop has its own quota of merchandise that is meant as much for show as for sale. It's almost as entertaining to watch the cooks stir up gooey batches of peanut brittle at the Main Street Confectionery as it is to actually savor a sweet sample. The shop windows, particularly at the Emporium, are also worth a look.

Once you start to meander along Main Street, be sure to notice the names on the second-story windows. Above the Uptown Jewelers store (near the Confectionery) is that of Walt's nephew, Roy E. Disney. And you'll see Walt's name above the ice cream parlor. Other names are those of people connected with The Walt Disney Company.

Note: Attractions in Main Street, U.S.A., are described in the order that they are encountered upon entering the park.

Stepping onto Main Street, U.S.A., is like jumping through a time portal. Welcome to turn-of-the-century America! Horse-drawn trolleys are the transportation of choice, peppy patriotic music underscores the bustle of merry, moving masses, and the tantalizing aroma of fresh-baked cookies constantly perfumes the air.

A rose-colored retrospective? Maybe. But this is Disney's version of a small-town Main Street—and the charm of this nostalgic land is lost on no one. Anchored by the old-fashioned train station at one end and a fairy-tale castle at the other, Main Street, U.S.A., whisks you from reality to fantasy in a few short blocks.

All of the addresses here feature just-dried coats of paint, curlicued gingerbread moldings, and pretty details. Add to that the baskets of hanging plants and genuine-looking gaslights, and Main Street, U.S.A., becomes a true showplace—both in the bright light of high noon and after nightfall, when the tiny lights edging all of the rooflines are flicked on.

The street represents an ideal American town. Although such a town never really existed, many claim to have served as the inspiration for it. Chances are Walt Disney got the idea from Marceline, Missouri, the tiny rural town that was his boyhood home.

WALT DISNEY WORLD RAILROAD: The best introduction to the Magic Kingdom, the 1½-mile journey on this rail line is as much a must for the first-time visitor as it is for railroad buffs. It offers an excellent orientation, as it passes by most of the park's major lands.

The 1928 steam engine happens to be exactly the same age as Mickey Mouse. Walt Disney himself was a railroad aficionado. During the early years of television, viewers watched films of him circling his own backyard in a one-eighth-scale train, the *Lilly Belle* (named for his wife).

The Walt Disney World Railroad also has a *Lilly Belle* among its quartet of locomotives. The others are named *Roy O. Disney*, *Walter E. Disney*, and *Roger E. Broggie* (a Disney Imagineer who shared Walt Disney's enthusiasm for antique trains). All of them were built in the U.S. around the turn of the century and later taken to Mexico to haul freight and passengers in the Yucatán, where Disney scouts found them in 1969. The United Railways of Yucatán was using them to carry sugarcane. Brought north once again, they were completely overhauled, and even the smallest of parts were reworked or replaced.

The train circles the park in 20 minutes, making stops in Frontierland, Mickey's Toontown Fair, and Main Street, U.S.A. Trains arrive in each station every 4 to 10 minutes. The line is usually shortest in Toontown, but there's rarely a long wait at any of the stations. The train is the most efficient way to reach the exit when parades take over Main Street, U.S.A.

Note: The Walt Disney World Railroad does not run during fireworks presentations.

MAIN STREET VEHICLES: A number of these can be seen traveling up and down Main Street—horseless carriages and jitneys patterned after turn-of-the-century vehicles (but fitted with Jeep transmissions and special mufflers that make a putt-putt-putting sound); a spiffy scarlet fire engine; and a troop of trolleys drawn by Belgians and Percherons, two strong breeds of horse that once pulled plows in Europe. These animals—weighing in at about a ton each, and shod with plastic (easier on their hooves)—pull the trolley the length of Main Street about two dozen times during each of their working days. Between shifts, they can be seen resting in Main Street's Car Barn. Feel free to stop by and say hello. At day's end they go to their barn at Fort Wilderness (where you can also visit them). The horses are often hosed down next to the Main Street firehouse. Youngsters love to watch.

TOWN SQUARE EXPOSITION HALL: A veritable shrine to photography, Town Square Exposition Hall does double duty as a museum and camera supply shop. Engaging exhibits take guests on a voyage through time, connecting the high-tech cameras of today with their primitive cousins of yesteryear. The humble beginnings of Mickey Mouse are celebrated here, too. *Steamboat Willie* and other classic Mickey toons (previously shown at the Main Street Cinema) are screened throughout the day.

Be sure to bring your own camera to the Hall—photo opportunities abound. Another item to have handy: the e-mail address of a friend or loved one. There are interactive stations from which to snap your picture and send it to someone over the Internet.

ADVENTURELAND

Adventureland seems to have even more atmosphere than the other lands. That may be a result of its neat separation from the rest of the Magic Kingdom by the bridge over Main Street on one end and by a gallerylike structure (where it merges with Frontierland) on the other, or possibly it's because of the abundance of landscaping.

The new, centrally located attraction, The Magic Carpets of Aladdin, sets the tone for this recently refurbished corner of the Kingdom. Still surrounded by tropical splendor, the area has taken on the look and feel of a bustling marketplace—the likes of which one might stumble upon in Agrabah. The shops here offer imports from around the globe.

As guests stroll away from Main Street, U.S.A., they just may hear the sound of beating drums, the squawks of parrots, and the regular boom of a cannon. Paces quicken. And the wonders soon to be encountered do not disappoint.

SWISS FAMILY TREEHOUSE: "Everything we need is right at our fingertips," said the father in Disney's 1960 rendition of the classic story *Swiss Family Robinson*. He was describing the treehouse that he and his kids built for the family after their ship was wrecked in a storm. When given a chance— several adventures later—to leave the island, all but one son decided to stay on. That decision is not hard to understand after a tour of the Magic Kingdom's version of the Robinsons' banyan-tree home. This is everybody's idea of the perfect treehouse, with its many levels and comforts—patchwork quilts, lovely mahogany furniture, candles stuck in abalone shells, even running water in every room. (The system is ingenious.)

The Spanish moss draping the branches is real; the tree itself—unofficially christened *Disneyodendron eximus*, a genus that is translated roughly as "out-of-the-ordinary Disney tree"—was constructed entirely by the props department. Some statistics: The roots, which are made of concrete, poke 42 feet into the ground, and about 300,000 life-like polyethylene leaves "grow" on the tree's 1,400 individual branches.

JUNGLE CRUISE: Inspired in part by the 1955 documentary film *The African Lion*, this ten-minute adventure is one of the crowning achievements of Magic Kingdom landscape artists for the way it takes guests through surroundings as diverse as a Southeast Asian jungle, the Nile Valley, and

an Amazon rain forest. Along the way, passengers encounter zebras, giraffes, lions, impalas, vultures, and headhunters (all of the Audio-Animatronics variety); they also see elephants bathing, and tour a Cambodian temple—while listening to an amusing, though corny, spiel delivered by the skipper. (Bet you didn't know that Schweitzer Falls was named after the famous doctor Albert . . . Falls.)

This adventure, which is best enjoyed by daylight, is one of the park's slower-moving attractions, and tends to be quite crowded from late morning until late afternoon.

THE ENCHANTED TIKI ROOM—UNDER NEW MANAGEMENT: Though cherished for their historical significance (the Tiki Birds starred in the first Audio-Animatronics attraction ever), the Tiki show was growing a bit tiresome. Now, thanks to clever new co-stars and zippy new tunes, the Tiki Room is rockin' once again.

The nine-minute show still features Michael, Pierre, Fritz, and José (who is pining for his beloved Rosita)—plus some 225 birds, flowers, and tiki statues singing up a tropical storm. But before long, their sweet serenade is interrupted by an unimpressed Iago (Jafar's partner in crime from *Aladdin*).

It seems that Iago, along with Zazu from *The Lion King*, is a new owner of the Tiki Room—and he has big changes in store for the show. In a fractured version of "Friend Like Me," the bratty Iago warns the Tiki

MAGIC KINGDOM

Birds that they'd "better get hip, or the audience will disappear." In a welcome twist, it is Iago who disappears, leaving the Tikis to prove just how hip they really are.

While it helps to have seen the old show to appreciate all of the silly humor, veterans and newcomers alike are sure to get a kick out of The Enchanted Tiki Room—Under New Management.

THE MAGIC CARPETS OF ALADDIN: Welcome to Agrabah! The Magic Kingdom's newest attraction is conveniently situated in the center of Adventureland. It features not one, but 16 carpets that fly through the air in a fashion similar to those airborne elephants over in Fantasyland. Each flying carpet accommodates four guest pilots at a time. The two in the front control vertical movement, while those in the back can tilt the carpet from side to side. The attraction is expected to open in the spring of 2001.

PIRATES OF THE CARIBBEAN: One of the very best of the Magic Kingdom's classic adventures, this ten-minute cruise is a Disneyland original, added to Walt Disney World's Magic Kingdom (in slightly revised form) due to popular demand. Here guests board a small boat and set sail for a series of scenes showing a pirate raid on a Caribbean island town, dodging cannon fire and weathering one small, though legitimate, watery dip

along the way. There are singing marauders, plastered pigs, and wily wenches; the observant will note that the leg of one rum-swilling swashbuckler, dangled over the edge of a bridge, is actually hairy.

While it's by no means the most politically correct attraction on-property, the rendition of "Yo Ho, Yo Ho; a Pirate's Life for Me"—the attraction's theme song—makes what is actually a rather brutal scenario into something that comes across as good fun.

Before entering the attractions' queue area, stop and give a nod to the parrot dressed in a pirate costume, near the Pirates of the Caribbean sign.

FRONTIERLAND

With the Rivers of America lapping at its borders and Big Thunder Mountain rising up in the rear, this re-creation of the American Frontier encompasses the area from New England to the Southwest, from the 1770s to the 1880s. Hosts and hostesses wear denim, calf-length cutoffs, long skirts, or similar garb. Additionally, the shops, restaurants, and attractions have unpainted barn siding or stone or clapboard walls, and outside there are several wooden sidewalks of the sort Marshal Matt Dillon used to stride along. The Walt Disney World Railroad makes a stop here.

Note: Attractions are described as they are encountered upon entering the land from the Hub, heading away from Cinderella Castle.

DIAMOND HORSESHOE SALOON REVUE: Singing cowboys, dancing girls, silly jokes—this western dance hall has it all. Each 30-minute show features a madcap mix of melodies and mirth.

The Prohibition-style saloon (translation: no alcohol) serves soft drinks, sandwiches, and snacks. There's no table service, so you'll have to belly up to the bar should you wish to indulge. See *Good Meals, Great Times* for details.

Reservations are not accepted and guests may drop in at any point during a performance. The entertainment varies from show to show. Check a guidemap for details and showtimes. (Get there about 15 minutes early to snag a seat.)

FRONTIERLAND SHOOTIN' ARCADE: This arcade is set in an 1850s town in the Southwest Territory. Gun positions overlook Boothill, a town complete with bank, jail, hotel, and cemetery. But bullets have given way to electronic beams at this shooting gallery.

Genuine Hawkins .54-caliber buffalo rifles have been refitted, and when an infrared beam strikes any of the targets, an interesting result is triggered. Struck tombstones rise, sink, spin, or change their epitaphs; hit the cloud and a ghost rider gallops across the sky; a bull's-eye on a gravedigger's shovel causes a skull to pop out of the grave. Sound effects—howling coyotes, creaking bridges, and shooting guns—are created by a digital audio system. Note that admission passes do not include use of the Frontierland Shootin' Arcade; there is an additional charge here.

COUNTRY BEAR JAMBOREE: The Country Bears may never make it to Broadway, but they don't seem to mind. Disney's brood of banjo-strummin' bruins has been playing to packed houses in Grizzly Hall for more than a quarter century. Judging by all the toe tappin' and hand clappin' that accompany each performance, the show remains a countrified crowd pleaser. As for the few folks who aren't charmed by the backwoods ballads and down-home humor, well, they just have to grin and *bear* it.

As guests are settling into their seats (all of which provide a decent view of the show), Buff, Max, and Melvin are already beginning to grumble. Despite their status as permanent fixtures in the theater, the mounted animal heads would rather not "hang around all day" waiting for the show to get going. The 17-minute review opens with a rousing ditty by the Five Bear Rugs. The wheels set in motion, the remaining songs come fast and furious. Together, they capture the spirit of a genre that has a tendency to celebrate and lampoon itself simultaneously.

For example, Bunny, Bubbles, and Beulah bemoan "All the Guys That Turn Me On Turn Me Down"; Henry, the emcee who sports a coonskin cap (which is still attached to the coon), belts out "The Ballad of Davy Crockett"; and Big Al, the tone-deaf fan-favorite, woefully croons "Blood on the Saddle," much to the delight of the giggle-prone audience.

Note that the bears present a special Christmas concert during the holiday season.

Timing Tip: Lines can get long during busy periods. It's worth noting, however, that huge groups are admitted together—so once a line starts moving, it dwindles rather quickly.

TOM SAWYER ISLAND: This small patch of land in the middle of the Rivers of America has hills to scramble up; a working windmill, Harper's Mill, with an owl in the rafters and a perpetually creaky waterwheel; and a few pitch-black (and scary) caves. To reach the island, guests take a raft across the river. (It's the only way to get there and back.)

Paths wind this way and that, and it's easy to get disoriented, especially the first time around. Keep an eye out for the large mounted maps scattered about the island.

There are two bridges here—a suspension bridge and a so-called barrel bridge, which floats atop some lashed-together wooden barrels. When one person bounces, everybody lurches—and all but the most chickenhearted laugh. Both bridges are easy to miss, so keep your eyes peeled and ask an employee for directions if the path eludes you.

Across the suspension bridge is Fort Langhorn. Inside the fort, there are about a dozen air guns for youngsters to fire in a ceaseless cacophony. Keep poking around and you'll discover a twisting, dark, and occasionally scary escape tunnel. Walk along the pathway on the banks of the Rivers of America and you'll find your way back to the bridges.

The whole island seems as rugged as backwoods Missouri, and, probably as a result, it actually feels a lot more remote than it is— enough to be able to provide some welcome respite from the bustle.

One particularly pleasant way to relax here is over lemonade and a snack at Aunt Polly's Dockside Inn. (The pickles are quite popular.) Restrooms are located at the main raft landing and inside Fort Langhorn.

Timing Tip: This attraction closes at dusk.

SPLASH MOUNTAIN: On the day this attraction made its official 1992 Walt Disney World debut, *everyone* got soaked— thanks in part to a particularly potent Florida rain cloud. But the rain wasn't entirely responsible

for the sea of soggy Magic Kingdom guests. The five-story drop into an aqueous briar patch was. And a steady stream of thrill seekers have been taking the plunge ever since.

In this guaranteed smile inducer, guests enjoy a waterborne journey through brightly colored swamps and bayous, and down waterfalls, and are finally hurtled from the peak of the mountain to a briar-laced pond five stories below.

Splash Mountain is based on the animated sequences in Walt Disney's 1946 film *Song of the South*. The scenery entertains as the story line follows Brer Rabbit through a variety of exploits as he tries to reach his "laughin' place." It's tough for a first-time rider to take in all the details, since the tension of waiting for the big drop is all-consuming.

It is a bit terrifying at the top, but once back on the ground, it seems most riders can't wait

for another trip—even though they may get drenched. (Water-wary guests are often seen wearing rain ponchos on this attraction. On the other hand, if you *want* to get wet, try to sit up front or on the right; seats in the back receive a smaller splash.)

By the second or third time around, it's possible to relax a bit, enjoy the interior scenes, and take in the spectacular views of the Magic Kingdom from the top of the mountain. At this point you may even manage to keep your eyes open for the duration of the final fall—or at least part of it.

If you'd like to get soaked on Splash Mountain, request a seat up front.

Splash Mountain's designers not only borrowed characters and color-saturated settings from *Song of the South*, but also used quite a bit of the film's Academy Award–winning music in this attraction. As a matter of fact, the song in Splash Mountain's final scene, "Zip-A-Dee-Doo-Dah," has become something of a Disney anthem over the years.

Note: You must be at least 40 inches tall to ride Splash Mountain. (There is a small play area nearby to keep little ones occupied.)

BIG THUNDER MOUNTAIN RAILROAD:

It's certainly not hard to spot Big Thunder, the lone red rock formation this side of the Mississippi. Even newcomers to the Magic Kingdom will be able to distinguish the landmark from its famed counterparts—Splash and Space mountains— because it's the only one that actually looks like a mountain range. The designers took Utah's Bryce Canyon as inspiration, and the resemblance is remarkable.

According to Disney legend, the 2.5-acre mountain is chock-full of gold. Unfortunately for the residents of Tumbleweed, the local mining town, a flood has ruined any chance of uncovering the remaining gold. Before these prospectors find drier land, they are having one last party at the saloon to celebrate their riches. Even though in danger of washing away, they don't seem too worried, and guests who decide to take a trip on the Big Thunder Mountain Railroad have nothing to worry about either.

As passengers board the 15-row train they are advised to "hang on to your hats and glasses 'cause this here's the wildest ride in the wilderness." Do heed the warning, but don't despair. The ride, though thrilling, is relatively tame, so relax and enjoy the sights. Note that passengers seated nearest the caboose experience a bit more turbulence than those up front.

A bleating billy goat atop a peak, a family of possums hanging overhead, and a dark cavern full of bats, not to mention chickens, donkeys, and washed-up miners, can be spotted along the way. Be sure to keep an eye out for the not-yet-sunken saloon—it's easy to miss the first time around.

A continuous string of curves and dips around Big Thunder's pinnacles and caverns is sure to please thrill seekers of all ages, but the adrenaline surge is caused by more than just the speed of the trip. The added sound of a rickety track, a steam whistle that blows right before the train accelerates into a curve, and an unexpected earthquake all compound the passengers' anticipation, making this attraction one of the Magic Kingdom's most popular. Note that you must be at least 40 inches tall to ride.

Timing Tip: Plan to visit early in the morning, during an evening parade, or just before park closing time, when lines are generally shorter.

LIBERTY SQUARE

The transition between Frontierland on one side and Fantasyland on the other is so smooth that it's hard to say just when you arrive at Liberty Square, yet ultimately there's no mistaking the location. The small buildings are clapboard or brick and topped with weather vanes; the decorative moldings are Federal or Georgian in style; the glass is sometimes wavy, and there are flower boxes in shop windows, brightly colored gardens, neatly trimmed borders of Japanese yew, and masses of azaleas in a number of varieties and shades of white, pink, and red. There's a bounty of good shops, most notably The Yankee Trader and Ye Olde Christmas Shoppe; plus two of the park's most famous attractions, The Haunted Mansion and The Hall of Presidents; and the Liberty Tree Tavern, one of the few full-service restaurants located within the Magic Kingdom.

Liberty Square is also home to one of the most delightful nooks in all the Magic Kingdom—the small, secluded area just behind Ye Olde Christmas Shoppe. There are tables with umbrellas, plenty of benches, and big trees to provide shade—and the crowds seem a million miles away.

Note: Liberty Square attractions are described in the order they are encountered upon entering the land from the Hub and heading away from Cinderella Castle.

THE HALL OF PRESIDENTS: This is not one of those laugh-a-minute attractions, like the Jungle Cruise or the Country Bear Jamboree; it's long on patriotism and short on humor. But the detail of this 20-minute show certainly is fascinating. After a film (presented on a sweeping 70mm screen) discusses the importance of the Constitution from the time of its framing through the dawn of the space age, the curtain goes up on what some guests have mistakenly called the "Hall of Haunted Presidents." A small portion of today's presentation of The Hall of Presidents derives from the Disney-designed Illinois Pavilion's exhibition Great Moments with Mr. Lincoln, from New York's 1964–65 World's Fair.

At the Magic Kingdom show, Bill Clinton and Abraham Lincoln have speaking roles. All of the chief executives are announced in a roll call and each responds with a nod; careful observers will note the others swaying and nodding, fidgeting, and even whispering to each other during the proceedings.

Costumes were created by two famous film tailors coaxed out of retirement. Not only are the styles those of the period in which each president lived, but so are the tailoring techniques and the fabrics. Some had to be specially woven for the show. Each of the Audio-Animatronics figures has at least one change of clothes—jewelry, shoes, hair texture, and even George Washington's chair are all re-created exactly as indicated by careful research of paintings, diaries, newspapers, and government archives. Perceptive viewers should be able to see the braces on Franklin Delano Roosevelt's legs. The effect is so lifelike that the figures look almost real, even at very close range.

Timing Tip: Planning to pop in on the presidents? Visit at quarter past or quarter till the hour. That's usually when the show starts.

LIBERTY BELLE RIVERBOAT: The *Liberty Belle*, built in dry dock at Walt Disney World, is a real steamboat. Its boiler turns water into steam, which is then piped to the engine, which drives the paddle wheel that propels the boat. It is not the real article in one respect, however: It moves through the half-mile-long, nine-foot-deep Rivers of America on an underwater rail.

The pleasant ride, with narration by an actor playing Mark Twain, is a good way to beat the heat on steamy afternoons. En route, a variety of props create a sort of Wild West effect: moose, deer, a burning cabin, and the like. The tour is completed within 17 minutes.

THE HAUNTED MANSION: This eight-minute experience is among the Magic Kingdom's most enjoyable. However, guests who expect to be scared silly when they enter the big old house, modeled after

those built in New York's Hudson River Valley in the 18th century, will be just a tad unfulfilled. In deference to the small children and other easily frightened souls who tour the Magic Kingdom on a daily basis, The Haunted Mansion steers clear of anything too terrifying, and a good-spirited voice-over keeps the mood light.

Once inside the portrait hall, which you enter after passing through the front doors, it's amusing to speculate: Is the ceiling moving up — or is the floor dropping? It's also where you meet your "Ghost Host" and learn how he met his untimely demise.

The spooky journey through the mansion takes place in a "Doom Buggy." The attraction is full of tricks and treats for the eyes; just when you think you've seen it all, there's something new: bats' eyes on the wallpaper, a plaque that reads "Tomb, Sweet Tomb," a suit of armor that comes alive, a terrified cemetery watchman and his mangy mutt, and the image of a creepy lady in a crystal ball.

One of the biggest jobs of the maintenance crews here is not cleaning up, but keeping things dirty. Since the mansion is littered with some 200 trunks, chairs, dress forms, harps, rugs, and assorted knickknacks, it requires a lot of dust. This is purchased by the five-pound bagful and distributed by a device that looks as if it were meant to spread grass seed — sort of a vacuum cleaner in reverse. Local legend has it that enough dust has been used since the park's 1971 opening to bury the mansion. (Which begs the question: Where did it all go?) Cobwebs are bought in liquid form and strung up by a secret process.

When waiting to enter, take note of the amusing inscriptions on the tombstones in the overgrown cemetery.

FANTASYLAND

Walt Disney called this a "timeless land of enchantment," and his successors termed it "the happiest land of all" — and it is, for some. It is the home of a number of rides that are particularly well liked by children. The nursery rhyme cadences of "It's a Small World" appeal to them, as do the bright colors of the trash baskets, the flowers, and the tentlike rooftops; and they delight in the fairy-tale architecture and ambience, reminiscent of a king's castle courtyard during a particularly lively festival.

CINDERELLA CASTLE: Just as Mickey stands for all the merriment in Walt Disney World, this storybook castle represents the hopes and dreams of childhood—a time in life when anything is possible.

At a height of about 190 feet, Cinderella Castle is nearly twice the height of Disneyland's Sleeping Beauty Castle. It was inspired by the architecture of 12th- and 13th-century France, the country where the classic fairy tale originated, as well as the Bavarian King Ludwig's fortress and designs prepared for Disney's 1950 classic, *Cinderella.*

Unlike real European castles, this one is made of steel and fiberglass; in lieu of dungeons, it has service tunnels. Its upper reaches contain security rooms; there's even an apartment originally meant for members of the Disney family (but never occupied). From any vantage point, Cinderella Castle looks as if it came straight from the land of make-believe.

Mosaic Murals: The elaborate murals beneath the castle's archway rank among the true wonders of the World. They tell the story of the little cinder girl and one of childhood's happiest happily-ever-afters, using a million bits of glass in some 500 different colors, plus real silver and 14-karat gold.

Cinderella Wishing Well: This pleasant alcove, nestled along a pathway that leads to Tomorrowland, is the perfect spot to gaze at the castle. Any coins tossed into the water are donated to children's charities.

CINDERELLA'S GOLDEN CARROUSEL: Not everything in the Magic Kingdom is a Disney version of the real article. This carousel, discovered at the now-defunct Olympic Park in Maplewood, New Jersey, was built back in 1917. That was the end of the golden century of carousel building that began around 1825. During the Disney refurbishing, many of the original horses were replaced with horses made of fiberglass.

FAIRY TALE GARDEN: This special, little corner of the Kingdom is tucked beside Cinderella Castle. Several times a day, Belle stops by to read a story and, afterward, mingle with guests. There is seating for about 20 at a time. Check a park guidemap for showtimes.

LEGEND OF THE LION KING: Based on the animated film *The Lion King*, this Fantasyland show combines 25 minutes of animation, puppetry, special effects, and music to make guests feel as if they walked into a cel from the film. In the pre-show area, guests meet Rafiki, the wise baboon who serves as the narrator. His voice is provided by stage and television actor Robert Guillaume. A clip from the film is shown and Rafiki recounts the legend that is about to unfold.

Once inside the 500-seat theater, visitors see the movie's Circle of Life scene presented on a stage. As the sun rises over Pride Rock, Mufasa assures his son, Simba, that he will always be with him. The characters are depicted by fully articulated puppets—when they speak, their mouths move accordingly.

Some of the puppets require up to five people to coordinate their head, foot, ear, and mouth movements. The story advances to other scenes, introducing the assorted characters. One of the few familiar voices you'll hear in the show belongs to Jeremy Irons who plays the evil Scar.

Guests experience environmental effects, including light winds during scenes in the Serengeti Plain and lightning during a dramatic storm. The climactic stampede scene begins on the screen; the noise builds and the theater shakes as smoke gives way to darkness. Note that small children may be frightened when the room goes dark.

PETER PAN'S FLIGHT: "Come on everybody, here we go!" So says Peter Pan at the start of this nonstop flight to Never Land. The three-minute adventure, which takes you

soaring in a pirate ship, fancifully retells the story of Peter Pan—a boy with a knack for flying and an immunity to maturity. The effects in this classic Fantasyland attraction are simple, but enchanting.

The journey starts in the Darling family nursery—which siblings Wendy, Michael, and John quickly abandon to follow Peter Pan on a trip to his homeland. As in Disney's animated feature, one of the most beautiful scenes—and one that makes this attraction a treat for grown-ups as well as smaller folk—is the sight of nighttime London, dark blue and speckled with twinkling lights. Keep your eyes peeled for such landmarks as Big Ben and London Bridge.

By the time you spot your first mermaid, you're deep in the heart of Never Land. Alas, something is terribly wrong—Captain Hook and his buccaneer buddies have taken the Darling kids captive. It's all really a trap for Peter (Hook is still peeved at Pan for serving his hand to a hungry crocodile). Does everyone live happily ever after? We'll *never* tell.

Timing Tip: The slow-moving lines for this popular attraction can be somewhat daunting. To avoid big crowds, plan to arrive close to when the park opens, late in the evening, or during any of the parades throughout the day.

DID YOU KNOW...

In all, Walt Disney World covers 47 square miles of property. That's twice the size of New York's Manhattan!

IT'S A SMALL WORLD: *Hola! Guten Tag! Hello!* No matter what language you speak, what you look like, or where you live, you still have a lot in common with folks the world over (including an especially high tolerance for a singsong melody that repeatedly reminds us that it's a small world after all). That's the message driving this ten-minute boat ride around the world.

HOT TIP Toddlers love to splash in the fountains near Ariel's Grotto (in Fantasyland) and Donald's Boat (in Toontown)—waterproof diapers are an absolute must.

Originally created for New York's 1964–65 World's Fair, the attraction is an oldie-but-goodie (and is quite popular with young children). The ride moves at slightly swifter than snail's pace, drifting past hundreds of colorfully costumed dolls from around the world—all of whom know all the words to the ride's infectious theme song.

A showcase of diversity, the attraction is a simple celebration of human similarities. It's also a relaxing alternative to many of the park's higher-tech, longer-line attractions.

DUMBO THE FLYING ELEPHANT: This is purely and simply a kiddie ride—though children of all ages have admitted to loving it. A beloved symbol of Fantasyland, the ride is most popular with the two- to seven-year-old set. Inspired by the 1941 film classic *Dumbo*, the attraction lasts two memorable minutes. Consider stopping here first thing in the morning, or during the afternoon parade, when the line—which is often prohibitively long—thins a bit. Incidentally, the mouse that sits atop the hot air balloon at the center of the circle of flying elephants is Dumbo's faithful sidekick, Timothy Mouse.

MAD TEA PARTY: The theme of this two-minute ride—in a group of oversize pastel-colored teacups that whirl and spin wildly—was inspired by a scene in the Disney Studios' 1951 movie production of Lewis Carroll's novel *Alice in Wonderland*. During the sequence in question, the Mad Hatter hosts a tea party for his un-birthday.

Unlike many rides in Fantasyland, this is not just for younger kids; the 9-to-20 crowd seems to like it best. Keep in mind that when the cups stop spinning, your head may continue to do so. Skip this ride if you suffer from motion sickness or if you've recently enjoyed a snack. Don't miss the woozy mouse that pops out of the teapot at the center of the platform—he ignored our advice.

THE MANY ADVENTURES OF WINNIE THE POOH: Perhaps as a tribute to the mischievous Mr. Toad, the host of the attraction previously housed here, everyone's favorite honey-lovin' cub treats Magic Kingdom guests to a wild and whimsical 3½-minute tour of his home turf.

The spirited attraction, which opened in 1999, features a most unlikely form of transportation: honey pots! They whisk (and bounce) guests through the pages of a giant storybook and into the Hundred Acre Wood, where the weather's

decidedly blustery. The wind is really ruffling the feathers of one of the locals. It seems Owl's treehouse has been shaken loose and just may topple to the ground—and onto the helpless honeypots below. Similar sight gags abound, from a bubble-blowing Heffalump (hey, this *is* Fantasyland) to a treacherous flood which threatens to sweep Tigger, Piglet,

HOT TIP

Many of the Fantasyland attractions are dark, and in some cases special effects may be too intense for small children.

and the rest of the gang away. When Pooh saves the day, it's time to celebrate—and everyone is invited to the party.

Note that, like other Fantasyland attractions, The Many Adventures of Winnie the Pooh takes place in the dark. Some youngsters may find the dark a bit unsettling.

SNOW WHITE'S SCARY ADVENTURES: This three-minute attraction takes guests on a twisting, turning journey through a few happy moments and several scary scenes from the Grimm brothers' fairy tale, which Walt Disney made into the world's first full-length animated feature in 1937. Snow White makes several appearances, as do the seven Audio-Animatronic dwarfs. But the wicked witch—evil, long-nosed, and practically toothless—shows up more than once with a suddenness that startles some youngsters. The adventure ends on an up note, as the dwarfs wave good-bye to Snow White and the prince.

Ariel's Grotto

The Little Mermaid's Ariel doesn't greet Magic Kingdom guests in the traditional way, since mermaids, like most fish, find it difficult to walk around theme parks. Instead, she invites folks of all ages to stop by her Fantasyland home away from home—a colorful grotto surrounded by starfish, coral, and waterfalls. Here guests can meet and pose for a picture with the ever-popular Disney heroine (don't forget to bring your camera). The area, which is especially popular with little ones, also features a soft-surface play zone filled with squirting fountains. Note that the line to meet Ariel is often long enough to scare Ursula herself.

MICKEY'S TOONTOWN FAIR

The newest neighborhood in the Magic Kingdom was built with little visitors in mind. Scaled-down buildings, vibrant colors, and an abundance of Disney characters make Mickey's Toontown Fair a veritable children's paradise. Not only do Mickey, Minnie, and their pals keep homes here, but the county fair is always in town. Tucked away behind Fantasyland, the area can be reached by taking a path from the Mad Tea Party or Space Mountain and via the Walt Disney World Railroad. Guests who arrive by stroller are advised to park their vehicles in the lot across from Pete's Garage. Keep in mind that the traffic here is heaviest early in the day.

Note: Attractions are described in the order in which they are encountered upon entering the area from Fantasyland and proceeding counterclockwise.

THE BARNSTORMER: At Goofy's Wiseacre Farm, guests of all sizes climb into crop dusters and follow the same fluky flight path taken by the Goof himself. The planes zip through the farm and crash through a barn, causing quite a ruckus among the chickens. Don't let the size fool you—this roller coaster proves that big thrills come in small packages. Although guests as young as three are allowed to ride, it may be too turbulent for some.

Take time to explore Goofy's Wiseacre Farm before lining up for the ride. Cotton, tomatoes, and other real crops have been spotted growing here. The observant may notice the unconventional parking spot that Goofy found for his plane (hint: Look up). Plan to swing by the farmers market on your way out. In addition to souvenirs, the shop sells cupcakes, bananas, and other simple snacks.

DONALD'S BOAT: If you're looking to cool off a bit, stop at Donald Duck's boat, the *Miss Daisy*. The vessel has sprung so many leaks, it looks like a fountain. It's almost impossible to walk across the "duck pond" without getting squirted once or twice. The ship's interior, though sparse, includes a captain's wheel and a whistle—pull it and water shoots out the top. Toddlers love it here.

MICKEY'S COUNTRY HOUSE: Don't bother knocking—the door is always open. Guests are welcome to peer inside each of the four rooms in this modest cottage: bedroom, living room, kitchen, and gameroom. The kitchen is being remodeled, but it's worth a peek (after which you'll vow never to hire Donald Duck and Goofy to redecorate your own home). As the gameroom shows, the Mouse is quite an accomplished sportsman, dabbling in everything from table tennis to football. (Is that a Heisman trophy on the shelf?!)

Despite all there is to see, one thing is conspicuously missing from Mickey Mouse's house. . . Mickey himself. Don't despair. The head judge of the county fair is in the Judge's Tent, where he greets guests all day long. (It's the best place to meet Mickey in all of Walt Disney World.) To get there, slip out the back door of the house and follow the path toward the tent. (Others can exit through the garage, which packs some surprises of its own.) It's fun to check out the backyard, where Mickey's award-winning garden is bursting with giant vegetables, many of which have mouse ears. This is also the spot to take a peek at Pluto's doghouse.

JUDGE'S TENT: A must for fans of the Mouse, this place is all Mickey all the time. The waiting area (and there is always a significant wait) features a pre-show video that highlights all of his county fair successes. All guests are treated to a private

The line to meet Mickey in the Judge's Tent can be quite lengthy. It's usually shorter late in the day and during parades.

meeting with the star, so have those cameras ready! To get to the Judge's Tent, take a trip through Mickey's Country House. The line is usually shortest late in the day or during a parade.

TOONTOWN HALL OF FAME: Just beyond Cornelius Coot Commons and across from Goofy's Wiseacre Farm is the Toontown Hall of Fame. The big tent is stocked with Disney souvenirs as well as some of the prize-winning entries from the Toontown Fair. (Only the former are for sale.) Beyond this area, three different rooms offer guests the opportunity to meet any number of Disney characters.

Note that there is a separate line for each room, and characters vary throughout the day. Signs above the queue area indicate which characters are on hand at any given moment. It's best to have cameras (and autograph books) ready before entering the character area.

MINNIE'S COUNTRY HOUSE: Since Minnie and Mickey are neighbors here in the country, Minnie's house is merely a hop, skip, and a jump from Mickey's. Young kids will love it here because the special toon furniture is meant for climbing. As they explore, guests can push a button to listen to answering-machine messages, open the refrigerator (Minnie has cheese chip ice cream in the freezer, which is actually chilly inside), and try in vain to snatch some chocolate chip cookies (it's a clever mirror trick, courtesy of Minnie herself).

The screen porch is quite lovely and full of some very special plants. Don't miss the palm tree (it's made of hands), the Tiger Lilies (feline faces), and the Twolips (no explanation necessary).

PETE'S GARAGE: This cleverly disguised restroom is the only place to make a pit stop in Mickey's Toontown Fair. The toon vehicle, which is parked out front, makes for an excellent photo opportunity. The lot across from Pete's is zoned for stroller parking.

The original Tomorrowland attempted a serious look at the future. But as Disney planners discovered, it isn't easy to portray a future that persists in becoming the present. So the old Tomorrowland has given way to a friendlier, space-age town whose neighborhood atmosphere is more in keeping with the other lands in the Magic Kingdom. This is the future that never was, the fantasy world imagined by the science fiction writers and moviemakers of the 1920s and '30s. It's a land of sky-piercing beacons and glistening metal, where shiny robots do the work, whisper-quiet conveyances glide along an elevated highway, and even time travel is possible.

Note: All Tomorrowland attractions are described in the order that they are encountered upon entering the land from the Hub and heading (roughly counterclockwise) away from Cinderella Castle.

THE TIMEKEEPER: A 20-minute multimedia presentation combining a Circle-Vision 360 film with Audio-Animatronics characters and special in-theater effects is hosted by Timekeeper, a wacky mad scientist robot. Inspired by the likes of Jules Verne and H. G. Wells, who wrote about fantastic visions of the future, Timekeeper has created the world's first and only working time machine (at least as far as we know). Assisting Timekeeper in his time voyage demonstration is 9-Eye, a flying robot camera who is the test pilot for Timekeeper's invention. She has volunteered to fly through history and transmit pictures back to guests in the

360-degree time chamber. Guests are able to experience what it was like to hear the young Mozart play his first composition and to see Leonardo da Vinci working on a masterpiece, among many other exciting stops on this whirlwind trip through time and space.

In a sweep of the 1900 Paris Exposition, guests see Jules Verne and H. G. Wells. When Verne hitches a ride to the present and beyond, he gets to see some of his visions realized. Guests may recognize the voice of Timekeeper as that of Robin Williams. Other stars featured are Rhea Perlman as 9-Eye, Jeremy Irons as H. G. Wells, and Michel Piccoli as Jules Verne.

THE EXTRATERRORESTRIAL ALIEN ENCOUNTER: The Tomorrowland Interplanetary Convention Center is the home of the Magic Kingdom's scariest attraction.

Created by Disney Imagineers and motion picture director George Lucas, Alien Encounter features some of the most elaborate special effects ever employed by a theme park.

The premise is this: The Convention Center is hosting X-S Tech, a mysterious corporation from a distant planet. X-S Tech's objective is to impress earthlings with its high-tech products. Following a brief preshow, guests are shown to a circular auditorium with a large teleporter (a machine that "beams" objects from place to place) in the center. Screens around the theater display a live transmission from their planet. Restraints are suddenly lowered onto guests' shoulders. (Don't panic—the experience is not rough, just scary. Sit up straight as the restraint comes down. It will enhance your enjoyment of the show.) Just then, X-S Tech's Chairman Clench volunteers to be teleported to the Magic Kingdom.

Special effects abound as guests await the arrival of Chairman Clench. But something goes wrong, and an angry alien is transported into the audience as the theater goes black. Next comes a series of creepy sensations designed to convince everyone that the monster has found its way to their side. And, no, you are not imagining it—something really is breathing down your neck.

Note: This 20-minute attraction may be too intense for some children. You must be at least 44 inches tall to enter Alien Encounter.

BUZZ LIGHTYEAR'S SPACE RANGER SPIN:

The Evil Emperor Zurg is up to no good. As soon as he swipes enough batteries to power his ultimate weapon of destruction—*KERPLOOEY!*—it's curtains for the toy universe as we know it. It's up to that Space Ranger extraordinaire Buzz Lightyear and his Junior Space Rangers (that means you) to save the day.

So goes the storyline of Tomorrowland's newest attraction, a video game-inspired spin through toyland. The adventure is experienced from a toy's point of view. Guests begin their 4½-minute tour of duty as Space Rangers at Star Command Action Center. This is where Buzz gives his team a briefing on the mission that lies ahead. Then it's off to the Launch Bay to board the ride vehicles. The ships feature duel laser cannons, glowing lights, and a piloting joystick.

In addition to Buzz and the evil Emperor, you may recognize some other toy faces swirling about—the little green, multi-eyed alien squeaky toys, best known for their awe of "the claw." The squeakies have been enlisted to help in the fight against Zurg. (They and their counterparts were animated by Pixar, the creative team responsible for the groundbreaking set of *Toy Story* films. *Toy Story* director, John Lasseter, was also on board to shape the ride's story line.)

Once Junior Space Rangers blast off, they find themselves surrounded by Zurg's robots, who are mercilessly ripping batteries from other toys. As Rangers fire at targets that are scattered about, beams of light fill the air. For every target hit, you'll be rewarded with sight gags, sound effects, and points. The points, which are tallied automatically, are accumulated throughout the journey. Although the vehicles follow a rigid flight path (they're on a track), the joystick allows riders to maneuver the ships, arcing from side to side or spinning in circles while taking aim at your surroundings.

When the star cruiser arrives at Zurg's spaceship, it's showdown time. Will good prevail over evil? Or has time run out for the toy universe? And, most important of all, will you score enough points to be a Galactic Hero?

TOMORROWLAND TRANSIT AUTHORITY:

Boarded near Astro Orbiter, these trains (formerly known as the WEDway People-Mover) move at a speed of about seven miles per hour along almost a mile of track, beside or through most of the attractions in Tomorrowland. They are operated by a linear induction motor that has no moving parts, uses little power, and emits no pollution.

The peaceful, breezy excursion through Tomorrowland takes about ten minutes. There is almost never a wait to board.

WALT DISNEY'S CAROUSEL OF PROGRESS:

First seen at New York's 1964–65 World's Fair and moved here in 1975, this 20-minute show features a number of tableaux starring an Audio-Animatronics family, and demonstrates the improvements in American life that have resulted from electricity. The audience moves around the scenes as on a carousel. An updated final scene has been added, in which guests see what life might be like in the near future: A grandmother plays a virtual reality game and the oven talks.

ASTRO ORBITER:

Here, passengers fly around for two minutes in machine-age rockets designed to look more like oversize Buck

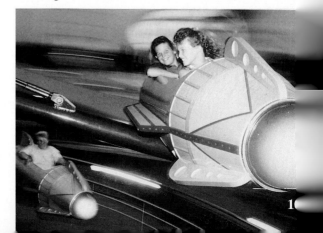

Rogers toys than 21st-century space shuttles. Riders are surrounded by vibrantly colored, whirling planets as they get an astronaut's-eye view of Tomorrowland.

SPACE MOUNTAIN: This attraction, which blasted onto the Magic Kingdom scene in 1975, is a can't-miss crowd pleaser for throngs of thrill seekers. Rising to a height of over 180 feet, this gleaming steel and concrete cone houses an attraction that most people call a roller

coaster. It's the Disney version—a roller coaster and then some.

While the 2-minute, 38-second ride may not precisely duplicate a trip into space, there are impressive effects— shooting stars and flashing lights among them—and the ride takes place in an outer space-like darkness that gets inkier and scarier as the journey progresses.

The rockets that roar through this blackness attain a maximum speed of just over 28 miles per hour. The Space Mountain experience is wild enough to send eyeglasses, purses, wallets, and even an occasional set of false teeth plummeting to the bottom of the track, so be sure to find a safe place for your possessions before the ride starts. It's also turbulent enough to upset the stomachs of

Not sure if you're able to handle Space Mountain? Take a trip on the Tomorrowland Transit Authority. It provides a turbulence-free tour of the popular roller coaster.

those so unwise as to ride it immediately after eating—but not so harrowing that knees shake for more than a minute or two after "touchdown." (Those who chicken out at the last minute have their own exit from the queue area.)

DID YOU KNOW...

Before Disney World opened in 1971, Roy O. Disney changed the resort's official name to *Walt* Disney World. Why? He wanted everyone to know that it was his brother's dream.

Note: Guests who are under 44 inches are not permitted to ride, and you must be in good health and free from heart conditions, motion sickness, back or neck problems, or other physical limitations to ride. Expectant mothers should skip the trip. Children under seven must be accompanied by an adult.

The Tomorrowland Light & Power Co., an arcade near Space Mountain's exit, is a great place to wait for your party if you skip the ride. An ATM is available.

TOMORROWLAND INDY SPEEDWAY: Little cars that burn up the tracks at this attraction provide most of the background noise in Tomorrowland. Kids love the ride and will spend as much time driving the gas-powered cars as they can.

Like true sports cars, the vehicles have rack-and-pinion steering and disc brakes, but unlike most cars, these run along a track. Yet, even expert drivers have trouble keeping them going in a straight line. (Don't panic when you notice the lack of a brake pedal— when you take your foot off the gas, the car comes to a quick, if not screeching, halt.) The one-lap trip takes about five minutes.

Note: You must be at least 52 inches tall to drive the cars by yourself.

SHOPPING

No one travels all the way to the Magic Kingdom just to go shopping. But as many a first-time visitor has learned with some surprise, shopping is one of the most enjoyable pastimes here.

The Magic Kingdom's boutiques and stores stock much more than just Disneyana. Along with the more predictable items in Main Street shops, it's possible to find cookbooks and stoneware dishes, pirate hats and toy frontier rifles, 14-karat gold charms and filigreed costume jewelry. In Adventureland, shops boast many items imported from the exotic regions the area represents. Throughout the park, stores generally have merchandise that complements the themes of the various lands.

In some shops, you can watch people at work—a candymaker pouring peanut brittle in the Main Street Confectionery, a glassblower crafting wares in Main Street's Crystal Arts, and the like. And every store offers a selection of items from the inexpensive to the somewhat costly.

Finally, some advice. We recommend shopping in the early afternoon, rather than at the end of the day, when the shops are more crowded. However, keep in mind that Main Street shops do stay open a half hour after park closing, in case you need any last-minute gifts on the way out of the park. Also note that purchases can be stored for the day in lockers under the Walt Disney World Railroad's depot or, in the case of very large items, sent to package pickup. WDW resort guests may arrange for purchases to be sent to their hotel rooms free of charge. Purchases may be shipped on request.

Main Street

THE CHAPEAU: This Town Square shop is the place to buy Mouse ears and have them monogrammed, and to shop for straw hats, baseball caps, and assorted other headgear.

CRYSTAL ARTS: Cut-glass bowls, vases, glasses, and plates glitter in the mirror-backed glass cases of this crystal-chandeliered emporium. An engraver or a glassblower is always at work by the bright light that floods through the big windows. There is a crystal castle on display in the window out front. Presented by the Arribas Brothers.

DISNEY & CO.: The wallpaper at this lovely shop on Center Street (the cul-de-sac just off Main Street) is Victorian and the woodwork elaborate; old-fashioned ceiling fans twirl slowly overhead. This store specializes in intimate apparel. It also carries infant and toddler clothing, and toys.

DISNEY CLOTHIERS: This shop features an array of clothing, including sweatshirts and flannel sleepwear, all of which incorporate Disney characters in some way. Bags, jewelry, watches, and other accessories round out the selection.

EMPORIUM: Framed by a two-story-high portico, this Town Square landmark, the Magic Kingdom's largest gift shop, stocks stuffed animals and toys, an array of dolls, sundries, film, T-shirts, and more.

The cash registers always seem to be busy, especially toward the end of the afternoon

Where to Eat in the Magic Kingdom

A complete listing of all eateries—full-service restaurants, fast-food emporiums, and snack shops—can be found in the *Good Meals, Great Times* chapter. See the Magic Kingdom section beginning on page 216.

and before park closing. It's a good place to shop, though, since it's only a few steps from lockers (under the train station) where packages can be stowed.

Don't forget to peer into the windows, which usually feature elaborate displays ranging from seasonal themes to character tableaux from the latest Disney movie.

FIREHOUSE GIFT STATION: Authentic firefighting paraphernalia provides the backdrop for a variety of *101 Dalmatians* products, Mickey Mouse firefighter souvenirs, and reproductions of historical firefighting objects.

HARMONY BARBER SHOP: The quaint, old-fashioned setting for this working shop (complete with occasional appearances by a harmonizing quartet) merits a peek even if you have no need for a trim. It's open from 9 A.M. to 5 P.M. daily.

MAIN STREET ATHLETIC CLUB: Sports-related gifts and apparel are the hallmarks of this shop. The merchandise features images of Disney characters pursuing their favorite sports. The shop also stocks golf shirts with a small Mickey embroidered on the pocket.

MAIN STREET CONFECTIONERY: Tasty chocolates are sold in this old-fashioned pink-and-white paradise. A delight at any time of day, but especially when the cooks in the shop's glass-walled kitchen are pouring peanut brittle onto a table to cool. Then the candy sends up clouds of aroma that you could swear were being fanned out onto the street. Several batches are made each day; the sweet product is for sale in small bags, along with jellybeans, marshmallow crispie treats, and dozens of other confections that will satisfy any sweet tooth.

MAIN STREET GALLERY: The focus here is on Disneyana—including limited-edition Disney plates, cels from Disney movies, and other collectibles. The store is located in the building formerly occupied by the bank.

MAIN STREET MARKET HOUSE: An old-fashioned spot, with cookies, candy, and housewares, including specialty tins, napkin rings, and espresso cups.

NEWSSTAND: No newspapers are sold in the Magic Kingdom—even at its newsstand, which is near the park entrance. (It's to the left, just inside the turnstiles.) The stand sells a small selection of character merchandise and souvenirs.

THE SHADOW BOX: Watching Rubio Artist Co. silhouette cutters snip black paper into the likenesses of children is one of Main Street's more fascinating diversions.

STROLLER AND WHEELCHAIR RENTAL: Inside the turnstiles on the right as you enter the Magic Kingdom, this rental concession offers a limited number of strollers and wheelchairs (available on a first-come, first-served basis). Souvenirs may also be purchased here.

TOWN SQUARE EXPOSITION HALL: A combination camera center and museum, Exposition Hall features exhibits celebrating the history of photography. This is the spot for film, batteries, photo albums, disposable cameras, two-hour film processing, and very minor camera repairs. It's also possible to have your photo snapped and superimposed onto a decidedly Disney background—be it in front of Cinderella Castle, beside Disney villains, or in the Hundred Acre Wood. These photos can be made into posters, plaques, or mousepads.

UPTOWN JEWELERS: Modeled after a turn-of-the-century collectibles shop, this store specializes in jewelry, china, and other gift items. One counter stocks souvenir charms in 14-karat gold and sterling silver, among them Tinker Bell, Cinderella Castle, and the Walt Disney World logo (a globe with mouse ears). There's also a selection of Disney character figurines, priced from $3.50 to $3,500. Clocks and watches in all shapes and sizes are available here, including Mickey Mouse watches in a variety of configurations.

Adventureland

Big changes are brewing in these parts. The new attraction, The Magic Carpets of Aladdin, is expected to trigger a bit of redecorating. Most obvious will be a metamorphosis of the area's shopping zone (which may take place by the time you visit). Expect the wares to complement the Agrabah atmosphere oozing from those magic carpets. The following descriptions were accurate at press time:

BWANA BOB'S: A colorful hut full of the critters you may have just seen on the Jungle Cruise or at the Enchanted Tiki Birds.

ELEPHANT TALES: A variety of women's and men's clothing with a safari theme is featured at this shop. Women's accessories and safari plush toys are also available.

ISLAND SUPPLY: This tropical surf shop features a vast assortment of surfing clothing and accessories.

TRADERS OF TIMBUKTU: Located opposite the Tiki Birds, this shop stocks the sort of trinkets that world travelers might come across in distant lands.

Caribbean Plaza

HOUSE OF TREASURE: A good spot to pick up pirate hats and shirts, this swashbuckler's delight adjoins Pirates of the Caribbean and stocks nautical gifts and pirate merchandise—a Pirate's Creed of Ethics, Jolly Roger flags, rings, pirate dolls, sailing-ship models, ships in a bottle, and eye patches.

PLAZA DEL SOL CARIBE BAZAAR: Located next to the Pirates, this market sells candy and snacks, straw hats (including colorful oversize sombreros), piñatas, pottery, straw bags, clothing, and artificial flowers.

Frontierland

BIG AL'S: Named for the most popular (and least talented) member of the Country Bears, this riverfront shop is the place to acquire leather goods, coonskin caps, assorted six-shooters, and other Wild West toys.

BRIAR PATCH: Toys and cuddly creatures from The Hundred Acre Wood—Winnie the Pooh, Tigger, and their pals—are featured at this shop, near the exit to Splash Mountain.

FRONTIER TRADING POST: Outfit a child like a true youngster of the Great Frontier. Cowboy hats or feathered headdresses and moccasins, sleeve garters, sheriff's badges, and turquoise jewelry should do the trick.

FRONTIER WOOD CARVING: The spot for wooden gifts with personalized carvings.

PRAIRIE OUTPOST & SUPPLY: Stop by this turn-of-the-century general store for candy, coffee, and cookies. Decorative items such as candles are also for sale.

TRAIL CREEK HAT SHOP: Hats of all kinds plus feathered hatbands and leather goods are on sale at this small shop tucked away near the Diamond Horseshoe Saloon Revue.

Liberty Square

HERITAGE HOUSE: Early American reproductions predominate in the stock of this store next to The Hall of Presidents. Parchment copies of famous American documents are popular with youngsters. Collectors might be tempted to snap up busts of the presidents, souvenir spoons, or documents signed by famous figures from American history. Campaign buttons, flags, T-shirts, and Statue of Liberty items are also available.

LIBERTY SQUARE PORTRAIT GALLERY: In the midst of Liberty Square, next to The Hall of Presidents, guests can sit to have their portraits drawn in this open-air studio.

MADAME LEOTA'S CART: This tiny shop gives guests on their way to The Haunted Mansion a taste of things to come, with horrific monster masks and ghoulish goodies. It's also the place to pick up an invisible pooch.

THE YANKEE TRADER: This quaint little shop, near The Haunted Mansion, is crammed with kitchen items. There are Mickey waffle irons and Mickey-shaped pasta, among other Disney-themed goods. The shop also stocks jams and jellies, cooking oils and sauces, pots, dishes, and other creative kitchenware.

YE OLDE CHRISTMAS SHOPPE: A wide variety of decorative Christmas items, including tree-top dolls, automated display characters, angel figurines, and souvenir ornaments—Disney-themed and traditional—is available year-round.

Merchandise found in shops at Walt Disney World is also available through mail order. Call 407-363-6200 for information.

Fantasyland

THE KING'S GALLERY: This shop, inside Cinderella Castle, features a line of knight-wear and other medieval items such as swords and shields. In addition, it stocks items related to Cinderella herself (including glass slippers), as well as her castle.

KODAK KIOSK: A convenient location to buy film and other photo supplies.

SEVEN DWARFS MINING CO.: This souvenir stand next to Snow White's Scary Adventures sells assorted Disney-motif key chains, candies, and stuffed animals, plus a colorful collection of Snow White merchandise.

SIR MICKEY'S: Expect to find all sorts of Disney souvenirs in this shop with a theme based on *The Brave Little Tailor*—the cartoon in which Mickey defeats a giant to win the hand of Princess Minnie. (It was one of the most elaborate and expensive Mickey Mouse cartoons ever made.) Notable items include embroidered denim jackets, character sweatshirts, and videos.

THE THOTFUL SPOT: Located at the exit of The Many Adventures of Winnie the Pooh, this shop has wall-to-wall wares featuring the folks from the Hundred Acre Wood. Oh, and it's not your imagination: this place really *does* smell like honey!

TINKER BELL'S TREASURES: One of the more wonderful boutiques in the Magic Kingdom. For sale are character clothing and costumes for kids, princess hats, stuffed animals, character toys, and an impressive array of Madame Alexander and other collector dolls.

Mickey's Toontown Fair

COUNTY BOUNTY: Disney character memorabilia, featuring all the favorites, can be found in this merchandise location under the big tent. Look for costumes, children's apparel, autograph books, key chains, candy, and more. Don't miss the doll-making exhibit or the winning entries from previous fairs, including the "most upside-down cake," baked by Daisy Duck.

Tomorrowland

GEIGER'S COUNTER: This small shop near the Tomorrowland Indy Speedway features a variety of souvenir hats, pins, and neon glow jewelry. It also monograms Mouse ears.

MERCHANT OF VENUS: The kinds of gifts and collector items that sci-fi enthusiasts love can be found here: futuristic toys, games, clothing, airbrushed shirts, and other such items. This is also the only shop that carries a selection of Alien Encounter merchandise.

MICKEY'S STAR TRADERS: This is one of the best places to go in the Magic Kingdom for Disney-themed items: plush toys, towels, hats, shirts, dishes, candy, etc. Film, sunglasses, and assorted sun care products are also available.

URSA'S MAJOR MINOR MART: A small spot tucked away to the right of Space Mountain (under the old Skyway station) that's great for discovering Disney souvenirs and Space Mountain T-shirts.

ENTERTAINMENT

In this most magical corner of the World, a tempting slate of live performances ranks among the more serendipitous discoveries. The Magic Kingdom's entertainment mix includes dazzling high-tech shows and old-fashioned numbers alike. To keep apprised of the offerings on any given day, stop at City Hall upon arrival at the park to pick up a current guidemap.

While the specifics are subject to change, the following listing is a good indication of the Magic Kingdom's extensive repertoire. As always, we advise calling 407-939-4636 to confirm entertainment schedules. For information on special events at the Magic Kingdom, see the "Holidays & Special Events" section of *Getting Ready to Go.*

ALL-AMERICAN COLLEGE MARCHING BAND: During weekdays in summer, this band, which features college students from around the country, performs throughout the Magic Kingdom in the afternoon and early evening.

CASEY'S CORNER PIANO: A pianist tickles the ivories of a snow-white upright daily at the centrally located Casey's Corner restaurant on Main Street.

DAPPER DANS: You just might encounter a barbershop quartet while strolling down Main Street. Conspicuously clad in straw hats and striped vests, the Dapper Dans tap-dance and let one-liners fly during their short four-part-harmony performances.

DIAMOND HORSESHOE SALOON REVUE: A Frontierland dance hall, such as those found in 19th-century Missouri, hosts this lively old-time show with cancan dancers several times daily. Guests may drop in at any time during the performances.

DISNEY'S MAGICAL MOMENTS PARADE: This 15-minute parade has an interactive twist: cameo appearances by about 900 randomly selected Magic Kingdom visitors. (Guests are selected for participation during the parade. Get there at least 45 minutes early to snag a good curbside spot and increase your chances of being chosen to join in the fun.) The parade, which has six floats inspired by classic Disney films, as well as every character imaginable, begins at 3 P.M. in Frontierland and winds its way up Main Street, U.S.A., stopping five times en route for special participatory sequences.

FANTASY IN THE SKY: This pyrotechnic extravaganza is presented during peak seasons and select weekends. The program opens with Tinker Bell's Flight, a dramatic sprinkling of pyrotechnic pixie dust over Cinderella Castle. The seven-minute fireworks presentation is ideally viewed from Main Street, but there are good viewing locations in Fantasyland, Tomorrowland, and Frontierland. It is presented rain or shine. (Fantasy in the Sky is often presented at 10 P.M. during peak periods, earlier during the rest of the year—check a park guidemap for specifics.)

FLAG RETREAT: At about 5:10 P.M. each day, patriotic music fills the air as a color guard marches to Town Square, in Main Street, U.S.A., takes down the American flag that flies from the flagpole, and releases a flock of snow-white homing pigeons symbolic of the dove of peace. Watch carefully: They flap away toward their home (behind the castle) practically before you can say "Cinderella." The entire flight takes 20 seconds.

KIDS OF THE KINGDOM: Often performing in front of Cinderella Castle, this group puts on a lively show, featuring singing and dancing to Disney tunes—plus appearances by such characters as the portly Winnie the Pooh and Mickey Mouse himself.

RHYTHM RASCALS: Specialty songs and comic ditties from the Roaring Twenties performed on washboards and banjos are their trademark; they appear on Main Street.

SWORD IN THE STONE CEREMONY: Several times each day, a child is appointed temporary ruler of the realm by pulling the magical sword, Excalibur, from the stone in front of Cinderella's Golden Carrousel. Merlin the Magician presides over the ceremony.

Holiday Happenings

It's a rare holiday that passes quietly in the Magic Kingdom. During certain holidays, such as Christmas, New Year's Eve, and the Fourth of July, this Kingdom usually breaks curfew, staying open extra late and stepping up its nighttime entertainment. On these occasions, special performances of Spectro-Magic and Fantasy in the Sky fireworks are often in store. Of course, entertainment plans are subject to change, so it's important to call 407-939-4636 for current schedules.

EASTER: An elaborate holiday parade on Main Street makes Easter an especially delightful, if a bit crowded, time to visit the Magic Kingdom.

FOURTH OF JULY: The busiest day of the summer—and with good reason: There's a double-size fireworks extravaganza whose explosions light up the skies not only above Cinderella Castle but also over Seven Seas Lagoon. It's a thrilling display.

HALLOWEEN: This most spooky of holidays is generally celebrated on several nights (though not necessarily on Halloween itself) with a special-ticket event: Mickey's Not-So-Scary Halloween Party. The park closes a bit early on nights when the party takes place.

CHRISTMAS: A towering Christmas tree goes up in Town Square, and the entire Magic Kingdom is decked out as only Disney can do it. On select evenings, the Magic Kingdom hosts a special-admission nighttime celebration called Mickey's Very Merry Christmas Party. The festivities, complete with hot chocolate and snow, include a running (or two) of Mickey's Very Merry Christmas Parade and other holiday shows. There are also special holiday performances during the day.

NEW YEAR'S EVE: It has always been true that on December 31 the throngs here are practically body to body. For a celebration of this nature, that can be lots of fun. Expect double-size fireworks and holiday decorations. There's plenty of nip in the air as the evening goes on, so dress accordingly. (It's not uncommon to see revelers clad in hats and scarves.)

Where to Find the Characters

Mickey's pals make appearances near City Hall throughout the day. Adventureland Character CongOasis is the spot to meet friends from *The Lion King*, *Aladdin*, and *The Jungle Book*. Alice and her Wonderland friends show up in Fantasyland, as does Ariel. Belle reads stories to guests in Fairy Tale Garden, near the Castle. The Fantasyland Character Festival is an excellent spot to see characters. The character meals at Crystal Palace, Cinderella's Royal Table, and Liberty Tree Tavern offer guests a chance to meet their favorites. But the best place is at Toontown Fair, where guests can meet Mickey and his buddies. Check a guidemap for updated information.

SpectroMagic is back!

After a nearly two-year hiatus, SpectroMagic is expected to rejoin the lineup of Magic Kingdom entertainment sometime in the spring of 2001. The dazzling parade, which first premiered during Walt Disney World's 20th anniversary celebration, has gotten rave reviews and taken its place among WDW's must-sees.

Fiber-optic cable and threads are the conduits for shimmering lights that create everything from the "hair" on King Triton's beard on one float to daisy petals on another. Some 600,000 miniature bulbs light up in wild, changing patterns, moving in perfect concert with sound effects and musical score.

SpectroMagic follows the traditional parade route (heading from Main Street, U.S.A., to Frontierland and vice versa). There are excellent viewing locations throughout the route, with many along the curbs of Main Street. It gets very crowded there, so you must plan to claim your foot of curb as much as an hour and a half ahead of time (particularly for the earlier running).

The parade lights up the Magic Kingdom during all peak seasons and select evenings throughout the year.

Timing tip: When the parade runs twice a night, the earlier presentation is always more crowded than the later one.

Note: SpectroMagic's return marks the end of the encore run of the beloved Main Street Electrical Parade. To find out if it will be presented during your visit, call 407-939-4636. Some performances may be canceled due to inclement weather.

HOT TIPS

• Each day, sections of one park are open up to 1½ hours early for WDW resort guests only. But keep in mind that the parks can get crowded on these days—that's when a park hopper pass comes in handy.

• If there are two performances of the evening parade, the later one tends to draw smaller crowds.

• Even if you are not staying at a Walt Disney World resort, plan to start out very early. Most people arrive between 9:30 A.M. and 11:30 A.M., and the roads and parking lots are jammed. If you're coming at Easter, Christmas, or in summer, plan to arrive before 8:30 A.M. or wait until late afternoon, when things are less hectic. Be at the gates to the Magic Kingdom when they open, and then be at the end of Main Street when the rest of the park opens.

• Wear very comfortable shoes: You'll be spending a lot of time on your feet. (Note that no bare feet are permitted in the park.)

• WDW resort guests (and those staying at the Swan and Dolphin) can have packages delivered to their hotels for free. (Keep in mind that it's often next-day delivery.)

• You can usually get in line for an attraction right up until the minute the park closes.

• Avoid the mealtime rush hours by eating early or late: before 11 A.M. or after 2 P.M., and before 5 P.M. or after 8 P.M.

• At busy times, take in these not-so-packed attractions: Walt Disney World Railroad, Liberty Belle Riverboat, Walt Disney's Carousel of Progress, and Tomorrowland Transit Authority.

• Check the Tip Boards for information on the wait times for popular attractions.

• Break up your day. Consider heading back to your hotel (if it's not too far) for some swimming. Be sure to have your hand stamped and hold on to your admission pass and your parking stub, so you can re-enter the Magic Kingdom.

• If your party decides to split up, set a meeting place and time. Avoid meeting in front of Cinderella Castle, since this area can become quite congested.

• Many Magic Kingdom attractions have two lines. The one on the left usually will be shorter, since most visitors automatically head for the one on the right.

• For a full-service meal in the Magic Kingdom, make advance priority seating arrangements by calling 407-WDW-DINE (939-3463).

• There are picnic facilities at the Transportation and Ticket Center (TTC).

• If you want a good spot for the Magical Moments parade, choose your spot at least 45 minutes early. Guests are randomly picked to participate from the parade route.

Epcot

121 Getting Oriented

122 Park Primer

123 Future World

135 World Showcase

149 Entertainment

150 Hot Tips

magine a place whose entertainment inventory includes both a rich sampling of world cultures and a fun, enlightening journey to the technological frontier. You now have an inkling of the eye-opening and mind-broadening potential of Epcot.

Walt Disney suggested the idea back in 1966: "Epcot will be an experimental prototype community of tomorrow that will take its cue from the new ideas and technologies that are emerging from the creative center of American industry." It would never be completed, he said, but would "always be introducing and testing and demonstrating new materials and systems." Now, more than ever, Walt Disney's dream is a reality. Innoventions is continually bounding into new territory in its mission to close gaps with technological destiny. The addition of Test Track puts guests on the thrilling inside track of the fast and perilous world of automobile testing. And the new Imagination! attraction, with its awe-inspiring special effects and interactive wonders, aspires to ignite the creative forces within us all.

The park consists of two distinct areas of exploration: Future World and World Showcase. The former examines the newest and most intriguing ideas in science and technology in ways that make them seem not only comprehensible but downright irresistible. The latter celebrates the diversity of the world's peoples, portraying a stunning array of nations with extraordinary devotion to detail.

Think of Epcot as Disney's playground for the curious and the thoughtful. The experiences it delivers—all of them wonders of the real world—never fail to amaze, delight, inspire, and (rest assured) entertain.

EPCOT

WORLD SHOWCASE

MOROCCO

FRANCE

JAPAN

INTERNATIONAL GATEWAY

THE AMERICAN ADVENTURE

UNITED KINGDOM

ITALY

CANADA

WORLD SHOWCASE LAGOON

IMAGINATION!

FUTURE WORLD

GERMANY

THE LAND

CHINA

INNOVENTIONS WEST

THE LIVING SEAS

NORWAY

SHOWCASE PLAZA

MEXICO

INNOVENTIONS EAST

TEST TRACK

WONDERS OF LIFE

SPACESHIP EARTH

UNIVERSE OF ENERGY

Entrance Plaza

To Buses

N

120

GETTING ORIENTED

Double the Magic Kingdom and you have an idea of the size of Epcot. As for layout, the park is shaped something like a giant hourglass. The pavilions of Future World fill the northern bulb, while the international potpourri called World Showcase occupies the southern bulb. Future World is anchored on the north by the imposing silver "geosphere" dubbed Spaceship Earth.

As you pass through Epcot's main Entrance Plaza, Spaceship Earth looms straight ahead. Pathways curve around either side of the 180-foot-tall geosphere, winding up at Innoventions Plaza. Here, in addition to a huge show fountain, you'll see signposts for Innoventions, whose two buildings cradle the east and west sides of the plaza. Beyond this central area, there are two roughly symmetrical north-south avenues; these are dotted with the seven pavilions that form the outer perimeter of Future World. Test Track, Wonders of Life, and Universe of Energy flank Spaceship Earth on the east, while Imagination!, The Land, and The Living Seas lie to the west.

In World Showcase, the international pavilions are arranged around the edge of sparkling World Showcase Lagoon, with The American Adventure directly south of Spaceship Earth on the lake's southernmost shore. A walkway from Future World leads to Showcase Plaza and World Showcase Promenade, a 1.2-mile thoroughfare that wraps all the way around the lagoon, winding past each World Showcase pavilion in the process. Proceeding counterclockwise around World Showcase, pavilions are encountered in the following order: Canada, the United Kingdom, France, Morocco, Japan, The American Adventure, Italy, Germany, China, Norway, and Mexico.

HOW TO GET THERE

Take Exit 26B off I-4. Continue along to the Epcot Auto Plaza; take a tram from the parking lot to the park's main entrance.

By WDW Transportation: From the Grand Floridian, Contemporary, and Polynesian: hotel monorail to the Transportation and Ticket Center (TTC), then switch for the TTC-Epcot monorail. From the Magic Kingdom: express monorail to the TTC, then switch for the TTC-Epcot monorail. From Fort Wilderness and Downtown Disney: buses to the TTC, then change for the TTC-Epcot monorail. From the Disney-MGM Studios, Animal Kingdom, all other WDW resorts, and the resorts on Hotel Plaza Boulevard: buses.

Note: A second Epcot entrance, called the International Gateway, provides entry directly to World Showcase. This gateway, which may be reached via scenic walkways and *FriendShip* water launches from the Swan, Dolphin, Yacht and Beach Club, and BoardWalk resorts, deposits guests between the France and United Kingdom pavilions. It is possible to purchase theme park admission here, at Epcot's "back door."

PARKING

All-day parking at Epcot is $6 for day visitors (free to Walt Disney World resort guests with a resort ID as well as annual passholders). Attendants will direct you to park in one of several lots named in honor of Future World pavilions. Trams circulate regularly, providing transportation between the lots and the main entrance. Be sure to note the section and aisle in which you park. Parking tickets allow for re-entry to the area (as well as other theme parks) throughout the day.

HOURS

Future World is usually open from 9 A.M. to 9 P.M. World Showcase hours are 11 A.M. to 9 P.M. During certain holiday periods and the summer months, Epcot's hours are extended. It's best to arrive at the park at least a half hour before the posted opening time, particularly during these busy seasons. Call 407-939-4636 for up-to-the-minute schedules.

GETTING AROUND

European-style water taxis, called *FriendShip* launches, ferry guests across the World Showcase Lagoon. Docks are located near Mexico, Canada, Germany, and Morocco. (The only other way to traverse the vast area is on foot.)

PARK PRIMER

EPCOT

BABY FACILITIES

There are changing tables and facilities for nursing mothers at the Baby Care Center in the Odyssey Center, between Test Track and Mexico. Disposable diapers are kept behind the counter at many Epcot shops; just ask.

CAMERA NEEDS

The Camera Center on the west side of the Entrance Plaza and World Traveler in International Gateway stock film, batteries, and disposable cameras. Film processing is available here and wherever you see a Photo Express sign. There is an additional camera shop inside the Imagination! pavilion. Film is sold in most Epcot shops. Attendants may be able to assist with minor camera repairs.

DISABILITY INFORMATION

Nearly all attractions, shops, and restaurants are barrier-free. Parking for guests with disabilities is available. Additional services are available for guests with sight and hearing disabilities. The *Guidebook for Guests with Disabilities* is available at Guest Relations. It provides a detailed overview of all services. For more information, turn to *Getting Ready to Go.*

EARLY-ENTRY DAYS

On Tuesday and Friday, Walt Disney World resort guests may enter Epcot up to 1½ hours before the posted opening time and enjoy selected attractions at Future World—usually Test Track, The Living Seas, The Land, Wonders of Life, and Spaceship Earth. Days and attractions are subject to change.

FIRST AID

Minor medical problems can be handled at the First Aid Center, located in the Odyssey Center, between Test Track and Mexico.

INFORMATION

Guest Relations, which is located next to Spaceship Earth, is equipped with guidemaps and a helpful staff.

LOCKERS

Lockers are found immediately west of Spaceship Earth. Cost is $5, including a $2 refundable deposit for unlimited use all day.

LOST & FOUND

The Lost and Found department is located at Guest Relations in Innoventions East. To report any lost items after your visit, call 407-824-4245.

LOST CHILDREN

Report lost children at Guest Relations or the Baby Care Center, or alert a Disney employee.

MONEY MATTERS

There are ATMs on the east side of the Entrance Plaza, on the path between Future World and World Showcase, and near Germany. Currency may be exchanged at Guest Relations or at the American Express Travel Office on the west side of the Entrance Plaza. Credit cards (American Express, JCB, Discover, Diner's Club, Visa, MasterCard, and The Disney Credit Card), traveler's checks, and WDW resort IDs are accepted for admission and merchandise, as well as meals at all full-service and fast-food restaurants.

PACKAGE PICKUP

Epcot shops can arrange for bulky purchases to be transported to the Gift Stop on the west side of the Entrance Plaza for later pickup. There is no charge for this service.

SAME-DAY RE-ENTRY

Be sure to have your hand stamped upon exiting the park and to retain your ticket if you plan to return later the same day.

STROLLERS & WHEELCHAIRS

Strollers, wheelchairs, and Electric Convenience Vehicles (ECVs) may be rented from venues on the east side of the Entrance Plaza and at the International Gateway entrance. Wheelchairs are also available at the Gift Stop. Cost is $6 for strollers and wheelchairs, plus a $1 refundable deposit; and $30 for ECVs, plus a $10 refundable deposit. Quantities are limited. Keep your rental receipt; it can be used that same day to obtain a replacement stroller or wheelchair at Epcot or at any of the other theme parks.

TIP BOARD

Check this digital board in Innovations Plaza throughout the day to learn current waiting times for the most popular attractions.

FUTURE WORLD

A brand-new Future World attraction is on the horizon—Mission: Space. The space-themed pavilion (which replaces Horizons) opens in 2003. The countdown has begun!

A mere listing of the basic themes covered by the pavilions at Future World—agriculture, communications, car safety, the ocean, energy, health, and imagination—tends to sound a tad academic, and perhaps even a little forbidding. But when these serious topics are presented with that special Disney flair, they become part of an experience that ranks among Walt Disney World's most exciting and entertaining.

Some of these subjects are explored in the course of lively and unusual Disney "adventures," involving a whole arsenal of remarkable motion pictures, special effects, and Audio-Animatronics figures so lifelike that it is hard to remain unmoved. And the new Innoventions offers an invitation to sample cutting-edge technology. The basic elements are also appealing in their own right, from the palm-dotted Entrance Plaza and the massive buildings of Innoventions to the stupendous fountain just past Spaceship Earth, the many-faceted "geosphere" that has become the universal symbol of Epcot.

There is so much to see and enjoy that it's hard to know just what to do first. Many guests simply stop at Spaceship Earth on their way into Epcot. As a result, they end up spending more time waiting in line than they need to. A wise alternative is to save Spaceship Earth for later in the day (when the lines inevitably thin out), and head for Test Track as soon as it opens (the line tends to stay long throughout the day). If you have young children, consider kicking things off with a visit to the colorful Wonders of Life pavilion. Then take in as many Future World attractions as time allows, making sure to see the Image Works playground in the Imagination! pavilion and

save World Showcase for the evening hours. This strategy works well for families. (Refer to page 26 for a detailed version of this recommended plan of attack.)

Another alternative—one that requires quite a bit of extra walking, but can help skirt a long line or two—is to explore Future World until World Showcase opens at 11 A.M. Then, in the afternoon, when many guests have shifted over to World Showcase, return to the Future World area. Innoventions is not only a fascinating spot to pass the busy hours after lunch, but also a pleasantly cool refuge when uncomfortably high temperatures prevail outdoors. And although queues can be found during peak seasons at Test Track, Imagination!, The Land, and Wonders of Life throughout most of the late morning and afternoon, the period from late afternoon until park closing is usually less hectic. But don't forget to make it back to World Showcase in time to see the nighttime spectacular, IllumiNations: Reflections of Earth.

Leave a Legacy

The Leave a Legacy program, held over from Disney's Millennium Celebration, invites guests to leave their mark on the park. This cluster of monoliths inside Epcot's main entrance is covered with images of Walt Disney World guests etched on one-inch square tiles on massive stone walls. (There is a second purchase location near the American Adventure in World Showcase.)

To purchase a tile, inquire at the information kiosk within the Leave a Legacy vicinity. The cost for a single-image tile is $35. A tile with two images (the maximum) is $38. Note that this exhibit is not expected to be a permanent one.

Spaceship Earth

As it looms impressively just above the earth, this great faceted silver structure—visible on a clear day from an airplane flying along either Florida coast—looks a little bit like a spaceship ready to blast off. It appears large from a distance, and it seems even more immense when viewed from directly underneath. It's no surprise that some visitors simply stop beneath it and gawk.

The show inside, which explores the continuing search by human beings for ever more efficient means of communication, remains one of Epcot's most compelling.

A common misconception about Spaceship Earth is that it is a geodesic dome. Not so. It is a *geosphere*. A geodesic dome is only half a sphere, while Spaceship Earth is almost completely round. Affectionately known to many simply as "the Ball," Spaceship Earth is indeed a sight to behold.

SPACESHIP EARTH RIDE: The noted science fiction writer Ray Bradbury, together with consultants from the Smithsonian Institution, the Los Angeles area's prestigious Huntington Library, the University of Southern California, and (among others) the University of Chicago, collaborated with Disney in developing this memorable 14-minute journey. It begins in an inky black time tunnel complete with a musty smell that suggests the dust of ages, and continues through history from the days of Cro-Magnon man (30,000 or 40,000 years ago) to the future.

The attraction features remarkable special effects, such as the flickering candles in the scene where a monk has nodded off, and the smell of smoke coming from the fall of Rome. Every scene is executed in exquisite detail. The symbols on the wall of that Egyptian temple really are hieroglyphics, and the content of the letter being dictated by the pharaoh was excerpted from a missive actually received by an agent of a ruler of the period.

HOT TIP The line for Spaceship Earth is usually quite long during the early morning hours and relatively short in the late afternoon and evening.

All of these sights are enough to keep heads turning as the "time machines" wend their way upward. The most dazzling scene is saved for the ride's finale, when the audience is placed in the heart of a communications revolution amid interactive global networks that tie all the peoples of the world together.

In the Global Neighborhood exhibit at the end of the journey, guests interact with emerging technologies such as voice-activated television and telephones with wacky sound effects.

GATEWAY GIFTS AND CAMERA CENTER:
These two shops are located near the entrance to Spaceship Earth. The former sells Epcot souvenirs—shirts, mugs, toys, etc.—as well as sunscreen, tissues, and the like. Film and various other Kodak products, including disposable cameras, are sold at the Camera Center. Film processing is available.

Innoventions

Where else but Walt Disney World would the information superhighway intersect with The Road to Tomorrow? It does so here, at the completely overhauled Innoventions—a forward-thinking showplace that encourages guests to experience futuristic technologies today. It's a golden opportunity to see, touch, and test products that will one day change the way we live and work. Equally important, Innoventions offers an unintimidating environment where you needn't know how to program a VCR to be able to try out supercomputers, experiment with electronic paper, and send video e-mail messages.

An introduction hosted by Tom Morrow 2.0, a mini-robot and "a friend to technology," provides an overview of the new Innoventions experience, as well as some navigational tips. Once Tom's had his say, it's time to follow The Road to Tomorrow, a winding thoroughfare that snakes throughout Innoventions, and along which the exhibits are found.

Ice Station Cool

Future World's Ice Station Cool is a great place to beat the heat. Located near Pasta Piazza Ristorante, it bears a striking resemblance to an iceberg—with one major difference: It has a door. Inside, an ice tunnel (with an average temperature of 32 degrees and constant snowfall) leads to Coca-Cola's International Tasting Station. Here, you can sample eight different soft drinks from around the world, some tastier than others.

After you've quenched your thirst, courtesy of the Coca-Cola Company, you may have a desire to do some shopping. Not coincidentally, there's plenty of Coke merchandise available to choose from (at this point, you will have to open your wallet if you'd like a souvenir).

At press time, Ice Station Cool was open for business during Epcot's regular operating hours.

The displays change often, making one of Walt Disney's original dreams for Epcot a reality. Employees will answer questions from curious—or skeptical—visitors.

Innoventions covers two buildings, referred to as Innoventions East and West. The outside area between the pavilions is filled with color, light, spinning mobiles, and sidewalks glistening with fiber-optic lighting effects. Inside, areas are divided by company (a sampling is described below). Since the exhibits change often, there may be many different technologies available when you visit.

> **HOT TIP**
> Keep an eye (or ear) out for a talking trash can inside the Electric Umbrella restaurant and a talking drinking fountain near the Imagination! pavilion.

Above all, count on spending time exploring the exhibit areas (at least an hour or two). There's so much to see and do that curiosity will often get the better of any schedule here.

INNOVENTIONS EAST: Exhibits on the east side of Innoventions include one by **Motorola**. The exhibit, which is divided into three sections, is designed as "A Quest for Personal Freedom." The first section is a theater called The Future Transporter. Here, an Audio-Animatronics host, Sky Starnac, narrates a video presentation highlighting technologies that allow people to feel more free. Among them are wireless video phones and a device that converts e-mail text into audio messages. The second section is a video presentation highlighting cutting-edge technologies.

The final section of the exhibit allows guests to try out these high-tech gadgets.

Disney Online sponsors an exhibit entitled "The Internet Zone." It is meant to show the Internet's ability to give users a sense of community. Here, guests can send video e-mail (a video clip of themselves) to their loved ones online. Kids can paint, play music, even make a comic book. The items can be posted on the Web for future viewing.

House of Innoventions is a sample kitchen, living room, laundry room, bathroom, and bedroom. Representatives demonstrate the latest ideas to help make home life a little easier by automating daily tasks. Some of the products include home security systems and a remote control toilet (with a heated seat). But our favorite is the Total Home—a computer that fully automates all of the above, plus the lighting, heating and cooling systems, most appliances, and more.

HOT TIP

Innovations Plaza is home to Pin Central. This area, between Innoventions East and West, is the pin-trading headquarters for Walt Disney World. (Of course, there are other trading areas throughout WDW.)

INNOVENTIONS WEST: Exhibits on the west side of Innoventions include the **Ultimate Home Theater** experience. Designed as a soundstage, guests enter what appears to be an ordinary living room. It's really the living room of most people's dreams, with remote control lighting; high definition TV; and a special acoustic design that enhances the overall sensory experience.

IBM features new ways to work and play with your computer. Try out some of IBM's newest technologies, such as speech recognition. Kids love getting a cartoon puppy to sit, roll over, and play fetch. (He understands several languages.) At the IBM Internet Postcards stations, visitors have their picture taken and superimposed on a cool background, and then send it across the Internet. (Remember to bring e-mail addresses with you.) Also of interest: a new pager system that allows users to transmit documents through physical touch.

The **RSNA** (Radiological Society of North America) sponsors an intriguing exhibit area that is dedicated to advances in medical technology. The **Monsanto** area focuses on life sciences, with a highlight being a video presentation with an interesting twist: The nature themed show is projected onto a screen of water.

Xerox allows guests to sample the latest forms of communication technology, with an emphasis on breaking down language barriers. One display to look out for: an instant language translator.

MOUSE GEAR: This enormous shop used to be called the Centorium. Though the name has changed, the quality remains top notch. Mouse Gear stocks Disney character memorabilia, key chains, T-shirts, pencils, hats, and much more—making this the number one source for character merchandise in Epcot. There are also items related to the park itself, such as Spaceship Earth picture frames, along with Disney-themed apparel and children's clothing. It is one of the best shops at Walt Disney World.

THE ART OF DISNEY EPCOT GALLERY: Formerly located on the second floor of the Mouse Gear shop, this is Epcot's spot for a unique assortment of Disney collectibles. The store showcases a wide variety of Disney animation art, including production cels, hand-painted limited-edition cels, maquettes (character models), fine-art serigraphs, and lithographs.

The Living Seas

The Living Seas is the largest facility ever dedicated to humanity's relationship with the ocean. It was designed by Disney Imagineers, in cooperation with a board of some of the world's most distinguished oceanographic experts and scientists.

The show also features a seven-minute film about how Earth's oceans were formed and about the diversity of the life that calls them home.

From there, a ride through a simulated Caribbean coral reef environment and the hands-on activities of Sea Base Alpha combine to prolong a visitor's stay.

CARIBBEAN CORAL REEF RIDE: To reach the sea cabs that make the trip to the coral reef, visitors enter "hydrolators," elevator-like capsules that create the illusion of diving deep under the sea while actually descending only about an inch. The man-made reef exists in an enormous tank that holds about six million gallons of water and more than 60 species of sea life. Among the 2,000 or so inhabitants are turtles, barracuda, angelfish, sharks, dolphins, and diamond rays. It's fun to stop by at around 10 A.M.—that's when breakfast is served to the fish!

Guests sometimes get to see scuba divers testing and demonstrating the newest diving gear and underwater monitoring equipment as they carry on training experiments with dolphins. Following the three-minute ride, guests are deposited at Sea Base Alpha. This pavilion is an especially big hit with young guests.

EPCOT

Under the Sea

Two behind-the-scenes tours offer guests a closer look at life in The Living Seas underwater environs. DiveQuest gives certified scuba divers the opportunity to explore one of the world's largest aquariums. Dolphins in Depth offers guests the chance to learn about dolphin behavior as they closely observe researchers and trainers interacting with dolphins. Reservations for either tour can be made by calling 407-WDW-TOUR (939-8687). For more information on both of these programs, turn to page 203 of the *Everything Else in the World* chapter.

SEA BASE ALPHA: This prototype undersea research facility, spread over two levels, includes a visitors center and six rooms, each dedicated to a specific subject. One focuses on ocean ecosystems and shows various forms of adaptation, including camouflage, symbiosis, and bioluminescence.

A tremendous tank displays another coral reef where Bermuda morays, barracuda, and bonnethead sharks swim about. Another room is dedicated to the study of porpoises and manatees. A tank features a step-in port, where guests can see the mammals up close.

Guests can try a cutaway suit and test its maneuverability. There are also video screens to test and expand your knowledge of oceanography.

Adjacent to the six rooms of Sea Base Alpha, the Sea Base Concourse features several interesting displays.

The Land

Occupying six acres, this enormous skylighted pavilion examines the nature of one of everybody's favorite topics—food. A film, *The Circle of Life*, uses characters from *The Lion King* to deliver an entertaining yet inspirational message about humanity and the environment. A boat ride explores farming in the past and future.

Guided tours give visitors the chance to learn about the experimental agricultural techniques being practiced in the pavilion. In addition, the subject of nutrition is touched upon in one of Epcot's wackiest attractions, a musical show called Food Rocks.

Timing Tip: During peak seasons, lengthy queues build up for the boat ride and *The Circle of Life*. It's best to visit early in the morning and have a quick breakfast at the food court. Or wait until late afternoon, when many people have moved on to World Showcase.

BEHIND THE SEEDS: For guests interested in a more detailed look at the growing areas at The Land, one-hour guided tours take place throughout the day. Tours travel through four greenhouses where plants are grown hydroponically (without soil).

Different areas of the greenhouses showcase pioneering research projects undertaken in cooperation with NASA and the U.S. Departments of Agriculture and Energy. Because this walking tour is an expanded version of the Living with the Land boat ride, the ride is suggested as a prerequisite.

Reservations, which are required, must be made in person on the day of the tour, inside the Green Thumb Emporium. Cost is $6 for adults and $4 for children ages 3 through 9. The first tour of the day begins at 10:30 A.M. The reservations desk opens at 9 A.M. Book your tour as early as possible.

LIVING WITH THE LAND: The 13½-minute boat ride through the rain forest and greenhouses in this pavilion opens with a dramatic storm scene. Guests sail through tropical rain forests, prairie grain fields, and a family farm. As the boat passes through each realistic setting, the guide offers commentary on humanity's ongoing struggle to cultivate and live in harmony with the land. Note some of the details that make each setting so convincing, such as sand blowing over the desert, and light flickering from the television set in the farmhouse window.

In the next segment, guests enter a plant research laboratory and solarium. Here, our planet's major food crops are being grown in research projects, along with rare new crops that may someday help meet Earth's ever-growing dietary needs.

HOT TIP

Epcot is bigger than it seems, so allow yourself plenty of time to get from place to place. (It takes about a half hour to walk from Spaceship Earth to The American Adventure in World Showcase.)

The guide on each boat provides information on the crops being grown. Also of interest are the experiments being conducted to explore the possibilities of raising fish like other farm products, and a desert farm area, where plants get nutrients through a drip irrigation system that delivers just the right amount of water—important in a dry climate.

As fantastic and unreal as they appear, all the plants on view in the experimental greenhouses are living. In contrast, those in the biomes (the ecological communities viewed from the boat ride) were made in Disney studios out of lightweight plastic that simulates the cellulose found in real trees. The trunks and branches were molded from live specimens; the majestic sycamore in the farmhouse's front yard, for example, duplicates one that stands outside a Burbank, California, car wash. Hundreds of thousands of polyethylene leaves were then snapped on.

FOOD ROCKS: Classic songs have been humorously altered to deliver a nutritional message at this 15-minute mock rock concert. The show is set in a kitchen of cartoonish proportions, and life-size characters make this an entertaining show. It is hosted by Füd Wrapper, who was inspired by rap artist Tone Loc.

The opening number, performed by a "heavy metal" group—giant kitchen utensils atop a cartoon stove—is Queen's "Bohemian Rhapsody" with new lyrics. Musical guests include the Peach Boys, Neil

Moussaka, Chubby Cheddar, the Get-the-Point Sisters, and (Little) Richard.

It's interesting to note that Tone Loc, Chubby Checker, Neil Sedaka, Little Richard, and The Pointer Sisters actually recorded the parodies of their music.

THE CIRCLE OF LIFE: This 20-minute film uses animation and live action to illustrate some of the dangers to our environment, as well as potential solutions. Presented as a fable featuring *The Lion King* favorites Simba, Timon, and Pumbaa, the film takes an optimistic approach to a serious subject. It is shown in the Harvest Theater, just inside the entrance to The Land.

Soon after the film begins, Simba's startled by the exuberant shout of "Timber!" and is drenched by the splash of a fallen tree in the water. The culprits are none other than his friends Timon and Pumbaa, who are clearing the savanna for the development of the Hakuna Matata Lakeside Village. Simba seizes the opportunity to tell them a tale about creatures who sometimes forget that everything is connected in the Circle of Life: humans.

Simba demonstrates to Timon and Pumbaa the consequences of progress, as his lessons are driven home by visual evidence of humans' mistreatment of the air, water, and land. (Timon: "And everybody was *okay* with this?") The effect is a compelling mix of entertainment and a valuable message about environmental responsibility.

GREEN THUMB EMPORIUM: This little shop between Sunshine Season Food Fair and Food Rocks stocks land-related merchandise, such as hydroponic plants, seeds, and gardening books, as well as kitchen accessories, candy, and home products.

Imagination!

The oddly shaped pyramids that house the recently refurbished Imagination! pavilion are quite striking. But they pale in comparison with the experiences inside, which are easily among the most whimsical at Epcot. The crown jewel here is a dazzling 3-D movie called Honey, I Shrunk the Audience. Guests are also invited behind the scenes of the Imagination Institute in an all-new attraction called Journey Into Your Imagination.

Another pavilion highlight is the pair of quirky fountains outside—the Jellyfish Fountains, which spurt streams of water that spread out at the top, looking for an instant like their namesake sea creature, and the Leap Frog Fountains, which send out smooth streams of water that arc from one garden plot to another in the most astonishing fashion. Kids just can't get enough of them.

Timing Tip: During peak seasons, the queue outside seems to be longest from about 10 A.M. to noon and remains fairly lengthy throughout most of the day. Count on spending an hour at the very least at this new and improved pavilion.

JOURNEY INTO YOUR IMAGINATION: The Imagination Institute is rolling out the red carpet, inviting guests to step behind the scenes and get a sneak peek at its latest groundbreaking project: The Imagination Scanner. It seems the prototype is nearly ready, save for a bit of routine testing. Fortunately, there's no shortage of test subjects here at Epcot. Guests are literally lining up for the chance to serve as human guinea pigs.

The Imagination Scanner-induced sensory experiences begin soon after test subjects board their ride vehicle. A series of perceptual experiments is intended to change the way people think and see the world. Above all, the Imagination Scanner endeavors to blast the cobwebs off even the most dormant of imaginations. Special effects and optical illusions are combined to create images as fanciful as the imagination itself. The trip lasts eight minutes. (Keep an eye out for the empty cage in which a enormous butterfly mysteriously appears. It's amazing.)

Note: Fans of Figment need not lament. Though the tiny purple dragon has retired from active attraction-duty, he does put in a special appearance inside the Imagination! pavilion.

IMAGE WORKS: KODAK "WHAT IF" LABS: It's a rare Image Works visitor who doesn't experience at least some of the emotion felt by one young girl who cried every time her parents tried to take her home. That's not surprising, because Image Works is filled with activities that give every visitor the chance to use his or her imagination.

Although this interactive wonderland recently underwent extensive refurbishment, it has retained some old favorites. A true highlight for youngsters (though guests of all ages appreciate it) is an area called Stepping Tones. It's hopscotch with a musical twist. Another popular attraction invites guests to wave their arms conductor-style and, by doing so, trigger a cacophony of sounds, some more melodious than others.

A recent addition to this imaginative playground encourages guests to morph pictures of themselves into flowers, puppies, and even cartoon characters. Once you've been transformed into a daisy or a superhero, you can send the image to friends (or yourself) via the Internet.

Plan to spend up to an hour exploring these entertaining labs.

IMAGE WORKS SHOP: This spot at the exit to the Image Works: Kodak "What If" Labs offers merchandise themed to the Imagination! pavilion. It also provides a service whereby your image can be captured by computer and reproduced onto items such as charms and crystal cubes. You can have your mug slapped onto a mouse pad, poster, or a variety of other accessories. Guests are invited to create custom Walt Disney World CDs here, too.

EPCOT

HONEY, I SHRUNK THE AUDIENCE:

Welcome to the Imagination Institute, workplace of Professor Wayne Szalinski, the featured character in the three "Honey" movies: *Honey, I Shrunk the Kids*; *Honey, I Blew Up the Kid*; and *Honey, We Shrunk Ourselves.*

Rick Moranis, Marcia Strassman, and the kids reprise their familiar film roles at this 25-minute attraction.

In the pre-show area, guests see a movie about imagination. Then they are welcomed to the Imagination Institute and given an overview of what they will see inside the theater. Szalinski is to be presented with the Inventor of the Year Award, and will demonstrate several of his inventions. On the way into the theater, guests are provided with "protective goggles" (3-D glasses), to shield their eyes from the flying debris that can come loose during new-product demonstrations.

Once the audience is seated, Szalinski is nowhere to be found. Then he zooms off the screen in his new HoverPod, out of control and miniaturized by his shrinking machine. Szalinski's son Nick steps in to demonstrate the "Dimensional Duplicator," a machine that can make exact copies of anything. As Nick switches on the machine, his little brother Adam drops his pet mouse into the duplicating chamber and hits the number 999. Suddenly hundreds of mice pour out of the screen in an almost 4-D effect that leaves guests squirming.

Nick quickly gets rid of the mice with Professor Szalinski's No-Mess Holographic Pet System, which projects a 3-D cat out into the audience to scare away the mice. The cat morphs into a lynx and a ferocious lion before overheating and exploding. Just then, Szalinski returns, blows himself up to normal size, and demonstrates his new, more powerful, shrinking machine. The machine spins out of control and accidentally shrinks the audience and Nick. While the audience is miniaturized the theater shakes with every on-screen footstep. When apparent giants crouch down to ogle

Honey, I Shrunk the Audience is known to frighten small children and more than the occasional grown-up (especially those afraid of snakes or mice).

guests in the theater, it's a rare person who doesn't feel diminished to ant proportions. The effects are very believable, particularly when Adam picks up the theater and shows it to his mom. Motion effects in the theater add to the realism, as does the full-size pet snake that gets loose. The audience is eventually brought back to normal size, of course, although not without incident. The attraction has one last surprise in store which we won't divulge.

CAMERAS AND FILM:
A good selection of film is for sale here, along with disposable cameras and various other photographic essentials.

Test Track

Fasten your safety belt! This industrial-looking pavilion puts guests through the frenetic motions of auto- mobile testing. As vehicles progress along the track, they whiz down straightaways, hug

hairpin turns, and face near-collisions—and not always in ideal road conditions. En route, riders learn how tests are performed in real facilities (called proving grounds) and discover why certain procedures are crucial to car safety.

Before developing the attraction, Disney Imagineers toured GM proving grounds around the country. The result: From the roll-up doors of its steely facade to the rows of authentic testing equipment inside, Test Track bears more than a passing resemblance to the real thing.

The experience begins with a pre-show walking tour of the plant that reveals the incredible amount of component testing performed before automakers commit to production. Guests witness automotive testing vignettes, with everything from human interface (our courageous, crash-prone counterparts) to tires, brakes, air bags, and even seats being put through their paces.

The computer-controlled six-seater vehicles are equipped with video and audio, but no steering wheels or brake pedals. The roads bear the familiar lines and signage of the real world, adding to the attraction's realism.

The five-minute ride begins with an uphill acceleration test. Then the suspension gets a

workout, as vehicles descend over a bumpy surface that puts the wheels at odds with one another. During environmental testing, riders feel the heat and get the shivers as vehicles pass first through a radiant heat chamber, then a cold chamber. Roadside robots pitch in by spraying the fenders and door panels with water to test for corrosion.

The ride takes a dramatic turn during the road-handling segment. Vehicles course along a winding road, complete with simulated mountain scenery, and into a darkened tunnel. Passengers hear a horn blast, see the

HOT TIP If you don't mind splitting up your party, jump on Test Track's "single riders" line. It moves much faster than the standby line.

blinding high beams of a tractor trailer, and swerve to avoid the truck. As they emerge and the light level picks up, there is a crash; guests round a corner to witness a barrier crash test. Their own vehicles then accelerate toward the same barrier.

A long straightaway feeds into a series of heavily banked turns and another straight shot that sends vehicles rocketing around the pavilion at top speed (up to 65 miles per hour). Strobe lights add to the effect.

Note: Children under seven must be accompanied by an adult; guests under 40 inches are not permitted to ride; passengers must be free of back problems, heart conditions, motion sickness, and other physical limitations. Pregnant women are advised to sit this one out.

TEST TRACK SHOP: This retail spot features General Motors merchandise as well as items with a Test Track theme. Impulse buyers take note: There are no actual automobiles available for purchase here.

Wonders of Life

The 72-foot-tall steel DNA molecule at the entrance to this popular pavilion beckons guests to humorous and informative experiences related to health. Housed in a geodesic dome and two attached buildings, this pavilion allows guests to enjoy both a serious and an amusing look at health, fitness, and modern lifestyles. Wonders of Life also boasts Body Wars, Epcot's dramatic simulator ride—a fast and furious journey through the human body.

Once inside the building, guests find themselves at the Fitness Fairgrounds. At the Fairgrounds, a variety of shows and activities for both children and adults are offered. *Goofy About Health* is an eight-minute multiscreen montage that sees Goofy go from a sloppy-living guy to a health-conscious fellow. Using old Goofy cartoons that haven't been seen for many years, the show traces Goofy's ups and downs, and winds up with new footage of Goofy at his doctor's office. The film is shown in an open theater where visitors can come and go as they please.

At the AnaComical Players Theater, a wacky (but informative) show is presented by an improvisational theater group. Audience members are asked to participate, and it's all a lot of fun. This theater seats 100 people.

The third theater at the Fitness Fairgrounds is enclosed. The 14-minute film shown here, *The Making of Me*, is a story starring Martin Short as a man who wonders how he came into existence. To find out, he travels back in time to the birth of his parents, their first few years together, and their decision to have a child—him. Footage from an actual delivery is part of the film; it is sensitively presented and provides an accessible and touching view of childbirth. It was written and directed by Glenn Gordon Caron, who directed the TV show *Moonlighting*.

Parents should be aware that the film is a bit graphic and may not be suitable for some children. It also leaves a few key questions unanswered, thereby allowing parents to satiate their kids' appetite for knowledge on a case-by-case basis.

There are plenty of hands-on activities in areas surrounding the theaters. Guests can ride Wonder Cycles, computerized stationary bicycles that enable guests to pedal through a variety of locales, including Disneyland and the Rose Bowl Parade. At Coach's Corner, golf, tennis, or baseball swings are analyzed, and a professional knowledgeable in each sport offers free, albeit taped, advice to help you on your way. The Sensory Funhouse offers hands-on activities for the young and young at heart. It's the Disney version of a children's museum, where education and entertainment go hand in hand.

At the Lifestyle Revue, guests punch in such information as age, weight, height, exercise habits, whether they smoke, and perceived stress levels at an interactive computer terminal. The computer then processes the information and offers some advice on how to lead a healthier and less stressful existence.

Frontiers of Medicine, located toward the back of the Fitness Fairgrounds, features the only completely serious segment of Wonders of Life. Here, guests can see scientific and educational exhibits of leading developments in medicine and health sciences. The exhibits change regularly.

WELL & GOODS LIMITED: Located near Body Wars, this shop offers a selection of athletic wear, most of which features classic Disney characters participating in sporting activities, as well as educational materials.

CRANIUM COMMAND: This area of the Wonders of Life pavilion welcomes guests into the mind of a 12-year-old kid. The pre-show sets the mood as a brief animated film explains what you are about to see.

General Knowledge is recruiting pilots for an assortment of new brains. There are jokes aplenty, many of which go right over the heads of young kids. Buzzy, our star pilot, fumbles through basic training and gets assigned to one of the most volatile brains of them all, that of an adolescent boy.

Inside a 200-seat theater, the enormously exaggerated head of our 12-year-old subject is piloted by Buzzy, a delightfully goofy Audio-Animatronics figure. The two large eyes are actually rear-projection video screens, and it is through them that the audience gets an idea of how a young boy thinks and reacts. The other animated participant, General Knowledge, helps Buzzy learn which portion of the mind is required for a particular situation.

The right and left sides of the brain, the stomach, the heart, and the adrenal gland are all represented by perfectly cast, celebrities. One such actor is George Wendt (Norm from *Cheers*), operating the stomach. Other characters include Bobcat Goldthwait as the adrenal gland, Dana Carvey and Kevin

Nealon (Hans and Franz of *Saturday Night Live* fame) as the heart, Charles Grodin as the left brain, and Jon Lovitz as the right brain.

Cranium Command is an altogether whimsical and entertaining show—one of Epcot's best. This 17-minute presentation is fast-paced and packed with so many details that you'll notice new things even after seeing it many times.

BODY WARS: The same state-of-the-art technology that sends guests on a rollicking ride through space at the Star Tours attraction at the Disney-MGM Studios also exists at Wonders of Life in the form

of this five-minute thrill ride. After boarding the vehicles, which are actually the same type of flight simulators employed by military and commercial airlines in pilot training, guests are whisked away on a rough and exciting ride through the human body. Movie buffs will think immediately of the films *Fantastic Voyage* and *Inner Space*.

The queue area features exhibits from a fictional company specializing in the latest technology in the miniaturization of people. Guests pass through two special-effects portals and are ready to do a routine medical probe of the human body—from the inside.

During the course of this bumpy trip, a scientist is dispatched to remove a splinter that has made its way beneath the patient's skin. Guests go along for the ride but end up on a rescue mission when the scientist is attacked by a white blood cell. Of course, there are some problems along the way, making this trip seem out of control.

Note: This is a somewhat rougher ride than Star Tours, its simulator-ride counterpart at the Disney-MGM Studios. Signs posted outside Body Wars warn that passengers must be free of back problems, heart conditions, motion sickness, and other such physical limitations. Pregnant women should not ride Body Wars. Children must be at least 40 inches tall to ride. Finally, if the sight of blood makes you woozy, this attraction is probably not for you.

Universe of Energy

Although it's easy to spot this pavilion's mirrored pyramid, the facade doesn't provide any clue at all to the 45 minutes of surprises in store. One of the most technologically complex experiences at Epcot, the

show consists of several movies and a ride-through segment. None of these is exactly what guests might expect. This is especially true after the pavilion's 1996 renovation, which repackaged the attraction, placing its legendary Audio-Animatronics dinosaurs and lofty environmental message in a decidedly funny and much more personal context.

The show begins with a film (featuring a few familiar faces). In it, a character named Ellen is watching *Jeopardy!*. One of the contestants is Ellen's annoying college roommate Judy.

Ellen plays along but keeps striking out, particularly in the ENERGY category. As she watches, her neighbor Bill Nye, the Science Guy, pops in and is aghast at Ellen's ignorance. Shortly thereafter, Ellen falls asleep.

Ellen dreams she is a contestant on the show, competing against her former friend Judy and Albert Einstein. This time, all of

133

the questions are about energy. As Einstein ponders and Ellen fumbles, Judy is racking up points. Ellen, who has a negative score ("this nightmare game is a lot harder than the home version"), decides to freeze her dream and ask Bill Nye, the Science Guy, for some help.

The second segment leads guests into a theater where Bill vows to educate Ellen about the importance of energy. He persuades her to travel back in time to see where some of our energy sources came from. Suddenly, the whole seating area rotates, then breaks up into six sections that move slowly forward.

The vehicles embark with Ellen upon an odyssey through the primeval world. Enormous prehistoric trees crowd the forest. Apatosauruses wallow in the lagoon out front. A lofty allosaurus battles with an armored stegosaurus, and an elasmosaurus bursts out of a tide pool with frightening suddenness—all under the vulturelike gaze of winged creatures known as pteranodons.

Next, guests move out of the forest and view a montage of pictures capturing the history of civilization, from cave dwellers to the present. (Keep your eyes peeled for the wacky caveman who discovers fire—chances are, you'll recognize him.) The issue of alternative energy sources is raised, and the message is that there is no save-all source, but rather there are many possibilities with promise.

The attraction winds up with Ellen returning to the game show of her dreams. This time, she's beating her friend Judy, who is not at all happy about how much Ellen has learned during the commercial break. Ellen bets everything in the final round. In order to win, she must name the one energy source that will never be depleted. (We won't reveal the answer, but we're not too proud to brag about getting it right!)

Almost as intriguing as the attraction is the technology behind it. The vehicles weigh about 30,000 pounds when fully loaded with passengers, yet are guided along the floor by a wire that is only *one-eighth inch thick*.

DID YOU KNOW...

There are two acres of solar panels on the rooftop of Future World's Universe of Energy pavilion. Together, they generate 15 percent of the energy it takes to power the attraction housed inside. (It's enough energy to run six average homes.)

WORLD SHOWCASE

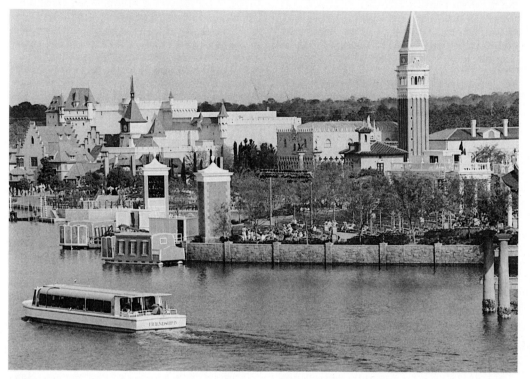

Noble sentiments about humanity and the fellowship of nations, which have motivated so many world's fairs in the past, also inhabit World Showcase. But make no mistake about it: This area of Epcot is unlike any previous international exposition.

The group of pavilions that encircles World Showcase Lagoon (a body of water that is about the size of 85 football fields, with a perimeter of about 1.2 miles) demonstrates Disney conceptions about participating countries in remarkably realistic, consistently entertaining styles. You won't find the real Germany here; rather, the country's essence, much as a traveler returning from a visit might remember what he or she saw.

Shops, restaurants, and attractions are housed in a group of structures that is an artful pastiche of all the elements that give that nation's countryside and towns their distinctive flavor. Although occasional liberties have been taken when scale and proportion required, careful research governed the design of every nook and cranny.

Equally impressive is the cuisine. With no fewer than eleven upscale eateries to choose from, it's no wonder some guests here do nothing but nosh. (That is especially true during Epcot's popular Food and Wine Festival, a time when dozens more nations contribute to an already fortified international menu. See page 12 for additional information.)

HOT TIP

World Showcase pavilions do not open until 11 A.M. However, guests may use the International Gateway entrance up to a half hour prior to Future World's official opening time.

In the shops, many of the wares represent the country in whose pavilion they are sold. Craftspeople are occasionally on hand to demonstrate their arts. Thanks to special cultural exchange programs and recruiting efforts, many World Showcase staffers hail from the countries the pavilions represent.

A diverse lineup of entertainment ensures that all visitors experience more than a little culture, foreign or otherwise. The entertainment is as authentic as the Disney casting directors can make it, with native performers commonly featured and new festivities always in the works.

Pavilions are described in the order in which they would be encountered while moving counterclockwise around the World Showcase Lagoon after crossing the bridge from Future World.

Canada

Celebrating the many beauties of the U.S.A.'s neighbor to the north, the area devoted to the Western Hemisphere's largest nation is complete with its own mountain, waterfall, rushing stream, rocky canyon, mine, and splendid garden massed with colorful flowers. There's even a totem pole, a trading post, and an elaborate, mansard-roofed hotel similar to ones built by Canadian railroad companies as they pushed west around the turn of the century. All this is imaginatively arranged somewhat like a split-level house, with the section representing French Canada on top, and another devoted to the mountains alongside it and below. From a distance, the Hôtel du Canada, the main building here, looks like little more than a bump on the landscape—as does Epcot's single Canadian Rocky Mountain. But up close they both seem to tower as high as the real thing.

The gardens were inspired by the Butchart Gardens in Victoria, British Columbia, a famous park created on the site of a limestone quarry. The hotel is modeled after Ottawa's Victorian-style Château Laurier. Lively, engaging entertainment is provided by a troupe of Celtic rock musicians called "Off-Kilter," and the Pipes of Nova Scotia.

O CANADA!: This 17-minute motion picture, presented in Circle-Vision 360 inside Canada's mountain, portrays the Canadian confederation in all its coast-to-coast splendor—the prairies and plains, sparkling shorelines and rivers, and the untouched snowfields and rocky mountainsides surround you. The Royal Canadian Mounted Police also put in an appearance. All the maritime provinces are pictured, with their covered bridges and sailing ships, as is Montreal, with its old-world cafes and churches; the scene in the Notre-Dame Basilica, with its organ booming and choirboys in attendance, is particularly stirring.

The great outdoors gets equal play. In one scene, snow geese take off all around the screen, and the beating of their wings is positively thunderous. Eagles, possums, mallards, bobcats, wolves, bears, deer, bison, and herds of reindeer can also be seen.

Filmed, too, were steers being roped at a rodeo and the chuck wagon race that takes place every year at that great provincial fair known as the Calgary Stampede. Skiers in the vast and empty Bugaboos, dogsledders, and ice-skaters are featured in the winter scenes; in a hockey game, the sound system almost perfectly conveys the scratch of skates on ice and the sharp whack of sticks slamming against the puck. And throughout, the motion picture provides a you-are-there feeling that makes all of this spectacular scenery still more memorable. Note that there are no seats in this theater.

NORTHWEST MERCANTILE: The first shop to the left upon entering the pavilion's plaza features merchandise by Roots, a Canadian apparel label. The Roots line features athletic attire, shoes, and fragrances. The shop also stocks plush toys, maple syrup, and other Canada-themed collectibles. Skeins of rope, tin scoops, lanterns, and antique ice skates hanging from the long beams overhead set the mood, together with the structure itself.

LA BOUTIQUE DES PROVINCES: This small shop inside Hôtel du Canada, which features a variety of items with an Anne of Green Gables theme, also proffers jewelry, prints, ceramics, and giftware.

United Kingdom

In the space of only a few hundred feet, visitors to this pavilion stroll from an elegant London square to the edge of a canal in the rural countryside—via a bustling urban English street framed by buildings that constitute a veritable rhapsody of historic architectural styles. But one scene leads to the next so smoothly that nothing ever seems amiss. Here again, note the attention to detail: the half-timbered High Street structure that leans a bit, the hand-painted "smoke" stains that make the chimneys look as if they had been there for centuries. When a thatched roof is required, it's right where it should be—though the roof may be made of plastic broom bristles because fire regulations prohibit the real thing. Off to the side is a pair of scarlet phone booths identical to those that used to be found all around the U.K. And there are eight architectural styles characteristic of the streetscapes, from English Tudor to Georgian and English Victorian.

There is no major attraction in this pavilion; instead, it features half a dozen fine shops and a pub that serves a selection of beers and ales that would be the toast of any first-class "local" in London itself. There's also plenty of good entertainment, including a group of comedians called the World Showcase Players, who, when not engaged in general clowning on the World Showcase Promenade, coax audience members into participating in their farcical playlets. In the pub, a pianist plays, takes requests, and interacts with guests late into the evening. A mop-topped quartet known as the British Invasion occasionally plays Beatles tunes in the garden courtyard.

Disney characters also make appearances and pose for photos in the garden courtyard throughout the day.

THE TOY SOLDIER: This delightful shop presents a variety of British toys, as well as a rather extensive selection of merchandise starring Winnie the Pooh, Piglet, Eeyore, and Tigger, too. Outside, the shop resembles a stone manor built during the last half of the 16th century.

THE CROWN & CREST: This shop looks like a backdrop for a child's fantasy of the days of King Arthur, with its high rafters decked out with bright banners, vast fireplace (and crossed swords above), and immense wrought-iron chandelier. English dart boards, fragrance products, "pub mugs," glasses that serve yards of beer,

limited-edition chess sets, and coin and stamp sets are the stock-in-trade at this emporium adjoining The Toy Soldier. Name histories and family crests are also available.

PRINGLE OF SCOTLAND: Shop here for apparel and accessories centered around uniquely British locales and events. You can expect to find a wide assortment of Wimbledon tennis garb, golf items from Scotland's Royal and Ancient Golf Club at Saint Andrews, plus Rugby shirts and Cambridge and Oxford University attire. Don't miss the tartan map on the wall opposite The Crown & Crest; it identifies plaids from Glen Burn and Gordon to Langtree and St. Lawrence.

> **HOT TIP**
>
> One of the best places to watch IllumiNations: Reflections of Earth is from a lagoonside table at the Rose & Crown Pub in the United Kingdom pavilion. Try to snag a table about 30 minutes before the show is scheduled to begin.

THE QUEEN'S TABLE: This shop (opposite Pringle of Scotland) may be one of the loveliest in Epcot. This is particularly true of the store's elegant Adams Room, embellished with elaborate moldings, hung with a crystal chandelier, and painted in cream and robin's-egg blue. The setting is a lovely background for the selection of superbly crafted collector's statuettes. Perfumes, soaps, fine china, and other items are also available.

Don't forget to inspect small, serene Britannia Square just outside the shop entrance farthest from World Showcase Promenade. But for its somewhat reduced scale and the distinctively Floridian climate, it feels almost like London itself.

THE MAGIC OF WALES: This small emporium offers pottery, jewelry, souvenirs, and handcrafted gifts from Wales. Despite its modest size, it does the highest volume of business among the United Kingdom shops.

THE TEA CADDY: Fitted out with heavy wooden beams and a broad fireplace to resemble the Stratford-upon-Avon cottage of William Shakespeare's wife, Anne Hathaway, this shop stocks English teas, both loose and in bags, in a variety of flavors. Other items include teapots, biscuits, and assorted candies.

International Gateway

GATEWAY GIFTS: Disney memorabilia, fresh coffee, convenience items, and a package pickup depot are located at this spot near the France entrance.

WORLD TRAVELER: Disney fashions and character merchandise plus film and a drop-off for two-hour film processing are conveniently located here.

STROLLER AND WHEELCHAIR RENTAL: Strollers and wheelchairs are available for rent at this location. Remember to keep your rental receipt; it can be used on the same day in the Magic Kingdom, the Disney-MGM Studios, Animal Kingdom, or again in Epcot should you leave and return at a later hour. It is also possible to get a replacement stroller at this location.

France

The buildings here have mansard roofs and casement windows so Gallic in appearance that you expect to see some sad bohemian poet looking down from above. A canal-like offshoot of the lagoon seems like the Seine itself; the footbridge that spans it recalls the old Pont des Arts. There's a kiosk nearby like those that punctuate the streets of Paris and a bakery whose heavenly rich aromas announce its presence long before it's visible.

Shops sell perfumes and other luxury items. Their roofs are of real copper or slate, and the cabinetry is finely crafted. Galerie des Halles—the iron-and-glass-ceilinged market that Paris once counted as one of its most beloved institutions—lives again (near the Palais du Cinéma exit). But perhaps most special of all are the people. Hosts and hostesses who hail from Paris and the French provinces answer questions in lyrically French-accented English. It's fun to take in the shows put on by The Statues, amazing white-robed performers who stand motionless and then suddenly change poses when you least expect it.

Some interesting background notes: The dusty rose–colored, lace-trimmed costumes that the hostesses wear were inspired by the

Where to Eat in Epcot

A complete listing of all eateries—full-service restaurants, fast-food emporiums, and snack shops—can be found in the *Good Meals, Great Times* chapter. See the Epcot section beginning on page 221.

dresses in *Le Bar aux Folies-Bergère* by the Impressionist painter Edouard Manet, and the main entrance to the pavilion recalls the architecture of Paris, most of which was built during the Belle Epoque ("beautiful age"), the last decades of the 19th century.

Don't miss the garden on the opposite side of this arcade. It is one of the most peaceful spots in World Showcase.

IMPRESSIONS DE FRANCE: Shown in the Palais du Cinéma, an intimate, elegant little theater that's not unlike the one at Fontainebleau, this enchanting 18-minute film takes viewers on a trip through France.

The film shows off a beautiful tree-dotted estate, fields and vineyards at harvest time, a flower market and a luscious pastry shop, the ribbed tongue of a glacier, and a harbor full of squawking gulls. Viewers visit the Eiffel Tower; Versailles and its gilt Hall of Mirrors (just outside Paris); Mont Saint Michel; the French Alps; and Cannes, the star-studded resort city on the Mediterranean coast. All this is even more appealing thanks to a superb sound track, consisting almost entirely of the music of French classical composers.

The exceptionally wide screen adds yet another dimension. This is not a Circle-Vision 360 film like the movies shown at China and Canada. The France film used only five cameras, and it is shown on five large projection surfaces—200 degrees around. It's a beautiful film, one of the park's best.

PLUME ET PALETTE: This is one of the loveliest shops in all of World Showcase. The Art Nouveau style is reflected in the curves that embellish the wrought-iron balustrade edging the mezzanine and the moldings that decorate cherry-wood cabinets and shelves.

LA SIGNATURE: Another beautiful spot, this boutique features a selection of Guerlain cosmetics and fragrances.

GALERIE DES HALLES: Souvenirs—from Eiffel Tower statues to CDs with music by French composers—are the stock-in-trade at this location near the exit of the cinema. Gifts themed to the artwork of French artists, such as Monet and Renoir. Mugs, tote bags, umbrellas, and picture frames are among the offerings. The area is based on Paris' now-demolished Les Halles, designed by noted architect Victor Baltard.

L'ESPRIT DE PROVENCE: This shop stocks dinnerware and kitchen accessories from the Provence region of Southern France.

LA MAISON DU VIN: Selections in this lovely wine shop range from the inexpensive to the pricey, from *vin ordinaire* going for several dollars to upward of $290 for a rare vintage. Wine tastings are held here to sample the offerings (a small charge is levied, but you get to make a souvenir of the glass). Those who don't want to carry their purchases may have them dispatched to Package Pickup for retrieval later in the day (allow at least two hours for arrival).

Morocco

Nine tons of tile were handmade, handcut, and shipped to Epcot to create this World Showcase pavilion. To capture the unique quality of this North African country's architecture, Moroccan artisans came to Epcot to practice the mosaic art that has been a part of their homeland for thousands of years. Koutoubia Minaret, a detailed replica of the famous prayer tower in Marrakesh, stands guard at the entrance. A courtyard with a fountain at the center leads to the Medina (Old City). Between the traditional alleyways and the more modern sections are the pointed arches and swirling patterns of the Bab Boujouloud gate, a replica of the one that stands in the city of Fez. An ancient working waterwheel irrigates the gardens, and the motifs repeated throughout the buildings include carved plaster and wood, tile, and brass. Mo'rockin takes over the courtyard, with musicians playing western music with an Arabic twist.

GALLERY OF ARTS AND HISTORY: This museum houses ever-changing exhibits of Moroccan art, artifacts, and costumes.

MOROCCAN NATIONAL TOURIST OFFICE: An information center offering literature useful in planning a visit to Morocco. This is also the place to inquire about a "Morocco Tour." The tour of the pavilion includes an in-depth description of the culture, history, and architecture of Morocco. Tours, which are held hourly and are free to Epcot guests, generally last from 20 to 45 minutes.

CASABLANCA CARPETS: Rabat carpets with colorful geometric designs, prayer rugs, wall hangings, and throw pillows are among the offerings here.

HOT TIP Don't try to fit all of the World Showcase movies into one day, especially if you are traveling with kids.

TANGIER TRADERS: This is the place to shop for a fez, woven belts, leather sandals and purses, and other traditional Moroccan clothing and accessories.

MARKETPLACE IN THE MEDINA: Hand-woven baskets, sheepskin wallets and bags, and assorted straw hats are available.

THE BRASS BAZAAR: Interspersed among the decorative brass items in this shop are ceramic pitchers, planters, pots, bottles of rosewater, serving sets, and soapstone carvings.

SOUK AL MAGREB: This small waterside enclave on the promenade spills over with crafted brasswork. Baskets and leather goods abound.

Japan

Serenity rules in Japan. Except, of course, when the pavilion resounds with traditional Japanese music performed by a drum-playing duo or group.

The landscaping, designed in accordance with traditional symbolic and aesthetic values, contributes to the pavilion's peaceful mood. Rocks, which in Japan represent the enduring nature of the earth, were brought from North Carolina and Georgia (since

boulders are scarce in the Sunshine State). Water, symbolizing the sea (which the Japanese consider a life source), is abundant; the Japan pavilion garden has a stream and pools inhabited by *koi* (fish). Evergreen trees, which in Japan are symbols of eternal life, are here in force.

Disney horticulturists created this very Japanese landscape using few plants native to that country because the climate there is so different from that of Florida. Among the few trees here native to Japan are the *sago* near the courtyard entrance to the Yakitori House; the two Japanese maple trees, identifiable by their small leaves, not far away (near the first stairway from the promenade on the left side of the courtyard as you face it); and the prickly monkey-puzzle trees near the walkway to the promenade, on The American

Adventure side of the pagoda. Needle-sharp thorns make the latter the only species of tree that monkeys cannot climb.

The pagoda was modeled after an eighth-century structure located in the Horyuji Temple in Nara, Japan. The striking *torii* gate on the shore of World Showcase Lagoon derives from the design of the one at the Itsukushima shrine in Hiroshima Bay.

BIJUTSU-KAN GALLERY: Housing a changing cultural display, this small art museum has offered, among other exhibitions, "Netsuke—Historic Carvings of Old Japan," a showcase of traditional Japanese art forms that features carved miniatures (from a private collection).

MITSUKOSHI DEPARTMENT STORE: There are kimonos in silk, cotton, and polyester; T-shirts bearing Japanese characters; traditional headdresses; and an excellent selection of bowls and vases meant for flower arranging. But on the whole, no one would ever apply the term *quaint* to this spacious store set up by Mitsukoshi—an immense, three-century-old retail firm.

The shop features a large selection of kimonos, as well as chopsticks, bonsai, jewelry, china, paper fans, and origami products. There is also a bounty of snacks, candies, and tea. The pleasant atmosphere and variety of merchandise make this establishment a rewarding experience for both the casual browser and the serious shopper.

The building's design was inspired by the Gosho Imperial Palace, which was constructed in Kyoto in 794 A.D.

The American Adventure

When it came to creating The American Adventure, the centerpiece of World Showcase, Disney Imagineers were given relatively free rein. So the 110,000 bricks of the imposing Colonial-style structure that houses a show, fast-food restaurant, and shop are of real brick—made *by hand* from soft Georgia clay.

The show inside stands out because of its wonderfully evocative settings, its detailed sets, and the 35 superb Audio-Animatronics players, some of the most lifelike ever created by the Disney organization. A superb a cappella vocal group called Voices of Liberty periodically serenades guests in the building's foyer. By all means catch a performance.

THE AMERICAN ADVENTURE SHOW: One of the truly outstanding Epcot attractions, this 26-minute presentation celebrates the American spirit from our nation's earliest years right up to the present. Beginning with

the arrival of the Pilgrims at Plymouth Rock and their hard first winter on the western shore of the Atlantic, the Audio-Animatronics narrators—an amazingly lifelike Ben Franklin and a convincing, cigar-puffing Mark Twain—recall key people and events in American history: the Boston Tea Party, George Washington and the grueling winter at Valley Forge, the influential abolitionist Frederick Douglass, the celebrated 19th-century Nez Percé chief Joseph, and many more. The Philadelphia Centennial Exposition is remembered, along with women's rights campaigner Susan B. Anthony, telephone inventor Alexander Graham Bell, and the steel giant and philanthropist Andrew Carnegie. Naturalist John Muir converses onstage with Teddy Roosevelt. Charles Lindbergh, Rosie the Riveter, Jackie Robinson, Marilyn Monroe, and Walt Disney are represented. So are John Wayne, Lucille Ball, Margaret Mead, John F. Kennedy, Martin Luther King Jr., and Billie Jean King.

The idea is to recall episodes in history, both negative and positive, that contributed to the growth of the spirit of America, either by engendering "a new burst of creativity," (in the designers' words) "or a better understanding of ourselves as partners in the American experience."

For information about how each of the historical figures spoke during his or her lifetime, researchers contacted historians and cultural institutions—the Philadelphia Historical Commission, Harvard's Carpenter Center of Visual Arts, the State Historical Society of Missouri, the Department of the Navy's Ships Historical Branch, and others. When recordings were not available, educated guesses were made: Alexander Graham Bell's voice was created on the basis of contemporary comments about his voice's clarity, expressiveness, and crisp articulation, combined with the fact that his father taught elocution.

A special highlight of the show is the majestic music played throughout by the Philadelphia Symphony Orchestra.

Seats in the front of the house give the optimal view of the Audio-Animatronics figures (although all of the seats provide an acceptable view of the show.) One of the best times to schedule a visit is during a performance of IllumiNations: Reflections of Earth (provided that you've already seen the nighttime spectacular). Check a park guidemap for exact showtimes. If you have some extra time before the show, be sure to read the inspirational quotes on the walls— Jane Addams, Charles Lindbergh, Herman Melville, and Ayn Rand are among the Americans who are quoted.

Timing Tip: As one of the best of all the World Showcase attractions, The American Adventure show is often quite busy. Perhaps the best time to schedule a visit is soon after World Showcase opens for the day or in the early evening. Make an effort to catch a performance by the talented Voices of Liberty—you won't regret it.

HERITAGE MANOR GIFTS: Visit this shop to find authentic Americana. Gifts include patriotic clothing, housewares, autographs of famous Americans, and books about American history.

AMERICA GARDENS THEATRE: An ever-changing slate of entertainment is presented throughout the week in this lakeside amphitheater in front of The American Adventure pavilion. Check your guidemap for details and exact times. Showtimes are also posted on the promenade at the east and west entrances to the theater.

Be sure to note the pruning of the western sycamores overhead: the old-fashioned pollarding method used, which involves trimming the treetops flat and allowing the lower branches to fill out and interlock, eventually produces a thick canopy. The flower beds outside are planted appropriately with red, white, and blue blossoms.

Italy

The arches and cutout motifs that adorn the World Showcase reproduction of the Doge's Palace in Venice are just the more obvious examples of the attention to detail lavished on the individual structures in this relatively small pavilion. The angel atop the scaled-down campanile was sculpted on the model of the original right down to the curls on the back of its head—then covered with real gold leaf, despite the fact that it was destined to be set almost 100 feet in the air.

The other statues in the complex, including the sea god Neptune presiding over the fountain in the rear of the piazza, are similarly exact. And the pavilion even has an island like Venice's own, its seawall appropriately stained with age, plus moorings that look like barber poles, with several distinctively Venetian gondolas tied to them. St. Mark the Evangelist is also remembered, together with the lion that is the saint's companion and Venice's guardian; these can be seen atop the two massive columns that flank the small arched footbridge that connects the island to the mainland. The only deviation from Venetian reality is the alteration of the site of the Doge's Palace in reference to the real St. Mark's Square.

The sounds of opera, accompanied by an accordion and guitar, frequently fill the courtyard. Some of the most interesting entertainment at this pavilion is provided by Nova Era, a contemporary group performing classically inspired music from Venice.

The pavilion is equally interesting from a horticultural point of view. The island boasts kumquat trees, citrus plants typical of the Mediterranean, and a couple of olive trees that can be seen on both sidewalls of the Delizie Italiane. Originally located in a Sacramento, California, grove, the olive trees arrived in Florida via flatbed truck a bit slimmer than when they started out. (Arizona border inspectors decreed that the trees be trimmed to the ten-foot width

required by state law; therefore, the ancient olives were shorn en route. The hardy trees survived, leaving only their scars to remind visitors of the ordeal; the darker bark is what remains of the original, while the lighter areas are new growth.) The tall, narrow trees that stand like dark columns are Italian cypresses, which are extremely common in their native country.

DELIZIE ITALIANE: This open-air market on the western edge of the piazza is a good spot for a sweet snack of tasty Italian chocolates and other goodies.

IL BEL CRISTALLO: There is an abundance of fine leather goods, including purses, wallets, bags, and belts at this shop (just off the promenade on the Germany side of the piazza). Delicate Armani porcelain figurines are also on display. Other featured wares include scarves, ties, fragrances and jewelry.

LA BOTTEGA ITALIANA: This gourmet shop tempts with an assortment of Italian pastries and desserts. Expect to find wines from some of the finest vineyards in Italy. Wine tastings are held here daily. An eclectic blend of decorative ceramics rounds out the selection.

Germany

There are no villages in Germany quite like this one. Inspired by various towns in the Rhine region, Bavaria, and the German north, it boasts structures reminiscent of those found in urban enclaves as diverse as Frankfurt, Freiburg, and Rothenburg. There are stair-stepped rooflines and towers, balconies and arcaded walkways, and so much overall charm that the scene seems to come straight out of a fairy tale. The beer hall to the rear is almost as lively as the one at Munich's famed Oktoberfest, especially late in the evening. The shops, which offer a range of merchandise from wine and sweets to ceramics and cuckoo clocks, toys, and books—and even art—are so tempting that it's hard to leave the area empty-handed.

The elements that constitute the Germany pavilion are described here as they would be encountered walking from west to east (counterclockwise) around the cobblestone-paved central plaza, which is known as the St. Georgsplatz, after the statue at its center. St. George, the patron saint of soldiers, is depicted with a dragon that legend says he slew during a pilgrimage to the Middle East.

Try to time your World Showcase peregrinations to bring you to Germany on the hour, when the handsome, specially designed glockenspiel at the plaza's rear can be heard chiming in a melody composed specifically for the pavilion. Check the guidemap to see if a German trio will be performing outside the Biergarten restaurant.

DAS KAUFHAUS: This two-story structure, whose exterior is patterned after a merchants' hall known as the Kaufhaus (located in the German town of Freiburg in Breisgau), stocks an assortment of limited-edition steins and glassware. (Film and sundries are also available.)

VOLKSKUNST: Small and exceptionally appealing, this establishment is filled with a burgher's bounty of German timepieces, plus

a smattering of other items made by hand in the rural corners of the nation. As for cuckoo clocks, some are small and unobtrusive, while others are so immense that they'd look appropriate only in some cathedral-ceilinged hunting lodge.

DER TEDDYBAR: Located adjacent to Volkskunst, this toy shop would be a delight if only for the lively mechanized displays: Some of the stuffed lambs and the dolls wearing folk dresses (called *dirndls*) have been animated so that tails wag and skirts swirl in time to German folk tunes. The shop is also home to one of WDW's best selections of toys, including an assortment of expensive stuffed keepsakes from Steiff. Colorful wooden toys are tempting as well, along with all kinds of building blocks. Last but not least, the dolls are simply wonderful—you can even have one customized to your personal specifications.

KUNSTARBEIT IN KRISTALL: This shop to the left of the Biergarten features Austrian and crystal jewelry, tall beer mugs, wineglasses in traditional German tints of green and amber, and crystal decanters. Guests can have glassware etched on the spot.

SUSSIGKEITEN: It's a mistake to visit this tiny confectionery shop on an empty stomach: Chocolate cookies, butter cookies, and almond biscuits mix with caramels, nuts, and pretzels on the shelves, and there are boxes upon boxes of *Lebkuchen*, the spicy crisp cookies traditionally baked in Germany at Christmas, not to mention Gummy Bears (which the packages announce as *Gummibaeren*). Be sure to note the attractive display of old Bahlsen sweets by the door.

WEINKELLER: The Germany pavilion's wine shop, situated between the cookie shop and the crystal shop toward the rear of St. Georgsplatz, offers about 250 varieties of German wine produced and bottled by H. Schmitt Söhne, one of Germany's oldest and largest vintners. Wine tastings are held here daily. The selection includes not only those vintages meant for everyday consumption, but also fine estate wines. These are white (with a few exceptions), because white wine constitutes the bulk of Germany's

vinicultural output. (Only 20 percent of all German bottlings are red.) The setting itself is quite attractive—low-ceilinged and cozy, and full of cabinets embellished with carvings of vines and bunches of grapes.

DIE WEIHNACHTS ECKE: This is a shop that can set a visitor's mind to thoughts of Christmas—even in the hottest dog days of summer. Ornaments, decorations, and gifts manufactured by various German companies line the shelves of this store. Among them are wood carvings made in the German town of Oberammergau, nutcrackers, and a whole collection of "smokers" (carved wooden dolls with a receptacle for incense and a hollow pipe for the smoke to escape).

GLAS UND PORZELLAN: Featuring glass and porcelain items made by the German firm of Goebel, this is an attractive establishment with rope-turned columns, curved moldings, delicate scrollwork, and tiny carved rosettes. But no matter how attractive the background, the stars of the show are the M. I. Hummel figurines that Goebel makes. Cherubic, rosy-cheeked children, shown carrying baskets, trays, umbrellas, and other items—depicted as in the drawings of a young German nun named Berta Hummel—are favorites of collectors around the world. There is always an elaborate showpiece at the center of the shop, and a Goebel artist is here to demonstrate the process by which Hummel creations are painted and finished.

China

Dominated by the Disney equivalent of Beijing's Temple of Heaven and announced by a pair of banners that offer good wishes to passersby (the Chinese characters translate: "May good fortune follow you on your path through life" and "May virtue be your neighbor"), this pavilion conveys a level of serenity that offers an appealing contrast to the hearty merriment of the bordering Germany and the gaiety of nearby Mexico. Part of this quiet environment is the by-product of the soothing traditional Chinese music. Live flute, zither, or dulcimer music is performed inside the Temple of Heaven, while agile acrobats do tricks in the courtyard. The gardens also make a major contribution. They are full of rosebushes native to China, and there is a century-old mulberry tree (to the left of the main walkway into the pavilion), with a pomegranate tree and a wiggly-looking Florida native known as a water oak nearby.

The number of stones in the floor of the pavilion's main structure is not random; the center stone is surrounded by nine stones because nine is considered a lucky number in China. Around the edge of the outer room rise 12 columns—because 12 is the number of months in the year and the number of years in a full cycle of the Chinese calendar. Be sure to stand on the round stone in the center: Every whisper is amplified.

A spacious emporium is devoted to Chinese wares, and two Chinese restaurants add to the overall atmosphere. However, all this is secondary to the motion picture shown inside the Temple of Heaven—a Circle-Vision 360 film that is one of the most diverting World Showcase attractions.

WONDERS OF CHINA: LAND OF BEAUTY, LAND OF TIME: This 19-minute presentation shows the beauties of a land that few Epcot visitors have seen firsthand—and does it so vividly that it's possible to see the film twice and still not fully absorb all the wonderful sights. The Disney crew was the first Western film group to shoot certain sites, and their remarkable effort includes such marvels as Beijing's Forbidden City; vast,

Village Traders

Located between Germany and China, this open-air shop sports a selection of gift items from Africa, India, and Australia. Browse through such souvenirs as boomerangs, handbags, hats, and of course, T-shirts.

wide-open Inner Mongolia and its stern-faced tribespeople; the 2,400-year-old Great Wall; the Great Buddha of Leshan; and the 3,000-year-old city of Suzhou. Its location on the Grand Canal, which is believed to be the largest man-made waterway in the world, led Marco Polo to call it the Venice of the East. Note that the theater has no seats.

HOUSE OF WHISPERING WILLOWS: When exiting, pass by the House of Whispering Willows, an exhibit of ancient Chinese art and artifacts. Changed about every six months, it invariably includes fine pieces from well-known collections.

YONG FENG SHANGDIAN: This vast Chinese emporium, located off the narrow, charming Street of Good Fortune, offers a huge assortment of merchandise—silk robes, prints, paper umbrellas, embroidered items, and more. Trinkets, moderately priced items, and expensive antiques are available in an array that may be matched in few places in the United States. The calligraphy on the curtains wishes passersby good fortune, long life, prosperity, and happiness.

Norway

Set between Mexico and China is Norway, a pavilion added to the World Showcase mix in 1988. Built in conjunction with many Norwegian companies, the pavilion celebrates the rich history, folklore, and culture of one of the Western world's oldest countries.

The cobblestone town square is an architectural showcase of the styles of such Norwegian towns as Bergen, Alesund, and Oslo. There's also a Norwegian castle fashioned after Akershus, a 14th-century fortress still standing in Oslo's harbor; the castle here houses the Akershus restaurant. Few can resist walking into the bakery for a taste of its treats. In a show of modernity, a statue of Norway's living legend, marathoner

Grete Waitz, stands behind the bakery. Shops stock handicrafts and folk items: hand-knit woolens, wood carvings, and glass and metal artwork.

For a free guided tour of the pavilion and a crash course in Norwegian culture and architecture, stop by the Norway Tourism desk. Consult a park guidemap for tour times.

MAELSTROM: Appropriately, visitors tour Norway by boat—16-passenger, dragon-headed longboats inspired by those Eric the Red and other Vikings used a thousand years ago. The five-minute voyage through time begins in a tenth-century Viking village where a ship is being readied to head out to sea. Seafarers then find themselves in a mythical Norwegian forest, populated by trolls who cause the boats to plummet backward, through a maelstrom to the majestic grandeur of the Geiranger fjord, where the vessel narrowly avoids spilling over a waterfall. Ultimately, after a plunge through a rocky passage, the boats wind up in the stormy North Sea. Lightning flashes reveal an enormous oil rig; as the boat passes the concrete platform legs, the storm calms and a coastal village appears on the horizon.

Survivors disembark and enter a small movie theater, where the journey continues on-screen for five additional minutes, giving visitors a sense of the scenic spectacles and unique personalities that make up modern Norway.

STAVE CHURCH GALLERY: Inside the wooden stave church, there is a small exhibit that explores Norwegian culture. It's interesting to note that only 28 stave churches remain in Norway today.

THE PUFFIN'S ROOST: Norwegian gifts, sweaters, activewear, fragrances, jewelry, fine leather goods, pewter, candy, toys, and trolls are the wares for sale at this shop.

Mexico

The tangle of tropical vegetation surrounding the great pyramid that encloses this pavilion and the Mexican restaurant at the lagoon's edge on the promenade provide only the barest suggestion of the charming area inside.

Dominated by a re-creation of a quaint plaza at dusk, the pyramid's interior is rimmed by balconied, tile-roofed, colonial-style structures. Crowding a pretty fountain area is a quartet of stands selling Mexican handicrafts, and to the left is a shop stocked with other handsome wares. The Mariachi Cobre band keeps things lively. To the rear, the San Angel Inn, a corporate cousin of the famous Mexico City restaurant, serves authentic Mexican fare. Behind it, the pavilion's main show chronicles Mexican culture from earliest times right up to the present.

Take a look at the cultural exhibit inside the pyramid entrance on the way in. Note that the pyramid itself was inspired by Meso-American structures dating from the third century A.D.

EL RIO DEL TIEMPO: THE RIVER OF TIME: Over the course of this six-minute boat trip, sprinkled with vignettes of pre-Columbian, Spanish colonial, and modern Mexican life, visitors greet a Mayan high priest, watch performers dance, and are assailed by vendors at a market. A band dressed to look like skeletons entertains at one juncture (in a reference to the Day of the Dead, a holiday celebrated in Mexico with candies and sweets shaped like skulls and skeletons). The cheery montage of film, props, and Audio-Animatronics figures is reminiscent of It's a Small World.

Timing Tip: During peak seasons, long lines, which prevail from late morning on, usually thin out in the afternoon.

PLAZA DE LOS AMIGOS: Brightly colored paper flowers, sombreros, malachite, peasant blouses, baskets, and pottery make this *mercado* (market) at the plaza's center as bright and almost as lively as one in Mexico itself. The colorful papier-mâché piñatas that figure strongly in the scenery here are so popular that Epcot has to buy them from suppliers by the truckload.

ARTESANIAS MEXICANAS: This shop carries Mexican-made home decor items. Among the featured items are candles, glasses, and pottery.

EL RANCHITO DEL NORTE: Gifts and souvenirs from northern Mexico are the featured items at this spot.

LA FAMILIA FASHIONS: Mexican fashions and accessories for families; silver and turquoise jewelry is available.

Showcase Plaza

PORT OF ENTRY: A children's shop carrying infants' and kids' clothing, girls' character dresses, plush dolls, and toys.

DISNEY TRADERS: Merchandise combining the charms of Disney characters and World Showcase themes is the primary stock-in-trade. Sunglasses, film, and sundries are also available.

ENTERTAINMENT

Epcot presents an intriguing array of live performances each day, making it very important for guests to consult an entertainment schedule when they arrive (it's printed on the park guidemap). For information about special events at Epcot, see the "Holidays & Special Events" section of *Getting Ready to Go*. For up-to-the-minute schedules call 407-939-4636.

AMERICA GARDENS THEATRE: The venue alongside the lagoon at The American Adventure pavilion hosts an ever-changing program of diverse live entertainment. Top name performers may appear throughout the summer. Check a park guidemap for current offerings.

FOUNTAIN OF NATIONS: This dramatic fountain in Future World's Innoventions Plaza breaks into a computer-choreographed water ballet every 15 minutes.

ILLUMINATIONS: REFLECTIONS OF EARTH: Unveiled during Walt Disney World's Millennium Celebration, this nighttime spectacular presents the entire history of our planet in 13 minutes—from its creation to the present and a look toward the future. A dazzling mix of lasers, fireworks, fountains, and original music, this show is a highlight of any Epcot visit. The extravaganza, visible from anywhere on the World Showcase Promenade, takes place nightly at closing time. There are excellent viewing locations all around the World Showcase lagoon. Note that additional viewing areas have been added to the stretch between the Germany and China pavilions.

KIDCOT FUN STOPS: There is an activity area in each of the countries of World Showcase. These spots allow young guests to play games and make crafts that are native to each country's culture. Note that these areas are best enjoyed by small children.

TAPESTRY OF NATIONS: Each evening, World Showcase puts on a festival—complete with giant puppets, primal percussion units, and tribal dances—to mark the beginning of the new millennium. Check a guidemap for showtimes. (At press time, this show was expected to run throughout 2001.)

WORLD SHOWCASE PERFORMERS: It's all but impossible to complete a circuit of World Showcase without catching a few performances en route. Keep an eye on the schedule to take in live entertainment at each pavilion, often performed by natives of the country represented. Among the possibilities: worldly comedians, a Mexican mariachi band, Moroccan belly dancers, Chinese acrobats, Canadian bagpipers, African drummers, and more. For details, see descriptions in the "World Showcase" section of this chapter.

Holiday Happenings

During certain holidays, such as the Fourth of July, Christmas, and New Year's Eve, Epcot usually stays open extra late and presents added entertainment for the occasion.

Note, too, that World Showcase keeps an international holiday calendar. January visitors might celebrate Scottish Heritage Day or Chinese New Year. In February there is the Black Heritage Celebration at The American Adventure. Constitution Day is celebrated in Norway on May 17. July packs France's Bastille Day, Japan's Tanabata Festival, and Canada's Dominion Day, in addition to the USA's Fourth of July. Germany's Oktoberfest and Morocco's Independence Day get their turn in October. Call 407-939-4636 to confirm schedules.

CHRISTMAS: Epcot celebrates the holiday in a big way, with a nightly tree-lighting ceremony, a lighted archway that hugs the pathway to Showcase Plaza, and a candlelight choral processional.

The Candlelight Processional, a beautiful presentation of traditional holiday songs, features a reading of the Christmas story by a celebrity narrator. This is a very popular event (and one of our favorites!).

HOT TIPS

- Stop by Guest Relations or any shop for a free guidemap. Consult the entertainment schedule first thing.

- Lines throughout Epcot are longest at midday and shortest in the early evening.

- During peak seasons, preferred priority seating times at Epcot's table-service restaurants book quickly—arrange for priority seating as far in advance as possible. However, some tables may be available on a first-come, first-served basis (with a bit of a wait).

- Most World Showcase restaurants seat guests until park closing. To make advance plans call 407-WDW-DINE (939-3463).

- Check the Tip Board in Innoventions Plaza for wait times at the most popular attractions and adjust your plans accordingly.

- If you plan to play at Image Works, the delightful interactive play area inside Imagination!, bring along the e-mail address of a friend. It may come in handy.

- Allow plenty of time to explore the hands-on exhibits at Innoventions East and West, and Image Works in Imagination!, as well as Fitness Fairgrounds inside the Wonders of Life pavilion.

- Guests staying at WDW resorts can have purchases delivered to their hotels for free.

- Although a *FriendShip* water taxi is unlikely to transport you across World Showcase Lagoon any faster than a brisk walk would, it is a peaceful, foot-friendly way to make the half-mile-plus journey.

- Several interactive fountain areas at Epcot provide guests of all ages with an opportunity to cool off. Be sure to pack swimsuits (or waterproof diapers) for little ones who will undoubtedly spend time splashing in the water.

Where to Find the Characters

Characters host each meal at The Land's Garden Grill restaurant and many appear in a special greeting area next to Mouse Gear. Goofy is often spotted at Wonders of Life. In World Showcase, characters often favor the country of their literary origin. You may discover *Snow White* characters in Germany, familiar faces from *Beauty and the Beast* and *The Hunchback of Notre Dame* in France, friends from *Aladdin* in Morocco, and the cast of *Mulan* in China. The United Kingdom has been home to Winnie the Pooh, Alice in Wonderland, Mary Poppins, and others. Note that characters are subject to change at any time. Check a guidemap for exact locations or ask a park employee.

EPCOT

150

Disney-MGM Studios

153 Getting Oriented

154 Park Primer

155 Main Attractions

163 Shopping

165 Entertainment

166 Hot Tips

Welcome to "the Hollywood that never was and always will be." So said Walt Disney Company chairman Michael Eisner when he officially opened the Disney-MGM Studios in April 1989. A bit hokey—but also true. Enter the gates and the mosaic of flashy neon, chromed Art Deco and streamlined architecture, and star-gazing street characters immediately plunge you into the Hollywood of the 1940s. A nostalgic view of the moviemaking capital has been combined with revealing backstage tours, a variety of entertaining attractions, and a delightful selection of eateries to create this Walt Disney World enclave.

The Studios' water tower, known to punsters (for obvious reasons) as the "Earffel Tower," is reminiscent of the structures looming over most Hollywood studios of the Golden Age. Here, however, it gets that special Disney touch—it's capped by a Mouseketeer-style hat.

Even as the Studios enters its second decade, the park continues to expand and evolve. Its eclectic lineup of classic attractions is joined by a trio of thrilling newcomers: an enhanced (and scarier) Tower of Terror, the rollicking Rock 'n' Roller Coaster, and an explosive struggle between good and evil in Fantasmic! Each adds a whole new dimension to the Hollywood term *action*.

What makes this area of Walt Disney World different from other Disney theme parks is the extent to which guests can participate in the attractions. Our best advice is to volunteer, wherever and whenever possible. It's fun, and it adds enormously to the experience.

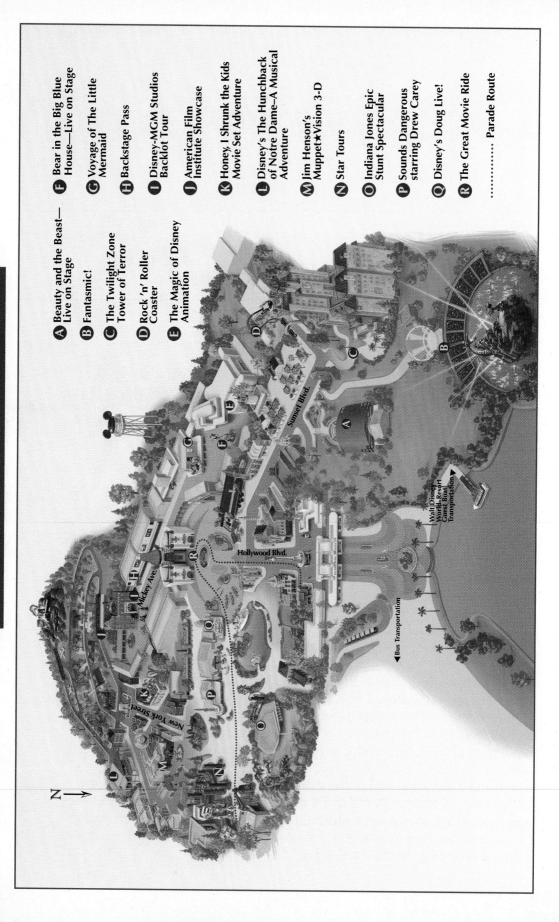

A Beauty and the Beast—Live on Stage

B Fantasmic!

C The Twilight Zone Tower of Terror

D Rock 'n' Roller Coaster

E The Magic of Disney Animation

F Bear in the Big Blue House—Live on Stage

G Voyage of The Little Mermaid

H Backstage Pass

I Disney-MGM Studios Backlot Tour

J American Film Institute Showcase

K Honey, I Shrunk the Kids Movie Set Adventure

L Disney's The Hunchback of Notre Dame—A Musical Adventure

M Jim Henson's Muppet★Vision 3-D

N Star Tours

O Indiana Jones Epic Stunt Spectacular

P Sounds Dangerous starring Drew Carey

Q Disney's Doug Live!

R The Great Movie Ride

••••••••• Parade Route

Sunset Blvd.

Hollywood Blvd.

New York Street

St. Mickey Ave.

Walt Disney World Resort Guest Boat Transportation ▶

▲Bus Transportation

N →

GETTING ORIENTED

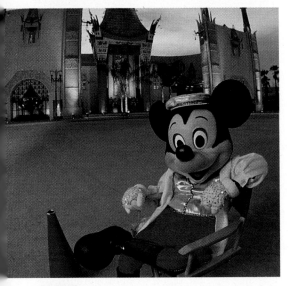

While the Disney-MGM Studios is much smaller than Epcot, the park has a sprawling layout with no distinctive shape or main thoroughfare. As such, the Studios can be a bit of a challenge to navigate. Be sure to study a guidemap as you enter.

The park entrance is at Hollywood Boulevard. This shop-lined avenue leads straight to Hollywood Plaza, address of the Studios' most central landmark, a replica of Mann's Chinese Theatre that doubles as the site of The Great Movie Ride. Walking along Hollywood Boulevard toward the plaza, you'll come to the first major intersection, Hollywood Junction. Here, a wide, palm-fringed thoroughfare known as Sunset Boulevard branches off to the right.

Stroll down Sunset Boulevard and you'll come across The Hollywood Hills Amphitheater, home of Fantasmic!, and Rock 'n' Roller Coaster starring Aerosmith. At the street's far end is The Hollywood Tower Hotel, home of The Twilight Zone Tower of Terror. The strip is also graced with shops, the Sunset Ranch Market, and the Theater of the Stars amphitheater, where Beauty and the Beast—Live on Stage is performed daily.

Stand in Hollywood Plaza facing the Chinese Theater, and you'll notice an archway just off to your right; this leads to Animation Courtyard, an area with a backstage feel to it. Mickey Avenue, the street veering off to the left of Animation Courtyard, leads to The Disney-MGM Studios Backlot Tour and Backstage Pass.

If you turn left off Hollywood Boulevard and proceed past Echo Lake, you are on course for such attractions as Disney's Doug Live!, Sounds Dangerous starring Drew Carey, Indiana Jones Epic Stunt Spectacular, and Star Tours. Just beyond Star Tours there is one more entertainment zone, near New York Street. The high-profile attractions here: Jim Henson's Muppet*Vision 3-D, Disney's The Hunchback of Notre Dame—A Musical Adventure, and the Honey, I Shrunk the Kids Movie Set Adventure.

HOW TO GET THERE

Take Exit 25 off I-4. Continue about a half mile to reach the parking area. Take a tram to the park entrance.

By WDW Transportation: From the Swan, Dolphin, Yacht and Beach Club, and Board-Walk: boat or walkway. From Fort Wilderness and Downtown Disney: bus to the Transportation and Ticket Center (TTC), then transfer to the Disney-MGM Studios bus. From the Magic Kingdom, Epcot, Animal Kingdom, all other WDW resorts, and the resorts on Hotel Plaza Boulevard: bus.

PARKING

All-day parking at the Studios is $6 for day visitors (free to WDW resort guests). Trams circulate regularly, providing transportation from the parking area to the park entrance. Be sure to note the section and the aisle in which you park. Also be aware that the parking ticket you receive allows for re-entry to the parking area throughout the day.

HOURS

The Disney-MGM Studios is usually open from 9 A.M. until about one hour after sunset. During certain holiday periods and summer months, hours are extended. It's best to arrive at least a half hour before the posted opening time, particularly during busy seasons. Depending on the season, some stage shows do not open until late in the morning.

Admission Prices

ONE-DAY TICKET
(Restricted to use only in the Disney-MGM Studios. Prices include sales tax and are subject to change.)

Adult	$48.76
Child*	$39.22

*3 through 9 years of age; children under 3 free

PARK PRIMER

BABY FACILITIES

Changing tables and facilities for nursing mothers can be found at the Baby Care Center in the Guest Relations lobby near the park entrance.

CAMERA NEEDS

The Darkroom on Hollywood Boulevard stocks film, batteries, and disposable cameras. Film processing is offered here and wherever you see a Photo Express sign. Film is sold in most Studios shops.

DISABILITY INFORMATION

Most Walt Disney World attractions, restaurants, shops, and shows are accessible to guests using wheelchairs. Additional services are available for guests with visual or hearing disabilities. For a detailed overview of the services offered, including transportation, parking, attraction access, and more, pick up a copy of the *Guidebook for Guests with Disabilities* at Guest Relations. For more information, see the "Travelers with Disabilities" section of *Getting Ready to Go.*

EARLY-ENTRY DAYS

On Wednesday and Sunday, WDW resort guests may enter the Disney-MGM Studios up to 1½ hours before the official opening time to enjoy such attractions as Tower of Terror, Jim Henson's Muppet*Vision 3-D, The Great Movie Ride, Rock 'n' Roller Coaster, and Star Tours. Early-entry days and attractions are subject to change.

FIRST AID

Minor medical problems can be handled at the First Aid Center, located next to Guest Relations at the park entrance.

INFORMATION

Guest Relations, located just inside the park entrance, has free guidemaps and an ever-resourceful staff. To make same-day dining arrangements for certain Studios eateries, go to the booth at the junction of Hollywood and Sunset boulevards.

LOCKERS

Lockers, found at Oscar's Super Service, near the entrance, cost $5 per day (including a $2 refundable deposit) for unlimited use.

LOST & FOUND

Located near the park entrance, past the turnstiles on the right. To report lost items after your visit, call 407-824-4245.

LOST CHILDREN

Report lost children at Guest Relations or alert a Disney employee to the problem.

MONEY MATTERS

There is an ATM just outside the park entrance, and one inside Toy Story Pizza Planet Arcade. In addition to cash, credit cards (American Express, Visa, Discover, JCB, Diner's Club, The Disney Credit Card, and MasterCard), traveler's checks, and WDW resort IDs are accepted for admission, merchandise, and meals at all restaurants.

PACKAGE PICKUP

Shops can arrange for cumbersome purchases to be transported to package pickup at the Lost and Found (near the park entrance), where they can be picked up later. There is no charge for this service.

SAME-DAY RE-ENTRY

Be sure to have your hand stamped upon exiting the park and to retain your ticket if you plan to return later the same day.

STROLLERS & WHEELCHAIRS

Strollers, wheelchairs, and Electric Convenience Vehicles (ECVs) may be rented from Oscar's Super Service, located just inside the park entrance on the right. Cost for strollers and wheelchairs is $6, plus a $1 refundable deposit. Cost for ECVs is $30, plus a $10 refundable deposit. Remember to keep your receipt, which can be used on the same day for a stroller or wheelchair replacement at the Magic Kingdom, Epcot, Animal Kingdom, or at the Studios (at The Writer's Stop shop). Quantities are limited.

TIP BOARDS

Check the boards at the junction of Hollywood and Sunset boulevards and on New York Street to learn the current waiting times for the most popular attractions in the park. Tip Boards also list showtimes. Hosts and hostesses stand nearby to provide additional information.

THE MAIN ATTRACTIONS

The Disney-MGM Studios has a brand of attractions altogether unique. Some offer guests behind-the-scenes looks at the creative and technical processes that generate television, movies, and animation. Others go so far as to allow guests to gain a bit of showbiz experience along with the insight. Still others resurrect popular characters and stories in new forms—from stage shows to thrill rides.

Because many shows and attractions are presented at scheduled times, it's very important to consult a guidemap or the park's Tip Board for starting times.

The Twilight Zone Tower of Terror

The Hollywood Tower Hotel is the decrepit home of an exhilarating ride— which is now, thanks to a dramatically altered

drop sequence and enhanced special effects, more thrilling than ever. On the facade of the 199-foot-tall building (the tallest attraction at any Disney theme park) hangs a sparking electric sign. As the legend goes, lightning struck the building during a storm on Halloween night in 1939. An entire guest wing disappeared, along with an elevator carrying five people.

BIRNBAUM'S ★BEST★

The line for the ride winds through the lobby, where dusty furniture, cobwebs, and old newspapers add to the eerie atmosphere. As guests enter the library, they see a TV brought to life by a bolt of lightning. Rod Serling intones a monologue, inviting them to enter The Twilight Zone.

Guests are led toward the boiler room to enter the ride elevator. (This is your chance to change your mind about riding. Simply ask the attendant to direct you toward the "chicken exit.") Once you take a seat in the elevator, the doors close and the room begins its ascent. At the first stop, the doors open and guests have a view down a corridor. Among the many effects is a ghostly visit by the hotel guests who vanished. The doors close again and you continue your trip skyward.

At the next stop, you enter the Fifth Dimension, a combination of eerie sights and sounds reminiscent of *The Twilight Zone* TV series. In fact, Disney Imagineers watched each of the 156 original *Twilight Zone* episodes at least twice for inspiration. Notice the clock that ticks incessantly as it hangs in midair, and the giant eyeball (watch it closely and you may see your image floating inside). This part of the ride is a disorienting experience, in part because the elevator is actually moving horizontally.

What happens next depends upon the whim of Disney Imagineers, who have programmed the ride so that the drop sequence can easily be changed. At press time, the elevator was taking an immediate plunge (of about eight stories) before traveling quickly back up to the 13th floor. At the top (about 157 feet up), passengers can look out at the Studios below. Once the doors shut, you plummet 13 stories. The drop lasts about 2 seconds, but it seems longer.

Just when you think it's over, the vehicle launches skyward, barely stopping before it plunges again. And again. As you exit, Rod Serling offers a helpful tip: Next time, use the stairs.

From the time you are seated in the service elevator, the trip takes about five minutes. Note that you must be at least 40 inches tall to ride. It is not recommended for pregnant women, those with a heart condition, or people with back and neck problems.

TOWER SHOP: Located near the attraction exit, this is the spot to shop for items featuring The Hollywood Tower Hotel logo.

Rock 'n' Roller Coaster starring Aerosmith

The newest and fastest roller coaster in Walt Disney World history is guaranteed to rock your world. Open since summer 1999, it's ideally suited for those who consider the Tower of Terror a little on the tame side.

The indoor attraction reaches a speed of 60 miles per hour—in 2.8 seconds flat. Other twists include two loops and a corkscrew—marking the first time Disney has ever turned guests upside down on American soil.

The ride's premise is this: The rock band Aerosmith has invited you to a backstage party. The only thing standing between you and the big bash is a classically chaotic Los Angeles Freeway.

To get to the party on time, you'll have to zip through the nighttime L.A. streets in a stretch limo. The ride vehicles (designed to resemble limousines) are equipped with a high-tech sound system (five speakers per seat make for a mega-decibel ride), and the remainder of the journey features rockin' synchronized sound—adding a dramatic dimension to the roller coaster experience most daredevils have come to expect.

HOT TIP You'll need to stop at a locker (near the park entrance) before riding Rock 'n' Roller Coaster— there's no place to store loose articles in the ride vehicles.

You must be free of back, neck, and heart problems to experience this topsy-turvy tour. Expectant mothers are advised to sit this one out. Guests must be at least 48 inches tall to ride.

Beauty and the Beast—Live on Stage

Here's the show that gave birth to the Broadway musical. Several times each day, Belle, Gaston, Mrs. Potts, and the rest of the cast of the Disney film *Beauty and the Beast* come to life at the 1,500-seat Theater of the Stars on Sunset Boulevard.

BIRNBAUM'S BEST

The 20-minute show is as entertaining as they come. The staging's just right and the music simply addictive as it traces the classic tale—from Belle's dissatisfaction with her life in a small French town to the climactic battle between the staff of the Beast's castle and Gaston and the townspeople. Lumière and friends perform the song "Be Our Guest" with a delightful display of dancing flatware. The happy-ending finale, complete with fluttering doves, is a delight. Although showtimes vary, the first performance of the day usually takes place in the morning.

The Magic of Disney Animation

This tour, which was recently revised and updated, gives guests an insider look at the creative process behind Disney's many animated blockbusters. In each 35-minute tour (which run continuously), guests learn about animation and watch Disney animators as they work their magic. (They are generally on duty weekdays until about 5 P.M.)

The tour begins with a hilarious film featuring Robin Williams and Walter Cronkite. It offers a lesson in the basics of animation. The film is followed by a meeting with an actual Disney artist. Feel free to ask any questions that cross your mind—this is an interactive, if informal, presentation.

Next stop: the recently expanded animation studio. Once inside the studio, guests see the story room, where plot lines are developed for animated features. Then it's off to the drawing boards, where characters undergo the metamorphosis from pencil sketch to moving picture. Working at their desks in full view of visitors, Disney animators are seen creating the drawings that will later appear in real films. A tour guide describes what the artists are doing at any given moment.

There's a special treat at the end of the tour: Copies of some of the many Academy Awards won by the Disney animation team are on display, along with drawings from famous films.

Before moving on, spend some time browsing at the Animation Gallery, where Disney animation cels, exclusive limited-edition reproductions, books, figurines, and many other collectibles are for sale.

Voyage of The Little Mermaid

One of the Disney-MGM Studios' most popular attractions, this is a 15-minute live musical production, adapted from the Disney animated classic. The show is presented in a theater with an underwater feel. In it, many of the film's animated characters, such as Flounder and Sebastian, are

HOT TIP

An elevated stage makes it tough for small children to see all the details in the Voyage of The Little Mermaid. The best vantage point is from the lap of a grown-up.

brought to life by puppeteers. The show opens with the lively song "Under the Sea," then animated clips from the movie are shown as actors join the puppets onstage.

Ariel is the star and performs songs from the film. Prince Eric makes an appearance, and an enormous Ursula glides across the stage to steal Ariel's voice. Of course, as in the movie, the happy ending prevails. The story line is a bit disjointed, hopping from scene to scene, and some of the signature songs are missing. However, most viewers are familiar with the plot of the film, so this choppiness doesn't detract much from the show.

There are excellent special effects, including cascading water, lasers, and a lightning storm that may be a bit intense for younger children. Note that many of the effects are best enjoyed from the middle to the rear of the theater.

Bear in the Big Blue House—Live on Stage

Put on your dancing shoes! Bear, Tutter, Pip, Pop, and the rest of the gang will be very disappointed if you don't join in the fun as they perform playful ditties from their Disney Channel show. Most popular with preschoolers, this stage show gets off to a bit of a slow start: Bear is sound asleep. Once audience members rouse him from his nap (no easy task), he bursts into song, welcoming one and all to his big blue house. Later, Bear invites his new friends to investigate the day's mail, pay tribute to his beloved home, search for Shadow, and, of course, do the Bear Cha Cha.

The performance space, which resembles a working television production studio, accommodates large crowds (of mostly tiny people) at a time. There are no seats per se, but there's plenty of room to sprawl out on the carpeted floor. Bear in the Big Blue House—Live on Stage is presented in the Animation Courtyard area of the park. Check a guidemap for showtimes.

Disney-MGM Studios Backlot Tour

Guests go backstage to see—and experience—some little-known aspects of TV and movie production on a tour of authentic sets and prop stations. Highlights of the 35-minute tour (which runs continuously throughout the day) include two special-effects sequences in which guests learn how natural disasters and waterborne scenes can be created on a studio set.

HOT TIP

Guests on the left side of the tram may get wet at Catastrophe Canyon, while those on the right stay dry. Choose accordingly.

First stop is an outdoor special-effects area, where two guests are tapped to hit the high seas. The show demonstrates the effects that can be used to reproduce battle scenes at sea in a water tank. Pyrotechnics, simulated depth charges, and torpedo blasts combine in an action-packed display.

Guests then board the trams that travel to the backlot area. Each trip begins with a look at the wardrobe department. More than 100 designers produce costumes for all of Disney's movie, TV, and other entertainment projects—and with 2.5 million garments, Walt Disney World has the world's largest working wardrobe. Famous costumes are on display.

The tram then passes through the camera, props, and lighting departments. A look into the scene shop reveals carpenters at work on sets that are later finished on the soundstages.

The tram turns into the backlot residential street, where empty, hollow facades give the outward appearance of a lovely neighborhood. Used mainly for exterior shots, the houses on this street include Vern's home from *Ernest Saves Christmas*, the facade of *The Golden Girls* home, and the house from *Empty Nest*.

Where in Central Florida can you find an active oil field in the middle of a dry, rocky, barren desert canyon prone to flash floods? In Catastrophe Canyon! As the guide will tell you, crews are filming a movie in which a backstage tram gets stuck in the canyon during a flash flood. But supposedly it's safe to go in because they're not filming today.

In a series of special effects, a rainstorm begins. Then there's an explosion, complete with flames that are so hot even riders on the right side of the tram feel them, followed by a flash flood that is so convincing it forces everyone to lean the other way. The road underneath the tram shifts and dips, lending even more reality to the adventure.

From Catastrophe Canyon, the tram rides by New York Street, where meticulously reproduced building facades line the urban street. Though the brickwork looks authentic, these backless facades are constructed mostly of fiberglass and Styrofoam. The skyscrapers, including the Empire State Building and the Chrysler Building, are actually painted flats. Forced perspective (the same technique that makes Cinderella Castle appear much taller than it is) makes the four-story Empire State Building appear as if it were the actual 104-story structure. After the tour, if crews are not filming, guests can explore New York Street on foot. Note that it is possible to visit New York Street without experiencing the backlot tour.

Timing Tip: Early morning tends to be the best time to visit this attraction.

Backstage Pass

This behind-the-scenes tour gives guests an inside look at movie and television production. The experience focuses on the TV sitcom *Home Improvement* and the creative processes that were necessary to produce it.

The 25-minute guided walking tour begins with a video clip. Guests are then led into a room called Jim Henson's Creature Shop, where they see all kinds of props used to produce TV and movie magic. The guide explains how certain props help filmmakers create action scenes that would otherwise be impossible to shoot.

Before the tour proceeds to the Special Effects Stage, a guest is randomly picked to participate as an actor in a scene from *Home Improvement*. The crowd learns how film or video shot against a blue screen can be superimposed onto any background. Then the "actor" is taped while performing in front of the blue screen. The footage is edited into a scene and shown to guests.

Then it's on to the soundstages, where soundproof catwalks allow visitors to gawk and talk all they want. The tour takes in three soundstages, where filming may (or may not) be in progress for movies or television shows.

American Film Institute Showcase

Though it is the final stop on the Disney-MGM Studios Backlot Tour, it is possible to visit this treasure chest of Hollywood memorabilia without taking the Backlot Tour itself. Costumes, props, and set pieces used in recent, as well as classic, movies and television programs are on display in this ever-changing exhibit.

Although showcased items may be different when you visit, displays have included Barbara Stanwyck's costume from *Sorry, Wrong Number*, the police car from *Dick Tracy*, an Academy Award won by the film *My Fair Lady*, concept artwork from *Toy Story*, and live-action sets and stop-motion puppets from *James and the Giant Peach*. Other props have come from *Star Wars, Evita, Armageddon, George of the Jungle*, and the television show *Home Improvement*.

The Great Movie Ride

Housed inside a full-scale reproduction of historic Mann's Chinese Theatre, this 22-minute attraction captivates guests' imaginations from the start. The queue area winds through the lobby and into the heart of film-making, where guests will see famous movie scenes on a large screen. The guided tour begins in an area reminiscent of the hills of Hollywood (which as the famous, now

abbreviated sign indicates, was once known as Hollywoodland) in its heyday. As a ride vehicle whisks guests under a vibrant marquee, they are transported to the celluloid world of yesteryear.

HOT TIP Parts of The Great Movie Ride may be a little intense for young children.

More than 60 dancing mannequins atop a cake greet guests in a replay of the "By a Waterfall" scene from the Busby Berkeley musical *Footlight Parade*. Gene Kelly's memorable performance from *Singin' in the Rain* is the next scene, in which rain seems to drench the soundstage but does not dampen the spirits of the Audio-Animatronics representation of Mr. Kelly. (Gene Kelly personally inspected his likeness.) Then Mary Poppins and Bert the chimney sweep entertain (Julie Andrews and Dick Van Dyke, respectively), as Mary floats from above via her magical umbrella and Bert sings "Chim Chim Cher-ee" from a rooftop.

From the world of musical entertainment, guests segue to adventure. James Cagney re-creates his role from *Public Enemy* as the ride proceeds along Gangster Alley. A mob shootout begins and puts guests in the midst of an ambush. An alternate route leads to a western town, where John Wayne can be seen on horseback eyeing some would-be bank robbers. When the thieves blow up the safe and flames pour from the building, heat can be felt from the trams.

As the ride vehicle glides into the spaceship from *Alien*, Officer Ripley guards the corridor while a slimy monster threatens riders from overhead. (Note that this and other scenes are presented in a dark setting and may upset young children.)

The legendary farewell from *Casablanca* is also depicted, complete with a lifelike Rick and Ilsa. (Ingrid Bergman's daughter Isabella Rossellini has brought her kids here to "see Grandma.") Guests are moved from the airfield to the swirling winds of Munchkinland, where a house has just fallen on the Wicked Witch of the East. Her sister, as portrayed by Margaret Hamilton, appears in a burst of smoke. This Audio-Animatronics figure is impressively realistic (and scary). But happy endings prevail, and guests follow Dorothy and company along the Yellow Brick Road to the Emerald City of Oz. As the ride draws to a close, guests view a montage of memorable moments from classic films.

Timing Tip: If the queue extends outside the building, you're in for a long wait. It takes about 25 minutes to reach the ride vehicles once you've entered the theater.

Sounds Dangerous starring Drew Carey

As you streak around a hairpin curve, precariously positioned in the driver's seat of a speeding car, you may want to check the security of your safety belt. Don't bother. There are no seatbelts. Why? As its name indicates, this attraction only *sounds* dangerous. The majority of the action takes place in your head, thanks to a personal headset and some remarkably convincing stereo sound effects.

This 3-D audio adventure occurs inside a television soundstage. Audience members (that's you) are on hand to watch a new show being filmed. The program, *Undercover Live*, follows a detective (played by Drew Carey) as he attempts to solve cases in the real world. Drew sports a tiny camera on his tie, so the audience can see and hear all the action.

Initially, all goes according to plan. Drew infiltrates a warehouse owned by the United Snowglobe Company. He suspects they are smuggling something, although can't put his finger on just what the contraband is. (Nor does he catch on after brushing past a box labeled SMUGGLED DIAMONDS, KEEP CLEAR.)

As Drew breaks into a suspect's office, he pulls the camera out of his tie tack, to give the audience a closer look at his lock-picking prowess. The unexpected appearance of a security guard sends a wave of panic over our hero and he quickly hides the camera . . . in his mouth. Snap, crackle, black-out — the camera's video feed shorts out. Fortunately, the audio is unaffected, so it's on with the show!

From here on in, it's all about 3-D sound. (Drew Carey actually wore tiny microphones on his ears to achieve this effect.) Drew's mad pursuit to catch the bad guys takes audience members everywhere from a room full of buzzing honeybees to a barber

shop for a quick trim and blow dry. The case is finally resolved at the circus, but not before a close encounter with a prancing pachyderm.

The show, which runs continuously, lasts about 12 minutes. Generally fun for everyone, it does have its dark and intense (remember the bees?) moments.

Disney's Doug Live!

A new superstar has moved into town, in an attraction that has replaced SuperStar Television. Perhaps you've heard of him: Doug Funnie? Whether you consider yourself

a fan or not, rest assured that this original musical production delivers an engaging theatrical wallop for everyone — even for those unfamiliar with the trials and tribulations of the angst-ridden 12-year-old from Bluffington.

The premise is this: The wildly popular rock group known as The Beets is breaking up, again. Doug and his best pal Skeeter have scored tickets to the sold-out event. In an admirable display of selflessness, Skeet suggests that Doug invite the girl of his dreams, Patti Mayonnaise, to the concert. Of course, the ever-insecure Doug has a bit of a breakdown at the thought (cue musical number!) but musters the courage to ask Patti out. Unfortunately, he's too late. Patti has already accepted an invitation from Roger, the notorious bully and Doug-taunter. It's all too much for poor Doug to bear and he slips into his ultra-suave alter ego Quailman.

In the following fantasy sequence, Quailman attempts to rescue Patti from the clutches of the evil Dr. Rubbersuit (Roger's alter ego). But he can't do it alone. Just when it looks like our hero is doomed, it's Quailkid to the rescue! (Quailkid's actually a young audience member selected during the preshow and wearing, among other things, a belt for a headband, and giant underpants.)

Once back in the real world, the kids—and the audience—groove to a brief concert by The Beets (four adult members of the audience, also picked at the preshow). After the out-of-control Roger is hauled off by security, Doug has the pleasure of walking Patti home. And all is right with the world.

The show wraps up with Doug writing about his experience in a journal. The lesson: It doesn't matter what you look like or how goofy you may think you are. Just be yourself—that's what people really like.

The 25-minute show is usually presented five times a day. Check a guidemap for exact times. Casting for the show (the five audience-participation parts) takes place five to ten minutes before showtime, once the audience has been seated in the auditorium.

Indiana Jones Epic Stunt Spectacular

Earthquakes, fiery explosions, and assorted other dramatic events give guests some insight into the science of movie stunts and special effects at this impressive 2,000-seat amphitheater. Stunt people re-create scenes from Indiana Jones films to demonstrate the skill required to keep audiences on the edge of their seats. Show director Glenn Randall, who served as stunt coordinator of such films as *Raiders of the Lost Ark*, *Poltergeist*, *Never Say Never Again*, *E.T.*, and *Jewel of the Nile*, calls the show "big visual excitement."

But the 30-minute show isn't all flying leaps. Guests also see how the elaborate stunts are pulled off—safely—while the crew and an assistant director explain what goes on both in front of and behind the camera.

In one segment, a scene from *Raiders of the Lost Ark* is staged. A 12-foot-tall rolling ball chases a Harrison Ford look-alike out of the temple. The steam and flames are so intense that the audience can feel the heat. The crew then dismantles the set, revealing the remarkable lightness of movie props, as assistants roll the ball uphill for the next show.

In a scene at a busy "Cairo" street market, "extras" chosen from the audience play the famous scene in which Indiana Jones pulls a gun while others are fighting with swords. The explosive action continues and leads to a desert finale in which the hero and his sweetheart make a death-defying escape.

There are moments during this show when audience members might wonder if something has actually gone wrong. But by revealing tricks of the trade, the directors and stars show that what appears to be dangerous is actually a safe, controlled bit of movie magic.

Star Tours

This attraction, which was inspired by George Lucas' blockbuster quartet of *Star Wars* films, offers guests the chance to board StarSpeeders that are the same type of flight simulator regularly employed by the military and commercial airlines to train pilots. By synchronizing a stunning film with the virtually limitless motion of the simulator, the ride allows guests to truly feel what they see.

Visitors enter an area where the famed *Star Wars* characters R2D2 and C-3PO are working for a galactic travel agency. They spend their time in a bustling hangar area servicing the Star Tours fleet of spacecraft. Riders board the craft for what is intended to be a leisurely trip to the Moon of Endor, but the five-minute ride quickly develops into a harrowing flight into deep space, including encounters with giant ice crystals and laser-blasting fighters. The flight is out of control from the start, as the rookie pilot comically proves that Murphy's Law applies to the entire universe.

This is a turbulent trip through the galaxy. Passengers must be free of back problems, heart conditions, motion sickness, and other physical limitations. Pregnant women are not permitted to board. Guests must be at least 40 inches tall, and children under seven must be accompanied by an adult; kids under three are not allowed to ride.

Jim Henson's Muppet*Vision 3-D

One of the most entertaining attractions at the Disney-MGM Studios, this 3-D movie is quite remarkable. As with so many other Disney theme park attractions, much of the appeal is in the details.

A funny 12-minute pre-show gives clues about what's to come. Once inside the theater, many will notice that it looks just like the one from the classic television series *The Muppet Show*. Even the two curmudgeonly fellows, Statler and Waldorf, are sitting in the balcony, bantering with each other and offering their typically critical commentary on the show.

The production comes directly from Muppet Labs, presided over by Dr. Bunsen Honeydew—and his long-suffering assistant, Beaker—and introduces a new character, Waldo, the "Spirit of 3-D." Among the highlights is Miss Piggy's solo, which Bean Bunny turns into quite a fiasco. Sam Eagle's grand finale leads to trouble as a veritable war breaks out, culminating with a cannon blast to the screen from the rear balcony, courtesy of everyone's favorite Swedish Chef.

The 3-D effects, spectacular as they may be, are only part of the show: There are appearances by live Muppet characters, fireworks, and lots of funny details built into the walls of the huge theater. Including the preshow, expect to spend about 25 minutes with Kermit and company. Shows run continuously throughout the day.

Disney's The Hunchback of Notre Dame—A Musical Adventure

A 30-minute musical based on the animated feature *Disney's The Hunchback of Notre Dame* is performed in the shaded comfort of the Backlot Theater—a canopied bleacher-style theater located just beyond New York Street. The show takes guests to the catacombs of 15th-century Paris, where gypsies reprise the tale of the bell ringer Quasimodo and his struggle to find love and happiness.

The show is characterized by an imaginative simplicity akin to street theater. Runway ramps that bring characters into the audience enhance the feeling of being part of the show.

The curtain opens on a gypsy campsite beneath the city. Here, Clopin and the gypsies create a colorful set filled with such treasures as Persian rugs and jewels. The gypsies impart the details of Quasimodo's life in the cathedral's bell tower, telling the story through song, costumes, masks, puppets, and dance. As the show evolves, the gypsies' theatrics reveal Quasimodo's oppression at the hands of Judge Claude Frollo, his love for Esmeralda, and the kindness of Phoebus, the guard who helps the lonely bell ringer.

Lest there be too much sorrow, the set again transforms and a wonderfully lively scene steals away to the streets of Paris for a thoroughly rambunctious revival of the Festival of Fools. Comic relief is provided by the gargoyles, Victor, Hugo, and Laverne, who collectively act as Quasimodo's conscience.

Honey, I Shrunk the Kids Movie Set Adventure

The set for the backyard scenes of the popular Disney movie has been re-created as an imaginative, oversize soft-surface playground. Enter it and experience the world from an ant's perspective.

Blades of grass soar 30 feet high, paper clips are as tall as trees, and Lego toys are practically big enough to live in. There are caves to explore (under the giant mushrooms) and many climbing opportunities (tremendous tree stumps and sprawling spiderwebs are among the better ones). Kids love to crawl into the discarded film canister and slide out along an oversize piece of film.

A leaky hose also provides entertainment as it squirts in a slightly different location each time. It's great fun, and the props make kids and adults look and feel as though they were indeed shrunk by *Honey, I Shrunk the Kids'* Professor Wayne Szalinski.

SHOPPING

Hollywood Boulevard

CELEBRITY 5 & 10: Modeled after a 1940s Woolworth's, this large shop carries Disney-MGM Studios logo merchandise, frames, clothing, and backpacks, as well as movie-themed items.

COVER STORY: Just through The Darkroom, this is where guests can have their images put on the front cover of a large selection of magazines. If you've had your picture taken by any of the park photographers, this is also the place to pick it up.

CROSSROADS OF THE WORLD: In the middle of the entrance plaza, Mickey Mouse keeps watch from atop this Hollywood Boulevard landmark. The small kiosk deals in souvenirs, sunglasses, film, rain gear, sundries, and guidemaps.

THE DARKROOM: The Art Deco facade of this shop allows guests to peer through an aperture-like window. Cameras (including the disposable kind), film, and camera accessories are sold.

KEYSTONE CLOTHIERS: Women's fashions and accessories are the specialties of the house. There is also a large selection of character ties and intimate apparel.

L.A. PROP CINEMA STORAGE: A great source for kids' stuff, with a variety of clothing, including costume pajamas. Many items feature characters from recent animated films, but classic Disney characters have a presence as well.

MICKEY'S OF HOLLYWOOD: The place to find character T-shirts, sweatshirts, hats, plush toys, watches, socks, wallets, tote bags, books, mugs, and sunglasses, plus items emblazoned with the Disney-MGM Studios logo or Walt Disney Studios logo.

MOVIELAND MEMORABILIA: This kiosk, located just to the left of the Disney-MGM Studios main entrance, stocks stuffed toys, hats, books, sunglasses, film, key chains, and other souvenirs.

OSCAR'S CLASSIC CAR SOUVENIRS & SUPER SERVICE: The 1949 Chevrolet Tow Truck parked out front gets plenty of attention. Automotive memorabilia, mugs, models, and key chains are for sale. (The truck, by the way, is not.) Services offered here include stroller, wheelchair, and locker rentals, plus a stamp machine.

SID CAHUENGA'S ONE-OF-A-KIND: Unique antiques and curios are the stock-in-trade here. Autographed photos of past and present matinee idols, old movie magazines and posters, and assorted Hollywood memorabilia, such as Clark Gable's pants and baubles once owned by Cher, are among the many celebrity-oriented collectibles with which Sid is willing to part—for a price. For movie buffs, a stop at Sid's is an absolute must.

Sunset Boulevard

THE BEVERLY SUNSET: All bad guys, all the time. That's the motto of this new shop, which has a killer selection of merchandise and candy featuring the dark side of Disney—the characters we love to hate.

LEGENDS OF HOLLYWOOD: A tribute to Disney's animated legend, Winnie the Pooh. Expect to find an abundance of shirts, hats, books, and other colorful merchandise featuring everyone's favorite chubby little cubby—plus his pals from the Hundred Acre Wood.

MOUSE ABOUT TOWN: The best source for men's golf apparel featuring the famed mouse subtly embroidered onto sportswear, sweatshirts, and jackets. The Mouse also purveys golf-related apparel and accessories.

ONCE UPON A TIME: The exterior of this shop replicates the Carthay Circle Theatre in Hollywood, where *Snow White and the Seven Dwarfs* premiered in 1937. The shop specializes in decorative gifts and Disney houseware items. For $25, a Disney artist will customize a character sketch for you.

PLANET HOLLYWOOD SUPERSTORE: This spot offers Planet Hollywood-brand items such as T-shirts, caps, and jackets.

SUNSET CLUB COUTURE: A sophisticated selection of jewelry and mostly Mickey watches includes limited-edition pieces and pocket watches. A Disney artist can customize character watches on the spot.

SUNSET RANCH: This open-air shop carries Disney character hats, totes, and apparel, plus sunscreen, film, and sundries.

Beyond the Boulevards

ANIMATION GALLERY: Don't overlook this shop in the Animation Building, where limited-edition figurines, Disney animation cels, and other collectibles ensure great browsing, even if buying isn't on your mind.

GOLDEN AGE SOUVENIRS: Located between Sounds Dangerous and Disney's Doug Live!, this shop stocks items such as hats, sunglasses, film, and souvenirs.

IN CHARACTER: In front of Voyage of The Little Mermaid, this costume shop has everything a child needs to dress up like his or her favorite Disney character.

INDIANA JONES ADVENTURE OUTPOST: Next to the Indiana Jones attraction, you'll discover adventure clothing, as well as memorabilia emblazoned with the Indy insignia.

IT'S A WONDERFUL SHOP: Tucked away behind Jim Henson's Muppet*Vision 3-D, this "snow-covered" shop—with Disney ornaments galore—feels like Christmastime all year round.

STAGE 1 COMPANY STORE: Near the exit of Jim Henson's Muppet*Vision 3-D, guests can find plush toys, shirts, figurines, and other merchandise with the likenesses of Muppet characters, in addition to a variety of items featuring the Disney gang.

THE STUDIO STORE: Expect to find T-shirts, hats, and accessories inspired by Disney films at this Animation Courtyard shop. Items featuring the Disney-MGM Studios logo are available, too.

TATOOINE TRADERS: This refurbished and expanded shop (formerly known as Endor Vendors) near the exit of the Star Tours attraction offers intergalactic souvenirs tied to the *Star Wars* films (including the most recent installment, *Episode I: The Phantom Menace*) and the Star Tours attraction. Among the wares are hats, T-shirts, and action figures, as well as Chewbacca masks, Darth Maul mugs, and C-3PO pens.

TOY STORY PIZZA PLANET GIFTS: Located next door to Toy Story Pizza Planet Arcade, this spot is second only to Andy's room when it comes to finding *Toy Story* and *Toy Story 2* collectibles.

THE WRITER'S STOP: This cozy nook next to the Sci-Fi Dine-In Theater has coffee, stationery, and a small selection of reading material. Ask about recent—and future—book signings. Even if you miss an author appearance, you may find an autographed copy of a book on the shelves. There's also a counter offering fresh-baked cookies and other tempting desserts.

Where to Eat at the Studios

A complete listing of eateries at the Studios—full-service restaurants, fast-food emporiums, and snack shops—can be found in the *Good Meals, Great Times* chapter. See the Disney-MGM Studios restaurant section, which begins on page 228.

ENTERTAINMENT

As you might expect from a park fashioned in the image of Hollywood's heyday, the Disney-MGM Studios knows how to put on a show. Celebrity appearances are a distinct possibility as well. Basically, in these parts, it's always showtime. So be sure to pick up a free guidemap (at Guest Relations or any shop), not only to check attraction starting times but also to find out what other entertainment is on tap.

While specifics may change, the following list is a good indication of the Studios' stage presence. As always, we advise calling 407-939-4636 for entertainment schedules. For information on special events, see the "Holidays & Special Events" section of *Getting Ready to Go*.

MULAN PARADE: The star of *Mulan*, Disney's 36th animated feature, rides down Hollywood Boulevard every afternoon. The colorful procession features music and characters inspired by the film, from Mushu the dragon to the villain Shan Yu (who has no choice but to participate—he is tied to a bed of skulls). Plan on staking out your piece of curb about 20 to 30 minutes early.

STREETMOSPHERE CHARACTERS: This troupe of performers infuses Hollywood Boulevard with old-time Tinseltown ambience. Would-be starlets searching for their big break, fans seeking guests' autographs, and gossip columnists chasing leads entertain daily.

Holiday Happenings

The Disney-MGM Studios usually stays open extra late to mark holidays such as New Year's Eve, the Fourth of July, and Christmas. During these times, lots of special entertainment is often in store. Call 407-939-4636 for up-to-the-minute schedules.

CHRISTMAS: The Osborne Family Spectacle of Lights is the Studios' brilliant, twinkling homage to the season. An extraordinary, luminous holiday display featuring about five million lights (provided by Little Rock businessman Jennings Osborne and his family) sets the backlot area of the Studios aglow. The display, which is lit nightly throughout the season, is truly spectacular. Check a park guidemap for exact times.

DISNEY-MGM STUDIOS

Trip the Light Fantasmic!

Fantasmic!, a lavish musical production, plays nightly at The Hollywood Hills Amphitheater on Sunset Boulevard. A dramatic mix of fireworks, fountains, lasers, special effects, and Disney characters, it invites guests to take a peek into the dream world of Mickey Mouse.

Though similar to its Disneyland counterpart, half of this 26-minute production is original. The action follows Mickey through a series of dreams. In the first dream, he appears on a mountain, shoots fireworks from his fingertips, and conducts an orchestra of colorful fountains. (Guests seated up front get spritzed.) Soon Mickey is plagued by nightmares as Disney villains take over his dreams. In the end, the Mouse and his pals prevail (of course!).

Seating begins about 90 minutes before showtime (though some guests line up even earlier). Check a guidemap for exact times. While all seats afford a good view, we recommend sitting toward the back. Note that there is standing room, too.

After the grand finale, plan to sit for a bit. It can take up to 20 minutes for the crowd to exit the theater.

Timing Tip: On nights when Fantasmic! is presented twice, see the last show. Afterward, as the masses exit the park, take some time to browse the shops that stay open after hours.

HOT TIPS

- Arrive at the Disney-MGM Studios before the posted opening time. The gates open at about 8:30 A.M. (Attractions open at 9 A.M.)

- Check the Studios Tip Board often to get an idea of showtimes and crowds.

- See Rock 'n' Roller Coaster, Voyage of The Little Mermaid, and Star Tours early in the day, before the crowds build up.

- Snag a spot along Hollywood Boulevard about 20 to 30 minutes before the parade.

- Tower of Terror is a popular attraction with long lines. Ride it very early or later in the day—and never right after eating a meal.

- The line for The Great Movie Ride is generally the longest early in the morning and immediately following the afternoon parade.

- For a full-service meal, make priority seating arrangements when you arrive, at either Hollywood Junction (at the corner of Sunset and Hollywood boulevards) or the eatery: 50's Prime Time Cafe, Hollywood Brown Derby, Sci-Fi Dine-In Theater, Hollywood & Vine, or Mama Melrose's Ristorante Italiano. For reservations, call 407-WDW-DINE (939-3463) up to four months ahead.

- Park hoppers take note: There is a water taxi link between the Disney-MGM Studios and Epcot. The boat docks to the left as you exit the Studios. You may also reach Epcot, as well as all other parks, by bus.

- The Hollywood Brown Derby and Mama Melrose's Ristorante Italiano offer a dinner-and-show combination: a meal followed by Fantasmic!, complete with V.I.P. seating. It's a great way to avoid the time-consuming hassle of waiting for the show.

- Many attractions and shows stop admitting guests prior to the park's official closing time. (Check a guidemap for schedules.) Attractions that you may enter up until the very last minute include Rock 'n' Roller Coaster, The Twilight Zone Tower of Terror, The Great Movie Ride, Jim Henson's Muppet*Vision 3-D, and Star Tours.

- The shops on Hollywood Boulevard are open a half hour past park closing.

Where to Find the Characters

You'll find Disney characters—such as Buzz Lightyear and Woody from *Toy Story*—strolling down Mickey Avenue and hanging out by Toy Story Pizza Planet. They are often joined by Minnie, Pluto, or other characters. Look for Mickey Mouse in the festive Animation Courtyard. Another good way to meet Disney characters is at the Hollywood & Vine restaurant. As always, check the guidemap or with a park employee for current details.

Disney's Animal Kingdom

169 Getting Oriented

170 Park Primer

171 Attractions

181 Shopping

182 Entertainment

182 Hot Tips

With a mix of lush landscapes, thrilling attractions, and spine-tingling encounters with exotic animals, this is clearly a theme park raised to another level of excitement. Here, guests do more than just watch the action—they live it. They become paleontologists, explorers, and students of nature. And if, by doing so, they leave with nothing more than a great big smile, Disney will have accomplished one of its major goals. But most guests will come away with a little bit more: a renewed sense of respect for our planet and for the life-forms we share it with (not to mention a few boffo souvenirs).

The attractions at Disney's Animal Kingdom are meant to engage, entertain, and inspire. They immerse guests in a tropical landscape and introduce them to wondrous creatures from the past and present—as well as a few that exist only in our collective imagination.

The park, which is accredited by the American Zoo and Aquarium Association, is home to more than 1,700 animals representing 250 different species. Most of the creatures are of the animate variety, as opposed to the Audio-Animatronics kind. Despite that, you won't see many beasts behind bars here. Instead, you'll see a menagerie of wild critters living in spacious habitats, with remarkably few separations visible to the naked eye.

The following pages will help you get the most out of your visit to Disney's Animal Kingdom. It is, after all, a jungle out there.

N ↓

AFRICA

A Kilimanjaro Safaris

B Pangani Forest Exploration Trail

C Wildlife Express to Conservation Station

D Conservation Station

SAFARI VILLAGE

E The Tree of Life

F Safari Village Trails

G It's Tough to be a Bug!

CAMP MINNIE-MICKEY

H Festival of the Lion King

I Pocahontas and Her Forest Friends

ASIA

J Flights of Wonder at Caravan Stage

K Maharajah Jungle Trek

L Kali River Rapids

DINOLAND U.S.A.

M Dinosaur

N The Boneyard playground

O Cretaceous Trail

P Tarzan™ Rocks!

GETTING ORIENTED

Though Disney's Animal Kingdom encompasses about five times the area of its Magic counterpart, one need not be in training for the Olympics to tackle it. By all estimates, pedestrians rack up about the same mileage in one day here as they do in a day at Epcot. (If you *want* to pack the hiking boots, by all means do — there are plenty of pretty areas to explore.)

The park's layout is reminiscent of the Magic Kingdom's: a series of sections, or "lands," connected to a central hub. In this case, the hub is Safari Village, an island surrounded by a river, and home to The Tree of Life, the park's icon. A set of bridges connects Safari Village with other lands: The Oasis, DinoLand U.S.A., Asia, Africa, and Camp Minnie-Mickey.

As you pass through Animal Kingdom's entrance plaza, you approach The Oasis. Feel free to meander at a leisurely pace, absorbing the soothing ambience of a thick, elaborate jungle, or you can proceed more quickly and plan to revisit this relaxing region later on. Each of several pathways deposits you at the foot of a bridge leading to Safari Village. As you emerge from The Oasis, you'll see the awe-inspiring Tree of Life, a 14-story Disney-made banyan tree, looming ahead. The tree, which stands near the middle of the island, is surrounded by Safari Village Trails. Off to the southwest is the character-laden land known as Camp Minnie-Mickey.

To the southeast lies DinoLand U.S.A., home of countless prehistoric animals, a fossil dig, and an attraction that's sure to induce a mammoth adrenaline surge: Dinosaur. Behind Safari Village and to the northwest is Africa, where guests can go on an African safari, explore a nature trail, and take a train to Conservation Station, the park's research and education center.

The park's newest land, Asia, is northeast of Safari Village. Here, guests may encounter tigers on the exotic Maharajah Jungle Trek, and take a daring journey through the rain forest on a raft at the splashy Kali River Rapids.

HOW TO GET THERE

Take Exit 25 off I-4. Then follow the signs to Disney's Animal Kingdom. Trams run continually between the parking lot and the main entrance.

By WDW Transportation: From all Walt Disney World resorts: buses. From Downtown Disney: bus to the Transportation and Ticket Center (TTC), then transfer to the bus for Disney's Animal Kingdom. From the Magic Kingdom, Epcot, the Disney-MGM Studios, and the resorts on Hotel Plaza Boulevard: buses.

PARKING

All-day parking at Animal Kingdom is $6 for day visitors (free to WDW resort guests with presentation of resort ID). Trams circulate regularly, providing transportation from the parking area to the park entrance. Be sure to note the section and aisle in which you park. Also, be aware that the parking ticket allows for re-entry to the parking area throughout the day.

HOURS

Although hours are subject to change, Animal Kingdom usually opens earlier than the other theme parks. Gates are generally open daily from about 8 A.M. until about an hour after dusk. During certain holiday periods and the summer months, hours may change. It's best to arrive at the park at least a half hour before the official opening time. Call 407-WDW-INFO (939-4636) for current schedules.

Admission Prices

ONE-DAY TICKET

(Restricted to use only in Disney's Animal Kingdom. Prices include sales tax and are subject to change.)

Adult...$48.76
Child*.......................................$39.22

*3 through 9 years of age; children under 3 free

PARK PRIMER

BABY FACILITIES

Changing tables and facilities for nursing mothers can be found at the Baby Care Center in Safari Village, behind Creature Comforts. Also, disposable diapers are kept behind the counter at many Animal Kingdom shops; just ask.

CAMERA NEEDS

Film may be left for processing at Garden Gate Gifts near The Oasis, Wonders of the Wild in Safari Village, Duka La Filimu and Mombasa Marketplace in Harambe, and Chester and Hester's Dinosaur Treasures in DinoLand U.S.A. The photo pickup location is at Garden Gate Gifts. Film is sold in most shops.

DISABILITY INFORMATION

Nearly all of the Animal Kingdom attractions, shops, and restaurants are accessible to guests using wheelchairs. Additional services are available for guests with visual or hearing disabilities. The *Guidebook for Guests with Disabilities* provides a detailed overview of the services available, including transportation, parking, and attraction access. (For additional information, refer to the *Getting Ready to Go* chapter.)

FIRST AID

Minor medical problems can be handled at the First Aid Center, located in Safari Village on the northwest side of The Tree of Life, near Creature Comforts.

INFORMATION

Guest Relations, located just inside the park entrance, is equipped with guidemaps and a helpful staff. Free guidemaps are also available in many shops.

LOCKERS

Lockers are found in two locations just inside the main entrance area: near Garden Gate Gifts and Guest Relations. Cost is $5 (including a $2 refundable deposit) for unlimited use all day.

LOST & FOUND

The department is located near the Baby Care Center, behind Creature Comforts in Safari Village. To report lost items after your visit call 407-824-4245.

LOST CHILDREN

Report lost children at Guest Relations, near the park entrance, or alert a Disney employee to the problem.

MONEY MATTERS

There is an ATM at the entrance to the park. It's just before the turnstiles and to the right, next to the kennel. Currency exchange can be handled at Guest Relations. Disney Dollars, in $1, $5, and $10 denominations, are also available at Guest Relations. (The bills feature Mickey, Goofy, and Minnie, respectively.) In addition to cash, credit cards (American Express, Diner's Club, Discover Card, JCB, Visa, MasterCard, and The Disney Credit Card), traveler's checks, and WDW resort IDs are accepted for admission and merchandise, and for meals at all full-service restaurants and fast-food spots. Many snack carts accept cash only.

PACKAGE PICKUP

Animal Kingdom shops can arrange for bulky purchases to be transported to Garden Gate Gifts for later pickup (packages will be ready for pickup three hours after purchase). The service is free. WDW resort guests can arrange for packages to be delivered to their resort at no extra charge.

SAME-DAY RE-ENTRY

Be sure to have your hand stamped upon exiting the park and to retain your ticket if you plan to return later the same day.

STROLLERS & WHEELCHAIRS

Strollers, wheelchairs, and Electric Convenience Vehicles (ECVs) may be rented at Garden Gate Gifts (the first shop on the right inside the park entrance, near the entrance to The Oasis). The cost is $6 for strollers and wheelchairs, plus a $1 refundable deposit; $30 for ECVs, with a $10 refundable deposit. Quantities are limited. Keep your receipt; it can be used the same day to get a replacement at the Magic Kingdom, Epcot, the Disney-MGM Studios, or at Animal Kingdom.

TIP BOARDS

There is a Tip Board in Safari Village. Check it throughout the day to learn the current wait times for the most popular attractions at Disney's Animal Kingdom.

THE OASIS

Traditionally, one has to travel across a long, sunbaked stretch of desert in order to experience the soothing atmosphere of a tropical oasis. With that in mind, think of the Animal Kingdom parking lot as a concrete version of the Sahara. Once you've trekked across it, your journey takes you through the park's front gate and entrance plaza. What's that up ahead? Could it be a towering banyan tree? Here in Central Florida? It must be a mirage.

But no. Within seconds you arrive at The Oasis, a thriving tropical garden filled with waterfalls, running streams, and lush vegetation. The transition is by no means a subtle one. You are immediately enveloped in a world of nature and animals. The peaceful setting is idyllic.

Though not a full-fledged "land" per se, this small jungle simply oozes atmosphere. It is thick and elaborate, and crawling with critters. (Some are more difficult to spot than others. When searching for the naturally camouflaged creatures, remember to look up occasionally.) As park visitors walk along the pathways, they will catch glimpses of all kinds of animals, from deer and iguanas to anteaters and sloths. As in the rest of Animal Kingdom, there is the illusion that guests are walking among the wildlife.

The Oasis is at once an exciting and calming experience. It sets the stage for what's to come. Guests have several options once they've entered The Oasis. They can continue on a northerly path, making tracks toward The Tree of Life and across a bridge to Safari Village. They can proceed at a more snail-friendly pace, keeping a tally of the various life-forms that slither by. Or they can simply take time to stop and smell the flowers.

"I have learned from the animal world. And what everyone will learn who studies it is a renewed sense of kinship with the earth and all of its inhabitants."

—Walt Disney

Timing Tip: Making a trip through The Oasis is the only way to get into (and out of) Disney's Animal Kingdom. Therefore, some of the smaller paths can become a bit congested during the hours closest to opening and closing times. To beat the crowds, use the paths farthest to the left when you enter and exit the park.

SAFARI VILLAGE

Once you've passed through The Oasis, you will come to a bridge spanning a peaceful river. The bridge leads to Safari Village, an island at the center of Animal Kingdom and the hub from which all other realms of the park may be reached.

Safari Village is defined by the brilliant colors, tropical surroundings, and equatorial architecture of Africa and the South Pacific. The facades of the buildings are all carved and painted based on the art of nations from around the world. Don't fail to notice all the bright, whimsical folk-art images representing various members of the animal kingdom.

This island is the shopping and dining center of Animal Kingdom. Many of the park's fast-food restaurants can be found here, including Pizzafari and Flame Tree Barbecue.

By far the most striking element in Safari Village is The Tree of Life. It is on the map, but chances are you'll have no trouble finding it. Rising from the middle of the island and as tall as a 14-story building, The Tree of Life is hard to miss.

The Tree of Life

The majestic Tree of Life is the dramatic 145-foot icon of Disney's Animal Kingdom. The imposing banyan-like tree, with its swaying limbs and gnarled trunk, looks an awful lot like the real thing—from a distance. Up close, it's apparent that this is a most unusual bit of greenery. Completely covered with more than 325 animal images, it is a swirling tapestry of carved figures, painstakingly assembled by a team of Disney artisans. The tree, though inorganic, stands as a symbol of the connected nature of life on Earth. We think Joyce Kilmer would have approved.

SAFARI VILLAGE TRAILS: Walkways that snake around The Tree of Life allow guests to get a close-up view of the trunk and even play a game of "spot the animals." (The spiraling animal images go all the way to the top of the tree. You'll need a pair of binoculars if you hope to see them all.)

HOT TIP

Take a moment to study a guidemap as you enter Animal Kingdom. It will give you a sense of the park's layout and provide information about showtimes for Festival of the Lion King and other attractions.

Scattered about the tree's base are a variety of animal habitats. Animals can be seen in a very open, somewhat traditional parklike setting, with lush grass, trees, and other vegetation. Among the creatures you may recognize are toucans, flamingos, and deer. Others to which you may be introduced for the very first time as you meander through the exhibits include capybaras (huge rodents with an affinity for swimming) and ring-tailed lemurs (not quite monkeys' uncles, more like cousins). The trails are accessible from several points around the tree.

 Children under age four may have loved the film *A Bug's Life*, but few of them fancy It's Tough to be A Bug! In fact, it terrifies them.

IT'S TOUGH TO BE A BUG!: Inside the trunk of The Tree of Life is a 430-seat auditorium featuring an eight-minute, animated 3-D movie augmented by some surprising "4-D" effects. The stars of the show are the world's most abundant inhabitants—insects. They creep, crawl, and demonstrate why, someday, they just might inherit the earth. It's a bug's-eye view of the trials and tribulations of their multi-legged world.

As guests enter "The Tree of Life Repertory Theater," the orchestra can be heard

warming up amid the sounds of chirping crickets. When Flik, the emcee (and star of *A Bug's Life*), makes his first appearance, he dubs audience m embers honorary bugs and instructs them to don their bug eyes (3-D glasses). Then the mild-mannered ant introduces some of his not-so-mild-mannered cronies, including a Chilean tarantula, dung beetles, and "the silent but deadly member of the bug world"—the stink bug. What follows is a manic, often hilarious, revue.

Note: The combination of intense special effects and frequent darkness tends to frighten toddlers and young children. In addition, anyone leery of spiders, roaches, and their ilk is advised to skip the performance, or risk being seriously bugged.

DISNEY'S ANIMAL KINGDOM

173

AFRICA

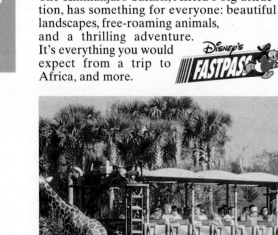

The largest section of Animal Kingdom, Africa is bigger than the Magic Kingdom all by itself. This 110-acre, truer-than-life replica of an African savanna is packed with pachyderms, giraffes, hippos, and other jungle beasts. Guests enter Africa through Harambe, a village based on a modern East African coastal town. It is the dining and shopping center of Animal Kingdom's Africa.

The instant you walk across the bridge to Harambe, you are transported to Africa. Everything here is authentic, from the architecture to the landscaping to the merchandise in the marketplace. The result was achieved after Disney Imagineers made countless trips to the continent. After seven years of observing, filming, and photographing the real thing, they re-created it here in North America.

The animals that live here, however, are not re-creations. They are quite real, most varied, and extremely abundant. In fact, this chunk of land puts the *animal* in Disney's Animal Kingdom.

Kilimanjaro Safaris

The Kilimanjaro Safaris, Africa's big attraction, has something for everyone: beautiful landscapes, free-roaming animals, and a thrilling adventure. It's everything you would expect from a trip to Africa, and more.

The 20-minute safari begins with a brief introduction from a guide who does double duty as your driver. Note that some of the guides actually come from various parts of the African continent.

Once on board the ride vehicle, look at the plates on the back of the seat in front of you. They will help you identify all the animals you see. And have those cameras ready!

As the open-air vehicle travels along dirt roads, you'll spot free-roaming wild animals: zebras, gazelles, hippos, elephants, warthogs, rhinos, lions, and more. Some of the animals wander near your vehicle, and others cross its path. (Relax. Only harmless creatures approach. Others, such as lions and cheetahs, only *appear* to invade your personal space.)

The majesty of the Serengeti may lull you into a state of serenity, but it's merely the calm before the storm. You will soon be jostled and jolted as the vehicle crosses pothole-filled terrain and rickety bridges—one of which puts you close to a hungry horde of sunbathing crocodiles.

The safari experience takes a sudden, dramatic turn when a band of renegade ivory poachers is discovered hunting for elephants. Your guide chooses to chase the outlaws and takes you along for the ride. The mad pursuit that follows is a brief but wild adventure.

Pangani Forest Exploration Trail

This self-guided walking trail winds past communities of gorillas and other rare African animals. It can be accessed at the end of the Kilimanjaro Safaris or by its entrance located in Harambe.

The first major stop on the trail, the name of which translates to "place of enchantment" in Swahili, is the Research Station. The station contains several exhibits, including naked mole rats. Just outside are a free-flight aviary and an aquarium teeming with exotic fish. Not far away is the hippo exhibit, which provides close-up views of hippopotamuses both in and out of water. Farther along the trail there is a scenic overlook point, where you can get an unobstructed view of the African savanna. This is also known as the "Timon" exhibit, featuring a family of perky meerkats. Afterward, you may catch an up-close glimpse (through a glass wall) of a cavorting gorilla or two.

As you come to the end of the suspension bridge, you'll find yourself in a beautiful green valley. Congratulations! You've finally reached the gorilla area—an experience well worth the wait. (Note that you may have to wait a little bit longer for that first gorilla sighting. Our evolutionary cousins have been known to play hide-and-seek in the lush vegetation.)

Conservation Station

On the east side of the village of Harambe is the Harambe Train Station. That's where you board the Wildlife Express and experience an interesting behind-the-scenes look at a Disney park while en route to Conservation Station.

As part of the 5½-minute trip, you'll glide past the buildings where elephants, rhinos, and giraffes sleep at night. You will also see the animal care facilities at Conservation Station and get a backstage view of the Kilimanjaro Safaris. A guide narrates throughout the trip. All guests disembark at Conservation Station. (You must reboard the train to return to Harambe.)

While Animal Kingdom's stories often carry a conservation theme, this part of the park really brings the message home. A veterinary lab, this facility is the park's conservation headquarters. It's also the research and education hub. Here, guests get a look at the way animals are cared for.

"Much of the world's wildlife is in imminent danger," says Judson Green, former chairman of Walt Disney Attractions. "Disney is working directly to save endangered animals, but we also hope to motivate our guests to support wildlife programs that are in urgent need of support." After spending time at Conservation Station, visitors just might have the motivation they need. Exhibits are geared to spark curiosity and awe about wildlife and conservation efforts around the world. Here are a few highlights of the area:

Affection Section: An animal encounter area with accessible, friendly critters to see and touch. Most of the animals are exotic breeds of familiar petting-zoo types: goats, sheep, pigs, etc. However, this is still a not-to-be-missed experience for young Animal Kingdom guests.

Animal Cams: Guest-operated video cameras that observe animals throughout Disney's Animal Kingdom as they go about their daily business.

Animal Health & Care: A tour of veterinary labs and research facilities.

Eco Heroes: A set of touch-sensitive video kiosks that allow guests to interact with famous biologists and conservationists.

EcoWeb: A computer link to conservation organizations around the world. Printouts are available.

Rafiki's Planet Watch: An interactive video, hosted by *The Lion King*'s Rafiki, that connects guests to information about endangered animals.

Song of the Rainforest: A not-to-be-missed "3-D" audio show that surrounds guests with the sounds of the rain forest.

The only way to get here is by taking the Wildlife Express. Conservation Station is about a five-minute walk from the train depot. Note that, in addition to its educational appeal, this is also one of the best places to cool off at Animal Kingdom.

Get Involved!

When it comes to conservation efforts, the folks at the Walt Disney Company want you to do as they say—*and* as they do: The Disney Wildlife Conservation Fund helps nonprofit groups protect and study endangered and threatened animals and their habitats. Among those groups are the ASPCA, Dian Fossey Gorilla Fund, Jane Goodall Institute, and the Wildlife Conservation Society.

Of course, as a trip to Disney's Animal Kingdom makes clear, there are many ways to help our planet's wild inhabitants. Be sure and stop by Conservation Station during your visit. There, you can get information about conservation efforts in your neck of the woods. Don't leave your enthusiasm behind when you leave the park!

On the far side of a Himalayan-style bridge, beyond an ancient temple, lies the tranquil village of Anandapur (Sanskrit for "place of delight"). The buildings' design was inspired by structures in Thailand, Indonesia, and other Asian countries known for their rich architectural history.

A product of Disney Imagineering, the village epitomizes the complex, enduring relationship between the animals and ecosystems of the Asian continent. The village borders an elaborate re-creation of a Southeast Asian rain forest. As such, Disney's Asia is an ideal location for trekking through the jungle, shooting the rapids on a raging river, and gazing upon the multi-hued inhabitants of this treasured terrain. This land is the newest in Disney's Animal Kingdom.

Kali River Rapids

Before guests board rafts at Kali (pronounced *KAH-lee*) River Rapids, a wise voice admonishes that "the river is like life itself, full of mysterious twists and turns." What the voice *doesn't* say is that the river is also full of splashing water and a blazing inferno. This may be business as usual for some daring souls, but for most of us, these elements make for one dramatic adventure.

All guests begin the journey in the offices of Kali River Rapids Expeditions, a river rafting company. A slide show offers information on the sometimes unscrupulous business of logging—how it has ravaged the rain forest and deprived animals of their habitats. However, thanks to ecotourism (among other things), there is hope. Peaceful voyages give people a new appreciation and sense of responsibility for this endangered land.

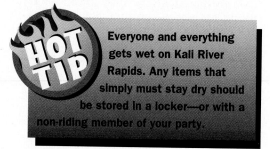

HOT TIP

Everyone and everything gets wet on Kali River Rapids. Any items that simply must stay dry should be stored in a locker—or with a non-riding member of your party.

A 12-seater raft whisks "ecotourists" up a watery ramp and through an arching tunnel of bamboo. It proceeds onward, through a hazy mist and past remnants of an ancient shrine. As the raft moves along curves of the river, guests enjoy spectacular views of undisturbed rain forest.

The tranquillity is shattered by a startling sight. A huge chunk of forest has been gutted by loggers. On both sides of the river, the forest has vanished. As guests absorb the image, they are besieged by more disturbing sights and sounds. Straight ahead, the river is choked with a tangled arch of burning logs—and the raft is headed straight for it. Suddenly, the rain forest isn't the only thing that is endangered.

Kali River Rapids is an especially drenching experience. It is the rare guest who leaves the ride without a thorough soaking. Should you wish to repel as much precipitation as possible, plan on purchasing a plastic poncho at the ride's entrance.

Note: This is a bumpy adventure. In order to experience it, you must be at least 42 inches tall. It is not recommended for pregnant women, those with a heart condition, people with back or neck problems, or anyone who wishes to stay dry.

Maharajah Jungle Trek

Welcome to the jungle! The Maharajah Jungle Trek is a self-guided walking tour of a tropical paradise, complete with roaming tigers, gushing waterfalls, and dense greenery. Throughout the expedition, trekkers encounter a deluge of flora and fauna typically found in the rain forests of Southeast Asia. Tapirs, Komodo dragons, and a conglomeration of colorful birds call this corner of Animal Kingdom home. Majestic Asian tigers can be spotted stalking ancient ruins, strategically separated from would-be prey. Deer and antelope graze and frolic nearby, blissfully oblivious of their fearsome neighbors' proximity.

Approximately midway through the thicket stands a rustic, tin-roofed assembly hall. Step inside to witness the breathtaking sight of giant fruit bats showing off their six-foot wingspans. As you look through the windows, thinking that the crystal-clear glass was cleaned by a super-diligent window washer, think again. There is no glass in some of the windows—and, therefore, *nothing* separating you from the giant creatures fluttering about on the other side. What keeps the big bats from getting up close and personal with guests? They're a lot less interested in humans than humans are in them. (Can't say that we blame them.) Note that some viewing areas are adorned with wire or glass—for guests who are more comfortable with a bat buffer.

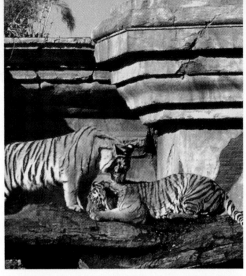

Flights of Wonder

A 1,000-seat, open-air theater, the Caravan Stage features performances by actors wearing nothing but feathers and the occasional crown. Members of more than 20 different bird species have starring roles in Flights of Wonder, a high-flying celebration of the winged wonders of the world. Hawks, falcons, and even chickens awe spectators as they swoop, soar, and strut their stuff in each 20-minute performance. Some demonstrate how they hunt. Others, such as Sluggo the Red-legged Seriema, display the fine points of pulverizing prey. And a few simply show off. (Case in point: Quasar the African Gray parrot, who may or may not be a math genius.) Check a park guidemap for showtimes.

DINOLAND U.S.A.

If the look and feel of DinoLand U.S.A. seems familiar, there's a reason: It was designed to capture the flavor of roadside America. It is a clever mixture of culture and kitsch—the likes of which you might stumble upon during a cross-country road trip. Here, you'll come face-to-face with fossil fanatics, jump into gigantic footprints, and browse through a typically tacky roadside souvenir stand, where you can pick up some dinosaur mementos for the folks back home.

This corner of Animal Kingdom comes complete with its own dramatic entrance: a 50-foot skeleton of a brachiosaurus. As guests stroll beneath the bones, they find themselves smack in the middle of a paleontological dig. Here, guests of all ages (especially little ones) have the chance to play paleontologist as they dig through a fossil-packed pocket of dino discovery.

The dinosaurs that dwell here, though often quite animated, are all of the inanimate variety. But do keep your eyes peeled for the prehistoric life-forms that actually *live* in this land. That is, for real creatures that exist in the here and now, but whose ancestors kept company with the likes of the carnotaurus and its cousins from the Cretaceous era.

The Boneyard

The Boneyard gives guests—especially the younger ones—an opportunity to dig for fossils in a discovery-oriented playground. They will excavate the ancient bones of a mammoth in this re-creation of a paleontological dig (think huge, prehistoric sandbox). They will also unearth clues that will help them solve the mystery of how and when the creature met its untimely demise.

For serious "boneheads" who just aren't satisfied with simple digging, there are plenty of other bone-related activities here. You can bang out a primitive tune on a bony xylophone (it's located near the car; to make a sound, simply press on a rib), zip down prehistoric slides, and work your way through a fossil-filled maze. While exploring, watch your step: If you accidentally wander into a giant dinosaur footprint, you'll be greeted with an ominous roar. Be sure to check out the OldenGate Bridge, too. It's a gateway structure made from the giant skeleton of a dinosaur. The bridge links one end of The Boneyard with the other. Note that this is a good place to take younger children while other members of your party ride Dinosaur.

Dinosaur

This thrilling attraction is dramatic with a capital *D*. The dizzying adventure begins with guests being strapped into high-speed vehicles and catapulted back in

time to complete a dangerous, albeit noble, mission: to rescue the last living iguan-

odon—a 16-foot plant-eating dinosaur that you may recognize from the Disney film *Dinosaur*—and bring him back to the present. The iguanodon, which lived more than 65 million years ago (during the Cretaceous period) just might hold the answer to the mysterious disappearance of his dino brethren.

Throughout the frenetic quest to locate the elusive iguanodon, you cling to an out-of-control vehicle while dodging blazing meteors and a mix of friendly and ferocious dinosaurs. Soon you encounter the carnotaurus—a fearsome, carnivorous dinosaur. The carnotaurus, which has horns like a bull, a face like a toad, and squirrel-like arms, is an unsightly specimen.

For a slightly less turbulent experience on the Dinosaur attraction, request an inside seat near the front of the ride vehicle.

All of the dinosaurs are especially fierce-looking and move as though they were alive. Even their nostrils move as they "breathe."

This 3½-minute attraction offers more than a thrill a minute. You rocket through time, are practically pelted by meteors, and narrowly escape becoming a dino dinner as the hungry carnotaurus turns the tables and chases after *you*.

Guests reach the attraction through the Dino Institute, a museumlike building deep in the heart of DinoLand. Here, you'll be treated to a pre-show by Bill Nye, the Science Guy (audio only) and see a dinosaur skeleton and an assortment of fossils and other artifacts.

This is an extremely intense attraction. You must be at least 40 inches tall to experience it. It is not recommended for pregnant women, those with a heart condition, or people with back or neck problems. Small children will be frightened.

Note: The Dinosaur attraction used to be known as Countdown to Extinction.

DID YOU KNOW...

The benches in Disney's Animal Kingdom are made of recycled plastic milk jugs. It takes 1,350 jugs to make a single bench!

Cretaceous Trail

Looking for something totally different from the high drama of the Dinosaur attraction? Head for the decidedly calmer Cretaceous Trail. This short and simple walking path is filled with living plants and some animals (like crocodiles and birds) that have survived from the Cretaceous period, the last time dinosaurs ruled the land.

Many of the land plants of the Cretaceous period were much like those that lived in the Jurassic period, the time that immediately preceded it, with a notable exception: the presence of angiosperms, or flowering plants. These and many other prehistoric flora evolved into the plants we see today.

Tarzan™ Rocks!

The huge, covered Theater in the Wild seats 1,500 guests at a time. Here, audiences are treated to a 30-minute rock concert featuring songs, dances, and characters based on those in Disney's animated feature, *Tarzan*.

This energetic, artistic interpretation of the Disney film includes appearances by Tarzan, Jane, and Terk, plus a cast of jungle gymnasts and other rock 'n' roll animals.

Like Animal Kingdom's other big-ticket performance, the Festival of the Lion King, the show aspires to dazzle guests with aerial spectacles, acrobatic stunts, and stirring sound. Tarzan Rocks! runs throughout the day, on most days. Check a guidemap for exact showtimes.

CAMP MINNIE-MICKEY

What would a theme park be without a gregarious cast of handshaking characters? You will find the patented Disney character experience in all of its animated glory in Camp Minnie-Mickey. Set deep in a dense forest, this land is really a summer camp frequented by Mickey Mouse and all of his pals.

To find the characters, guests follow one of four short trails. Each one leads to an open-air hut, occupied by the likes of Mickey, Minnie, Winnie the Pooh, Goofy, Tigger, and Timon. Different characters make appearances at these meet-and-greet pavilions throughout the day.

Keep in mind that this is one of the few places in all of Disney's Animal Kingdom to schmooze with the characters. Therefore, if you are traveling with small children, this area is not to be missed.

Camp Minnie-Mickey is also the home of two engaging theater shows, starring the cast of *The Lion King* and the heroine of the Disney film *Pocahontas*. Both shows are presented daily. Check a guidemap for times.

Festival of the Lion King

In addition to rustling up grubs in Camp Minnie-Mickey, the cast of *The Lion King* performs a 30-minute stage show in the Lion King Theater.

Presented in the round, this lavish outdoor revue is as bright and boisterous as they come. The dramatic opening features a parade of performers in colorful animal costumes. What follows is an intriguing, energetic interpretation of the film, including songs, dances, and acrobatics. With the exception of Timon, who plays himself, lead characters are portrayed by humans draped in bold African costumes. The rolling stages come courtesy of Disneyland. They were used in the park's *Lion King* parade.

Songs include Scar's nasty version of "Be Prepared," as well as "Can You Feel the Love Tonight?," "The Circle of Life," and a rousing audience-participation rendition of "The Lion Sleeps Tonight."

Timing Tip: Although this covered theater accommodates 1,400 guests at a time, we recommend arriving at least 45 minutes before the scheduled performance time—since the show is extremely popular. Take our word for it: it's worth the wait.

Pocahontas and Her Forest Friends

The forest is in trouble, and Pocahontas is worried. "It is being cut down limb by limb," she tells Grandmother Willow (the wise old tree from Disney's *Pocahontas*). "They are leaving nothing in their path."

And so the stage is set for this 12-minute presentation in Grandmother Willow's Grove. The grim premise soon gives way to a more positive outlook, as Grandmother Willow reminds Pocahontas that there is one creature of the forest who has the power to protect it. But which one?

Pocahontas begins a quest to find the creature. Along the way, she learns that many forest dwellers have special talents. Among them are possums, porcupines, skunks, rabbits, and even snakes. Her encounters with these real live critters are interspersed with heartfelt verses of the song "Colors of the Wind." At the end of this sweet and simple musical fable, Pocahontas learns a very important lesson about preserving the forest—as do many members of the audience.

Note: The small theater space isn't entirely canopied. Wear sunscreen. Also, because live animals star in the production, no food is permitted in the seating area. The cast includes a few live rats and one live snake (just a warning).

SHOPPING

Entrance Area

GARDEN GATE GIFTS: Located near the entrance to The Oasis, this is the place to rent strollers and wheelchairs. Film and disposable cameras are for sale, as is a selection of shirts, hats, and other merchandise. This is also the park's package pickup location.

OUTPOST: This small shop, located just outside the park entrance, features a variety of character merchandise and Animal Kingdom souvenirs.

Safari Village

BEASTLY BAZAAR: Safari hats with Mickey, Pooh, or Pluto ears; Disney's Animal Kingdom logo watches; character figurines; and plush toys clad in safari garb are among the wares offered in this shop, designed as a celebration of aquatic animals.

CREATURE COMFORTS: This open-air shop offers items for kids—toys, clothes, costumes, hats, and more.

WONDERS OF THE WILD: Nature-themed gifts and apparel are the stock-in-trade here. In addition to men's and women's clothing, you'll discover items such as wind chimes, fountains, and aromatic candles. Make a point of checking out the authentic carved animal totem poles in the center room—they are most impressive.

ISLAND MERCANTILE: This sprawling shop is themed as a shipping company that celebrates working animals—camels, elephants, beavers, and others. Here, you'll find character merchandise, clothing, candy, and Disney paraphernalia. Note that it stays open about a half hour after the park closes for the day.

Africa

DUKA LA FILIMU: Situated near the entrance to Kilimanjaro Safaris, this is an ideal place to load up on film for your trip. You will find it comes in handy when you need to develop the film after your visit to the African savanna, too.

MOMBASA MARKETPLACE AND ZIWANI TRADERS: An African marketplace and trading company, these connected shops feature animal toys, safari clothing, T-shirts, books, and Africa-themed gifts such as pottery, masks, and musical instruments.

DID YOU KNOW...

Many of the costumes worn by Animal Kingdom cast members are made of wood—actually, a natural fabric called lyocell, made from wood pulp. The pulp is harvested from trees grown specifically for this purpose.

OUT OF THE WILD: Located just outside the exit of Conservation Station, this open-air shop stocks souvenirs with a conservation theme, including shirts, hats, books, toys, and even items for the bath.

DinoLand U.S.A.

CHESTER & HESTER'S DINOSAUR TREASURES: Themed as an American roadside souvenir stand, this shop pays homage to all reptiles and prehistoric animals. Its dinosaur focus is reflected in an assortment of wacky dino-inspired items.

ENTERTAINMENT

AFRICAN ENTERTAINMENT: Contemporary sounds of Africa often fill the air as live bands serenade guests passing through the village of Harambe. Storytellers perform animal tales throughout the day.

ANIMAL ENCOUNTERS: Enjoy up-close encounters with some of the smaller members of the animal kingdom as they wander the park with their human keepers.

DINOLAND U.S.A. ENTERTAINMENT: There's a bunch of loud-mouthed dinosaur groupies on the loose in DinoLand U.S.A. This raucous troupe of improv performers will stop at nothing to get your attention— and make you dig 'em.

HOT TIPS

- Island Mercantile in Safari Village stays open a half hour after the park closes.

- Most of Animal Kingdom's attractions take place outdoors. Don't become overheated! Make a point of slipping into an air-conditioned shop or restaurant from time to time to cool off.

- Narrow, winding paths; grooved pavement; and hilly terrain make this the most challenging Disney theme park in which to navigate a wheelchair.

- Arrive at the park at least a half hour before the posted opening time.

- Check the Animal Kingdom Tip Board often to get an idea of showtimes and crowds.

- The line for Kilimanjaro Safaris tends to dwindle a bit by midday. See it then (the experience is enjoyable at any time of day).

- Make priority seating arrangements *in advance* for the character breakfast at Restaurantosaurus in DinoLand U.S.A.

- Rainforest Cafe generally keeps longer hours than the park does.

- When the weather gets steamy, keep a refillable water bottle with you at all times.

- WDW resort guests can have packages delivered to their hotels free of charge.

Where to Eat in Animal Kingdom

A complete listing of eateries at Disney's Animal Kingdom—table-service restaurants, fast-food spots, and snack stands—can be found in the *Good Meals, Great Times* chapter of this book. See the Animal Kingdom restaurant section, which begins on page 231.

Everything Else in the World

184 Downtown Disney

191 BoardWalk

192 Water Parks

198 Fort Wilderness

201 WDW Spas

202 Fireworks Cruises

203 Behind-the-Scenes Tours

While the total turf of the World encompasses 47 square miles, the theme parks cover less than 1,000 acres. Much of the remaining Walt Disney World terrain is crammed with irresistible activities of a variety and quality seldom found anywhere else.

There's superb golf and tennis, beaches for sunbathing, lakes for speedboating and sailing, canoes to rent and winding streams to paddle along, bicycles for hire, campfire sites, nature trails, and picnic grounds. The recreation options continue with River Country, Disney's old-fashioned swimming cove; Typhoon Lagoon, a state-of-the-art water park complete with surfing lagoon; and Blizzard Beach, a thrilling watery wonderland that translates the hallmarks of a ski resort to the realm of swimming.

A triumverate of lavish spas provides guests with ample opportunity to pamper themselves silly. Intriguing "backstage" programs invite the curious to slip behind the scenes and learn about the workings of Walt Disney World. Add to all that Downtown Disney, a dining, shopping, and amusement district encompassing Pleasure Island, an after-dark entertainment complex; the Marketplace, a colorful assortment of shops and restaurants; and the West Side, a cluster of themed eateries, unique shops, and interactive entertainment experiences. It seems this really is a World without end.

DOWNTOWN DISNEY

prinkled across 120 waterfront acres are the shops, nightclubs, restaurants, and entertainment sites that collectively make up Downtown Disney. Like the downtown area of any thriving metropolis, Disney's Downtown consists of several distinct neighborhoods. In this case, they are the Marketplace, Pleasure Island, and the West Side. Unlike a typical downtown, however, the Disney depiction dispenses with the downside. You won't see litter on the streets, unsightly storefronts, or weary workers rushing home at 5 o'clock. You *will* see a series of spirited spots designed solely for your dining, shopping, and partying pleasure.

Judging by the throngs that descend upon this place, Downtown Disney is *the* place to be after dark. That said, it can get a tad congested—especially on the roads leading here. Whether you are traveling by bus or car, allow plenty of extra time to get to and from this fun zone. Note that all three sections are connected by walking paths, and the West Side and Marketplace are linked by water taxi service (after 6 P.M.).

Downtown Disney Essentials

GUEST SERVICES: Next to Toys Fantastic in the Marketplace, and at the AMC Theatres on the West Side, these information centers are also the place to go for priority seating assistance, Lost and Found, stroller and wheelchair rental, theme park ticket purchase, and more. There is an ATM near Guest Services in the Marketplace, next to Forty Thirst Street on the West Side, and near the Rock N Roll Beach Club at Pleasure Island.

HOW TO GET THERE: Downtown Disney is accessible from exits 26B and 27 off I-4.

By WDW Transportation: From the Disney Institute: walkway or bus. From Port Orleans, Dixie Landings, and Old Key West: boats or buses. From the Magic Kingdom, Epcot, Grand Floridian, Contemporary, and Polynesian: monorail to the Transportation and Ticket Center (TTC), then transfer to a Downtown Disney bus. From the Disney-MGM Studios, Animal Kingdom, Wilderness Lodge, and Fort Wilderness: bus to the TTC, then switch to a Downtown Disney bus. From all other WDW resorts: buses. For more information, turn to the *Transportation & Accommodations* chapter.

By Taxi: Yellow cabs, operated by several different companies, service the Downtown Disney area. The cost to most WDW resorts is usually $5 to $15.

Note: We recommend sticking with authorized yellow cabs, and avoiding the independent cabs. Their fees are not regulated and are often outrageous.

West Side

Pleasure Island

Downtown Disney Marketplace

Located on the shores of Lake Buena Vista, the Marketplace is a relaxing setting for shopping, dining, and much more. The waterside enclave is sprinkled with gardens featuring whimsical topiaries. Kids are fond of the Downtown Disney Marketplace Carousel, (tucked between Pooh Corner and Gourmet Pantry.) And adults may enjoy a drink at the area known as Sunset Cove.

While many guests opt to eat in a restaurant, others grab a bite from the Gourmet Pantry and sit at waterfront tables. (Refer to *Good Meals, Great Times* for restaurant information.) Afterward, some gravitate toward the marina for boating or fishing. (See *Sports* for details.)

Shopping

The descriptions below suggest the types of wares each store offers. Most shops are open daily from 9:30 A.M. to 11 P.M. Note that delivery to a Walt Disney World resort is free. (Keep in mind that packages may take up to two days to arrive at your resort.)

THE ART OF DISNEY: Disney animation cels, porcelain figures, ceramics, and collectibles are the goods available at this gallery next to 2R's Reading and Riting.

DISNEY AT HOME: You'll find an eclectic selection of items for the bedroom and bath here. Among the wares once on display were Pooh sheets, bathroom carpets shaped like Mickey's head, and lamps, rocking chairs, and even beds with a Mickey theme (some designs are more subtle than others).

DISNEY'S DAYS OF CHRISTMAS: Here's the best place to deck the halls Disney-style—it's the largest Christmas shop on Disney property. In addition to character items, the shop, which smells of cinnamon, boasts a large assortment of handcrafted ornaments. Other items to look for: Christmas cards, candles, Santa hats with Mouse ears, pajamas, and books. Many items can be personalized.

EUROSPAIN: This shop sells handcrafted items from Spanish artisans and designers. Large cut-glass bowls and vases are available, along with mugs, sculptures, and other wares, all of which can be engraved.

GENERATION BENEFITS: Designed to have the appearance of a Bermuda plantation home, this shop boasts a sizable stock of traditional and casual men's and women's clothing from designers such as Nautica, Ralph Lauren, Liz Claiborne and Tommy Hilfiger. It is located near Toys Fantastic.

GOURMET PANTRY: Though escargots and smoked oysters can be found here, there are also breads and pastries, meats and cheeses, beer, wine, soft drinks, and much more. Unusual teas and specially blended coffees are available, as are chocolates, sandwiches, and salads. Free tastes are occasionally offered to lucky passersby. Guests staying at the nearby villas, take note: Purchases can be delivered to your room; if you aren't going to be there, the delivery person will even stash perishable items in your refrigerator. To order by phone, call 407-828-3886.

Marketplace

LEGO IMAGINATION CENTER: World of Disney's next-door neighbor, this shop is a showcase for larger-than-life Lego models, including dinosaurs and scary aliens. It also invites guests to flaunt their creativity in an outdoor play area. The store stocks a variety of Lego products and educational toys. By the way, that fire-breathing sea serpent in Lake Buena Vista is also made of Legos.

POOH CORNER: Searching for that perfect plush Pooh? You'll find him here, along with his pals from the Hundred Acre Wood. Also on hand are kitchen items, stationery, books, sweatshirts, T-shirts, and other clothing for adults and kids. The shop itself is quite soothing, with the ceiling painted to look like a blue sky with puffy clouds drifting by. Pooh videos are shown on screens behind the counter.

RESORTWEAR UNLIMITED: An excellent source of bright and sophisticated fashions for women. An assortment of sportswear is enhanced by bold jewelry and handbags. Lancôme cosmetics are available.

STUDIO M: Here guests can have a portrait taken with Mickey Mouse and have their image added to photos of Disney characters. It's also possible to create a custom CD of classic Walt Disney World music and dialogue.

SUMMER SANDS: A beach lover's delight, this shop stocks swimwear, kids' clothing, sun care products, straw hats, and bags.

TEAM MICKEY'S ATHLETIC CLUB: A cavernous store with a locker-room motif, this shop is the perfect setting for sports clothing, activewear, and sports equipment.

You'll find many items with Disney characters in sporting poses emblazoned on them. There is also a large selection of golf apparel.

TOYS FANTASTIC: This fun spot stocks a wide variety of Mattel toys and games, including the newest playthings featuring Disney characters, a full line of Hot Wheels action toys, and Barbie fashions.

2R'S READING AND RITING: Books on many subjects can be found here. Located close to the bus stop, at the far end of the Marketplace, this shop also has greeting cards and stationery. You can sip cappuccino while browsing.

VILLAGE TOWER: This shop boasts a broad selection of Disney merchandise, which changes several times a year.

WORLD OF DISNEY: A sprawling space stuffed with a tremendous selection of Disney merchandise, this is the place for one-stop shopping. In fact, it's the largest Disney character shopping experience in the World. Twelve themed rooms provide the backdrop for the huge array of goods. The enchanted dining room from *Beauty and the Beast* was the inspiration for the culinary section; Disney villains are celebrated in a room that's filled with items such as clocks, watches, candles, and frames; and fairies from *Cinderella* and *Sleeping Beauty* can be seen floating through the intimate apparel department. Disney characters are available on everything from hats and shirts to sleepwear and bags.

Engraving and personalization services are available for many items. A concierge can help locate any item in the store, then arrange for delivery home or to a WDW resort.

Where to Eat at Downtown Disney

A complete listing of restaurants, bars, and snack spots can be found in the *Good Meals, Great Times* chapter. See the Downtown Disney restaurant listing, beginning on page 233. Most restaurants here are open from about 11:30 A.M. to midnight. Planet Hollywood serves until 1 A.M. West Side spots serve as late as 2 A.M.

Downtown Disney Pleasure Island

A six-acre nighttime entertainment complex, Pleasure Island delivers a wealth of options that nicely top off a day in the parks. In addition to clubs, there are several restaurants and shops here in the central area of Downtown Disney.

Most clubs open at 7 P.M. or 8 P.M. and don't close until 2 A.M. There is no fee to explore Pleasure Island before clubs open or to eat at its restaurants. A single admission of $20 (including tax) allows access to clubs and nightly street party. Ultimate Park Hopper Passes include Pleasure Island admission. It's also an option with a Park Hopper Plus Pass. An annual pass costs $58.25 ($47.65 to renew). Guests under age 18 must be accompanied by a parent or guardian. Valet parking costs $6. Guidemaps provide showtime information.

Cocktails and soft drinks are available at all of the clubs. The drinking age in Florida is 21. Guests who are 18 and older will be admitted to the clubs (except Mannequins and BET SoundStage Club) but will not be served alcohol. A valid U.S., foreign, or international driver's license with a photo, an active U.S. military identification card, or a passport must be presented as proof of age.

Clubs

ADVENTURERS CLUB: "Explore the unknown, discover the impossible" states the credo posted at the entrance. The place is modeled after the paneled libraries and elegant salons of similar clubs of the 19th century and is packed with memorabilia. Most of the items on display were collected at garage sales, antiques shows, and shops from around the world by Disney Imagineers.

The two-story club is littered with "stuff," so stroll around and snoop all you like. If you have a seat at the bar, ask the bartender to work some magic; your stool may slowly sink toward the floor. In the library, a haunted organ sets the scene for outrageous storytellers. The show is a little silly, but entertaining.

BET SOUNDSTAGE CLUB: Dancing and other audience-engaging activities combine to make BET SoundStage Club a unique entertainment experience. Located in the space previously occupied by the Neon Armadillo Music Saloon, the club welcomed its first visitors in summer 1998. (It's operated by BET Holdings, Inc., which owns Black Entertainment Television.)

In keeping with the BET musical tradition, the club features the best in rhythm and blues and hip-hop. Early in the evening, a veejay cues up videos by contemporary urban artists from Mariah Carey to Sean "Puffy" Combs and encourages everyone to take to the dance floor. A tempting selection of appetizers is available.

Although big-name talent does perform here on occasion, a Downtown Disney Pleasure Island pass is all you need to enter. Shows are often announced several weeks ahead. Call 407-934-7781 for information. Note that BET SoundStage is restricted to guests 21 and older.

COMEDY WAREHOUSE: A comedy troupe performs five times each evening from 7 P.M. to 1 A.M. There are five comedians and one musician. It's a funny, entertaining show that features improvisational comedy based on audience suggestions. Every seat offers a good view, even if the stools are a little tough on bad backs. Popcorn is the snack of choice.

8TRAX: Got a penchant for the Partridge Family? Do the Bee Gees have a special place in your heart? If so, make tracks for 8TRAX. Music from the early seventies and the disco era fills this dance spot. To keep things in a 1970s mode, the staff even dresses in polyester. The club also has eighties nights every Thursday for the seventies-challenged.

MANNEQUINS: This is the place to head to dance the night away. Guests enter through an elevator that rises to the third floor. Lights, contemporary dance music, and an overall exuberant atmosphere dominate the scene. The name of the club comes from the many mannequins serving as props.

The main dance floor is actually a big turntable, and the music is provided by a deejay. The lighting is a major attraction, with 60 robotically controlled lighting instruments and a matrix of lights behind the stage. Mannequins house dancers occasionally perform on an elevated stage area.

Note that guests must be at least 21 (with valid proof of age) to enter Mannequins.

PLEASURE ISLAND JAZZ COMPANY:
Reminiscent of jazz clubs from the 1930s, the interior of this spot resembles an old warehouse. There is live entertainment nightly, featuring jazz from the 1930s to the present. Guests sit at tables. The music is not too loud, so conversation is possible. Tapas-style appetizers are served.

ROCK N ROLL BEACH CLUB: A combination of dancing and surfer-style decor awaits guests here. The dance floor is on the lowest level of the building, and there are billiard tables and games on the other two floors. Live bands perform hits from the 1960s to the present. The atmosphere is a little frenetic but nonetheless exciting. Light snacks are available.

Note that during the refurbishment a second staircase was added out front, allowing for quicker entrances and exits.

WILDHORSE SALOON: A dance club, restaurant, and concert hall all wrapped up in one, Wildhorse appeals to the fun-lovin' cowpoke in all of us. With an emphasis on new country, the daytime deejay cues up everyone from Garth Brooks to the Dixie Chicks. The atmosphere is casual even into the night (they may blame it all on your roots if you *don't* show up in boots), and live music keeps the joint jumpin'. After midnight, it's "wild time"—when the musical repertoire expands to include all genres.

Free dance lessons are offered daily, beginning at about 6 P.M. There is no admission charge prior to 7 P.M. After that, guests have three options. They can buy a Pleasure Island pass, which includes admission to Wildhorse; purchase a Wildhorse-only pass, which can be upgraded to include the rest of Pleasure Island; or buy a ticket to a premium concert—a show by a big name such as Toby Keith or Diamond Rio—which includes admission. Call 407-827-4947 for information.

Open from 11:30 A.M. to 2 A.M., the kitchen serves lunch, dinner and late night snacks. Priority seating is available. For more information, turn to the *Good Meals, Great Times* chapter.

Entertainment

LATE-NIGHT STREET PARTY: At Pleasure Island, every night is New Year's Eve. There's a fireworks display, special-effects lighting and confetti, and a troupe of dancers entertaining on an outdoor stage.

WEST END STAGE: Bands perform here nightly. The Explosion Dancers, Pleasure Island's own dance troupe, also entertains.

Shopping

The following Pleasure Island shops are all open from 11 A.M. to 1 A.M.:

CHANGING ATTITUDES: This shop reveals its hip young style with an assortment of shirts, accessories, jewelry, bags, and other goods.

DTV: A collection of fun and colorful contemporary fashions featuring Mickey Mouse and his friends is available here.

ISLAND DEPOT: The shop has a nice selection of surfwear and activewear, including shirts, shorts, backpacks, and hats, plus wristwatches and jewelry.

MOUSE HOUSE: A showcase of Disney character items, golf clothing, and souvenirs.

MUSIC LEGENDS: CDs, T-shirts, and music memorabilia are available at this location. There are three sections, highlighting different types of music.

REEL FINDS: Movie- and TV-themed memorabilia constitute the stock here. Items once owned by celebrities are for sale.

SUPERSTAR STUDIOS: Guests lip-synch to favorite songs to create video recordings. A particular favorite with teens.

SUSPENDED ANIMATION: Posters, prints, lithographs, cels, and original Disney animation art are sold here.

Shopping at Crossroads

Constructed by the WDW folks, the Crossroads of Lake Buena Vista shopping center, near the resorts on Hotel Plaza Boulevard, is a convenient dining and shopping area. The center is anchored by a Gooding's supermarket, which is open 24 hours a day. In addition to the many shops and services, there's a miniature golf course dubbed Pirate's Cove Adventure Golf.

Downtown Disney West Side

When Disney's shopping and entertainment district underwent its latest growth spurt, it did so in true American style: It went west. The West Side boasts a wide variety of restaurants, shops, movies, and clubs. Although it does not have an admission fee, some venues may charge a cover.

AMC THEATRES: The most popular multi-screen movie theater complex in the state of Florida is also the largest. The 24 screens show an impressive selection of current movie releases. The seats are roomy and comfortable, and the sound system is first-rate. (It was developed by George Lucas, the creative force behind the series of *Star Wars* blockbusters.) For current schedules, call 407-298-4488.

BONGOS CUBAN CAFE: Situated across from the AMC Theatres on the edge of Lake Buena Vista, Bongos echoes the style of clubs in Miami's South Beach. Created by Gloria Estefan and her husband, it features the flavors and rhythms of Cuba and other Latin American countries. The bold design is dramatic, yet whimsical. Guests dine and, if the mood strikes, even dance amid the colorful, tropical decor (and one remarkably oversized pineapple, which houses a multi-level cocktail lounge).

There is entertainment nightly. The food here moves to a Latin beat as well, with its slate of traditional and nouvelle Cuban dishes. (For more information, refer to *Good Meals, Great Times.*)

CIRQUE DU SOLEIL: The building that towers over all the others at Downtown Disney West Side is actually a tent—a circus tent. It's the home of a most extraordinary entertainment experience: Cirque du Soleil. This original show, titled La Nouba, premiered for Walt Disney World resort guests in winter 1998.

Known for its high energy and artistic performances, Cirque du Soleil shows feature a unique mix of acrobatics and modern dance combined with outrageous costumes, magical lighting, and dramatic original music. A cast of more than 60 international performers showcase their physical talents twice a day, five days a week.

Tickets for the show can be purchased up to six months in advance. Call 407-939-7600 for information or to order tickets. If you have not already purchased tickets, stop by the Cirque du Soleil box office at Downtown Disney West Side—seats are often available. Note that the show is quite popular. Get your tickets as early as possible.

DISNEYQUEST: This imaginative entertainment complex features high-tech activities that engage kids and grown-ups alike. Best described as a self-contained, interactive theme park, the five floors under the DisneyQuest roof are divided into four "zones": Explore, Score, Create, and Replay.

Each zone features rides and games from the simple (classic video games like Asteroids, in Replay) to some of the most technologically advanced (e.g., Create's CyberSpace Mountain, in which guests not only design gravity-defying roller coasters but actually get to ride their creations in a simulator).

Other stops on the tour include Buzz Lightyear's AstroBlaster (wacky bumper cars that shoot balls at other drivers), Mighty Ducks Pinball Slam (which transforms players into human joysticks), Sid's Create-a-Toy (a computer terminal that allows guests to assemble their own twisted toys), the family-oriented Virtual Jungle Cruise (a turbulent river raft ride into a primeval world), and Pirates of the Caribbean: Battle for Buccaneer Gold (a swashbuckling shipboard adventure).

Hunger pangs can be quelled in two areas run by the Cheesecake Factory Express: The Wonderland Cafe, featuring snacks and drinks, and, FoodQuest, which has tempting sandwiches, burgers, salads, and more.

Expect to be fully engaged for two to three hours at a stretch (or until sensory overload sets in). DisneyQuest is open daily from late morning till midnight.

HOUSE OF BLUES: A combination restaurant-music hall with room for 2,000, House of Blues (HOB) was inspired by one of America's most celebrated musical traditions. Lest too much of the blues bring you down, there is a lively dose of jazz and country, plus a little bit of R & B and some rock 'n' roll thrown into the music mix. The old-fashioned southern cooking lures diners here—especially on Sunday mornings, when the chefs prepare an all-you-can eat buffet feast, complemented by live gospel music. Tickets can be purchased through Ticket-Master (407-839-3900; *www.ticketmaster.com*) or the House of Blues box office (407-934-2583). Prices range from about $5 to $30, depending on the performer.

The House of Blues restaurant features an interesting mélange of Delta-inspired cuisine, including jambalaya, étouffée, and bread pudding. (Refer to the *Good Meals, Great Times* chapter for additional information.)

WOLFGANG PUCK CAFE: This restaurant brings the L.A. chef's creative California cuisine to the fore in Florida. There are three dining areas in this two-story restaurant—an express counter, a cafe, and a more formal dining room on the second floor—plus a sushi bar. All feature the celebrated chef's signature pizzas, rotisserie chicken, and other specialties.

Shopping

ALL STAR GEAR: This shop specializes in sports gear, hats, shirts, and other items stamped with the Official All Star Cafe logo.

CANDY CAULDRON: Stop here for some homemade southern-style sweets in an open candy kitchen.

CELEBRITY EYEWORKS STUDIO: Looking to change your eyeglass image? Slip into some shades that have been sported by the stars—or at least convincing replicas of their shades. Celebrity Eyeworks has designer styles modeled in the movies.

GUITAR GALLERY: Whether you prefer it plugged or unplugged, this spot can satisfy all of your guitar needs. A vintage guitar display entices buyers and browsers alike.

HOYPOLOI: The glass, ceramics, sculpture, jewelry, and other decorative items on display here make this shop seem more like an art gallery. Designed as a "soothing retreat," it is meant to communicate an ambience of harmony, balance, and serenity.

MAGNETRON: Your fridge will never be the same once you've visited this specialty magnet shop with its eclectic assortment of 50,000 magnets.

SOSA FAMILY CIGARS: In addition to offering premium cigars, this shop showcases the art of hand-rolling.

STARABILIAS: The spotlight here is on memorabilia—music, television, movie, political, and historical—allowing you to bring a piece of Hollywood to the folks back home.

VIRGIN MEGASTORE: This store stocks a huge selection of music, from classical to contemporary. Much of it can be sampled with headphones at one of many CD listening stations. Videos and books are also available. Outside, a stage is used for live performances.

WILDHORSE STORE: Before you step onto the Wildhorse dance floor, you might want to step into this shop. It has western-style duds, including denim shirts and bandannas. Also for sale: baseball caps, leather jackets, and Wildhorse logo merchandise.

BOARDWALK

A stroll at Disney's BoardWalk is a journey back in time. Inspired by the Middle Atlantic seaside attractions of the early 1900s, BoardWalk recaptures the carefree atmosphere of that bygone era. The resort is surrounded by restaurants, clubs, and amusements similar to those enjoyed by beachgoers of yesteryear. It's bordered by a wood-planked walkway, which hugs the shore of Crescent Lake. By day, BoardWalk is a peaceful place to soak up sun, enjoy lunch, or simply walk the boards. After dark, the place turns into a twinkling center of nighttime activity—some of it elegant, some of it downright raucous.

Wyland Galleries, which features the world's foremost marine environmental art, is one of the more calming diversions. Wild-Wood Landing challenges onlookers to test their luck and skill at a collection of classic carnival games. And strolling performers enchant passersby of all ages with magic shows, balloon tricks, and more.

BoardWalk is open to everyone. Although there is no admission price, individual venues may charge a cover. There is a $6 charge for valet parking after 5 P.M. for guests who are not staying at a Walt Disney World resort. Self-parking is free. (For more restaurant information, refer to *Good Meals, Great Times*.)

Clubs

ATLANTIC DANCE: Elegant and nostalgic, this is a delightful place to dance the night away. A deejay cranks up tunes, tempting guests to twist, shout, and swing on the spacious dance floor. Live bands, some big, some small, play on select occasions.

In addition to traditional cocktails, the club offers 25 specialty drinks. Sample one at a table in the "big room" or on the more private waterfront balcony.

You can swing and sway here from 8 P.M. until 2 A.M. nightly. Guests must be 18 or older, with a legal ID, to enter. The cover charge is usually $5, though it varies depending on the act scheduled to perform.

Note that a deejay often spins discs just outside the club, turning the boardwalk into a rockin' dance party. Guests of all ages are welcome to join the fun.

ESPN CLUB: This club aims to please sports enthusiasts of all kinds, from the casual armchair quarterback to the most rabid fanatic. It includes a multimedia center (complete with an Internet connection), broadcasting facility, arcade, and table-service restaurant and bar.

More than 80 televisions broadcast live sports events, so guests always know the score. (Need to make a pit stop at a crucial moment of the game? Don't sweat it—there are even TVs in the bathrooms.)

The ESPN Club has three sections. As you enter, you're on the 50-yard line at The Sidelines. You can catch a game on a television monitor above the "penalty box" bar or sit at a nearby table (from which you can pick up the sound of any TV in the room). Beer, wine, and soft drinks are available, as is the usual pub fare.

Sports Central, the main dining area, has a big screen, showing—what else—the big game. The kitchen is open until 11:30 P.M. for meals, 1 A.M. for appetizers.

The Yard Arcade, a gameroom with an "urban playground" motif, lets you play the latest sports-themed video games while listening to the big game of the moment.

JELLYROLLS: You might want to warm up your vocal cords before crossing the threshold. They don't call it a sing-along bar for nothing: Guests are expected to sing, clap, and join in the fun at this rollicking warehouse, home of dueling pianos. You'll hear everything from Gershwin to *Grease*. The piano players take requests, so plan ahead. Write the request—a cocktail napkin will do—and slip it onto the piano. (Although it's not required, we recommend slipping a tip along, too. It will increase the odds of your hearing the request *and* help the musicians pay their rent.)

Jellyrolls is open from 7 P.M. until 2 A.M. nightly. There is usually a $5 cover charge to enter. (Note that the cover charge may vary.) To get in, you must be at least 18 years old and willing to prove it.

WATER PARKS
Typhoon Lagoon

A furious storm once roared 'cross the sea,
Catching ships in its path, helpless to flee,
Instead of a certain and watery doom,
The winds swept them here to Typhoon Lagoon!

So reads the legend that guests see as they approach Typhoon Lagoon, a 56-acre aquatic park. The watery playground was inspired by an imagined legend: A typhoon hit a tiny resort village many years ago, and the storm—plus an ensuing earthquake and volcanic eruption—left the village in ruins. The locals, however, were resourceful and rebuilt their town as this "wateropolis."

The centerpiece of Typhoon Lagoon is a huge watershed mountain known as Mt. Mayday. Perched atop its peak is the *Miss Tilly*, a marooned shrimp boat originally from Safen Sound, Florida. *Miss Tilly*'s smokestack erupts every half hour, shooting a 50-foot flume of water into the air.

The surf lagoon is huge: Thrilling slides snake through caves, tamer ones offer twisting journeys, and tiny slides entertain small kids. Note that children under ten must be accompanied by an adult.

SURF POOL: The main swimming area contains nearly three million gallons of water, making it one of the world's largest wave pools. The Caribbean-blue lagoon is surrounded by a white-sand beach, and its main attraction is the waves that come crashing to the shore every 90 seconds. The less adventurous can loll about in two relatively calm tide pools, Whitecap Cove and Blustery Bay.

CASTAWAY CREEK: This 2,100-foot circular river that winds through the park offers a lazy, relaxing orientation to Typhoon Lagoon. Tubes may be borrowed for free and are the

most enjoyable way to make the trip along the three-foot-deep waterway. The ride takes guests through a rain forest, where they are cooled by mists and spray; through caves and grottoes that provide welcome shade on hot summer days; and through an area known as Water Works, where "broken" pipes from a water tower unleash showers on helpless passersby. The current

Modest maidens beware! A one-piece suit is far safer than a two-piece on many of the more adventurous water slides—especially Typhoon Lagoon's Humunga Kowabunga and Blizzard Beach's Summit Plummet.

is calm, and aside from a few floating props and the occasional whirlpool, the journey is unimpeded. There are exits along the way, where guests can hop out for a while and do something else, or just dry off a bit and then jump right back into the water. It takes 20 to 35 minutes to ride around the park without taking a break.

GANGPLANK FALLS, KEELHAUL FALLS, AND MAYDAY FALLS: These three whitewater rides offer guests a variety of slippery trips, two of them in inner tubes. All of the slides course through caves and waterfalls, and past intricate rockwork, making the scenery an attraction in itself. Gangplank Falls gives families a chance to ride together in a three- to five-passenger craft.

HUMUNGA KOWABUNGA: These three speed slides, reported to have been carved into the landscape by the historic earthquake, will send guests zooming through caverns at speeds of 30 miles per hour. The 214-foot slides each offer a 51-foot drop, and the view from the top is a little scary. But it's over before you know it, and once-wary guests hurry back for another try. Guests are also warned that they should be free of back trouble, heart conditions, and other physical limitations to take the trip. Guests must be at least four feet tall to ride any of the Humunga Kowabunga speed slides. Pregnant women are not permitted to ride.

STORM SLIDES: The Jib Jammer, Rudder Buster, and Stern Burner body slides send guests off at about 30 miles per hour down winding fiberglass slides, in and out of rock formations and caves, and through waterfalls. It's a somewhat tamer ride than Humunga Kowabunga, but still offers a speedy descent. The slides run about 300 feet, and each offers a different view and experience.

SHARK REEF: Guests obtain free snorkel equipment for a swim through a coral reef, where they come face-to-face with sharks and tropical fish. The reef is built around a sunken tanker (where non-swimming guests can get a close look from the portholes). The sharks, by the way—leopard, nurse, and bonnethead— are passive members of the species. All guests must shower before entering. Kids must be at least ten years old to experience Shark Reef.

KETCHAKIDDEE CREEK: Open only to those four feet tall or under, this area has small rides for pint-size visitors. Children must be accompanied by an adult. There are slides, fountains, waterfalls, squirting whales and seals, a mini-rapids ride, an interactive tugboat, and a grotto with a veil of water that kids love to run through.

SURFING: Surf clinics are offered on select mornings before the park opens. For information, call 407-WDW-SURF (939-7873).

Essentials

WHEN TO GO: Typhoon Lagoon gets very crowded early in the day. When the park reaches peak capacity, no one will be admitted until crowds subside (usually after 3 P.M.). Hours vary seasonally, but the park is generally open from 10 A.M. to 5 P.M., with extended hours in the summer months. All of the pools are heated in the winter. Note that Typhoon Lagoon is usually closed for refurbishment during certain winter months, typically November and December. The park may also close due to inclement weather. Call 407-939-4636 for schedules.

HOW TO GET THERE: Buses from the Transportation and Ticket Center (TTC) and all Walt Disney World resorts, except the Grand Floridian, Contemporary, Polynesian, Wilderness Lodge, and Fort Wilderness (which require a transfer at the TTC). Parking is free.

LOCKER ROOMS: Restrooms with showers and lockers are located close to the entrance. Other restrooms are available farther into the park. These are labeled "Buoys" and "Gulls." Small lockers cost $3 plus a $2 deposit to rent for the day, while large lockers cost $5 plus a $2 deposit. Towels rent for $1; life jackets and tubes are available free of charge.

WHERE TO EAT: Both of the Typhoon Lagoon restaurants offer similar fare and outdoor seating. Leaning Palms, which was known as Placid Palms before the typhoon hit, was renamed to fit its somewhat unorthodox architecture. Burgers, pizza, salads, ice cream, and assorted snacks are sold here. Typhoon Tilly's Snack Shack serves fish and chips and has a separate area just for ice cream and frozen yogurt. Let's Go Slurpin offers frozen drink specialties and spirits. Also on hand are picnic areas, where guests can bring their own food or enjoy a sampling from the restaurants. Note that no alcoholic beverages or glass containers can be brought into the park.

FIRST AID: A first-aid station capable of handling minor medical problems is located just to the left of Leaning Palms.

BEACH SHOP: Singapore Sal's, located to the right of the park's main entrance, is set in a ramshackle building left a bit battered by the typhoon. Bathing suits, sunglasses, hats, towels, sunscreen, souvenirs, thong sandals, and beach chairs are for sale here.

Admission Prices

ONE-DAY TICKET
(Prices include sales tax and are subject to change.)

Adult..$29.63
Child*......................................$23.85

ANNUAL PASS
Adult..$105.95
Child*......................................$85.33

Note: Admission is included with an Ultimate Park Hopper or Premium Annual Pass. It is an option with a Park Hopper Plus Pass.

*3 through 9 years of age; children under 3 free

Blizzard Beach

A wintery, watery wonderland, Blizzard Beach is said to be the result of a freak storm that dropped a mountain of snow onto Walt Disney World, prompting the quick construction of Florida's first ski resort. When temperatures soared and the snow began to melt, designers prepared to close the resort. But when they spotted an alligator sliding down the slopes, they realized that they had created an exhilarating water adventure park! The slalom and bobsled runs became downhill water slides. The ski jump is one of the world's tallest (120 feet), fastest (60 miles per hour), free-fall speed slides.

The centerpiece of Blizzard Beach is the snow-capped Mt. Gushmore and its Summit Plummet. Most of the more thrilling runs are found on the slopes of this mountain, which tops out at 90 feet. At the summit, swimmers have a choice of speed slides, flumes, a white-water raft ride, and an inner-tube run. There is also an observation tower that offers a spectacular view. Guests may reach the top of Mt. Gushmore via chairlift. The lift is equipped with a gondola for guests with disabilities. There are also three sets of stairs for those who prefer to scale the mountain on foot.

This is the most action-packed Disney water park yet, with enough activities for the entire family to fill at least a day. Note that kids under ten must be accompanied by an adult.

MELT-AWAY BAY: This one-acre pool at the base of Mt. Gushmore is equipped with its own wave machine. No tsunamis here, however—just a pleasant bobbing wave.

CROSS COUNTRY CREEK: This meandering 3,000-foot waterway circles the entire park. A slow current keeps visitors moving along. Inner tubes, which are free, are the most pleasant way to travel. The ride includes a trip through a bone-chilling ice cave, where guests are splashed with the "melting ice" from overhead.

SUMMIT PLUMMET: The big thrill ride begins 120 feet in the air on a platform built 30 feet above the top of Mt. Gushmore. (In other words, it's high! If you suffer from vertigo, pass on this plummet.) Brave souls travel about 60 miles per hour down a 350-foot slide. Near the top, guests pass through a ski chalet. To those watching from below, riders seem to disappear into an explosion of mist. Guests must be at least four feet tall to take the plunge.

SLUSH GUSHER: This relatively tame, double-humped water slide offers a brisk journey through a snow-banked mountain gully. Topping out at 90 feet, Slush Gusher is the tallest slide of its kind. You'll find it on Mt. Gushmore, next to Summit Plummet. Guests must be at least four feet tall to ride.

TEAMBOAT SPRINGS: The longest family white-water raft ride in the world takes five-passenger rafts down a twisting, 1,200-foot series of rushing waterfalls.

TOBOGGAN RACERS: An eight-lane water slide sends guests racing over a number of dips. They lie on their stomachs on a mat and travel headfirst down the 250-foot route.

SNOW STORMERS: A trio of flumes descends from the top of the mountain. Guests race down on a switchback course that includes ski-type slalom gates.

RUNOFF RAPIDS: On this inner-tube run, guests careen down three twisting, turning flumes in a single, double, or triple tube.

DOWNHILL DOUBLE DIPPER: Guests travel down these two parallel 230-foot-long racing slides at speeds of up to 25 miles per hour. The partially enclosed water runs feature ski-racing graphics, flags, and time clocks. You must be 48 inches tall to ride.

SKI PATROL TRAINING CAMP: An area designed specifically for preteens. Frozen Pipe Springs looks like an old pipe and drops sliders into eight feet of water. The Thin Ice Training Course tests agility as kids try to walk along broken "icebergs" without falling into the water. Snow Falls' "wide" slides allow a parent and child to ride together. At the Ski Patrol Shelter, guests grab on to a T-bar for an airborne trip. At any point in the ride they can drop into the water below. Ski patrol participants also experience Cool Runners, where riders can count on hurtling and whirling over lots of moguls on twin inner-tube slides. No bunny slopes for these brave daredevils.

TIKE'S PEAK: A kid-size variation of Blizzard Beach, this attraction features miniature versions of Mt. Gushmore's slides and a snow-castle fountain play area.

Essentials

WHEN TO GO: As the World's largest water park, Blizzard Beach becomes very crowded early in the day. When the park reaches peak capacity, no one is admitted until crowds subside (usually after 3 P.M.). Hours vary seasonally, but the park is generally open from 10 A.M. to 5 P.M., with extended hours in summer. All pools are heated in winter. Blizzard Beach is often closed for refurbishment during certain winter months, typically January and February. It may also close due to inclement weather. For schedules, call 407-WDW-INFO (939-4636).

HOW TO GET THERE: Buses are available from the Transportation and Ticket Center (TTC) and all WDW resorts. Parking is free.

LOCKER ROOMS: There are restrooms with showers near the main entrance. Other restrooms and dressing rooms are located around the park. Small lockers cost $3 plus a $2 deposit for the day, while large lockers cost $5 plus a $2 deposit. Towels rent for $1, and life jackets and tubes may be used for free.

WHERE TO EAT: Burgers, hot dogs, fruit salads, and drinks are available at Lottawatta Lodge, in the main village area. Two snack stands with limited offerings are located in more remote areas: Avalunch and The Warming Hut. Frostbite Freddie's Frozen Frosty Freshments offers drink specialties and spirits. There are picnic areas for those who prefer to pack their own. No alcoholic beverages or glass containers are permitted in the park.

FIRST AID: Minor medical problems are handled at this station near the main entrance.

BEACH SHOP: The Beach Haus stocks bathing suits, T-shirts, shorts, sunglasses, hats, sunscreen, beach towels, and more.

Admission Prices

ONE-DAY TICKET
(Prices include sales tax and are subject to change.)
Adult..$29.63
Child*......................................$23.85

ANNUAL PASS
Adult $105.95
Child* $85.33

COMBO TICKET (Includes one-day admission to Blizzard Beach and Disney's Winter Summerland miniature golf course.)
Adult..$37.05
Child*......................................$29.63

Note: Admission is included with an Ultimate Park Hopper or Premium Annual Pass. It is an option with a Park Hopper Plus Pass.

*3 through 9 years of age; children under 3 free

River Country

It's next to impossible to go through childhood reading such classic books as *The Adventures of Tom Sawyer* and *The Adventures of Huckleberry Finn* (and other great tales of growing up) without developing a few fantasies about what it would be like to swim in the perfect swimming cove. A group of Imagineers concocted a Disney version on a somewhat larger scale at River Country, a water-oriented playground that occupies a corner of Bay Lake near Fort Wilderness campground.

Fred Joerger—the same Disney rock builder who created the Magic Kingdom's Big Thunder Mountain, Schweitzer Falls at the Jungle Cruise, and the caves of Tom Sawyer Island—also helped design the rocks used to landscape one of the largest swimming pools in the state of Florida. The rocks, scattered with real pebbles acquired from streambeds in Georgia and the Carolinas, look so real that it's hard to believe they aren't.

More to the point, the place is great fun. Slipping and sliding down the curvy water chutes at top speed, floating along White Water Rapids, and slamming into the water from the swimming pool's high slides make even carewarn grown-ups smile, grin, giggle, chortle, and roar with delight. People who climb to the top of the Raft Rider Ridge with trepidation may be surprised to find themselves rushing back for more. Line-haters queue up—over and over again. Those who associate lakes with muck and weeds get ecstatic over the way the soft sand on the River Country bottom squishes between their toes. Kids under ten must be accompanied by an adult.

WHAT TO DO: There are several sections to River Country: the 330,000-gallon swimming pool; Bay Cove, the big walled-off section of Bay Lake that most people consider the main (and best) part of River Country; Kiddie Cove, an adjoining junior version of the above for small children, with its own beach; and the grassy grounds, with picnic tables and Indian Springs, a squirting fountain in which to play. On the edge of the lake there's also Cypress Point, a boardwalk nature trail through a lovely cypress swamp, and a wide (if not terribly long) white-sand beach.

The large swimming pool that's known as Upstream Plunge is heated in winter. It has a pair of Slippery Slide Falls water slides that begin high enough above the water to make an acrophobe climb right down again. They plunge at such an angle that it's impossible to see the bottom of the slide from the top. Daredevils who don't chicken out are shot into the water from a height of about seven feet—hard enough, as one commentator observed, to "slap your stomach up against the roof of your mouth." Gutsy kids adore the experience; those who like their thrills a bit tamer might prefer to watch.

The heart of River Country, Bay Cove, is actually a part of Bay Lake (and quite chilly during cooler months). It's fitted out with a rope climb, a ship's boom for swooping and plunging, and other constructions designed to put hearts into throats as swimmers plunge from air to water. The big deals, however, are the two flume rides—one 260 feet long and a smaller one, 100 feet shorter (accessible by a stairway to the left)—and a white-water raft ride called White Water Rapids.

The flumes, which are steep-sided water slides, corkscrew through the greenery at the top of the ridge, sending even the most stalwart shooting into the water, usually like greased lightning. White Water Rapids involves a more leisurely trip through a series of chutes and pools in an inner tube from the crest of Raft Rider Ridge (adjoining Whoop-'N-Holler Hollow) into Bay Cove. It's not a high-speed affair like the flumes, but some people like it better.

Essentials

WHEN TO GO: Daytime temperatures in Florida are such that it's possible to enjoy River Country almost all year round, though it is perhaps most pleasant in spring, when the weather is getting hot but the water is still on the cool side. In summer, the place can be very busy indeed. When the park reaches capacity, no one will be admitted until the crowds subside. Things usually quiet down after 3 P.M. Although hours vary, River Country often opens at 10 A.M. and closes at 5 P.M. During the summer it's open till 7 P.M. River Country is usually closed for refurbishment during off-peak months, typically September and October. Call 407-939-4636 for up-to-the-minute schedules. Note that River Country may also close as a result of inclement weather.

The warmer months are especially festive here. Independence Day is celebrated from late spring through early September. The All-American Water Party features appearances by Goofy and other Disney characters, games, and a parade. For details, call 407-939-4636.

HOW TO GET THERE: From the TTC, buses drop off passengers within walking distance of River Country. It's also possible to travel by boat. Launches leave regularly from the dock near the gates of the Magic Kingdom. Guests arriving at River Country by car may take a bus from the Fort Wilderness visitor parking lot to the entrance.

LOCKER ROOMS: Dressing rooms with showers and lockers are available. Small lockers cost $3 plus a $2 deposit to rent for the day; large lockers cost $5 plus a $2 deposit. Towels are available to rent for

$1 each at the concession window, but they are small, so you'll probably want to bring a beach towel.

WHERE TO EAT: Pop's Place has foot-long hot dogs, chicken strips, meatball subs, baked beans, brownies, ice cream, apple pie, and peanut butter and jelly sandwiches. The Waterin' Hole offers a limited selection during peak seasons. Picnicking is permitted (no alcohol or glass containers allowed). Eat on the beach or at a shaded table.

FIRST AID: A first-aid station capable of handling minor medical problems is located near the locker rooms.

BEACH SHOP: Film, towels, sand pails, sunscreen, sunglasses, and other beach essentials are available at the River Relics stand.

Admission Prices

ONE-DAY TICKET
(Prices include sales tax and are subject to change.)
Adult $16.91
Child* $13.25

Note: Admission is included with an Ultimate Park Hopper or Premium Annual Pass. It is an option with a Park Hopper Plus pass.

*3 through 9 years of age; children under 3 free

FORT WILDERNESS

In a part of the state where campgrounds tend to look like dried pastures—barren and very hot—the Fort Wilderness Resort and Campground, located almost due east of the Contemporary resort, is an anomaly—a forested, 700-acre wonder of tall slash pines, white-flowering bay trees, and ancient cypresses hung with Spanish moss. Seminole Indians once hunted and fished here.

There are more than a thousand campsites arranged in several campground loops; among them, Wilderness Cabins are available for rent, completely furnished and fitted with all the comforts of home. For information about lodging options, see *Transportation & Accommodations*.

Scattered throughout the campground loops are sporting facilities, including two tennis courts, and many tetherball, basketball, and volleyball courts. Fort Wilderness has riding stables, two swimming pools, a marina full of boats, a canoe livery, a beach, bikes and golf carts for rent, and a nature trail. Some facilities are available to campground guests only; some are open to guests at WDW-owned resort hotels and villas as well; some can also be enjoyed by guests lodging at the resorts on Hotel Plaza Boulevard as well as off the property.

There's also a petting farm and a barn that's home to the horses that pull the Magic Kingdom's Main Street trolleys. The barn houses a small museum that celebrates horses and the role they've played in Disney history.

Two stores—the Settlement Trading Post and the Meadow Trading Post—stock campers' necessities, groceries, and souvenirs. And then there's Pioneer Hall, the home of the

Hoop-Dee-Doo Musical Revue dinner show (described in the *Good Meals, Great Times* chapter). This rustic structure (made of white pine shipped all the way from Montana) also has a buffet-style restaurant and a small lounge area.

Last but not least in the Fort Wilderness neighborhood is River Country. The eight-acre expanse of water-oriented recreation embodies everyone's idea of a perfect old-fashioned swimming area. Note that it's a separate attraction, with its own hours and admission fee.

BEACHES AND SWIMMING: The beach on the shore of Bay Lake is a delightful spot for sunning or snoozing in a hammock. There are also two pools for campers' use. Note that beaches and pools are open to Fort Wilderness guests only.

BIKE RENTALS: A variety of bikes can be rented at the Bike Barn for trips along the bike paths and roadways of Fort Wilderness—or just for getting around. Bikes cost about $6 per hour or $14 per day.

BLACKSMITH SHOP: The pleasant fellow who shoes the draft horses that pull trolleys in the Magic Kingdom is on hand most mornings to answer questions and talk about his job; occasionally, guests can watch him at work, fitting the big animals with the special polyurethane-covered, steel-cored horseshoes that are used to protect the horses' hooves. This shop is located at the Tri-Circle-D Ranch.

BOATING: Fort Wilderness is ribboned with tranquil canals that make for delightful canoe trips of one to three hours—or longer if you take fishing gear and elect to wet your line. Canoe rentals are available at the Bike Barn for about $6 per half hour or $12 per hour. Pedal boats (about $6 per half hour or $12 per hour) can also be rented here for use in the canals. For a trip around Bay Lake, zippy little Water Mouse boats, canopy boats, and pontoon boats are available for rent at the marina, at the north end of the campground. (See the *Sports* chapter for details and fees.)

CAMPFIRE PROGRAM: Held nightly (weather permitting) near the Meadow Trading Post at the center of the campground, this evening program features Disney movies, a sing-along, and cartoons. It's open to WDW resort guests only (no charge). Also, Chip and Dale often put in an appearance.

ELECTRIC CART RENTALS: Available at the Bike Barn ($36 to $40 for 24 hours) for sightseeing or transportation. Renters must be 18 years old and have a valid driver's license. Reservations are necessary; call 407-824-2742 for reservations and additional information.

ELECTRICAL WATER PAGEANT: This twinkling cavalcade of lights (described in more detail in the *Good Meals, Great Times* chapter) can be seen from the beach here nightly at 9:45 P.M.

FISHING EXCURSIONS ON BAY LAKE: Walt Disney World's restrictive fishing policy means plenty of angling action—largemouth bass weighing two to eight pounds, mainly—for those who sign up for the special fishing excursions. The fee is about $150 for up to five people for a two-hour excursion (one additional hour is about $60) and includes gear, a guide, and refreshments; no license is required. Note that all fishing is strictly catch-and-release. Call 407-WDW-PLAY (939-7529) for exact times and to make reservations.

FISHING IN THE CANALS: In addition to largemouth bass, catfish and panfish can be caught here as well. Those without their own gear will find cane poles and lures for sale at the trading posts; equipment is also available for rent at the Bike Barn. Cane poles are about $4 per hour or $7 for the whole day. Rods and reels are about $5 per hour or $9 per day. Bait costs about $3.50. No license is required. Fort Wilderness resort guests may toss their lines in right from the shore.

HAYRIDES: The hay wagon departs from Pioneer Hall at 7 P.M. and 9:30 P.M., and carries guests on a trip through wooded areas near Bay Lake. Each ride lasts about an hour and concludes at Pioneer Hall. Purchase tickets from the hayride host: $6 for adults, $4 for children three through nine. Children under ten must be accompanied by an adult.

LAWN MOWER TREE: The tree that somehow, mysteriously, grew around a lawn mower is a Fort Wilderness point of interest worth hunting down. It's just off the sidewalk leading to the marina.

PETTING FARM: This fenced-in enclave just behind Pioneer Hall is home to some friendly goats, sheep, rabbits, chickens, and other barnyard critters. (A colony of prairie dogs didn't work out because its members persisted in burrowing out of their compound; no sooner would their Disney caretakers try to thwart them—by digging a bigger hole and installing a below-ground-level wire fence—than the little creatures would gnaw through it.) Pony rides are available between 9 A.M. and 5 P.M. for $2. (The pony-ride weight limit is 80 pounds.) Though designed with kids in mind, the Petting Farm is also fun for adults, and a good place to pass the time before the Hoop-Dee-Doo Musical Revue.

TENNIS: Two tennis courts are available; play is on a first-come, first-served basis.

TRAIL RIDES: Guided horseback trips depart four times daily from the Trail Blaze Corral and take riders on a leisurely, meandering ride through the Florida wilderness, where it is not uncommon to see birds, deer, and even an occasional alligator. Galloping is not part of the ride, so you don't need riding know-how to sign up. Cost is about $23 per person. No children under nine are allowed to ride. There is a weight limit of 250 pounds. Reservations are necessary; call 407-WDW-PLAY (939-7529) up to 30 days in advance.

TRI-CIRCLE-D RANCH: This corner of Fort Wilderness is the place that the world champion Percherons and the draft horses that pull trolleys down Main Street in the Magic Kingdom call home. You can watch them chomping on their food, and occasionally see young colts and fillies as well. The Tri-Circle-D insignia above the barn door—two small circles atop a large one with the letter *D* inside—is the WDW brand. The barn is also the site of a museum that pays tribute to horses and their role in Disney history.

VOLLEYBALL, TETHERBALL, AND BASKETBALL COURTS: Open only to guests at WDW–owned properties, these are scattered throughout the camping loops. No charge.

WILDERNESS SWAMP TRAIL: A three-quarter-mile trail, this smooth footpath into the woods skirts the marshes along the shore of Bay Lake, then plunges into a forest thick with tall, straight-standing cypress trees. It is near Marshmallow Marsh, at the northern end of the campground.

Essentials

HOW TO GET THERE: From outside the World, take Magic Kingdom Exit 25 off I-4 onto U.S. 192, go through the Magic Kingdom Auto Plaza, and, bearing to your right, follow the Fort Wilderness or River Country signs. This is the most expeditious way to go, even for WDW resort guests.

By WDW Transportation: There is a direct bus (or bicycle path) from the Wilderness Lodge to Fort Wilderness. From Epcot, the Contemporary, Polynesian, and Grand Floridian resorts, take the monorail to the Transportation and Ticket Center (TTC), and transfer for the bus to Fort Wilderness. From Disney-MGM Studios, Animal Kingdom, Downtown Disney, and the resorts on Hotel Plaza Boulevard, take a bus to the TTC. Change there to the bus

School's Out

Disney Institute scholars take note: At press time, the Disney Institute announced plans to suspend its traditional roster of guest-enrichment and behind-the-scenes programs. The property will, however, continue to operate as a full-service Disney resort, complete with tennis facilities, pools, and an excellent spa, as well as the usual Disney resort perks.

For up-to-the minute information on the Disney Institute's status, call 407-WDW-INFO (939-4636). For more details on the guest accommodations currently available at the Disney Institute, refer to page 72.

to Fort Wilderness. From all other WDW resorts, take a bus to Downtown Disney, switch for the bus to the TTC, then take the Fort Wilderness bus. Allow yourself plenty of time to make transfers.

Boats are also available from Magic Kingdom marinas (about a 30-minute ride) and from the Contemporary and Wilderness Lodge resorts (about a 25-minute ride). For details about Walt Disney World Transportation, see the *Transportation & Accommodations* chapter.

WHERE TO EAT: For a description of the Trail's End Buffet at Fort Wilderness, see the *Good Meals, Great Times* chapter. The Settlement Trading Post, located not far from the beach at the north end of the campground, and the Meadow Trading Post, located near the center of Fort Wilderness, also offer food staples.

WDW SPAS

For many guests, a day at the theme parks is an exciting test of physical endurance—complete with sprinting (say from Dumbo to Space Mountain before that Fastpass time expires), weightlifting (toting tired toddlers), and long-distance hiking (covering more than a mile to reach the American Adventure pavilion from Epcot's front gate—and back again!). Fortunately, there are many ways to rest and rejuvenate weary bones, throbbing feet, and noise-addled noggins. Chief among them is a visit to a soothing spa (ahhhh). There are three such spots on Disney property, all open to WDW resort guests and day visitors alike.

Grand Floridian Spa: A short walk from the Grand Floridian Resort, this relaxing retreat is located right next to the health club (across from the wedding pavilion). With saunas, steam rooms, and whirlpools, even the locker rooms promote pampering.

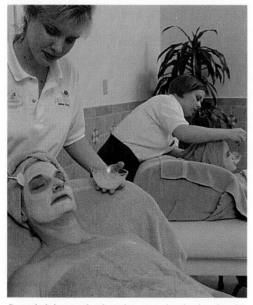

Specialties of the house include baths steeped in flowers, a deluxe facial, complete with hand and foot massage, and a cooling lavender oil wrap, guaranteed to take the sting out of any sunburn. Other services include hydrotherapy, aromatherapy, and massage (including shiatsu, Swedish, sports, and one specially designed for expectant mothers). Manicures, pedicures, and other hand and foot treatments are also available.

Hours are generally from 6 A.M. to 9 P.M., but vary seasonally. Prices (which include 18 percent gratuity) run about $50 for a 25-minute massage and about $90 for a facial. Full- and half-day packages are available.

For additional information, call 407-824-2332. Reservations are accepted up to one month in advance.

The Spa at the Disney Institute: Terracotta-colored tiles and teal towels accent this spa's ten treatment rooms. Signature services include the Warm Seafoam Mud Wrap and Seaweed Hydro-Massage. Also on tap: aromatherapy, reflexology, sports and Swedish massage, and hydrotherapy, plus a variety of body wraps and scrubs. Manicures, pedicures, and facials are also an option. The locker rooms are equipped with a steam room, sauna, and whirlpool.

Located on the shore of Lake Buena Vista, near Downtown Disney, the spa is inside the Fitness Center at the Villas at the Disney Institute. Hours are generally from 8 A.M. to 8 P.M., but vary seasonally. A 25-minute massage costs about $50, with facials going for about $85 (including 18 percent gratuity). Full- and half-day packages are available. For additional information, call 407-827-4455. Reservations are taken up to six months ahead.

The Spa at Wyndham Palace: A plush, peaceful place, this spa is as well-equipped as they come. One-way glass provides natural, picture-window views from (but not into) the 14 treatment rooms. High-tech chairs with whirlpool foot baths and back massage capability make getting a pedicure a real event. And a cool-mud Theme Park Leg Relief Wrap can put the spring back in the step of even the most labored lower limbs. Landscaped, outdoor whirlpools, plus locker room saunas and steam rooms are there to aid the relaxation process.

Among the many treatments from which to choose are aromatherapy and massage, including sports, shiatsu, Swedish, deep-tissue, reflexology, and hydrotherapy. A variety of special facials (including one for sun-stressed skin), baths (herbal, mud, mineral, and seaweed), scrubs, and wraps are available. An adjacent salon offers the usual lineup of services.

The Wyndham Palace Resort & Spa is situated opposite the Downtown Disney Marketplace, on Buena Vista Drive. Hours are usually 6 A.M. to 9 P.M., but vary seasonally. A 25-minute massage costs about $50 and facials are about $85 (including 18 percent gratuity). Full- and half-day packages are available, as are custom packages. For additional information, call 800-981-1472. Spa reservations are accepted up to one month in advance.

FIREWORKS CRUISES

At Walt Disney World, every evening ends with a bang—which comes in the form of elaborate pyrotechnic displays. Two such presentations, the Magic Kingdom's Fantasy in the Sky fireworks and Epcot's IllumiNations: Reflections of Earth, are seen by thousands of park-goers on a nightly basis. However, these dazzling displays are also enjoyed by a privileged few, far removed from the hubbub of the theme park crowds, yet close enough to marvel at the subtleties of each brilliant burst. These are the guests who chose to book a boat for a special fireworks cruise. This vintage vantage point is available to everyone, provided that the rates don't break the budget and and that reservations are made in advance.

As if a private screening of the nightly fireworks weren't enough, it is also possible to go for the dinner and a show option: Disney chefs will cater the event for you. Reservations are accepted up to 24 hours beforehand; advance reservations, accepted up to 90 days ahead, are strongly recommended. While specifics may change, the following is a good indication of what was available at press time.

HOT TIP If you plan to enjoy a scenic fireworks cruise, pack a sweater. It can get chilly out there on the open seas—even during summer!

The Grand 1: This striking 44-foot Sea Ray escorts up to 12 guests at a time. A private tour of the Seven Seas Lagoon and Bay Lake culminates with a front-row seat for the Magic Kingdom's Fantasy in the Sky fireworks. (The vessel drops anchor in the vicinity of the park entrance, aligning itself as closely with Cinderella Castle as possible.) Chefs from the Grand Floridian can cater the affair, providing anything from shrimp cocktail and champagne to a complete dinner for everyone on board. (Note that food and drink are not included in the rental fee.)

The *Grand 1* departs from the Grand Floridian marina, but may stop at the Polynesian, Contemporary, Wilderness Lodge, or Fort Wilderness Lodge on request. It costs about $275 per hour to rent, with the per-boatload fee covering up to 12 guests, plus a driver and deck hand. Call 407-824-2439 to book the boat. For information about having the trip catered, call 407-934-3946.

Pontoon Boats: More practical than luxurious, Disney's fleet of pontoon boats still deliver a crowd-pleasing cruise experience. The boats, which accommodate up to ten, take guests on tours of the Seven Seas Lagoon and Bay Lake, near the Magic Kingdom, as well as Crescent Lake, near Epcot's World Showcase. Those in the Magic Kingdom area are treated to VIP viewing of that park's Fantasy in the Sky fireworks, while Epcot-area cruisers take in IllumiNations: Reflections of Earth. Guests who want to dine while at sea can order (in advance) everything from appetizers to a complete meal.

Pontoon fireworks cruises last about one hour, beginning 30 minutes before the fireworks are scheduled to start. Fantasy in the Sky excursions depart from the Grand Floridian, Polynesian, Contemporary, Wilderness Lodge, and Fort Wilderness marinas. IllumiNations cruises leave from BoardWalk and Yacht and Beach Club marinas. The cost (which includes a driver) is about $120 per boatload. Call 407-WDW-PLAY (939-7529) for reservations. For catering information, contact Guest Services at the resort from which you wish to depart.

The Breathless: This elegant, open-air motor boat, is a sleek 24-foot reproduction of a 1930s mahogany runabout. Named after the Dick Tracy character, the vessel is equipped with bench seats and fits up to seven guests.

Moored at the Yacht and Beach Club marina, the *Breathless* escorts private parties around Crescent Lake and adjoining waterways by day and night. All cruises depart from the Yacht and Beach Club, but requests for pick-ups at the BoardWalk will be honored. From 2:30 P.M. to 5:30 P.M. daily, 10- and 30-minute trips are available. At dusk, one-hour trips culminate with a voyage to Epcot to watch IllumiNations.

Ten- and 30-minute trips cost about $25 and $75 respectively. The one-hour IllumiNations cruise runs about $160. Prices are per boatload (for up to seven people) and include a driver. Refreshments may be ordered in advance. Call 407-WDW-PLAY (939-7529) for reservations.

BEHIND-THE-SCENES TOURS

Disney Adult Discoveries programs offer the chance to experience Walt Disney World from the inside out. These guided behind-the-scenes tours (with the exception of the Disney's Family Magic Tour) are only open to visitors 16 and older. Tours and prices (which include tax) are subject to change; for additional information or to make reservations call 407-WDW-TOUR (939-8687).

Backstage Magic (Monday through Saturday): This is Walt Disney World's most popular program. Highlighting the 7-hour exploration of the Magic Kingdom, Disney-MGM Studios, and Epcot is an underground tour of the Magic Kingdom's Utilidors—Disney's tunnel system. Lunch is included, as are few special surprises. Cost is $199 per person. Theme park admission is not required, or included.

Backstage Safari (Monday, Wednesday, Friday): This 3-hour tour takes guests through backstage animal facilities, such as the nursery and elephant barn at Disney's Animal Kingdom. The cost is $60, plus theme park admission.

Keys to the Kingdom (daily): This 4½-hour tour offers an on-site orientation to the history and workings of Walt Disney World's original theme park, the Magic Kingdom. Guests visit an attraction (waiting in the regular attraction line) and take a peek at the Production Center and the Utilidors (the legendary tunnels underneath the park). Cost is $45, plus theme park admission.

Disney's Family Magic Tour (daily): Guests of all ages can participate in this 2-hour Disney-themed scavenger hunt through the Magic Kingdom. The cost is $25 per adult, $15 per child age 3 through 9, plus park admission.

DiveQuest (daily): The highlight of the 2½-hour program is a 30-minute underwater adventure—complete with sharks, turtles, rays, and other tropical fish—in The Living Seas aquarium. Participants must present proof of current scuba "open water" adult certification. Cost per person is $140. All gear is provided. Park admission is not required, or included.

Dolphins in Depth (weekdays): This 3½-hour program teaches guests about dolphin behavior as they interact with the animals and observe researchers and trainers working with them. The cost is $140, and park admission is not required, or included. For more information, call 407-939-8687.

Gardens of the World (Tuesday, Thursday): Hosted by a Disney horticulturist, this 3-hour program guides guests through a study of plants, flowers, and trees at Epcot's World Showcase. Cost is $49, plus admission to the park.

Hidden Treasures of World Showcase (Tuesday, Thursday, Saturday): This 3-hour tour takes guests to the international pavilions at Epcot's World Showcase. The focus is on the art, architecture, and traditions of our international community. Cost is $49, plus park admission.

Hidden Treasures of World Showcase Plus (Wednesdays): This 5-hour journey takes guests to all World Showcase pavilions, through Epcot's wardrobe department, and includes lunch in Morocco. Park admission is not required or included. Cost is $85 per person.

Inside Animation (Tuesday, Wednesday, Thursday, Friday): This 2½-hour program takes place at the Disney-MGM Studios. Participants learn about the art and history of animation, discover how the classics are brought to life, and create their own Mickey Mouse cel. Cost is $49. Park admission is not required, or included.

It's a Celebration!

What happens when a little bit of Disney magic spills into the real world? A town called Celebration, Florida. Founded in 1996 by a subsidiary of the Walt Disney Company, the town is surrounded by 4,700 acres of protected greenland.

The homes, with their front porches and picket fences, hark back to a much simpler time in American history. Built along a scenic lakeside promenade, downtown Celebration is a pleasant place to relax outdoors.

With the addition of the Celebration Hotel, which opened in fall 1999, guests can do more than just visit this quaint little town—they can move in! (If temporarily.)

The 115-room, four-star hotel is situated lakeside in downtown Celebration. It features 105 double, queen, or king rooms and 10 double queen suites. Guest accommodations include an environmental sound and music system, phone with data port, hair dryer, iron with board, and a safe. There is ample meeting space in addition to a pool, whirlpool, fitness center, lobby bar, and breakfast buffet. Note that breakfast is the only meal served here—but guests need only cross the street to find tempting restaurant options.

Architect Graham Gund based the design of the hotel on a turn-of-the-century Florida wood-frame look. With its big roofs, low eaves and dormers, and wraparound porches, the hotel reinforces the small town theme of Celebration, Florida.

Guests may shop, stroll, skate, or simply enjoy a picnic by the lake. There are several village parks, miles of nature trails, and an 18-hole public golf course (rates range from $32 to $120). Near the par-72 course is a 3-hole youth course where the Tiger Woods of tomorrow can practice their golf swings today.

The community's retail and business district invites visitors to enjoy a variety of dining (the award-winning Front Street Grille is a crowd-pleaser), shopping, and entertainment spots, including a bookstore, antiques shop, ice cream parlor, diner, and movie theater.

Located southeast of the intersection of U.S. 192 and I-4 near Kissimmee, Celebration is about a ten-minute drive from Walt Disney World. For information, call 407-566-2200, or write: Celebration Information; 200 Celebration Place; Celebration, FL 34747.

Sports

206 A Matter of Courses

208 Tennis Everyone

209 Waters of the World

212 Disney's Wide World of Sports Complex

213 More Sporting Fun

Many first-time visitors don't realize that Walt Disney World provides a plethora of sporting opportunities. Within WDW's 27,000-plus acres there are more tennis courts than at most tennis resorts, and more holes of championship-caliber golf than at most golf centers, plus so many other diversions—from fishing and bicycling to boating, swimming, and horseback riding—that the quantity and variety are matched by few other vacation destinations.

So while the family golfers are pursuing a perfect swing on one of five first-rate 18-hole courses, tennis buffs can be wearing themselves out on the courts, sailors can be sailing, waterskiers can be skimming back and forth across powerboat wakes, and anglers can be dangling a cane pole in hopes of hooking a big bream. Those who prefer to spectate rather than participate can visit a virtual sports mecca at Disney's Wide World of Sports complex, an enormous state-of-the-art facility that hosts a staggering array of sporting events, both amateur and professional.

Instruction, as well as guides, drivers, and assorted supervisors, makes every sport as much fun for beginners as for hard-core aficionados. Moreover, the ready accessibility of WDW sporting activities—via an excellent system of public transportation (see *Transportation & Accommodations*)—means that no family member need curtail play time to chauffeur others around.

Note: All prices are subject to change.

A MATTER OF COURSES

Most people don't immediately think of Walt Disney World when they contemplate a golf vacation. Yet there are six superb courses here: The Magnolia, the Palm, and the Oak Trail are situated across from the Polynesian resort and extend nearly to the borders of the Magic Kingdom. Just a short drive away is the Lake Buena Vista course, whose fairways are framed by the Disney Institute and Old Key West resort. Osprey Ridge and Eagle Pines play from the Bonnet Creek Golf Club near Fort Wilderness.

While the original Joe Lee–designed courses (the Palm, Magnolia, and Lake Buena Vista) won't set anyone's knees to knocking in terror from the regular tees, all three are demanding enough to have merited the status of a stop on the PGA Tour tournament trail.

Tom Fazio designed Osprey Ridge to offer a reasonable challenge for beginners as well as more advanced players. Eagle Pines, designed by Pete Dye, is a low-profile layout built level with, or lower than, the surrounding land.

Depending on the tee from which a golfer opts to play, the Disney courses will prove challenging and/or fun, and all are constructed to be especially forgiving for the midhandicap player.

PALM & MAGNOLIA: The wide-open, tree-dotted Magnolia measures 5,232 yards from the front tees, 6,642 from the middle, and 7,190 from the back. The Palm is tighter, with more wooded fairways and nine water hazards; it measures 5,311 yards from the front, 6,461 from the middle, and 6,957 from the back. Both courses have received a four-star ("outstanding") rating from *Golf Digest* magazine. The Magnolia and Palm share two driving ranges and two putting greens.

Oak Trail: This nine-hole 2,913-yard layout, a walking course tucked in a corner of the Magnolia, was designed for beginners, but it has some tough holes, including two par 5s.

OSPREY RIDGE & EAGLE PINES: These two par-72 courses play from the Bonnet Creek Golf Club. The Tom Fazio-designed Osprey Ridge measures 5,402 yards from the front tees, 6,680 from the middle, and 7,101 from the back. It takes guests into remote areas of WDW property as it winds through wooded landscape near Fort Wilderness. Dramatic contouring puts some tees 20 to 25 feet above the basic grade. In contrast, the Pete Dye-designed Eagle Pines is a low-profile layout. It plays 4,838 yards from the front tees, 6,309 from the middle, and 6,772 from the pro tees. Many fairways are bordered by scrub and pine needles; water comes into play as well. Osprey Ridge and Eagle Pines share a driving range and a putting green.

LAKE BUENA VISTA COURSE: This Joe Lee design measures 5,194 yards from the front tees, 6,268 from the middle, and 6,819 from the rearmost markers. Among the shortest of the 18-hole, par-72 courses, it has a fair amount of water, and its tree-lined fairways are Walt Disney World's narrowest. The course is well suited for beginners but equipped to challenge experienced players. A driving range and putting green are available.

Essentials

WHEN TO GO: January through April is peak golfing season. To beat the crowds, play on a Monday or Tuesday, tee off in the late afternoon, and take advantage of low summer rates. From May 17 through October 2, guests pay about $50 at Osprey Ridge and Eagle Pines, and about $50 at Lake Buena Vista, Palm, and Magnolia after 10 A.M. After 3 P.M., the price drops significantly at Osprey Ridge, Eagle Pines, Palm, and Magnolia. Annual Golf Memberships (available to Florida residents only for $53) net steep discounts during this period, too.

RESERVATIONS: Call 407-WDW-GOLF (939-4653) to confirm rates and to secure tee-off times. From January through April, morning and early afternoon tee times should be reserved well in advance; starting times after 3 P.M. are often available at the last minute. Those buying a golf package can reserve tee times up to 90 days prior to their check-in date. Guests with confirmed reservations at a WDW resort or at one of the resorts on Hotel Plaza Boulevard can also reserve 90 days ahead. Others can book tee times 30 days ahead. All reservations must be made with a major credit card. Cancelations must be made at least 48 hours in advance to avoid paying the full fee.

FEES: At the 18-hole courses, greens fees (including a required cart) vary with the course and season. Rates range from about $90 to $160 for guests at Walt Disney World resorts and the resorts on Hotel Plaza Boulevard, and from about $95 to $165 for day visitors. Twilight rates, usually in effect from mid-January through early October, beginning at 3 P.M. daily are about $53 to $80. Cost for adults to play Oak Trail ranges from about $16 to $34 for 9 holes; juniors (17 and under) pay about $11 to $21 for 9 holes. Prices include tax and are subject to change.

INSTRUCTION: At the WDW Golf Studio at the Palm and Magnolia, private lessons cost $63.60 per half hour for adults; $31.80 for juniors. Pros offer 45-minute video sessions; cost is $79.50. Nine-hole playing lessons in which a pro golfer gives instruction in club selection, strategy, and more, cost $159 for adults and $106 for juniors. Reservations are necessary for lessons; call 407-WDW-GOLF (939-4653). The Bonnet Creek Golf Club offers the Golf Experience: a system that lets golfers evaluate their swings, and compare clubs and balls. The 45-minute session is free. For information, call 888-223-7842.

DRESS: Proper golf attire is required. Shirts must have collars and any shorts must be Bermuda length.

EQUIPMENT RENTAL: Equipment can be rented at all courses; golf club rentals range from $35 to $45 for men and $25 to $35 for women, depending on the season. A photo ID and major credit card (for the $500 refundable deposit) are required for club rentals. Range balls ($5 per basket) are also among the items available.

Tournaments

The National Car Rental Golf Classic is among the biggest spectator events on Disney's sports calendar. It features most of the PGA Tour's top players and takes place from October 14 to 22. Guests who plan to golf during their WDW vacation are advised not to visit during tournament week. (You can, however, play with the pros if you are willing to pay for it.)

For additional information about the National Car Rental Golf Classic and other special Walt Disney World golf events, call 407-WDW-GOLF (939-4653). Private tournaments may be arranged by calling the same number.

TENNIS EVERYONE

No one comes to Walt Disney World strictly for a tennis vacation; it just doesn't exude the country-club ambience of a tennis resort where everyone is totally immersed in the game. But the facilities and instruction programs here are extensive enough that such holidays are possible. Certainly, playing a couple of sets of tennis on one of the World's 25 resort courts is a good way to unwind after a mad morning in the parks.

With six courts and a professional shop, Disney's Racquet Club at the Contemporary resort is Walt Disney World's major tennis facility for guest use. Located just beyond the hotel's north wing, the club features state-of-the-art hydrogrid clay courts. Elsewhere on property, The Villas at the Disney Institute, with four hydrogrid clay courts, merit attention. The Grand Floridian boasts a pair of clay courts. All other WDW tennis is played on hard courts. Fort Wilderness, Yacht and Beach Club, and BoardWalk have two; Old Key West has three; and the Swan and Dolphin share a four-court facility.

Essentials

WHEN TO GO: Courts are generally open from 7 A.M. to 7 P.M. daily (hours are seasonal, so call ahead for exact times); courts at the Swan and Dolphin are open 24 hours a day; lighted courts are available at each of the above-mentioned resorts. In February, March, April, June, and July the courts endure fairly heavy use, but there is usually a lull between noon and 3 P.M., and again from dinnertime until closing time. January, October, and November are prime months for tennis enthusiasts.

RESERVATIONS: Tennis courts may be reserved up to 90 days in advance for play at Disney's Racquet Club at the Contemporary, the Yacht and Beach Club, and the Disney Institute by calling 407-WDW-PLAY (939-7529), and as far ahead as desired for courts at the Swan and Dolphin (407-934-4396). Other courts are available on a first-come, first-served basis. Individual players seeking partners can find them through the player-matching program at Disney's Racquet Club (407-824-3578). During very busy periods, the length of time a single group of players can occupy a court is restricted to two hours on any morning, afternoon, and evening.

FEES: Play is $15 per hour at the Contemporary, Grand Floridian, Swan, and Dolphin. Courts at the Disney Institute are available with a $15 one-day health club pass. All other courts are free.

INSTRUCTION: The tennis program at WDW is under the direction of Peter Burwash International (PBI). PBI has trained pros staffing the resort programs (except at the Swan and Dolphin).

Pro Drill Sessions and Non-Stop Tennis are one-hour high-energy programs available for $15. One-and-a-half-hour daily clinics that focus on the fundamentals are $25. Private, semiprivate, and group lessons (for three to five people) are available for $50, $60, and $70, respectively. Special "hit with the pro" sessions are available for $40 per hour.

For information about tennis opportunities or to make reservations, call 407-WDW-PLAY (939-7529).

TOURNAMENTS: Private tourneys may be arranged by calling 407-827-4433. For information on tournaments at Disney's Wide World of Sports complex, call 407-363-6600.

DRESS: Tennis whites are appropriate, but not required, for play on Disney's courts.

EQUIPMENT RENTAL: Ball machine rental is $12.50 per half hour; good-quality (adult or child) racquets may be rented for $5. New balls sell for about $6 per can.

LOCKERS: Lockers are available at the Contemporary and Grand Floridian resorts.

WATERS OF THE WORLD

Boating

Walt Disney World is the home of the country's largest fleet of pleasure boats. Cruising on Bay Lake and the Seven Seas Lagoon can be excellent sport, and a variety of boats are available for rent at WDW resort marinas. Bay Lake excursions originate from the Contemporary, on the lake's western shore; Wilderness Lodge, on the south shore; and Fort Wilderness, which occupies the lake's southeastern shore. The Polynesian and Grand Floridian resorts send boaters out from their marinas on the southern shore of Seven Seas Lagoon. The Caribbean Beach resort leases watercraft for use on its own 45-acre Barefoot Bay. The Yacht and Beach Club, BoardWalk, Swan, and Dolphin share a boating haven in 25-acre Crescent Lake. And marinas at Dixie Landings, Port Orleans, Old Key West, and the Downtown Disney Marketplace set guests up to cruise the waterways adjoining the 35-acre Lake Buena Vista. Guests at Coronado Springs may rent watercraft for use on the 15-acre Lago Dorado.

To rent, day visitors and resort guests alike must show a resort ID, a driver's license, or a valid passport. Rental of certain craft may carry other special requirements (described below). Note that no privately owned boats are permitted on any of the WDW waters. Also, all prices are subject to change.

CANOEING: A long paddle down the smooth, wooded Fort Wilderness canals is such a tranquil way to pass a misty morning that it's hard to remember that the bustle of the Magic Kingdom is just a launch ride away. Canoes are available for rent at the Bike Barn at Fort Wilderness (about $6 per half hour, $12 per hour). Most trips last one to three hours; those with fishing gear can easily stay out longer. Canoes may also be rented at the Caribbean Beach, Port Orleans, The Villas at the Disney Institute, and Dixie Landings marinas. Ocean Kayaks (open-top kayaks) may be rented at La Marina at Coronado Springs and at the marinas at Port Orleans and Dixie Landings (about $6 per half hour, $12 per hour).

CANOPY BOATS: These 16-foot, V-hulled motorized boats with canopies are a good choice for relaxing cruises. They accommodate up to eight adults, and can be rented for about $20 per half hour at the Downtown Disney Marketplace, Polynesian, Contemporary, Grand Floridian, Wilderness Lodge, Yacht and Beach Club, Old Key West, Port Orleans, Caribbean Beach, Dixie Landings, and Fort Wilderness marinas.

PARASAILING: Excursions are offered at the Contemporary resort arena. Each seven- to ten-minute flight costs about $75 for one person, $115 for two to ride tandem. Reservations are necessary and may be made up to 90 days ahead; call 407-WDW-PLAY (939-7529).

PEDAL BOATS: These craft rent for about $6 per half hour or $12 per hour at the Caribbean Beach, Port Orleans, Disney Institute, Old Key West, Dixie Landings, Coronado Springs, Old Key West, and Swan and Dolphin marinas. Watercraft are available to all guests at all locations. Hydro Bikes (boats resembling bicycles affixed to pontoons) may be rented at the Swan and Dolphin when it isn't too windy; single-bike units cost about $8 per half hour at each location; doubles, about $16 per half hour at the Swan and Dolphin.

PONTOON BOATS: Motorized, canopied platforms on pontoons are perfect for families, inexperienced sailors, and visitors more interested in serenity than in thrills. Available at most resort marinas, the 20-foot craft hold up to ten adults and cost about $29 per half hour, $48 per hour. Guests must be at least 19 years old to rent a pontoon boat.

SAILBOATS: The running room and usually reliable winds of Bay Lake and Seven Seas Lagoon make for good sailing, and the Grand Floridian, Polynesian, Contemporary, and Wilderness Lodge marinas rent a variety of craft so that guests might get a little wind in their sails on the 650-acre expanse. Various types of sailboats are available; models accommodate two to six people and rent for about $12 to $20 per hour. Experience is required for rental of catamarans, available at the Contemporary, Polynesian, and Grand Floridian.

Sailing conditions are usually best in March and April, and before the inevitable late-afternoon thundershowers in the summer—and that's when demand is greatest.

SPEEDBOATS: Particularly when the weather is warm, there are always dozens of small boats zipping back and forth across Bay Lake, Seven Seas Lagoon, Lake Buena Vista, Crescent Lake, and Barefoot Bay. These are called Water Mouse boats, and they're just as much fun as they look. The boats, which move as fast as 22 miles per hour, are so small that a rider feels every bit of speed, and they whiz around quickly enough so that a lot of watery terrain can be covered in a half-hour rental period (for about $19).

Water Mouse boats can be rented at the Grand Floridian, Polynesian, Wilderness Lodge, Contemporary, Yacht and Beach Club, Fort Wilderness, Caribbean Beach, Coronado Springs, and Downtown Disney Marketplace marinas. When the weather is warm, lines form at about 11 A.M. and stay fairly constant until about 4 P.M. Guests must be at least 12 years old and five feet tall to rent Water Mouse boats. Kids under the minimum age and height may ride as passengers but are not allowed to drive.

WATERSKIING AND WAKEBOARDING: Ski boats with Sammy Duvall instructors and equipment ($100 an hour, for one to five guests) are available at the Contemporary resort marina. Reservations must be made at least 24 hours in advance and can be made up to 90 days ahead; call 407-WDW-PLAY (939-7529).

Fishing

The 70,000 bass with which Bay Lake was stocked in the mid-1960s have grown and multiplied as a result of WDW's restrictive fishing policy. (It's strictly catch-and-release.) No angling is permitted on Bay Lake or the Seven Seas Lagoon, except on the guided fishing expeditions. Largemouth bass weighing two to eight pounds are the most common catch. Excursions depart from the marinas daily (call 407-939-7529 for exact times and prices); five people can be accommodated on a trip. The trip lasts two hours and includes guide, gear, and refreshments (coffee and soft drinks). Guides will pick up guests at the Contemporary, Polynesian, Grand Floridian, Fort Wilderness, and Wilderness Lodge marinas.

Other trips depart from Downtown Disney Marketplace marina at 6:30 A.M. and 9 A.M. for fishing on Lake Buena Vista and adjoining waterways. Guides will also pick up guests at Old Key West, Dixie Landings, and Port Orleans. Two-hour excursions accommodate up to five anglers and include guide, gear, and refreshments.

At Dixie Landings, a two-hour trip tours Sassagoula River and Lake Buena Vista. Daily excursions usually depart at 6:30 A.M. and 9 A.M. and can accommodate up to five people; includes guide, gear, artificial bait, and soft drinks. Kids under ten must be accompanied by an adult.

Anglers might also consider two-hour tours that depart from the Yacht and Beach Club at 7 A.M. and 11 A.M. The former is a trip for up to four people, the latter accommodates five. Two-hour trips depart the BoardWalk dock at 7 A.M. and 1 P.M. daily. A guide, gear, and refreshments are included.

Special fishing excursions for kids ages 6 through 12 depart Monday through Friday from the Contemporary, Grand Floridian, Polynesian, Fort Wilderness, and Wilderness Lodge. Refreshments are provided, as is bait.

Reservations for all fishing excursions must be made at least 24 hours in advance and can be made up to 90 days ahead; call 407-WDW-PLAY (939-7529).

Fishing on your own—again, strictly catch-and-release—is permitted off the dock at the Downtown Disney Marketplace and Board-Walk; in the canals near The Villas at the Disney Institute, and at Fort Wilderness; and at the stocked fishing hole at Dixie Landings.

Fort Wilderness guests may toss in lines from any campground shore. Licenses are not required. Canoes, rods and reels, and cane poles are available for rent at the Fort Wilderness Bike Barn. Bait (in the form of worms) can be purchased. Poles may also be rented at Dixie Landings, BoardWalk, and the Downtown Disney Marketplace.

Swimming

Between Bay Lake and Seven Seas Lagoon, Walt Disney World resort guests have five miles of powdery white-sand beach at their disposal. Although the beaches are strictly for sunbathing, swimmers can splash in one of the many pools that come in every shape and size imaginable. River Country, Typhoon Lagoon, and Blizzard Beach (see *Everything Else in the World*) only add to the fun.

BEACHES: When Walt Disney World was under construction during the mid-1960s, Bay Lake had an eight-foot layer of muck on its bottom. The lake was drained and cleaned, and below the muck, engineers unearthed the pure, white sand that now edges Walt Disney World resort shorefronts, most notably at the Contemporary, Grand Floridian, Caribbean Beach, and Fort Wilderness. These four sections of beach, plus the ones at the Polynesian, Wilderness Lodge, Yacht and Beach Club, Coronado Springs, and Swan and Dolphin, make up WDW's sandy areas. They aren't walk-forever strands, but they are long enough that most people don't bother to go to the end. Note that all Walt Disney World resort beaches are open only to those guests staying at the respective hotels.

POOLS: WDW resorts have at least one pool apiece. With the exception of the sister resorts (Yacht and Beach Club; Dixie Landings and Port Orleans; All-Star Movies, All-Star Music, and All-Star Sports; and Swan and Dolphin), which share some of their recreational facilities, WDW hotel pools are open only to guests staying at those resorts. This policy was initiated to prevent overcrowding. Note that most of the pools are heated in winter.

Featuring one pool apiece are the Grand Floridian, Animal Kingdom Lodge, and Port Orleans. The Contemporary, Polynesian, Fort Wilderness, Wilderness Lodge and the All-Star resorts have two pools each. Board-Walk features three pools, Coronado Springs and Old Key West have four swimming holes each, Dixie Landings and The Villas at the Disney Institute have six apiece, and Caribbean Beach has seven. The Yacht and Beach Club resorts have between them two unguarded pools plus a small water park, called Stormalong Bay, that features slides, jets, and a sand-bottomed wading area. The Swan and Dolphin share a themed grotto pool with a slide, one huge rectangular pool, and a third smaller pool. For descriptions of the themed pools at WDW resorts, consult *Transportation & Accommodations*.

There are no diving boards; swimmers in search of a big splash should head for River Country, Blizzard Beach, or Typhoon Lagoon. Lifeguards are on duty during most daylight hours at the resort's main pools. In addition, each of the resorts on Hotel Plaza Boulevard has its own pool.

SPORTS

HOT TIP

As signs posted along the beaches indicate, swimming is not permitted in any of Walt Disney World's lakes. It's Disney's way of protecting guests from naturally occurring bacteria common to lakes in the state of Florida. Wading, however, is perfectly safe.

DISNEY'S WIDE WORLD OF SPORTS COMPLEX

Variety is the name of the game at Disney's Wide World of Sports complex. The multimillion-dollar complex invites athletes and spectators alike to dive into more than 30 types of sporting experiences. It's a grand slam for die-hard sports fans.

The 200-acre facility hosts amateur and professional events in everything from archery to wrestling. The home of the Amateur Athletic Union (AAU) is also the training site for Major League Baseball's Atlanta Braves.

Designed as a modern vision of old-time Floridian building styles, the architecture harks back to the days when sports facilities were extensions of their neighborhoods; to that end there is even a town commons.

The complex includes a baseball stadium; a field house that accommodates basketball, wrestling, and volleyball; a track-and-field complex; tennis courts; and multipurpose fields fit for football, soccer, and more. Given the possibilities, sports-loving spectators have a world of choices on their hands.

For those looking to flex a muscle or two, the NFL Experience may be just the ticket. This interactive football playground, like those built in Super Bowl host cities, gives fans of all ages a chance to test their football ability in a series of skills challenges.

A general admission ticket costs $9 for adults and $7 for kids ages 3 through 9. Tickets can be purchased at the gate and allow guests to watch "nonpremium" events and do the NFL Experience.

Tickets to premium events such as Atlanta Braves games (beginning in late February), and Orlando Rays (AA minor league baseball) games (April through September) may be purchased through TicketMaster (www.ticketmaster.com; 407-839-3900) and include general admission. Premium tickets may also be purchased at the Wide World of Sports complex box office on the day of an event, depending on availability. Prices vary, depending on the event.

WHERE TO EAT: The big-ticket eatery here is the Official All-Star Cafe. Don't worry about missing anything while you dine. TVs and a deejay keep you posted with current scores from the sports world.

There are more than 30 concessions for those seeking a lighter bite. They offer hot dogs, popcorn, and beer (not to mention peanuts and Cracker Jack), as well as a few more substantial, yet just as portable, snacks.

WHERE TO SHOP: D-Sports Shop, located just outside the baseball stadium (on the third baseline side), features a powerful lineup of NBA, NFL, and NHL merchandise, as well as other sports-themed items. Disney's Clubhouse, which is inside the stadium, is a hit with the baseball-loving crowd.

Essentials

HOW TO GET THERE: WDW resort guests can take a bus to Blizzard Beach and transfer to a bus headed for the complex from 10 A.M. to 6 P.M. From 6 P.M. to 11 P.M., take a bus to Downtown Disney and transfer there. Allow at least an hour for the bus commute. If you are driving, take the Magic Kingdom exit (25) off I-4. The complex is between U.S. 192 and Osceola Parkway. Parking is free.

Touch Base

Get the scoop on all the action at Disney's Wide World of Sports complex by calling 407-363-6600 or visiting the website: www.disneyworldsports.com.

MORE SPORTING FUN

BIKING: Pedaling along the rustic pathways and lightly trafficked roads at Fort Wilderness and The Villas at the Disney Institute can be a pleasant way to spend a couple of hours. Both areas are spread out so that bicycles are a practical way to get around. Bikes are available for rent at Fort Wilderness, Old Key West, Wilderness Lodge, Port Orleans, Caribbean Beach, Dixie Landings, BoardWalk, The Villas at the Disney Institute, and Coronado Springs. The cost is about $5 an hour or $12 per day; tandem bicycles are offered at some locations. Bikes with training wheels or baby seats are available. Helmets are free.

JOGGING: Except from late fall to early spring, the weather is usually too steamy in Central Florida for jogging. If you run very early in the morning in warm seasons, the heat is somewhat less daunting. The 1.4-mile promenade around the lake at the Caribbean Beach resort is ideal for jogging, as is the three-quarter-mile promenade surrounding Crescent Lake, the waterway that's bordered by the Swan and Dolphin, Yacht and Beach Club, and BoardWalk resorts, and the three-quarter-mile path around Coronado Springs' Lago Dorado. Fort Wilderness and the Wilderness Lodge share a three-quarter-mile path with exercise stations. Dixie Landings and Old Key West also have scenic routes. Courses range from one mile to about three.

MINIATURE GOLF: The Fantasia Gardens Miniature Golf complex, located near the Swan, Dolphin, and BoardWalk resorts, offers players two 18-hole courses themed to the Disney film. Disney's Fairways offers a difficult layout sure to tantalize serious golfers. It features traditional golf obstacles, such as sand traps, water hazards, doglegs, and roughs. Don't be fooled by the small size of the course—the challenges are big. (At press time, the record for the par-61 course was 50.)

Fantasia Gardens, on the other hand, is all in fun, with clever things (a dancing hippo, xylophone stairs, brooms dumping buckets of water) at every hole. The degree of difficulty varies from hole to hole, but overall this is an easy course to conquer. There are a few challenges out there, however. Hole 15, for example, is one of the trickier ones. Here golfers aim through four mini-geysers that randomly squirt water into the air.

The newest mini-golf option at Walt Disney World, Disney's Winter Summerland, is a mere stone's throw from the Blizzard Beach water park. Designed as a vacation retreat for Santa and his elves, the two 18-hole courses boast a delightfully festive atmosphere, complete with Christmas carol soundtracks. The sandy-surface course is slightly more challenging than its snowy-surface counterpart.

A round on any course costs $9.25 for adults, $7.50 for kids ages 3 through 9. The second round is half price. Typical playing time is about an hour. Hours are generally 10 A.M. to 11 P.M., but vary seasonally. For information, call 407-560-8760.

ROCK CLIMBING: For those daring souls not satisfied by simply sliding down a snow-covered mountain, Blizzard Beach offers this challenging option: climb Mount Gushmore. The supervised expeditions, which scale 15 to 35 feet, last about 25 minutes. All equipment is provided. To make the climb, guests must be at least nine years old. The Mount Gushmore Expedition Climbing Experience takes place continuously throughout the day and is located at the Ski Patrol Training Camp in Blizzard Beach. For more information, call 407-WDW-PLAY (939-7529).

SPAS AND HEALTH CLUBS: While some of the fitness centers within WDW hotels are reserved for guests staying at the resort that houses them, several have open-door policies and are accessible to all WDW resort guests. Health clubs include the Olympiad at the Contemporary, Sturdy Branches at Wilderness Lodge, Zahanati at Animal Kingdom Lodge, La Vida at Coronado Springs, Muscles & Bustles at BoardWalk, and Ship Shape at the Yacht and Beach Club. Rates are $10 per day, $20 per length of stay, and $35 for a family length of stay (up to five people). The Olympiad health club has Nautilus equipment, cardiovascular machines, and massage. The others have more extensive equipment. Ship Shape has a whirlpool and steam room. Muscles & Bustles has a steam room, tanning bed, and massage services. La Vida has a tanning bed and massage.

Body By Jake at the Dolphin, the fitness center at the Swan, and R.E.S.T. at Old Key West round out the health club options. Body By Jake ($8 per day or $16 for length of stay) is open to guests staying on or off Disney property. The facility at the Swan is free to the hotel's guests. R.E.S.T. is free to all Walt Disney World resort guests.

The spas are located at the Grand Floridian Spa & Health Club, the Disney Institute Spa and Fitness Center, and the Wyndham Palace Resort & Spa. The Fitness Center at the Disney Institute ($15 per day, $35 for a length of stay, $50 for a family of four length of stay) has aerobics, a gymnasium, and a modern facility with the best lineup of Cybex machines on Disney property. The Grand Floridian Spa & Health Club ($12 per day, $30 for three days, and $31.50 for length of stay) has all that plus a luxurious ambience. There are special spa packages available at each of these resorts.

STOCK CAR RACING: The Richard Petty Driving Experience (RPDE) takes motorsports fans out of the grandstands and into a scene that most can only dream about: behind the wheel of a stock car. The RPDE, located at the Walt Disney World Speedway, near the Magic Kingdom guest parking lot, is a training ground for racer wannabes. It offers two levels of actual driving experience: "Rookie Experience" and "Experience of a Lifetime." For the less "driven" daredevils, there is the "Riding Experience," which sends guests zooming around the track at blazing speeds while still maintaining their passenger status. No reservations are required for the Riding Experience. Rides begin at 9 A.M. daily. The cost is about $90.

The Rookie Experience includes instruction, eight high-speed (up to 145 miles per hour) laps around the one-mile oval track, as well as a warm-up and a cool-down lap. The three-hour program costs about $400. Reservations are required.

The Experience of a Lifetime is a 30-lap program completed over three sessions. Participants work on building speed and establishing a comfortable driving line. The cost is about $1,100. Reservations are a must.

The RPDE operates daily year-round, with the exception of dates on which actual races are held at the WDW Speedway. Shuttle transportation is provided from the Transportation and Ticket Center (TTC). Call 800-237-3889 for information or to make reservations. Prices are subject to change.

TRAIL RIDES: Guided horseback rides into pine woods and scrubby palmetto country set off from the front of Fort Wilderness four times daily. This trip is not meant for seasoned gallopers—you can't wander off on your own. The horses have been culled for gentleness, so trips are especially suitable for novices. Cost is about $25 per person for a 45-minute tour. Kids under nine are not allowed to ride, and there's a weight limit of 250 pounds. (Younger kids can saddle up on ponies at the Fort Wilderness Petting Farm.) Reservations are necessary, and can be made up to 30 days ahead by calling 407-WDW-PLAY (939-7529).

VOLLEYBALL & BASKETBALL: Except for the volleyball courts at River Country and Typhoon Lagoon, courts are reserved for WDW resort guests. The Grand Floridian, Contemporary, Yacht and Beach Club, Fort Wilderness, Wilderness Lodge, Swan and Dolphin, Coronado Springs, Old Key West, and The Villas at the Disney Institute have volleyball courts. Contemporary, Fort Wilderness, and Old Key West have basketball hoops.

Good Meals, Great Times

216 In the Theme Parks

233 In Downtown Disney

236 In the WDW Resorts

244 Restaurant Round-Up

249 Lounges of WDW

Although fast food is in great supply, it is hardly the entire Walt Disney World dining story. Epcot adds international flavors to the WDW menu. Tempting options at the other theme parks, Board-Walk, and Downtown Disney—not to mention new dining frontiers in the ever-growing brood of WDW resorts—make deciding where to eat a mouthwatering dilemma. Disney's ongoing effort to expand its culinary horizons has certainly been successful, producing prominent palate pleasers such as California Grill and Cítricos, plus family favorites like Chef Mickey's and Crystal Palace.

Because there's such a large number and variety of eateries around the World, this chapter presents dining information in two formats. First, we've included an area-by-area rundown—a comprehensive section whose precise descriptions of food purveyors, including sample menu options, will prove most helpful when you get hungry in a particular part of the World. Second, we've compiled a collection of what we consider to be the best restaurants in a particular category. To select these standouts we looked at the menu, theme, and overall enjoyability of each restaurant on property.

Finally, in the chapter's last section, we offer a guide to the varied lounges of Walt Disney World, along with a briefing on dining with Disney characters and Disney's dinner show options—and assurance that great times are destined to follow.

RESTAURANTS OF WDW
In the Magic Kingdom

The lion's share of eateries here in Walt Disney World's first theme park are fast-food spots. These establishments' colorful facades and costumed servers are natural extensions of the fantasy surrounding the park's seven distinct "lands." The healthy variety of food available on the fly is a testament to Magic Kingdom visitors' typical preference for a quick bite with no need for firm plans. For those who prefer an all-out meal, the park's small handful of table-service restaurants offer fine mealtime escapes in magical settings that only Disney could create. Visitors interested in character meals have breakfast, lunch, and dinner options here (see page 242 for additional details).

First Things First

- The letters that conclude each entry are a key to meals served there: breakfast (B), lunch (L), dinner (D), or snacks (S).

- As an indication of what you should expect to spend for a meal, we've classified restaurants as inexpensive (under $10); moderate ($10 to $20); expensive ($21 to $45); or very expensive ($46 and up). Prices are based on an adult-size dinner consisting of a beverage; entrée; and either one appetizer, side order, or dessert (not including tax or tip). These classifications are reflected by dollar symbols at the end of each entry (all symbols are defined in the key at the bottom of each page). Note that lunch and breakfast generally cost less.

- All Walt Disney World restaurants and fast-food spots (except some with outside seating or at the Swan and Dolphin resorts) are nonsmoking only. Some restaurants at BoardWalk and Downtown Disney have special sections set aside for smokers.

- Priority seating arrangements for most table-service restaurants should be made in advance by calling 407-WDW-DINE (939-3463). For complete details, see page 248 of this chapter.

- We advise guests to call 407-WDW-DINE (939-3463) to confirm all restaurant information.

Adventureland
FAST FOOD & SNACKS

Aloha Isle: This snack stand located near the Swiss Family Treehouse sells pineapple spears and juice, along with other tropical offerings, including pineapple floats and the especially refreshing Dole Whip pineapple soft serve. S. $

El Pirata Y el Perico: The Spanish name of this snack stand, located directly across from the Pirates of the Caribbean attraction, translates to "The Pirate and the Parrot." The offerings here include several traditional Mexican items, such as tacos, taco salads, and nachos, as well as hot dogs with chili and cheese. L, S. $

Oasis: Tucked away near the Jungle Cruise, this is the perfect spot for a soft drink. Open seasonally. S. $

Sunshine Tree Terrace: Offerings at this snack spot located near The Enchanted Tiki Room—Under New Management are some of the tastiest in the Magic Kingdom: orange slushes, nonfat frozen yogurt, and a tasty citrus swirl—soft-serve nonfat frozen yogurt swirled with frozen juice concentrate. Cappuccino, espresso, and soft drinks are also available. S. $

Fantasyland
TABLE SERVICE

Cinderella's Royal Table: Hostesses at this festive establishment wear French Renaissance-style gowns, while hosts sport medieval tunics with pirate-style blouses, pants, and long vests. The hall itself is high-ceilinged and as majestic as the old mead hall it is designed to represent. Its second-story setting offers a pleasantly peaceful view of Fantasyland. Decor tends to royal blues and purples, with tapestry-backed chairs. Cinderella is usually on hand to greet children and grown-ups alike in the restaurant's lobby. As guests of the princess, visitors dine on salads and sandwiches on the midday menu. Dinner includes prime rib (queen and king cuts, of course), spice-crusted salmon, coconut fried shrimp on chilled noodles, and herbed chicken with sautéed vegetables over polenta.

The Once Upon A Time character breakfast is held every morning. This all-you-can-eat

B breakfast **L** lunch **D** dinner **S** snacks **$** under $10 **$ $** $10–$20 **$ $ $** $21–$45 **$ $ $ $** $46 and up

216

GOOD MEALS, GREAT TIMES

breakfast is $14.95 for adults and $7.95 for children ages 3 through 11. Priority seating suggested (book *early*). B, L, D. `$$$`

FAST FOOD & SNACKS

Enchanted Grove: A small stand that's the perfect spot to cool off with a lemonade, lemonade slush, or strawberry soft-serve swirl. S. `$`

Hook's Tavern: Soft drinks and potato chips are available at this small refreshment stand just to the west of Cinderella's Golden Carrousel. S. `$`

Mrs. Potts' Cupboard: Ice cream gets top billing at this small spot near The Many Adventures of Winnie the Pooh attraction. There are soft-serve cones in chocolate, vanilla, and swirl; hot fudge, strawberry shortcake, and brownie sundaes; and shakes and floats. S. `$`

Pinocchio Village Haus: Located near It's a Small World (some tables offer a peek at the attraction via sizable picture windows), this is another one of those Magic Kingdom restaurants that seem a lot smaller from the outside than they really are, thanks to a labyrinthine arrangement of a half-dozen rooms decorated with antique cuckoo clocks, oak peasant chairs, and murals depicting characters from Pinocchio's story—Figaro the Cat, Cleo the Goldfish, Monstro the Whale, and Geppetto, the puppet's creator. The menu offers hot dogs, burgers, turkey sandwiches, and pasta salad. L, D, S. `$`

Scuttle's Landing: Soft drinks and shaved ice are the big draw at this snack spot located near Dumbo the Flying Elephant. Open seasonally. S. `$`

Frontierland

FAST FOOD & SNACKS

Aunt Polly's Dockside Inn: The much trumpeted sense of getting away from it all that islands always convey can also be found on Frontierland's Tom Sawyer Island. Though only a couple of minutes' ride across the Rivers of America via the Tom Sawyer Island rafts, this landfall manages to seem remote even when there are dozens of youngsters clambering through its caves, over its hills, and across its rickety barrel bridges. Therein lies the charm of Aunt Polly's. While the adults in a party get some much needed rest and relaxation sipping lemonade in the shade of the old-fashioned porch and watching the riverboats chugging by, the kids can go exploring. This is also a lovely, removed spot from which to observe the afternoon parade as it makes its way through Frontierland.

It doesn't even matter that Aunt Polly's offers a selection barely wider than the fare that the lady might have served to young Tom Sawyer himself—peanut-butter-and-jelly and ham-and-cheese sandwiches, apple pie, soft-serve ice cream, root beer floats, cookies, iced tea, lemonade, and soda. L, S. `$`

Diamond Horseshoe Saloon Revue: From about 10 A.M. until early evening, a troupe of singers and dancers presents a sometimes silly, occasionally hilarious, always entertaining musical show in this Wild West dance hall saloon. Stop by anytime for sandwiches, salads, hard ice cream, dill pickles, and other snacks. Note that this is one of those rare saloons in which no alcohol is served. L, S. `$`

All WDW table-service restaurants provide a menu geared to kids, and most fast-food spots offer kid-size value meals. Just ask!

Pecos Bill Cafe: This is not one of those Magic Kingdom eateries so tucked away that only those who hunt will find it. Sooner or later, almost every guest passing from Fantasyland into Frontierland—ambling along the banks of the river on their way to Splash Mountain—walks by Pecos Bill Cafe. Cheeseburgers, sandwiches, salads, and hot dogs are the staples. The expansive fixin's bar (which includes fresh lettuce and tomato, sautéed mushrooms and onions, and cheese sauce) and ample seating make this spot one of the most popular fast food restaurants in the Magic Kingdom. L, D, S. `$`

B breakfast **L** lunch **D** dinner **S** snacks `$` under $10 `$$` $10–$20 `$$$` $21–$45 `$$$$` $46 and up

Liberty Square

TABLE SERVICE

Liberty Tree Tavern: At this pillared and porticoed eatery opposite the riverboat landing, the floors are wide oak planks, the wallpaper looks as if it might have come from Williamsburg, the curtains hang from cloth loops, and the venetian blinds are made of wood. The rooms are chock-full of mementos that might have been found in the homes of Thomas Jefferson, George Washington, and Ben Franklin, and the window glass was made using 18th-century casting methods. Such charming environs make the food served therein seem almost secondary.

The à la carte lunch includes fish, pot roast, turkey, beef stew in a bread bowl, sandwiches, and soups.

Dinner, an all-you-can-eat feast served family-style, is hosted by Disney characters. Menu items include salad, roast turkey, flank steak, honey-glazed ham, macaroni and cheese, mashed potatoes, garden vegetables, and Stouffer's stuffing. The Patriot's Platter character dinner costs $19.95 for adults and $9.95 for children ages 3 through 11. Note that desserts and some beverages cost extra. Priority seating suggested. L, D.　$ $

FAST FOOD & SNACKS

Columbia Harbour House: A fast-food fish house with just a touch of elegance. Fried fish, fried chicken strips, vegetarian chili or clam chowder in a crusty bread bowl, and assorted sandwiches grace the

Healthier Options

Health-conscious folks need not abandon all restraint for want of suitable sustenance. Most restaurants offer low-fat, low-cholesterol, low-salt, and vegetarian entrées. Even fast-food stands now feature healthier fare such as fresh salads, grilled chicken sandwiches, fresh fruit, turkey burgers, and nonfat frozen yogurt.

menu. The food is excellent, and there are enough antiques and other knickknacks decking the halls to raise this establishment, located near the Liberty Square entrance to Fantasyland, well above the ordinary. Model ships, copper measures, harpoons, nautical instruments, little lace tie-back curtains, and low-beamed ceilings give the restaurant a cozy air. The upstairs dining area is particularly peaceful. L, D, S.　$

Sleepy Hollow: Ice cream cookie sandwiches, warm cobblers prepared with seasonal fruits, caramel corn, and other desserts—all made fresh before your eyes—are the sweets for sale at this savory snack stand located in The Hall of Presidents neighborhood, near the Liberty Square bridge. It's pleasant to eat on the secluded brick patio outside. It has a lovely view of Cinderella Castle. L, D, S.　$

B breakfast **L** lunch **D** dinner **S** snacks　$　under $10　$ $　$10–$20　$ $ $　$21–$45　$ $ $ $　$46 and up

Main Street

TABLE SERVICE

Crystal Palace: One of the Magic Kingdom's landmarks, this restaurant takes its architectural cues from a similar structure that once stood in New York, and from San Francisco's Conservatory of Flowers, which still graces that city's Golden Gate Park. The place is huge but not overwhelming, because the tables are scattered amid a Victorian-style indoor garden, complete with fresh flowers and hanging greenery. Tables in the front look out on flower beds, while those at the east end have views of a courtyard. The restaurant is located on a pathway at the end of Main Street, U.S.A., heading west toward Adventureland.

Four topiaries—Winnie the Pooh, Tigger, Eeyore, and Piglet—greet guests at the entrance, a sign of the character presence here. None other than Winnie the Pooh himself and his pals circulate throughout meals.

Offerings vary according to season and available produce. The all-you-can-eat buffet features a full variety of traditional breakfast items every morning; a salad bar, deli bar, pasta dishes, chicken, and fish for lunch; and spit-roasted beef, paella, chicken, pastas, fish, carved meats, and inventive sides for dinner. The evening salad bar, with its grilled vegetables, peel-and-eat-shrimp, cold pasta salads, and variety of greens and grains, is first-rate. Kids particularly like the ice cream sundae bar offered at lunch and dinner. Cost for breakfast is $14.95 for adults and $7.95 for children ages 3 through 11; lunch is $15.95 for adults and $8.25 for children; dinner is $19.95 for adults and $9.95 for children. Priority seating suggested. B, L, D. `$$-$$$`

The Plaza: This airy, many-windowed establishment, around the corner from the Plaza Ice Cream Parlor, is done up in mirrors with sinuous Art Nouveau frames. The menu offers chef's salads, burgers, and hot and cold sandwiches—plus hard ice cream, milk shakes, floats, and the biggest sundaes in the Magic Kingdom. Café Mocha, which combines chocolate and coffee, is another refreshing specialty. Priority seating suggested. L, D, S. `$$`

Tony's Town Square: The decor comes straight out of Walt Disney's film *Lady and the Tramp*. The terrazzo-style patio offers a fine view of Town Square. Breakfast options include eggs, *Lady and the Tramp* character waffles, cereals, and freshly baked sweet rolls. The lunch menu offers Italian specialties, including chicken Parmesan and turkey piccata. Pizzas with selected toppings are good bets. Other staples include Caesar salad, sandwiches, and a variety of pastas. At dinner select from country penne, sautéed shrimp, and chicken Florentine, along with a variety of daily specials. For dessert, tempting Italian sweets complement a cup of freshly brewed espresso or cappuccino. Priority seating suggested. B, L, D. `$$$`

FAST FOOD & SNACKS

Casey's Corner: The small round tables at this old-fashioned red-and-white stop on the west side of Main Street (adjacent to Crystal Palace) spill out onto the sidewalk. Except when the weather is hot, this baseball-themed spot is great for ballpark favorites—hot dogs in jumbo sizes, fries, brownies, peanuts, soft drinks, and coffee. During daytime hours a pianist plinks away on the restaurant's white upright. L, D, S. `$`

B breakfast **L** lunch **D** dinner **S** snacks `$` under $10 `$$` $10–$20 `$$$` $21–$45 `$$$$` $46 and up

Main Street Bake Shop: If the sight of this old-fashioned storefront doesn't lure you in, the heavenly aroma most certainly will. A genteel little tearoom with prim tables and cane chairs, the Main Street Bake Shop is a pleasant place for a light breakfast, midmorning coffee break, or midafternoon rest stop. Assorted pastries, cakes, and pies are the main temptations. Also offered are fresh cookies: chocolate chunk, oatmeal raisin, sugar, and Nestlé's Original Toll House recipe. Ice cream cookie sandwiches are "built to order." Cinnamon rolls are baked on the premises. B, S. $

Plaza Ice Cream Parlor: Ice cream lovers from all over the country converge on this corner of the park, which boasts the Magic Kingdom's largest variety of hard ice cream flavors. S. $

Tomorrowland

FAST FOOD & SNACKS

Auntie Gravity's Galactic Goodies: This small spot located across from the Tomorrowland Indy Speedway (between Merchant of Venus and Mickey's Star Traders) offers refreshing strawberry smoothies, soft-serve ice cream, sundaes, floats, fruit cups, juice, and soft drinks. S. $

Cosmic Ray's Starlight Cafe: The largest fast-food location in the Magic Kingdom is located directly across from the Tomorrowland Indy Speedway. Three different menus are offered at separate sections along the lengthy counter. *Cosmic Chicken* serves rotisserie chicken; *Blastoff Burgers* has cheeseburgers, vegetarian burgers, and hot dogs; and *Starlight Soup, Salad, Sandwich* offers soups, Caesar salads, chef's salads, grilled chicken sandwiches, and cheese steak sandwiches. An Audio-Animatronic lounge lizard known as Sun E. Clipse entertains diners with cheesy songs and (bad) jokes in the main dining area. L, D, S. $

Lunching Pad at Rockettower Plaza: Located at the base of the Astro Orbiter in the center of Tomorrowland's sprawling concrete plaza, this small dining spot offers sizable smoked turkey legs, character cookies, frozen soda slushies, and soft drinks. S. $

Plaza Pavilion: Just east of The Plaza restaurant on Main Street, U.S.A, this sleek spot on the edge of Tomorrowland serves pan pizzas, fried chicken strips, Italian specialty sandwiches, and salads. There are some particularly pleasant tables situated toward the water that look past the graceful willow trees nearby, an impressive topiary sea serpent, and Cinderella Castle. L, D, S. $

Magic Kingdom Mealtime Tips

- The hours from 11 A.M. to 2 P.M., and again from about 5 P.M. to 7 P.M., are the mealtime rush hours in Magic Kingdom restaurants. Try to eat earlier or later whenever possible.
- When a fast-food restaurant has more than one service window, don't just amble into the nearest queue. Instead, inspect them all, because, occasionally, the one farthest from an entrance will be wait-free (or nearly so).
- Table-service restaurants offering full-scale meals are usually less crowded at lunch than they are at dinner.
- To avoid queues, eat lunch or dinner at a restaurant that offers priority seating—Tony's Town Square, Crystal Palace, or The Plaza restaurant on Main Street; Liberty Tree Tavern in Liberty Square; or Cinderella's Royal Table in the castle. Priority seating arrangements can be made in advance by calling 407-WDW-DINE (939-3463). Check for same-day seating at the individual restaurant or City Hall. Refer to page 248 for further details.
- Consider taking the monorail to the Contemporary, Polynesian, or Grand Floridian to have lunch or dinner in a resort restaurant, and then return to the Magic Kingdom later. (Remember to have your hand stamped and keep your ticket for re-entry to the park.)

B breakfast **L** lunch **D** dinner **S** snacks $ under $10 $ $ $10–$20 $ $ $ $21–$45 $ $ $ $ $46 and up

In Epcot

The various areas that make up Epcot offer a spectrum of eating options that extends from the usual burgers and fries to mouthwatering international specialties. Future World counts a please-all food court among its fast-food spots, plus two table-service restaurants whose menus and atmosphere innovatively reflect the themes of the pavilions they inhabit. World Showcase, on the other hand, is characterized by international flavors. Here, the cuisine of each country is served in settings that strive to transport visitors, if just for the duration of their meal. While the abundance of appealing table-service restaurants makes World Showcase a very popular dining destination, the promenade is also ringed with fast-food spots, most of which feature international fare. Priority seating is an important part of the Epcot dining equation (for complete details, turn to page 248). Character meals are options for breakfast, lunch, and dinner in Future World (for specifics on dining with Disney characters, see page 242).

Future World

TABLE SERVICE

Coral Reef (The Living Seas): Decorated in cool greens and blues to complement its surroundings, this restaurant offers diners a panoramic view of the coral reef through large windows. The windows are eight feet high and more than eight inches thick. The dining room has several tiers, so all guests get a decent view. The menu features a bounty of fresh fish and shellfish—including Florida snapper, mahimahi, shrimp, and salmon—prepared in a number of delectable ways. Landlubber selections are also available. The menu may vary seasonally. Priority seating suggested. L, D.   **$ $ $**

Garden Grill (The Land): Sleek upholstered wood-trimmed booths illuminated with handsome brass lamps help to make this an exceptionally attractive eatery. The restaurant itself revolves (very slowly), moving past a mural of giant sunflowers and above scenes of the thunderstorm, sandstorm, prairie, and rain forest featured in the Living with the Land boat ride. The scenes were designed with diners in mind, and provide them with a peek into a farmhouse window that's out of viewing range of the waterborne passengers.

B breakfast **L** lunch **D** dinner **S** snacks **$** under $10 **$ $** $10–$20 **$ $ $** $21–$45 **$ $ $ $** $46 and up

Mickey and his friends host three character meals here each day. The all-you-can-eat country breakfast is $14.95 for adults and $8.25 for children ages 3 through 11. Lunch and dinner menus feature rotisserie meats, grilled flank steak, and fried catfish. There is a separate menu for children. The character lunch costs $16.95 for adults and $9.95 for children. Dinner is $18.95 for adults and $9.95 for children. Beverages and dessert are included. Priority seating suggested. B, L, D. **$$-$$$**

Fast Food & Snacks

Electric Umbrella (Innoventions): This large fast-food establishment is decorated in shades of blue, mauve, and magenta. It's a particularly good bet when the weather is temperate enough to allow dining at the tables on the terrace outside—or when bound for World Showcase with finicky eaters in tow. Offerings include chicken sandwiches, grilled ham-and-cheese sandwiches, grilled vegetable pita sandwiches, hot dogs, burgers, fruit salad, and chef's salad. L, D, S. **$**

Fountain View Espresso and Bakery (Innoventions Plaza): Fresh baked goods and desserts—such as croissants, cheesecake, tiramisu, and more—can be found at this spot across from the Fountain of Nations. Espresso, cappuccino, wine, and beer are among the assorted beverages available here. B, S. **$**

Pasta Piazza Ristorante (Innoventions): Pizza, pasta, and antipasto salad are among the menu items at this eatery located opposite the Electric Umbrella restaurant in Innoventions Plaza. B, L, D, S. **$**

Pure and Simple (Wonders of Life): This spot offers a variety of healthy treats, including oat bran waffles with fruit toppings, frozen yogurt, yogurt shakes, muffins, fruit juices, and more. Vegetable pizzas, soups, Caesar salad with chicken strips, and chicken wrap sandwiches are among the lunch options. B, L, S. **$**

Sunshine Season Food Fair (The Land): One of the most interesting of the Future World dining options, and a true standout in the Walt Disney World fast-food scene, this handful of diverse counter-service stands is on the lower level of the Land pavilion. Each stand in the food court has a farm-style facade done in bright colors, not unlike those that might be found in agricultural exhibit buildings at a midwestern state fair. With bright, umbrella-topped tables nearby, the effect is quite cheery. Because of the wide variety of foods available here, this is one of the best places in Epcot for a family that can't agree on what to eat—there's something for everyone.

Soup, Salad, & Sandwich offers Florida seafood chowder, fruit salad, rotini pasta salad, Caesar salad, and sandwich wraps. The *Bakery Shop*'s tasty morning offerings include fresh fruit, bagels with cream cheese, jumbo cinnamon rolls, Danish pastries, and muffins. After 11 A.M., cheesecake appears, along with chocolate cake, strawberry shortcake, rich double-chocolate brownies, and large cinnamon cookies—plus tasty chocolate chip cookies baked on the premises.

The *Barbecue* stand sells barbecued chicken and ribs smoked on the premises; barbecued pork or chicken breast sandwiches, and corn-on-the-cob. The *Pasta and Potato* stand offers Mickey macaroni and cheese; vegetable lasagne; and baked potatoes stuffed with Asian-style chicken and vegetables, cheddar cheese and bacon, and other fillings. An *Ice Cream Stand* tempts guests with cooling cones and cups, frozen yogurt, and sundaes. B, L, D, S. **$**

World Showcase

Table Service

Akershus (Norway): The Norwegian castle of Akershus dominates Oslo's harbor, and is the most impressive of all Norway's medieval fortresses. It is actually half fortress and half palace, and many of its grand halls continue to be used for elaborate state banquets. At Epcot's castle-like Akershus, guests are treated to an authentic royal Norwegian buffet called the *koldtbord*, literally "cold table." The diverse mix of offerings includes both hot and cold meats and seafood, and a selection of salads, cheeses, and breads. Traditional Norwegian desserts are also available for an extra charge, as are cocktails and Norwegian beer. Hosts and hostesses are on hand to answer any questions about the buffet that guests may have. Priority seating suggested. L, D. `$$-$$$`

Biergarten (Germany): Located at the rear of the St. Georgsplatz in the Germany pavilion, this huge tiered restaurant is every bit as jolly as Alfredo's restaurant in the Italy pavilion. This is partly because of the long tables that encourage a certain togetherness among guests—and partly because Beck's beer is served in 33-ounce

steins. But equal credit for the gemütlich atmosphere must go to the restaurant's lively entertainment. A German trio performs during lunch. At dinner, yodelers and other traditional Bavarian musicians—each clad in lederhosen or dirndl—play accordions, cowbells, a musical saw, and a harplike stringed instrument known as the "wooden laughter." The entertaining dinner shows take place at scheduled times in the dining room. Diners are usually invited to join the fun onstage.

The food is hearty and presented as an all-you-can-eat buffet, featuring all sorts of sausages (bratwurst, *Debrizinger*, *Bauernwurst*), frankfurters, rotisserie chicken, homemade spaetzle, assorted cold dishes, potato salad, cucumber salad, and many more German specialties. Because entertainment is intermittent, there's plenty of time to enjoy the pleasant setting. Priority seating highly recommended, particularly during peak seasons (book as early as possible). L, D. `$$-$$$`

Bistro de Paris (France): One flight above Les Chefs de France, this restaurant evokes the charm of early 20th-century Paris. A traditional bistro menu (created by the same trio of French chefs responsible for the fare at Chefs de France, see below) features such robust "preludes" as triple beef and black truffles consommé baked in a puff pastry, and skewers of scallops and jumbo shrimp with country salt pork in a lemon tomato fondue. The brief entrée menu includes honey-roasted rack of lamb with grilled vegetables; and a double cut white veal chop with roasted garlic cloves, potato puree, and spinach. The heartiness of the fare makes it an especially good dining choice in cool weather. Priority seating suggested. D. `$$$-$$$$`

Le Cellier Steakhouse (Canada): Tucked away on the lowest level of the pavilion near Victoria Gardens, this low-ceilinged, lantern-lighted, stone-walled establishment looks a little like the ancient wine cellars for which it is named. It offers a full menu of Canadian foods, with hearty open-face steak sandwiches and steak salads also available for lunch, and roast prime rib and steak added to the offerings at dinner. Excellent maple-glazed salmon, and penne in a pesto sauce (also with chicken or shrimp) round out the selection of entrées. For dessert, try the royal bread pudding or chocolate "moose" with raspberry sauce. Canada's own Molson and Labatt's beers and Inniskillin wine are served. This tempting menu makes Le Cellier Steakhouse a prime destination. Priority seating suggested. L, D. `$ $`

Les Chefs de France (France): This charming restaurant has a bright, airy feel, with yellow and cream-colored walls drenched in natural light. It boasts a large glass-enclosed "outside" dining area with a conservatory motif.

Behind the restaurant's well-appointed scenes, a team of internationally acclaimed chefs—Paul Bocuse, Roger Vergé, and Gaston Lenôtre—have prepared a tempting nouvelle menu. Bocuse operates a restaurant outside Lyons, France, and Roger Vergé runs one just north of the French Riviera. Together with Gaston Lenôtre (widely recognized as France's premier preparer of pastries and other delicious dessert delicacies), they form a most unusual, and absolutely formidable, gastronomic trio. Their menu features fresh ingredients readily available from Florida purveyors. In addition, the restaurant imports as many key ingredients from France as possible.

As you might expect, the fare here is fiercely French, but the foundation of the menu is nouvelle cuisine, which involves lighter sauces using much less cream and butter than in classic French cooking. Menu items include sautéed chicken breast with wild mushrooms, grilled salmon on polenta, and braised beef in red Burgundy wine beside spinach ravioli. Soups and appetizers, such as onion soup and escargot, are all-day staples. Apple tart, chocolate crêpes, peach melba, and chocolate mousse cake are the dessert specialties of note.

Be aware that this can be one of the most expensive of all World Showcase restaurants. Priority seating suggested (book as *early* as possible). L, D. **$$$**

L'Originale Alfredo di Roma Ristorante (Italy): This restaurant's trompe l'oeil paintings make diners believe they're seeing real scenes rather than mere murals, and lend character to the decor of this popular establishment. As in the famous Roman restaurant of the same name, the house specialty is fettuccine Alfredo—wide, flat noodles tossed in a sauce made of butter and imported Parmesan cheese. But many other sizes and shapes of pasta, all of it made right on the premises, are also available; they are significantly enhanced by tomato, meat, pesto (basil, garlic, and Parmesan), or carbonara (egg, bacon, cream, and pecorino romano cheese) sauces. There are also a number of less familiar Italian preparations involving chicken, eggplant, seafood, sausage, and veal, all of which are good. For dessert, choose from specialties such as ricotta cheesecake, spumoni, tortoni, or gelato. Even if you don't eat here, it's fun to stop and just peer through the glass kitchen windows to watch the cooks cranking out the rigatoni, ziti, linguine, lasagne, fettuccine, and spaghetti (which, the menu reminds guests, were brought from Europe to America by Thomas Jefferson in 1786). Priority seating suggested. L, D. **$$$**

Marrakesh (Morocco): The most savory part of the Morocco pavilion features a variety of examples of traditional and modern Moroccan cuisine. Waiters are dressed in traditional Moroccan costumes. Menu specialties include roast lamb, chicken brochette, and couscous (steamed semolina served with your choice of lamb, chicken, or vegetables). Sampler platters are also available. The beautiful tilework was done by Moroccan craftsmen. Belly dancers and musicians entertain diners at dinner. Priority seating suggested. D. **$$$**

Mitsukoshi (Japan): A complex of dining and drinking spots, all run by the Japanese firm for which it is named, occupies the second level of the large structure on the west side of the Japan pavilion. There are two options. *Tempura Kiku* occupies a small corner of the Mitsukoshi building that's devoted to the batter-dipped, deep-fried chicken, beef, seafood, and fresh vegetables that are collectively known as tempura. The individual tidbits are crisp and delicious. Priority seating not available. L, D. *Teppanyaki Dining Rooms* is composed of five rooms not unlike those popularized by the Benihana

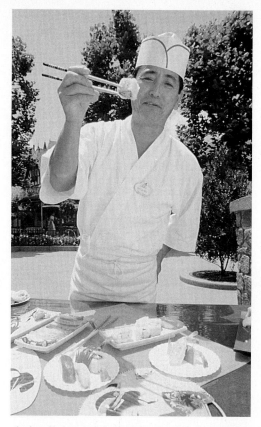

chain all around America. Guests sit counter-style around large flat grills while white-hatted chefs chop vegetables, meat, and fish at lightning speed and then stir-fry it all just as quickly. Whether the chopping and cooking accompany a mildly comic routine depends on the chef, but in any case the establishment is quite convivial. The seating arrangements make it natural to strike up a conversation with fellow diners; in fact, it's almost impossible to keep to yourself. Priority seating suggested. L, D. **$$$**

Nine Dragons (China): This stop on Epcot's varied international restaurant tour offers meals prepared in provincial Chinese cooking styles, including Mandarin, Cantonese, Hunan, Szechuan, and Kiangche. Entrées include Hong Kong-style sirloin, Kang Bao chicken (stir-fried chicken, peanuts, and dried hot peppers), and Nine Dragons Imperial Pine Cone fish. Appetizers range from Chinese pickled cabbage to pan-fried dumplings and hot-and-sour soup. A selection of Chinese teas, beers, and wines is available. The varied dessert menu features red-bean ice cream, toffee apples, and assorted Chinese pastries. Priority seating suggested. L, D. **$$$**

Rose & Crown Pub and Dining Room (United Kingdom): The fare here tends toward pub grub—that is, fish-and-chips and traditional meat pies. For lunch, however, it's also possible to order Bangers and Mash

B breakfast **L** lunch **D** dinner **S** snacks **$** under $10 **$$** $10–$20 **$$$** $21–$45 **$$$$** $46 and up

224

(sausages with mashed potatoes and Yorkshire pudding), vegetable curry, prime rib, or the Ploughman's Lunch (sliced turkey and ham, English cheeses, and fresh bread). At dinner the standard offerings are supplemented by roast prime rib with horseradish sauce, and fresh salmon. For an appetizer, we recommend the sautéed mushrooms in cream sauce on puff pastry. For dessert there's traditional sherry trifle, a confection of layered whipped cream, custard, strawberries, and sherry-flavored sponge cake; Guinness mousse; and chocolate cake. Bass ale from England, Tennent's lager and McCaffrey's Cream Ale from Scotland, and Harp lager and Guinness stout, both from Ireland, are on tap. (They're served cold, in the American fashion, not at room temperature, as the British prefer.)

The decor is beautiful, mainly polished woods, etched glass, and brass accents. In fine weather it's pleasant to lunch under a canopy on the terrace outside and watch the *FriendShip* water taxis cruising across World Showcase Lagoon; a late dinner on the water has an added perk—front-row seating for the nightly fireworks show. On the little island just to the east, the wind ruffles the leaves of the Lombardy poplars, a species of tree that is found along roadsides all over Europe.

As for the pub's architecture, it incorporates three distinct styles. The wall facing the World Showcase Promenade is reminiscent of urban establishments popular in Britain since the 1890s, while that on the south side evokes London's 17th-century Cheshire Cheese pub, with its brick-walled flagstone terrace, slate roof, and half-timbered

exterior. The canal facade, with its stone wall and clay-tile roof, reminds visitors of the charming pubs so common in the English countryside.

The pub section of the Rose & Crown serves such snacks as Stilton cheese and fresh fruit platters, and fish-and-chips—along with all the brews noted above and traditional British mixed drinks, such as shandies (Bass ale and ginger ale), lager with lime juice, black velvets (Guinness stout and champagne), and black and tans (Bass ale and Guinness stout). This drinking and snacking spot is quite popular, so it's often necessary to queue up at the door. But the wait is seldom very long, since few guests choose to linger over their drinks. Note that the pub section also spills out onto the World Showcase promenade—where the first-come-first-served waterside tables make for a nice spot to sip a drink and possibly enjoy some fish-and-chips from a nearby stand. Priority seating is not available in the pub area, but suggested for the adjacent dining room. L, D, S. $ $ $

| **B** breakfast | **L** lunch | **D** dinner | **S** snacks | **$** | under $10 | **$ $** | $10–$20 | **$ $ $** | $21–$45 | **$ $ $ $** | $46 and up |

San Angel Inn (Mexico): The food at this establishment located to the rear of the plaza inside the Mexico pyramid (a corporate cousin of the famous Mexico City restaurant of the same name) may come as a surprise to most visitors. Although the tacos and tortillas and other specialties that usually fall under the broad umbrella of Mexican food are available, the menu also offers a wide variety of more subtly flavored fish, poultry, and meat dishes.

To start, there's *queso fundido* for two (melted cheese and Mexican pork sausage with corn or flour tortillas). As entrées, the menu offers grilled tenderloin of beef served with a chicken enchilada, guacamole, and refried beans; *plato de la frontera* (beef taco, chicken burrito, rice and beans); *ensalada mexicana* (mixed greens with grilled chicken, tomatoes, avocado, turnip, cheese, and cactus strips tossed in a tortilla shell); plus much more that is good and tasty. Mexican desserts are largely unfamiliar to North Americans, with the possible exception of the custard known as flan, but are well worth trying. Dos Equis beer and margaritas make good accompaniments. Priority seating suggested. L, D. 　$ $ $

FAST FOOD & SNACKS

Boulangerie Patisserie (France): This bakery and pastry shop in the France pavilion is not hard to find: Just follow the wonderful aroma, then watch the crowds line up to consume the establishment's flaky croissants, éclairs, fruit tarts, and chocolate mousse. The treats are served under the management of the stellar trio of chefs who operate the popular Les Chefs de France restaurant not far away—Paul Bocuse, Roger Vergé, and Gaston Lenôtre. Hint for those who hate to wait: This has become a favorite snacking stop among Epcot veterans; your best bet is to stop here as soon as World Showcase opens at 11 A.M. or half an hour before park closing. S. 　$

Cantina de San Angel (Mexico): Located along the World Showcase Promenade, just outside the entrance to Mexico's pyramid, this fast-food stand serves beef-filled soft tortillas; *tacos al carbón*, flour tortillas filled with grilled chicken breast strips, onions, and peppers, served with refried beans and salsa; and *churros*, a sort of fried dough rolled in cinnamon and sugar. The Cantina is first-rate for a tasty rest stop, and even more so for its outdoor lagoonside seating. Dos Equis beer and margaritas are available. L, D, S. 　$

Kringla Bakeri og Kafe (Norway): Tucked between the Norway pavilion's wooden church and a cluster of shops, this popular eating spot serves *kringles*, sweet candied pretzels reserved for special occasions in Norway; *vaflers*, heart-shaped waffles topped with powdered sugar and jam; *kransekake*, almond-pastry sticks; and *smørbrøds*, open-face sandwiches of smoked salmon, roast beef, or turkey. Ringnes beer, brewed in Norway, is also available. There is also a pleasant, shaded outdoor eating area. L, D, S. 　$

Liberty Inn (The American Adventure): To many visitors from other countries, American food means burgers, hot dogs, and fries, and these are the staples at the Liberty Inn, located near the entrance to The American Adventure show on the far end of the World Showcase Lagoon. Salads, grilled chicken sandwiches, ice cream, apple pastries, and chocolate chip cookies round out the selections. As a result, the place is a good choice for small children, and also a pleasant spot for their parents. L, D, S. 　$

Lotus Blossom Cafe (China): Adjacent to Yong Feng Shangdian shopping gallery in the China pavilion, this fast-food counter offers sweet-and-sour pork, egg rolls, and soup. There is a covered outdoor seating area nearby. L, D. 　$

Refreshment Outpost (between Germany and China): This is a perfect spot for a refreshing cold drink. Frozen yogurt and ice cream are also served. S. 　$

Refreshment Port (Canada): Another good spot for a quick thirst quencher. Canadian beer, wine coolers, iced tea, and lemonade are served, plus hot dogs, nachos, fresh fruit, and frozen yogurt. S. 　$

B breakfast　**L** lunch　**D** dinner　**S** snacks　$ 　under $10　$ $ 　$10–$20　$ $ $ 　$21–$45　$ $ $ $ 　$46 and up

Sommerfest (Germany): Bratwurst sandwiches, soft pretzels, Black Forest cake, apple strudel, Beck's beer, and wine are offered at this outdoor establishment, located toward the rear of the pavilion; seating is nearby. L, D, S. `$`

Tangierine Cafe (Morocco): Named for the Morroccan city of Tangier, this casual spot serves lentil salad, hummus, and tabbouleh, as well as rotisserie chicken, beef, and lamb presented as sandwiches (served on Morroccan bread) and combination platters. Specialty coffees and pastries are also available. L, D, S. `$`

Yakitori House (Japan): Located in the gardens to the left of the plaza, the restaurant occupies a scaled-down version of the 16th-century Katsura Imperial Summer Palace in Kyoto; sliding screens, lanterns, and kimono-clad servers add to the atmosphere. *Guydon* is a stewlike concoction flavored with soy sauce, spices, and the Japanese rice wine known as sake, served over rice. That staple, along with skewered chicken known as *yakitori* (it's basted with soy sauce and sesame oil as it broils), teriyaki chicken sandwiches, and Japanese sweets and beverages, typifies the offerings here. L, D, S. `$`

Epcot Mealtime Tips

• The international restaurants of World Showcase offer some of the best dining on the property. Since many of them are very popular, it's a good idea to arrange advance priority seating for any table-service restaurants by calling 407-WDW-DINE (939-3463) long before arriving. However, it's important to note that many tables are left available for same-day seating. To make arrangements, head to Guest Relations first thing in the morning or to the kiosk located by the Tip Board in Innoventions Plaza. Meals can also be booked at the individual restaurants. Refer to page 248 for more details.

• If you aren't able to secure priority seating for dinner, don't despair. There are tasty alternatives to a table-service meal. Japan has Tempura Kiku, a full-service spot with batter-dipped, deep-fried meats and vegetables (and no priority seating available), and Yakitori House, good for skewered bits of barbecued beef and chicken. Sample Mexican specialties at Cantina de San Angel (whose lagoonside tables provide a fine view of the sun setting behind Epcot). Also try the open-face sandwiches at Kringla Bakeri og Kafe in Norway, or the sweet-and-sour pork at China's Lotus Blossom Cafe.

• Cravings for more conventional fast foods will be satisfied at the Electric Umbrella in Innoventions and at the Liberty Inn in The American Adventure. The Pasta Piazza Ristorante in Innoventions serves Italian fare. The Sunshine Season Food Fair in The Land pavilion offers a little bit of everything.

• The most unadventurous eaters can still find something pleasing—even in the more exotic restaurants of World Showcase. If you're undecided, ask at Guest Relations to see a booklet describing each of the menus.

• Don't dismiss the idea of an early seating if you can get it: If you have lunch at 11 A.M., a 5 P.M. dinner will not only be welcome, but more important, it will provide the opportunity to spend the most pleasant and uncrowded evening hours enjoying the Epcot attractions.

• Lunch provides guests with another chance to enjoy the most popular Epcot restaurants. It also has an additional appeal: With priority seating for 1 P.M., it's possible to spend some of the most crowded hours in the park consuming a pleasant meal while less fortunate visitors are waiting in some of the longest lines of the day.

B breakfast   **L** lunch   **D** dinner   **S** snacks   `$` under $10   `$ $` $10–$20   `$ $ $` $21–$45   `$ $ $ $` $46 and up

In the Disney-MGM Studios

The eateries at the Disney-MGM Studios are a breed apart. Some feature decor that returns guests to a bygone era; others recapture memorable moments from the big or small screen. All reprise a beloved part of Hollywood's star-studded heritage. The Studios has five full-service restaurants, whose atmospheres and menus are so distinct they satisfy altogether different moods and whims. Priority seating is available for these dining rooms (for details, turn to page 248). Hollywood & Vine offers character meals (see page 242 for specifics). A solid—and fairly diverse—ensemble of fast-food places hits the spot for eaters on the move.

TABLE SERVICE

50's Prime Time Cafe: The setting is straight out of your favorite sitcoms of the 1950s. Each of the plastic-laminate kitchen tables is set under a pull-down lamp, evoking a suburban kitchenette. Televisions around the room broadcast black-and-white clips from favorite fifties comedies (all related to food). Guests are waited on by "Mom" (and other family members) with considerable enthusiasm—they make recommendations, and encourage everyone to keep their elbows off the table and clean their plates (*or no dessert!*).

The menu is packed with "comfort foods." For openers there's a choice of homemade

chicken noodle soup, or Dad's chili. Specialties of the house include Magnificent Meat Loaf, served with mashed potatoes and mushroom gravy; fried chicken; and Granny's Pot Roast. There are also Caesar

salads, sandwiches, and Aunt Selma's Chicken Salad. Milk shakes, ice cream sodas, and root beer floats are filling accompaniments. And when you've finished everything on your plate, "Mom" will ask if you'd like dessert. Standouts include s'mores, a graham cracker topped with chocolate and toasted marshmallows (you'll feel like you're back at summer camp); sundaes; banana splits; and

B breakfast   **L** lunch   **D** dinner   **S** snacks   **$**   under $10   **$ $** $10–$20   **$ $ $** $21–$45   **$ $ $ $** $46 and up

228

apple pie à la mode. A full bar is available. Kids love this place. Priority seating suggested. L, D. `$$-$$$`

Hollywood & Vine: The distinctive Art Deco facade ushers guests into a contemporary version of a 1950s diner—all stainless steel with pink accents. An elaborate 42-by-8-foot wall mural depicts notable Hollywood landmarks, including the Disney Studios, Columbia Ranch, and Warner Brothers (back

HOT TIP Hollywood Brown Derby and Mama Melrose's Ristorante Italiano (and other eateries) offer a "dinner and a show" deal. Simply make arrangements upon arrival at the Studios to get special seating (no waiting!) at that evening's performance of Fantasmic! For details, go to Guest Relations.

when they were the only studios in the San Fernando Valley). At the center of the mural is the Carthay Circle Theatre, where *Snow White and the Seven Dwarfs* premiered in 1937.

Starlet Minnie Mouse is joined by Goofy, Pluto, Chip, and Dale, in welcoming and entertaining guests at this 334-seat restaurant. (Note that these characters were appearing at press time, but are subject to change.) The all-you-can-eat buffet offers a bounty of fresh selections. For breakfast there's eggs, chocolate french toast, fritatas, pancakes, Mickey waffles, potatoes, bacon, sausage, and more. The tempting lunch buffet features rotisserie turkey, flank steak, seafood, a selection of pastas, sautéed vegetables, macaroni and cheese, fried chicken, and hot dogs, plus a variety of pastries and a make-your-own-sundae bar. Cost for breakfast is $14.95 for adults and $7.95 for children ages 3 through 11; lunch is $16.50 for adults and $8.95 for children. Priority seating suggested. B, L. `$$$`

Hollywood Brown Derby: The home of the famous Cobb salad is alive and well. This re-creation of the former Vine Street mainstay is quite faithful, right down to the caricatures (reproduced from the original Derby collection) that cover the walls. Arch gossip queen rivals Louella Parsons and Hedda Hopper (portrayed by convincing actresses) may still be spotted dining here, just as they did in the heyday of the real Brown Derby. The restaurant is decorated predominantly in teak and mahogany, and the elegant chandeliers and perimeter lamps (shaped like miniature derbies) are reminiscent of those in the original eatery.

The menu features the famed Cobb salad, created by owner Bob Cobb in the 1930s. It's a mixture of ever-so-finely chopped fresh salad greens, tomato, bacon, turkey, egg, blue cheese, and avocado, served with french dressing. A modern incarnation of the salad is available with shrimp or chicken. Other menu selections of note include pan seared jumbo shrimp and penne pasta in a sundried tomato and goat cheese cream sauce, and roasted double-cut lamb chops with buttermilk blue cheese mashed potatoes and portobello mushrooms on the side. The dessert tray is tempting—particularly the grapefruit cake, a Brown Derby institution. The slightly formal atmosphere is not likely to enchant most kids. Priority seating suggested. L, D. `$$$`

Mama Melrose's Ristorante Italiano: This quirky Italian restaurant (with a California twist) is located in a warehouse that has been converted into a dining room. Appetizer pizzas are prepared in a wood-burning oven. The menu also features risotto, chicken, prime rib, pasta, and vegetarian options. More creative dishes include linguini with clams, shrimp, mussels, and calamari in a spicy marinara sauce; and potato and Parmesan encrusted veal scallopini. Note that the dinner hour ends a bit earlier than usual here. Priority seating suggested. L, D. `$$-$$$`

Sci-Fi Dine-In Theater: This 250-seat eatery re-creates a 1950s drive-in theater. The tables are actually flashy, 1950s-era cars, complete with fins and whitewalls. Fiber-optic stars twinkle overhead in the "night sky," and real drive-in theater speakers are mounted beside each car. All the tables face a large screen, where a 45-minute compilation of the best (and worst) of science fiction trailers and cartoons plays in a continuous loop.

The restaurant is also notable for its huge hot and cold sandwiches. Selections include club sandwiches, barbecue pork sandwiches, and flame-broiled hamburgers. There's also a slate of tempting desserts, including cheesecake, milk shakes, and The Sci-Fi Sundae (a colossal sundae made with vanilla ice cream and many toppings). Priority seating suggested. L, D. $$$-$$$$

FAST FOOD & SNACKS

ABC Commissary: This restaurant located near the Chinese Theater features savory grilled chicken breast sandwiches, quesadilla club sandwiches, red beans and rice, fresh tomato salad, fruit pies, and milk shakes. The kids' meals are sure to please. As fast food eateries go, this spot is a true standout. L, D. $

Backlot Express: This fast-food spot looks like the old crafts shops on a studio backlot. There's a paint shop, stunt hall, sculpture shop, and model shop. The paint shop has paint-speckled floors, chairs, and tables; the prop shop is decked out in car engines, bumpers, and fan belts. There is outdoor seating amid stored streetlights, plants, and trees. Menu offerings include burgers, hot dogs, chicken Caesar salad, grilled chicken sandwiches, tuna subs, and chili. For dessert, there's chocolate-chip cheesecake, brownies, and fresh fruit. Beer is available. L, D, S. $

Dinosaur Gertie's: "Ice Cream of Extinction" claims the sign at this giant dinosaur set on Echo Lake. And indeed, a selection of ice cream bars and soft serve ice cream disappear rather quickly. S. $

Min & Bill's Dockside Diner: "There's good eats in our galley" proclaims the welcoming sign posted on the *S.S. Down the Hatch*, a bit of "California crazy" 1950s architecture. The little tramp steamer, complete with a cartoonlike smokestack, mast, and booms, never actually sets sail. Min & Bill's sweet offerings include ice cream soda floats, sundaes, and downright delicious shakes. Soft-serve ice cream is also available in cups or cones with a variety of toppings. S. $

Starring Rolls Bakery: Freshly baked rolls, pastries, muffins, croissants, and sugar-free desserts are sold at this sweet-smelling shop. Coffee, tea, and soft drinks are also served, making this a good place for an eat-and-run breakfast. For lunch, ready-made sandwiches with ham and cheese, chicken salad, or tuna salad are available. B, L, S. $

Studio Catering Co.: Situated next to the Honey, I Shrunk the Kids Movie Set Adventure, the eatery offers a selection of hearty double-decker sandwiches. The

choices include a club sandwich, and a turkey and cheddar cheese sandwich served on wheat bread with lettuce and tomato. There is a separate line for cones and sundaes made with chocolate and vanilla soft-serve ice cream. Beer is available at a nearby stand. S. $

Sunset Ranch Market: Several well-stocked food stands on Sunset Boulevard offer snacking opportunities and quick bites. Yellow and white umbrellas dot the outdoor seating area. *Rosie's All-American Cafe* specializes in burgers, sandwiches, and soups. *Catalina Eddie's* offers plain, pepperoni, and vegetable pizzas, plus salads, brownies and cookies. Fresh fruit and vegetables, fruit juices, and soft drinks are available at *Anaheim Produce*. The turkey leg cart also offers baked potatoes with toppings, foot-long hot dogs, and soft pretzels. L, D, S. $

Toy Story Pizza Planet: This arcade looks as if it were plucked out of the film *Toy Story*. The centerpiece is a Space Crane, complete with aliens and mechanical grabber. Video games line the walls. A perfect spot for children with endless energy and parents who need to rest their feet while enjoying a leisurely lunch. The limited menu includes individual pizzas, salads, desserts, and juice. Cappuccino and espresso are also available. L, D, S. $

B breakfast   **L** lunch   **D** dinner   **S** snacks   **$**   under $10   **$$** $10–$20   **$$$** $21–$45   **$$$$** $46 and up

230

GOOD MEALS, GREAT TIMES

In Animal Kingdom

Whether you eat like a bird or more like a horse, you'll have no trouble finding something to sink your teeth into at one of Animal Kingdom's many eateries. The emphasis at Disney's newest theme park is on fast food, with Rainforest Cafe as the only traditional table-service establishment. The menagerie of quick-service options cater to carnivores and herbivores alike, featuring everything from freshly tossed Caesar salad to chicken roasted in a 16-foot "wall of flames." Beer, including Safari Amber specialty brew, and wine are served at most restaurants.

TABLE SERVICE

Rainforest Cafe: Like The Oasis, the region of Animal Kingdom that it borders, this cafe is a lush, soothing tropical jungle. Unlike The Oasis, any quiet moment here is merely a calm before the storm—as brief, dramatic thunderstorms occur throughout the day *inside* the restaurant. Gushing waterfalls,

twisting tree trunks, and colorful fish add to the ambience. The environmentally conscious cuisine includes items like Planet Earth Pasta and the Plant Sandwich. (The Calypso Dip—fresh salmon, artichoke hearts, onions, spices, and cheese served with warm pita—is an especially tantalizing appetizer.) There's no net-caught fish on the menu, nor beef from countries that destroy rain forest land to raise cattle.

Note: The restaurant and shop are accessible from both inside and outside Animal Kingdom, so admission to the park is not necessary to enter. It is located to the left of the park's entrance plaza. Priority seating suggested for breakfast (available 30 days ahead) and lunch and dinner (just 7 days prior). B, L, D, S. **$$-$$$**

FAST FOOD & SNACKS

Anandapur Ice Cream: Cool off with a soft-serve from Asia's local ice cream truck. The refreshing snack is available by the cone, in a soda float, or blended into a flavorful smoothie. S. **$**

Chakrandi Chicken Shop: In Asia, there is a walk-up window dispensing chicken satay dipped in peanut sauce, noodle bowls, corn on the cob, and soft drinks. S. **$**

Chip 'n' Dale's Cookie Cabin: For a sweet treat, head to Camp Minnie-Mickey for delicious, freshly baked cookies (chocolate chip, macadamia nut, and sugar) and ice cream sandwiches. S. **$**

Dino Diner: In DinoLand U.S.A., near the entrance, is a small wagon that sells pastries and muffins at breakfast and desserts throughout the day. S. **$**

Flame Tree Barbecue: You will probably start licking your chops before you even arrive here, as the aroma of barbecue wafts not-so-subtly by. This fast-food establishment serves up a savory selection of barbecued sandwiches and platters, all wood-roasted and fresh from the smoker. Sample the tomato-based barbecue sauce or the mustard-based Carolina-style sauce with your smoked beef brisket, St. Louis ribs, and pulled pork. Smoked turkey, a vegetarian wrap, and apple pie round out the options. There's endless outdoor seating along the river. Located in Safari Village, near the bridge to DinoLand U.S.A. L, D, S. **$**

Harambe Fruit Market: A healthy choice for snacking at Disney's Animal Kingdom is this fruit stand near the entrance to Kilimanjaro Safaris. S. **$**

Kusafiri Coffee Shop & Bakery: The bakery inside Tusker House provides a steady stream of fresh-from-the-oven breakfast treats and assorted desserts, plus cappuccino and espresso. B, S.

Mr. Kamal's Burger Grill: Located on the path between Africa and Asia, this spot offers juicy broiled burgers served with chips. The seating area nearby is small, but has a great view of The Tree of Life. L, D, S. **$**

Munch Wagon: Head to this stand at Conservation Station for tasty hot dogs and snacks. L, D, S. **$**

Pizzafari: Individual pizzas are available plain, with pepperoni, and deluxe (with a variety of meats and vegetables). In addition to the cheese-laden bill of fare, the options

B breakfast **L** lunch **D** dinner **S** snacks **$** under $10 **$$** $10–$20 **$$$** $21–$45 **$$$$** $46 and up here include pasta, a Caesar salad with grilled chicken, and a small roast vegetable calzone. Brightly colored animal murals decorate this counter-service restaurant, located in Safari Village, near the bridge to Camp Minnie-Mickey. L, D, S. $

Restaurantosaurus: Located deep in the heart of DinoLand U.S.A., this spot is themed as a campsite for student paleontologists. It's filled with fossils, bones, and such; class notes line the walls. This eatery offers "dino-mite" fast food at lunch and dinner: burgers, chicken salad, hot dogs, and salads—plus McDonald's french fries, chicken nuggets, and Happy Meals. Breakfast is an all-you-can-eat character-hosted buffet,

Still hungry? Vendors roaming throughout Animal Kingdom offer soft pretzels, popcorn, and ice cream bars imprinted with Simba's paw, among other treats.

called Donald's Prehistoric Breakfastosaurus. It's an entertaining meal, powered by the amusing antics of resident students, who wait tables between classes and banter about who left dirty laundry in their dorm lofts. Cost is $14.95 for adults; $8.95 for kids ages 3 through 11. Priority seating suggested for the breakfast buffet. Book as *early* as possible. B, L, D, S. $

Tamu Tamu Refreshments: Got a hankering for something cool and creamy? Stop by this snack spot in Africa's Harambe (across from Tusker House). Here you can indulge a sweet tooth with soft-serve frozen yogurt and ice cream cones, floats, and sundaes. There's a small outdoor seating nook next door. S. $

DID YOU KNOW...

Tusker House: Harambe village sets the stage for an exceptional dining adventure at this top-notch fast-food restaurant, themed as a safari orientation center. Seating inside is quite civilized, with cherry-wood-colored tables and carved chair backs; there's also outdoor seating under the thatched roof. The far-reaching menu—which happens to be one of the best in the park—features rotisserie chicken cooked in a 16-foot "wall of flames." Other highlights include the grilled chicken salad served in a bread bowl, beef stew, roast vegetable sandwiches served with tabbouleh, and grilled chicken with ham and cheese. Fried chicken, and side dishes such as chicken salad, fresh vegetables and garlic-mashed potatoes round out the creative options. L, D, S. $

Animal Kingdom Mealtime Tips

- Restaurantosaurus and Rainforest Cafe are the only restaurants to offer full breakfasts; a handful of stands, including Dino Diner, supply light options.
- The only restaurant that offers priority seating for all meals is Rainforest Cafe. To arrange for priority seating in advance, available 4 months ahead for all meals, call 407-WDW-DINE (939-3463). Refer to page 248 for details. To obtain same-day seating, go straight to the restaurant. Without priority seating, expect to wait a bit, since this is the only table-service restaurant in the park.
- The many seating pavilions along the river near Flame Tree Barbecue provide waterside dining that's nicely removed from the hubbub of Safari Village; it may be relatively calm here even during prime mealtimes.
- A great place to meet Donald, Mickey, Pluto, and Goofy is at Restaurantosaurus during the daily character breakfast. Don't forget to make priority seating arrangements.

B breakfast **L** lunch **D** dinner **S** snacks **$** under $10 **$ $** $10–$20 **$ $ $** $21–$45 **$ $ $ $** $46 and up

In Downtown Disney

The vast region known as Downtown Disney encompasses the Marketplace, Pleasure Island, and the West Side. While an admission fee applies after 7 P.M. for Pleasure Island club-goers, there is no charge simply to dine at any of Pleasure Island's full-service restaurants. (There is never a fee to roam the West Side or Marketplace.) On average, Downtown Disney restaurants operate from 11 A.M. to midnight; most of the snack spots are open from 11 A.M. to 2 A.M. For up-to-the-minute details on hours call 407-939-4636. It's worth noting that while the restaurants really hop at dinnertime, they are not terribly crowded at lunch (except, possibly, on the weekend).

Bongos Cuban Cafe (West Side): This creation of Gloria Estefan and her husband spices up the Downtown Disney dining repertoire with a menu driven by Cuban and Latin American flavors. Its slate of traditional and nouvelle Cuban dishes, such as black bean soup, plantains, steak topped with onions, and flan, tempt taste buds. Indoors, the elaborate mosaic mural and palm-leaf railings set the scene; the balcony for outdoor seating wraps around a three-story pineapple. A take-out window provides snacks on the go. Priority seating is not available. L, D, S.   **$$-$$$**

Cap'n Jack's Restaurant (Marketplace): This pier house juts right out over Lake Buena Vista, providing water views. The appetizer menu is so full of tasty things—peel-and-eat shrimp, garlic oysters, and clam chowder—that it's as good for a light lunch or dinner as it is for a snack. Entrées extend to crab cakes, lobster, mahimahi, and "landlubber" specials. There is a tempting variety of wines, microbrew beers, and other cocktails—and the house's special frozen margaritas are as tasty as they are beautiful. Cap'n Jack's is a terrific place to be, especially in late afternoon, as the sun streams through the narrow-slatted blinds and glints on the polished tables and the copper above the bar. L, D, S.   **$$**

Cheesecake Factory Express (West Side): Located on the top three floors of DisneyQuest, this fast food restaurant serves much more than the sumptuous sweets it is famous for. The daily offerings are prepared fresh from the four main counters. Highlights include warm spinach and artichoke dip served with chips and salsa, grilled portobello mushroom sandwiches, barbecue chicken pizza, and lasagne in a chicken bolognese sauce. Also available are a selection of hearty soups and salads, tasty sandwiches, and several specialty burgers and hot dogs. Temptations abound at the dessert counter—they come in the form of frozen mud pie, hot fudge brownie sundaes, cookies, cakes, and, of course, cheesecake. Note that DisneyQuest admission is required for access to the Cheesecake Factory Express. L, D, S.   **$**

D-Zertz (Pleasure Island): Pastries, chocolates, candy, frozen yogurt, and other confections are the desserts available here. Coffee and cappuccino are also served, making it a pleasant spot for a quick snack. S.   **$**

Forty Thirst Street (West Side): For a refreshing treat, this place is a fine choice. Smoothies, frozen yogurt, coffee coolers, pastries, and other sweet solutions are the bill of fare. There's also a wide selection of specialty coffees and cappuccino. S.   **$**

Fulton's Crab House (Between Pleasure Island and Marketplace; 407-934-2628): This traditional seafood house, operated by Levy Restaurants, occupies the three-deck riverboat formerly known as the *Empress Lilly*. Permanently docked on the western edge of Lake Buena Vista, it is a tribute to Robert Fulton, who invented the steamboat. The place is so serious about seafood that it has hooked up with fishermen worldwide to ensure that the truckloads of fish and shellfish arriving daily at Fulton's back door are at their freshest.

B breakfast   **L** lunch   **D** dinner   **S** snacks   **$** under $10   **$$** $10–$20   **$$$** $21–$45   **$$$$** $46 and up

233

GOOD MEALS, GREAT TIMES

The menu changes each day to reflect new arrivals, but is always filled with several types of crabs, oysters, and fish, plus lobster, steaks, grilled chicken, grilled vegetables, and combination platters. Signature dishes include cioppino, a savory San Francisco–style seafood stew with a tomato broth base. Accompaniments extend to corn-whipped potatoes and grilled asparagus. Desserts, coffee, and specialty drinks are also served.

Fulton's handsome polished-wood interior is awash in nautical knickknacks and nostalgia. Seating on the deck is sometimes available. The adjoining Stone Crab lounge has an excellent raw bar—the perfect place for lunch or a savory snack. Advance dining arrangements suggested for breakfast and dinner. B, L, D, S. **$ $ $ $**

Ghirardelli Soda Fountain and Chocolate Shop (Marketplace): San Francisco's famous sweetmaker finally comes east with a soda fountain extraordinaire. Stop in for a chocolaty treat, root beer float, or refreshing malt. Antique chocolate-making equipment demonstrates how the famous Ghirardelli chocolate got its start. There's no better place to please a sweet tooth. S. **$**

Gourmet Pantry (Marketplace): Though it's technically a shop, this food-oriented establishment is positively brimming with sweet and savory possibilities. Among the delectables standing by for snackers and impromptu picnickers are specialty salads and sandwiches, tasty heros sold by the inch, fresh-baked cookies and desserts, Godiva chocolates, nuts, beer, wine, spirits, and gourmet coffees. Seating is available right outside and also along the waterfront on Lake Buena Vista. B, L, D, S. **$**

House of Blues (West Side): The nightclub that Blues Brother Dan Aykroyd helped launch doubles as a Mississippi Delta–inspired dining spot. House of Blues gives Downtown Disney a culinary boost from the bayou—namely home-style Cajun and Creole cooking. Finally, WDW has a haven for diners desperately seeking their fill of such savory things as jambalaya, étouffée, and homemade bread pudding. A gospel brunch is presented on Sundays. Priority seating is available for groups of 6 to 19 only. L, D, S. **$**

McDonald's (Marketplace): The Golden Arches and all of its Mc-specialties (plus pizza) are on hand until the wee hours in this installation of the familiar fast-food establishment, located on the western edge of the Marketplace. B, L, D, S. **$**

Missing Link Sausage Co. (Pleasure Island): Hot dogs, bratwurst, kielbasa, and sausages (including a chicken-apple variety, and both mild and hot Italian links) dominate the menu of this snack spot across from 8TRAX. Cheese steaks are also available. L, D, S. **$**

Planet Hollywood (West Side): This branch of the international restaurant chain is a standout for its spherical silhouette. Built on three levels, this colossal globe is jam-packed with classic movie and television memorabilia.

The creative, wide-ranging menu features first-rate salads, sandwiches, pasta dishes, burgers, appetizer pizzas, fajitas, and dessert specialties. Be sure to consider sampling the blackened shrimp, Far East chicken salad, vegetable burger, or pasta primavera. Cap off the meal with a piece of butter rum cake. Priority seating is available for lunch only. Smoking is permitted. L, D, S. **$ $-$ $ $**

Portobello Yacht Club (Pleasure Island; 407-934-8888): The elegant Bermuda-style house combines high gables and beamed ceilings, bright Mediterranean colors and earthy tones. The establishment is divided into several informal dining rooms, each of which displays an interesting collection of maritime memorabilia.

The bustling open kitchen turns out grilled meat and fish, and delicious small gourmet pizzas baked in a wood-burning oven. Try the *quattro formaggi*, a four-cheese pie that's a true taste treat and a great appetizer or snack. Pasta offerings include *spaghettini alla Portobello* (pasta with shrimp, scallops, clams, mussels, crab legs, tomatoes, garlic, olive oil, wine, and herbs) and *penne all'arrabiata* (long pasta tubes with plum tomatoes, mushrooms,

B breakfast   **L** lunch   **D** dinner   **S** snacks   **$** under $10   **$ $** $10–$20   **$ $ $** $21–$45   **$ $ $ $** $46 and up

pancetta, garlic, onions, and fresh herbs). Be sure to save room for desserts such as *crema brucciata*, white chocolate custard with a caramelized sugar glaze; or *cioccolato paradiso*, a layer cake with chocolate ganache frosting, chocolate toffee crunch filling, and warm caramel sauce. Portobello also offers a selection of specialty coffees and an impressive wine list. Priority seating suggested. L, D, S. `$ $ $`

Rainforest Cafe (Downtown Disney Marketplace): There's no mistaking the environmental orientation of this Amazon-emulating eatery near Cap'n Jack's Restaurant. The atmospheric dining environs transport guests to a makeshift rain forest, complete with banyan trees, tropical fish, gushing waterfalls, and a friendly population of hand-raised parrots. A talking tree offers a constant stream of ecological insights, and animal experts are on hand to field questions. Sophisticated special effects envelop guests in tropical storms, complete with lightning and thunder. Menu items include Planet Earth Pasta, Island Hopper Chicken, and the Plant Sandwich (portobello mushrooms, zucchini, roasted red peppers, and fresh spinach). A merchandise shop stocks logo clothing. Priority seating suggested. B, L, D, S. `$$-$$$`

Wildhorse Saloon (Pleasure Island; 407-827-4947): The restaurant in this club serves up old-fashioned country cooking. There's smoked pork sandwiches, chicken fried steak, barbecued ribs, and, of course, grits to accompany the live country bands and line dancing. There may be an entertainment charge in the evening. Reservations available for dinner. L, D, S. `$$-$$$`

Wolfgang Puck Cafe (West Side): Wolfgang Puck's choice of Walt Disney World for his Florida debut is sure to spur a surge in cravings for his trademark California cuisine. Among his specialties are gourmet pizzas, Thai chicken satay pastas with fresh vegetables, Chinois Chicken Salad, and

rotisserie chicken. The menu is equal parts sophisticated and straightforward—and ever so fresh. There's also an attractive sushi bar. Colorful mosaics decorate his restaurants. Priority seating is not available. L, D, S. `$ $ $`

Wolfgang Puck Cafe—The Dining Room (West Side): The formal upstairs area in the cafe is devoted to the more elaborate of Wolfgang Puck's cuisine. Consider baby vegetable risotto and grilled chicken with squash ravioli in a sage brown butter sauce. Priority seating suggested. D. `$$$-$$$$`

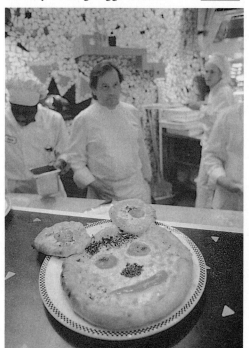

Wolfgang Puck Express (Marketplace and West Side): Renowned chef Wolfgang Puck turns his talents to fast service and signature treats, including gourmet wood-fired pizzas, rotisserie chicken, seasonal soups, focaccia sandwiches, and fresh salads—including his famous Chinois Chicken Salad. Inexpensive. L, D, S. `$`

Crossroads of Lake Buena Vista

WDW visitors can get everything from soup to McNuggets at the Crossroads of Lake Buena Vista shopping center, near the resorts on Hotel Plaza Boulevard. Choices include Pebbles (the best bet for adults), Perkins (popular with families), T.G.I. Friday's, Red Lobster, McDonald's, Taco Bell, Jungle Jim's, Pacino's, Chevy's Mexican Restaurant, and Pizzeria Uno.

GOOD MEALS, GREAT TIMES

In the WDW Resorts

Among the more pleasant surprises at Walt Disney World is the delightful theming of the Disney hotels. Each resort sports a fanciful setting quite foreign to Central Florida, reminiscent of such places as the Pacific Northwest; the more regional-minded offer a tasty sampling of the native cuisine to complete the picture. Whereas the deluxe properties provide a variety of dining options, including at least one full-service restaurant, moderate resorts feature a food court plus an informal dining room, and the value-oriented All-Star resorts keep guests' appetites in check with huge food courts.

Suffice it to say that the possibilities range from hearty dinners served family-style to innovative cuisine you might not expect from Disney, presented in settings worthy of special occasions. Priority seating is an important part of the resorts' full-service dining circuit (for details turn to page 248). Character meals are an option for breakfast, Sunday brunch, and dinner (see page 242).

All-Star Resorts

Each of these resorts features a themed central food court. The **End Zone** food court in Stadium Hall at the All-Star Sports resort, the **Intermission** food court in Melody Hall at the All-Star Music resort, and the **World Premiere** food court in Cinema Hall at the All-Star Movies resort have similar food stands. The selections include pasta, pizza, chicken, ribs, burgers, hot dogs, sandwiches, salads, frozen yogurt, and a wide variety of breakfast and baked goods. B, L, D, S. $

Animal Kingdom Lodge

Boma—Flavors of Africa : Big and bustling, this family restaurant, designed to resemble an African marketplace, features fare from around the world. Priority seating suggested. B, D. $$-$$$

Jiko—The Cooking Place: Food with an African flare fills the menu at this sophisticated eatery. Priority seating suggested. B, D. $$-$$$

The Mara: An enormous fast-food restaurant located near the pool. B, L, D, S. $ - $$

BoardWalk

Big River Grille & Brewing Works: Guests observe (and later sample) as the brewmaster creates three flagship ales and two seasonal brews at this working brewpub. The menu features a selection of sandwiches and salads, plus creative variations on pub favorites, such as veal meatloaf with Tilt Pale Ale sauce and lobster pot pie. L, D, S. $$

BoardWalk Bakery: The aromas wafting from Spoodles' next-door neighbor on the boardwalk reveal the fresh-baked goods therein. Display windows allow guests to watch bakers at work. B, S. $

ESPN Club: A sports bar-family restaurant one-two punch, ESPN Club surrounds guests with no fewer than 80 TV monitors, so no one misses a play. The fare includes burgers, sandwiches, and a variety of salads and entrées. L, D, S. $$

Flying Fish Cafe: This upbeat eatery delivers creative seasonal menus with an emphasis on seafood and healthy options. As an example of the entrées created in the open

"on-stage" kitchen, consider the potato-wrapped yellowtail snapper. While seafood is the specialty, steaks are also served. Save room for the chocolate lava cake. Priority seating suggested. Seating is available at the chef's counter. D. $$$

Seashore Sweets': Located next to the Flying Fish Cafe, this old-fashioned spot sates sweet tooths with candies, saltwater taffy, and ice cream and frozen yogurt. Specialty coffees are also offered. S. $

Spoodles: This family-oriented restaurant with butcher-block tables and Mediterranean tastes is on the boardwalk between Seashore Sweets' and the BoardWalk Bakery. The lunch and dinner menus highlight specialties from Greece, Spain, Northern Africa, and Italy, and encourage diners to share dishes and try new foods. Offerings range from pizzas baked in wood-burning ovens to braised lamb shank with a creamy herb polenta. The breakfast buffet features eggs, meats, fish, cereal, and french toast. A take-out window allows passersby to get pizza by the slice. Priority seating suggested. B, L, D. $$-$$$

B breakfast **L** lunch **D** dinner **S** snacks $ under $10 $$ $10–$20 $$$ $21–$45 $$$$ $46 and up

GOOD MEALS, GREAT TIMES

Caribbean Beach

Captain's Tavern: Prime rib, chicken, and pork loin are on the menu at this cozy restaurant within Old Port Royale. Tropical drinks, beer, wine, and cocktails are also served. Priority seating suggested. D, S. $$-$$$

Old Port Royale: The food court in Old Port Royale features a large dining area and the following fast-food eateries. *Bridgetown Broiler* offers spit-roasted chicken and home-style meals. *Cinnamon Bay Bakery* serves croissants, freshly baked rolls, pastries, ice cream, and other high-calorie treats. Italian specialties are the order at the *Kingston Pasta Shop*. Soups, salads, and hot and cold sandwiches make up the selections at *Montego's Deli*. Burgers and grilled chicken sandwiches are among the offerings at *Port Royale Hamburger Shop*. And pizza is available by the slice or the pie at *Royale Pizza Shop*. B, L, D, S. $

Contemporary

California Grill: Perched on the hotel's 15th floor, with terrific views of sunsets and Magic Kingdom fireworks, this acclaimed restaurant offers the best in West Coast cuisine in a stylish, relaxing atmosphere. (It has been named "restaurant of choice" by *Orlando Magazine*.) The ever-changing menu is defined by sophisticated use of fresh produce. Wood-fired California pizzas, alderwood-smoked salmon, sushi, spit-roasted chicken, and jumbo soufflés are made to order in an open kitchen. Grilled pork tenderloin with polenta and balsamic-vinegar-smothered cremini mushrooms suggest the chef's culinary prowess. There's even a vegetarian zone on the menu. The excellent wine list is updated daily. Priority seating suggested (book as *early* as possible). D. $$$

Chef Mickey's: Chef Mickey and his pals host this buffet-style feast, with dramatic views of the monorail passing above. Colorful

life-size illustrations of Disney characters decorate the room. The changing menu takes advantage of seasonal offerings; a sundae bar provides a sweet finish. Priority seating suggested. B, D. $$-$$$

Concourse Steakhouse: This spot offers omelettes, pancakes, and fresh fruit for breakfast. At lunch there are salads, soups, burgers, pizzas, and sandwiches. Dinner adds steaks, seafood, and oak-roasted prime rib to the menu. The wine list is updated daily. Priority seating suggested. B, L, D. $$$

Food and Fun Center: On the first floor by the arcade, this spot serves light fare 24 hours a day. B, L, D, S. $

Coronado Springs

Maya Grill: The only full-service restaurant at this resort, it features Latin American dishes. Signature items include grilled chicken breast with black beans and a Mayan salsa, pumpkin-seed-encrusted snapper filet, and broiled beef tenderloin with *chimichurri* sauce. Many items are cooked over an open-pit wood-fired grill. Breakfast is presented as an all-you-can-eat buffet. Maya Grill is located next to the Pepper Market food court. Priority seating suggested. B, D. $$$

Pepper Market: This food court, modeled after an open-air market, has a large seating area and lots of stands where vendors sell pizza, sandwiches, salads, burgers, stir fry, Mexican specialties, baked goods, margaritas, and more. Note that a ten percent gratuity is automatically added to the bill when you eat in the dining area. B, L, D, S. $ - $$

Disney's Old Key West

Good's Food to Go: Hamburgers, cheeseburgers, grilled chicken sandwiches, salads, ice cream, and frozen yogurt are among the offerings. L, D, S. $

Olivia's Cafe: An assortment of Key West favorites, including Key lime pie and conch fritters, are featured alongside contemporary southern fare. The menu changes seasonally. A Winnie the Pooh-themed character breakfast is held Sunday, Monday, and Wednesday. Priority seating suggested. B, L, D. $$

Dixie Landings

Boatwright's Dining Hall: Be sure to notice the boat that's being built in this table-service eatery. The specialties of the house include Cajun dishes as well as American home-style favorites. Priority seating suggested. B, D. $$-$$$

B breakfast **L** lunch **D** dinner **S** snacks $ under $10 $$ $10–$20 $$$ $21–$45 $$$$ $46 and up

Colonel's Cotton Mill: This high-ceilinged food court styled in the image of a working cotton mill offers half a dozen food counters and a sprawling seating area. Collectively, the stands offer pizza; pasta; calzone; fried, grilled, and spit-roasted chicken; burgers; barbecued ribs; salads; sandwiches; and fresh baked goods. For guests on the go, the food court's deli does double duty as a convenience store, stocking sandwiches, beer, wine, snack items, and prepared salads. B, L, D, S. $

Fort Wilderness

Most people cook their own meals here; ample supplies are available at both the Meadow Trading Post and the Settlement Trading Post (open from 8 A.M. to 10 P.M. in winter, to 11 P.M. in summer).

Trail's End Buffet: This informal log-walled restaurant offers an inexpensive, all-you-can-eat breakfast, including grits, biscuits, gravy, and a "breakfast pizza" that vaguely resembles an omelette. Hearty lunches and dinners feature barbecued chicken, fish, chicken pot pie, and spare ribs. There are sandwiches and a taco bar at lunch. Pizza is served every night from 9:30 P.M. until 11 P.M. (until midnight on weekends). Beer and wine are served by the glass or by the pitcher. B, L, D, S. $-$$

Grand Floridian

Cítricos: The most recent addition to the Grand Floridian's impressive restaurant lineup specializes in market-fresh Southern French cooking. The fare varies seasonally but may include sautéed tiger shrimp with ziti, artichokes, bell peppers, and roasted garlic in a spicy wine sauce; or braised veal shank with orzo pasta and a soy sauce glaze, presented with stylish simplicity. The menu suggests a wine from the extensive international list for each appetizer, entrée, and dessert; for $22 the waiter will bring one for each of three courses. The stunning view of the Seven Seas Lagoon is a year-round staple. A private dining room is available for parties up to 14 people. Priority seating suggested. D. $$$-$$$$

Gasparilla Grill & Games: Grilled chicken, hamburgers, pizza, hot dogs, and soft-serve ice cream are the mainstays at this 24-hour take-out, self-service restaurant near the pool. Continental breakfast is also available. B, L, D, S. $

Grand Floridian Cafe: Southern cooking is the specialty at this picturesque spot. Although the menu varies, selections may include fried chicken and Atlantic swordfish. There are also salads and an assortment of more traditional entrées. Priority seating available. B, L, D. $$$

Narcoossee's: The partially open kitchen is the focal point at this casual, airy octagonal dining spot on the shores of the Grand Floridian beach. Specialties of the house, which vary seasonally, may include turkey-portobello meat loaf with red-skin mashed potatoes and porcini cream sauce, or seared tuna with chilled vegetable couscous. Staples include charbroiled meats, Florida seafood, and vegetarian options. Priority seating suggested. D. $$$

1900 Park Fare: A sophisticated buffet menu and subtle decor make this the most elegant character restaurant on property. Big Bertha, a band organ built in Paris nearly a century ago, sits 15 feet above the floor in a proscenium. Mary Poppins and friends (characters vary) mingle with guests during the bountiful daily breakfast. Disney characters visit the dining room during dinner. Dinner features seafood, salads, pastas, vegetables, breads, and prime rib. The offerings change weekly. Priority seating suggested. B, D. $$$

Victoria & Albert's: The premier restaurant of not only the Grand Floridian, but probably the entire Walt Disney World complex. The intimate dining room seats only 60, and elegant touches include Royal Doulton china, Sambonet silver, and Schott-Zweisel crystal. The menu is customized daily. Each night there are fish, fowl, red meat, veal, and lamb selections, which depend on the best ingredients in the market and are described in detail by your waiter. The chef may even make a personal appearance to accommodate any special requests from patrons, or guests may choose to dine at the chef's table in the kitchen (for an additional charge). There are also choices of two soups, two salads, and desserts, including specialty soufflés of fresh berries, chocolate, or Grand Marnier. There is an extensive wine list, and wine pairings are available with each course.

Once guests have made their selections, they are presented a personalized menu as a souvenir of the event. At the completion of the meal, women receive a long-stemmed rose. Jackets are required. One oddity of note: Every host and hostess at the restaurant is named Victoria or Albert. Priority seating is necessary. D. $$$$

Polynesian

Captain Cook's Snack Company: A good spot for continental breakfast, hamburgers, hot dogs, fruit salad, and snacks; cans of beer are also available. Open 24 hours. B, L, D, S. $

Kona Cafe: Located on the second floor of the Great Ceremonial House, just around the corner from 'Ohana, this casual restaurant features a South Seas decor and an exotic menu. Lunch and dinner menus feature

Asian-influenced entrées. Possibilities include calamari in a sweet chili-mint sauce; char-grilled ahi tuna with pan fried noodles and bok choy; and char-crusted strip sirloin in a teriyaki marinade. A variety of tempting desserts are among the offerings (you can get a preview at the display counter). Adjoining the cafe is a coffee counter that's perfect for a quick bite en route to the monorail. Priority seating is available at the restaurant. B, L, D, S. $$-$$$

'Ohana: On the second floor of the resort's Great Ceremonial House, this restaurant features a 16-foot-long open fire pit. Dinner choices in the all-you-can-eat family-style feast include shrimp, poultry, pork, and beef, all roasted on skewers up to three feet long. Meats are marinated in original combinations of soy, ginger, lemongrass, or garlic, and are served family-style with an assortment of vegetables, salads, and homemade bread. The meal ends with fresh pineapple with caramel dipping sauce, or additional dessert offerings (for an extra charge) such as banana tarts. The room itself is large and open and offers fine views across the Seven Seas Lagoon all the way to Cinderella Castle. Minnie's Menehune character breakfast is held here daily. Polynesian singers entertain at dinner, while periodic hula hoop and coconut rolling contests amuse young children. Priority seating suggested. B, D. $$$$

Port Orleans

Bonfamille's Cafe: The name of this full-service restaurant derives from the Disney movie *The Aristocats*. Steak, seafood, and Creole cooking highlight the menu. Breakfast is also served. Priority seating suggested. B, D. $$

Sassagoula Floatworks & Food Factory: The stands at this festive food court feature pizza, pasta, gumbo, burgers, sandwiches, soups, salads, spit-roasted chicken, barbecued ribs, ice cream, and a full selection of fresh bakery products, including beignets. B, L, D, S. $

Swan & Dolphin

Cabana Bar & Grill: Burgers, grilled chicken sandwiches, fresh fruit, and yogurt are offered at this full-service poolside eatery. L, S. $

Coral Cafe: Buffets are offered for breakfast and dinner in this bright and casual restaurant. An à la carte menu is also available, offering turkey burgers, chicken, club sandwiches, pasta, and cheese steaks. Located at the Dolphin. B, L, D, S. $$

Dolphin Fountain: Homemade ice cream is the palate-pleasing highlight here. Flavors include dark chocolate, cappuccino, and mint chocolate chip. Oreo and Heath Bar mixes are available in waffle cones, cups, or as part of super sundaes. Burgers, shakes, and malts are also available. The old-time 1950s atmosphere is enhanced by an energetic staff that breaks into song and dance several times a day. L, D, S. $-$$

Garden Grove Cafe (407-934-1609): Situated in a five-story greenhouse, this Swan dining spot offers a full breakfast menu, and fresh fish and shellfish at lunch. At dinner, the restaurant is transformed into Gulliver's Grill, where gargantuan servings are presented before you, and a magician is on hand to entertain. Desserts are baked fresh daily in an open pastry kitchen. As you approach the restaurant, take a look through the glass windows to see the chefs

B breakfast **L** lunch **D** dinner **S** snacks $ under $10 $$ $10–$20 $$$ $21–$45 $$$$ $46 and up at work. Character breakfasts and dinners are held here on certain days. Reservations suggested for dinner. B, L, D, S. $ $ $

Juan & Only's (407-934-1609): This festive Dolphin restaurant features authentic Southwestern food. Specialties include fresh *pico de gallo* served with blue corn and spicy red chips; grilled beef, chicken, shrimp, and vegetarian fajitas from the fajita bar; chimichangas; burritos; lobster tacos and more. Reservations suggested. D. $ $ $

Palio (407-934-1609): This Italian bistro gets high marks for its bruschetta, focaccia, pasta, and pizza. Other specialties include

veal and fish dishes. A strolling musician adds to the ambience. Reservations suggested. Located at the Swan. D. $ $ $

Shula's Steak House (407-934-1609): Like the original Shula's in Miami, this new Dolphin dining spot specializes in generous portions of certified Angus beef, in addition to chicken and fresh fish dishes. The eatery pays tribute to the 1972 Miami Dolphins—the year

Par for the Course

The pleasant **Sand Trap Bar & Grill** in the Bonnet Creek Golf Club is a convenient dining option for golfers playing the adjacent Eagle Pines and Osprey Ridge courses. It's also close to the Magic Kingdom resorts. In addition to the traditional breakfast items, the Sand Trap serves a variety of appetizers, burgers, soups, and sandwiches. There is a full bar; ice cream and milk shakes are also available. Moderate. B, L, S.

legendary Coach Don Shula lead his team to a perfect NFL season. Photos and souvenirs abound. Reservations recommended for dinner. D. $ $ $

Splash Grill: Burgers and other grilled fare join ice cream and frozen yogurt on the menu at this Swan poolside spot. Beer and frozen drinks are served. Prepackaged snacks are also on hand. L, S. $

Tubbi's: Checkerboard decor and a jukebox raise this cafeteria above the norm. The food, including meatball subs and pizza, is fresh, and the lines are seldom long. The adjoining convenience store (which is open 24 hours) has assorted snacks and sundries. B, L, D, S. $

Wilderness Lodge

Artist Point: Decorated with artwork representing painters who first chronicled the Northwest landscape, this fine dining spot offers a creative menu that incorporates wild game in addition to more traditional

items such as steak, as well as salmon and other Pacific seafood. The solid wine list spotlights wines from the Pacific Northwest. A family-style character breakfast hosted by Winnie the Pooh and friends is served every morning. Priority seating suggested. B, D. $ $ $

Roaring Fork Snacks: Salads, burgers, sandwiches, yogurt, chili, and snacks are available at this simple nook adjacent to the hotel's arcade. B, L, D, S. $

Whispering Canyon Cafe: This family-friendly restaurant is open for all-day dining. Hearty all-you-can-eat fare includes smoked barbecued meats with a variety of sides and salads, plus homemade desserts (for an extra charge). Assorted sandwiches and entrées are available à la carte at lunch and dinner. Priority seating suggested. B, L, D. $ $ $

B breakfast **L** lunch **D** dinner **S** snacks **$** under $10 **$ $** $10–$20 **$ $ $** $21–$45 **$ $ $ $** $46 and up

240

GOOD MEALS, GREAT TIMES

The Villas at the Disney Institute

At press time, the restaurants at the Disney Institute, like the resort itself, were experiencing a bit of an identity crisis. While all of the old eateries, such as Seasons and Reflections, are gone, they may be replaced in the near future. For information, call 407-934-4889. In the meantime, hunger pangs may be quelled at nearby Downtown Disney.

Yacht & Beach Club

Beaches & Cream Soda Shop: This restaurant lies between the Yacht and Beach Club. It features oversize sundaes, cones, floats, shakes, and sodas, as well as the Fenway Park Burger—which can be ordered as a single, double, triple, or home run. Breakfast items are available as well. B, L, D, S. **$ - $$**

Cape May Cafe: A wonderful all-you-can-eat New England clambake is held each evening at the Beach Club. A cooking pit used for steaming is in full view of diners, and favorite menu items include clams, mussels, chicken, shrimp, red-skin potatoes, and chowder. Lobster is available for an extra charge. There is a character breakfast buffet each morning. Priority seating suggested. B, D. **$$-$$$**

Hurricane Hanna's Grill: Located in the Stormalong Bay area. Hot dogs, burgers, sandwiches, and ice cream are on the menu. There is also a full bar. L, S. **$**

Yacht Club Galley: Vivid ceramic-tile tabletops emphasize the nautical theme at the Yacht Club. Breakfast features a buffet and a full menu; lunch and dinner are à la carte only. Priority seating suggested. B, L, D. **$ $**

Yachtsman Steakhouse: As its name implies, beef is the specialty of the house. Guests can watch the butcher choosing cuts of meat in the glassed-in shop, and observe as meals are being prepared in the display kitchen. Fresh seafood and chicken are also available. Located at the Yacht Club. Priority seating suggested. D. **$ $ $**

B breakfast **L** lunch **D** dinner **S** snacks **$** under $10 **$ $** $10–$20 **$ $ $** $21–$45 **$ $ $ $** $46 and up

Dining with Disney Characters

At some sites, food takes second place to Mickey Mouse, Minnie Mouse, Goofy, and the rest of the Disney gang, who take turns making special appearances at these especially delightful affairs. Options abound, as the characters host meals throughout the day all over the World. Unless otherwise noted, character meals below are offered daily, and priority seating arrangements can generally be made up to four months in advance by calling 407-WDW-DINE (939-3463). We strongly suggest making these arrangements prior to your visit, especially during busy seasons. Walk-ins are possible, but highly unlikely for any except the Swan's first-come, first-served character breakfast (held Saturday at the hotel's Garden Grove Cafe). Bottomless buffets and all-you-can-eat family-style dining (a set menu served at each table) are the rule, particularly for breakfast, but specific offerings vary from place to place. Finally, keep in mind that the lineup of characters is subject to change.

Character Restaurants: Meals with the Disney characters have become so popular that there are now several restaurants dedicated to providing them all day long. Winnie the Pooh characters entertain during the buffet-style meals at Crystal Palace in the Magic Kingdom. Epcot has its popular, family-style Garden Grill restaurant, with homey fare and Chip and Dale appearances. In the Disney-MGM Studios, Minnie and friends sign autographs at a buffet-style breakfast

Picky eaters might prefer the selection at the buffet-style character meals over the limited menu at the family-style alternatives.

and lunch at the Hollywood & Vine restaurant. At the Contemporary, Chef Mickey and his crew cook up a buffet-style breakfast and dinner (at Chef Mickey's restaurant). Breakfast costs $13.95 to $14.95 for adults and $7.95 to $8.25 for children 3 through 11. For other meals, costs run from $14.95 to $19.95 for adults, and from $7.95 to $9.95 for children.

Breakfast: Guests may have breakfast with characters at 1900 Park Fare in the Grand Floridian resort (Mary Poppins may drop in); at Artist Point in the Wilderness Lodge (Winnie the Pooh and friends host a rustic affair); at Cape May Cafe in the Beach Club resort (Goofy runs the show); at Olivia's Cafe at Old Key West (Pals of Pooh are here on Sunday, Monday, and Wednesday); and at 'Ohana in the Polynesian resort (where Minnie's Menehune breakfast carries a South Seas theme). Character breakfasts are also served in the theme parks. Among the more popular is the Once Upon A Time breakfast at Cinderella's Royal Table in the Magic Kingdom. Donald's Prehistoric Breakfastosaurus is held at Restaurantosaurus in Animal Kingdom. Prices range from $12.95 to $15.95 for adults, and from $7.95 to $9.95 for children.

Dinner: The Liberty Tree Tavern in the Magic Kingdom hosts a character supper. Dinners are also held at 1900 Park Fare in the Grand Floridian (they feature appearances by classic Disney villains). Gulliver's Grill at Garden Grove in the Swan holds a character dinner on select nights; call 407-934-1609 to make reservations. Prices are about $19.95 to $21.95 for adults, $9.95 to $12.95 for children 3 through 11; the à la carte meal at the Swan may run higher.

Wonderland Tea Party: A one-hour tea party hosted by *Alice In Wonderland* characters. Open to kids ages 3 through 10, the party costs $22.95 per child. In addition to sipping tea and eating cupcakes, kids listen to a story and play games. The party takes place at 1900 Park Fare at the Grand Floridian on select afternoons. For information and to make reservations, call 407-WDW-DINE (939-3463). See page 243 for details.

Dinner Shows

The fact that Disney is the expert in family entertainment is nowhere more strongly apparent than amid the whooping and hollering troupe of singers and dancers who race toward the stage at Fort Wilderness resort's Pioneer Hall. As guests plow through barbecued ribs, fried chicken, and strawberry shortcake, these enthusiastic performers sing, dance, and joke up a storm. It's all in the course of an evening at the **Hoop-Dee-Doo Musical Revue**, presented nightly at 5 P.M., 7:15 P.M., and 9:30 P.M. Cost is $46.33 per adult and $23.78 for children (ages 3 through 11).

The Hoop-Dee-Doo Musical Revue is a tremendously popular show. Make your reservations as soon as possible!

Also presented at Fort Wilderness is **Mickey's Backyard Barbecue**. A country band gets guests out on the floor to kick up their heels (the line dance lessons help, too), and Disney characters join in the fun. Dinner consists of plenty of picnic favorites: barbecued ribs and chicken, corn on the cob, and baked beans. The seasonal dinner show costs $37 per adult and $25 for children.

The **Polynesian Luau** at the Polynesian resort also has its moments. The show is presented Tuesday through Saturday at 5:15 P.M. and 8 P.M. The performers' dancing is some of the most authentic this side of Hawaii. A complete Polynesian-style meal, including roasted chicken, island pork, and a fruity dessert is served. Cost is $46.33 for adults and $23.78 for children.

Plan to arrive at least 15 minutes before showtime, and allow extra time for transportation and parking. (Note that prices include tax and gratuity, and are subject to change.)

Wonderland Tea Party, presented Monday, Wednesday, and Friday at 1:30 P.M. at the Grand Floridian's 1900 Park Fare, is an experience for the younger set. The party, hosted by characters from Disney's *Alice in Wonderland*, includes lunch and cupcakes (which kids decorate), storytime, and games. The cost is $22.95 per child, ages 3 through 10.

Reservations: Arrangements for dinner shows can be made up to two years in advance (except for the Backyard Barbecue which accepts reservations up to one year ahead) by calling 407-WDW-DINE (939-3463). Groups of eight or more should call 407-939-7707. Note that a credit card number is required for all dinner show reservations. *Also, it's very important to remember that cancelations for any dinner shows must be made at least 48 hours prior to showtime to avoid paying full price.*

RESTAURANT ROUND-UP

Dining Disney-style is one of the most enjoyable aspects of the vacation for many Walt Disney World visitors. But with so many different restaurants to choose from, it can be difficult to select the spots that will best suit your family. Regulars to WDW are quick to recommend their favorites to newcomers. We, of course, are no exception to the rule. What follows is a rundown of the restaurants that we always try to include in our trips to the World and whole-heartedly recommend to those who are planning a visit. To pick these Birnbaum's Bests, we considered such factors as food quality, restaurant atmosphere, location, and overall value.

TOP WDW RESTAURANTS FOR FAMILIES

TABLE SERVICE

Cape May Cafe . . . . Beach Club resort (p. 241)
Chef Mickey's . . . . Contemporary resort (p. 237)
Cinderella's Royal Table . . . . Magic Kingdom (p. 216)
Coral Reef . . . . Epcot (p. 221)
Crystal Palace . . . . Magic Kingdom (p. 219)
50's Prime Time Cafe . . . . Disney-MGM Studios (p. 228)
Garden Grill . . . . Epcot (p. 221)
Rainforest Cafe . . . . . Animal Kingdom and Downtown Disney (p. 231)
Sci-Fi Dine-In Theater . . . . Disney-MGM Studios (p. 229)

FAST FOOD

Cheesecake Factory Express . . DisneyQuest, admission required (p. 233)
Columbia Harbour House . . . . Magic Kingdom (p. 218)
Pecos Bill Cafe . . . . Magic Kingdom (p. 217)
Pinocchio Village Haus . . . . Magic Kingdom (p. 217)
Sunset Ranch Market . . . . Disney-MGM Studios (p. 230)
Sunshine Season Food Fair . . . . Epcot (p. 222)
Tusker House . . . . Animal Kingdom (p. 232)

BEST CHARACTER MEAL

Chef Mickey's . . . . Contemporary resort (p. 237)

RUNNERS-UP

Crystal Palace . . . . Magic Kingdom (p. 219)
Garden Grill . . . . Epcot (p. 221)
Hollywood & Vine . . . . Disney-MGM Studios (p. 229)
1900 Park Fare . . . . Grand Floridian resort (p. 238)

BEST KID'S MEAL PRESENTATION

Old Port Royale . . . . Caribbean Beach resort (p. 237); The meal comes in a sand bucket with a shovel.

RUNNER-UP

Sci-Fi Dine-In Theater . . . . Disney-MGM Studios (p. 229); Dessert is served on a glow-in-the-dark Frisbee.

BEST PLACE TO CELEBRATE A CHILD'S BIRTHDAY

Chef Mickey's . . . . Contemporary resort (p. 237)

RUNNER-UP

Cinderella's Royal Table . . . . .Magic Kingdom (p. 216)

BEST FIREWORKS VIEW

California Grill . . . .Contemporary resort (p. 237)

BEST VEGETARIAN MEALS

Artist Point
Wilderness Lodge (p. 240)

BEST SPLURGE FOR GROWN-UPS

California Grill . . . . Contemporary resort (p. 237)

RUNNERS-UP

Cítricos . . . . Grand Floridian resort (p. 238)
Les Chefs de France . . . . Epcot (p. 223)
L'Originale Alfredo di Roma Ristorante . . . . Epcot (p. 224)
Victoria & Albert's . . . . Grand Floridian resort (p. 238)
Wolfgang Puck Cafe . . . . Downtown Disney (p. 235)

BEST DINNER SHOW

Hoop-Dee-Doo Musical Revue: This crowd-pleasing saloon hall show has been going like gangbusters since 1974. Kids enjoy the silly humor, while adults eat up the bottomless buckets of ribs, fried chicken, and other downhome dishes. Presented at Fort Wilderness (p. 243).

RUNNER-UP

Mickey's Backyard Barbecue: If it were offered year-round, this would be our number one choice. It's a big, informal party, complete with a kickin' country band, games for the kids, and line dancing with Disney characters. The self-serve, all-you-can-eat barbecue fare is first-rate. Presented at Fort Wilderness (p. 243).

BEST PIZZA FOR GROWN-UPS

Portobello Yacht Club ....Downtown Disney, West Side (p. 234)
House of Blues ....Downtown Disney, West Side (p. 234)

BEST PIZZA FOR KIDS

Tony's Town Square ....Magic Kingdom (p. 219)

BEST FIXIN'S BAR

Pecos Bill Cafe ....Magic Kingdom (p. 217)

BEST BUY

Clam Bake at the Cape May Cafe
Beach Club resort (p. 241)

BEST ITALIAN FARE

Mama Melrose's Ristorante Italiano ....Disney MGM-Studios (p. 229)

BEST ROOM SERVICE

Swan and Dolphin resorts ....(p. 239)

BEST THEME

50's Prime Time Cafe ....Disney MGM-Studios (p. 228)

RUNNER-UP

Sci-Fi Dine In Theater ....Disney MGM-Studios (p. 229)

BEST OUTDOOR CAFE

Aunt Polly's Dockside Inn ... Tom Sawyer Island, Magic Kingdom (p. 217)

BEST FRESH-BAKED COOKIES

Main Street Bake Shop ....Magic Kingdom (p. 220)

BEST SEAFOOD

Coral Reef . . . . .Epcot (p. 221)

RUNNERS-UP

Cape May Cafe . . . . .Beach Club resort (p. 241)
Fulton's Crab House . . . . .Downtown Disney (p. 233)

BEST CRAB CAKES

Stone Crab Lounge . . . . .Fulton's Crab House,
Downtown Disney Marketplace (p. 234)

RUNNER-UP

Ale and Compass . . . . .Yacht Club resort (p. 251)

BEST BLOODY MARY

Stone Crab Lounge . . . . .Fulton's Crab House,
Downtown Disney Marketplace (p. 234)

BEST MILK SHAKE

Min and Bill's Dockside Diner
Disney MGM-Studios (p. 230)

BEST ICE CREAM

The Plaza . . . . .Magic Kingdom (p. 219)
Ghirardelli Soda Fountain and
Chocolate Shop . . . . .Downtown Disney Marketplace (p. 234)

BEST STEAK

Le Cellier Steakhouse . . . . .Epcot (p. 223)

RUNNERS-UP

Yachtsman Steakhouse . . . . .Yacht Club resort (p. 241)
Shula's Steak House . . . . .Dolphin resort (p. 240)

BEST SUSHI

Wolfgang Puck Cafe . . . . . .Downtown Disney West Side (p. 235)

RUNNER-UP

Matsu No Ma Lounge . . . . .Epcot (p. 250)

All About Priority Seating

Priority seating has replaced reservations at most of WDW's full-service restaurants. Disney started the policy to provide the assurance of a reservation without delays caused by no-shows and late-comers. Ideally, the system ensures that guests are not left waiting if a table is available. Here's how it works: You call ahead to request a priority seating time; you arrive 15 minutes before the assigned time and check in at the podium; you receive the next available table that can accommodate your party. The system works very much like reservations, so you will always be seated before any walk-ins.

At most WDW restaurants priority seating arrangements are scheduled in five- or ten-minute intervals. If they don't have a 6:00 P.M. availability, ask about a 6:05 P.M.

We strongly recommend making advance arrangements. Priority seating times can generally be secured up to four months ahead by calling 407-WDW-DINE (939-3463). Hours are Monday through Friday from 7 A.M. to 10 P.M.; Saturday, Sunday, and holidays from 7 A.M. to 8 P.M. The number of tables available in advance varies. If you are unable to book a table ahead of time, try to make same-day arrangements.

Most WDW resorts have at least one telephone in the main lobby that provides direct contact with the "Dine Line." Simply touch 55—the call is free. From other locations, dial 407-WDW-DINE. Once at the theme parks, priority seating arrangements can be made at the restaurant itself; at City Hall in the Magic Kingdom; in Epcot at Guest Relations in Innoventions Plaza; by Hollywood Junction in the Disney-MGM Studios; and at Guest Relations in Animal Kingdom. Bookings can also be made at Guest Services in Downtown Disney Marketplace and at the West Side.

While the priority seating system is almost always successful, there *are* times when the wait for a table can be unexpectedly long. This is most likely to occur during peak mealtimes at restaurants that offer buffets or family-style meals, where patrons will often opt for seconds (or thirds). For this reason, be sure to check in at the restaurant particularly early for all character-hosted meals.

Priority seating is the prevalent policy at WDW restaurants, but there are some exceptions where tables may be booked solely via traditional reservations. Most notably, reservations are necessary for all dinner shows—the Hoop-Dee-Doo Musical Revue, Mickey's Backyard Barbecue, and the Polynesian Luau; they can be made by calling 407-WDW-DINE (939-3463). With the exception of Mickey's Backyard Barbecue, dinner show reservations can be booked up to two years in advance; the Barbecue accepts reservations one year ahead. If you can't get a table for an early performance, consider a later one (they are usually less heavily booked).

There are some full-service restaurants that fall outside the priority seating domain. They are Shula's Steak House and Juan and Only's at the Dolphin, Palio and Garden Grove Cafe at the Swan (407-934-1609), and Fulton's Crab House (407-934-2628), Portobello Yacht Club (407-934-8888), and Wildhorse Saloon (407-827-4947) in Downtown Disney.

Note: Because the dining scene at WDW is tremendously dynamic and procedures have changed more than a few times over the years, we advise calling 407-WDW-DINE (939-3463) to confirm current priority seating policies.

Advance Planning

While some WDW restaurants always seem to have an available table, others are booked far in advance. The restaurants for which careful planning is essential include: Cinderella's Royal Table in the Magic Kingdom; Les Chefs de France in Epcot; Donald's Prehistoric Breakfastosaurus (Restaurantosaurus's daily character breakfast) in Animal Kingdom; and California Grill in the Contemporary resort.

No one ever said the Magic Kingdom's no-liquor policy means that everyone in the World is a teetotaler. Actually, some of WDW's tastiest offerings are liquid (and decidedly spirited), and some of its most entertaining places are its bars and lounges.

Hours vary depending on the locale, but generally, watering holes at Epcot, Disney-MGM Studios, and Animal Kingdom shut their doors at park closing. Pool bars at the resorts generally keep daytime pool hours. Last call at lounges in the resorts is anywhere from 10 P.M. to midnight. Downtown Disney Marketplace spots stay open until the shops close, usually 11 P.M. The clubs at Pleasure Island and the West Side keep things going until 2 A.M. Note that specialty drinks sans alcohol are available at all establishments.

ALL-STAR MOVIES, ALL-STAR MUSIC & ALL-STAR SPORTS

Silver Screen Spirits at All-Star Movies, **Singing Spirits** at All-Star Music, and **Team Spirits** at All-Star Sports serve beer, wine, and specialty drinks by the pool.

ANIMAL KINGDOM

Dawa Bar: Enjoy Safari Amber beer and African music out under the thatched roof.

Rainforest Cafe: The Magic Mushroom bar serves fruit blends and specialty drinks.

ANIMAL KINGDOM LODGE

Capetown Lounge and Wine Bar: Sip African wines at this atmospheric spot near Jiko—The Cooking Place.

Uzima Springs: Poolside bar serving cocktails and snacks during pool hours.

Victoria Falls: Mezzanine-level lounge offering coffee, tea, wine, and other spirits.

BOARDWALK

Atlantic Dance: This dance hall showcases hors d'oeuvres, desserts, a full bar, 25 specialty drinks, and premium cigars.

Belle Vue Room: Snacks and a full bar accompany old-time tunes from antique radios in this lobby cocktail lounge.

Big River Grille & Brewing Works: A working brewpub where patrons can order appetizers at the bar and sample the brewmaster's flagship ales and specialty beers.

ESPN Club: The ultimate sports bar provides live radio and television broadcasts along with a menu of ballpark favorites.

Jellyrolls: Dueling pianos and lively sing-alongs are the draw at this unique club, serving beer and other drinks.

Leaping Horse Libations: The pool bar offers cocktails, tuna sandwiches, fruit salad, and garden salads in a carnival setting.

BONNET CREEK GOLF CLUB

Sand Trap Bar & Grill: Appetizers and sandwiches supplement the array of libations offered at this fully stocked bar.

CARIBBEAN BEACH

Banana Cabana: All types of drinks and fast-food items are served at this poolside bar.

Captain's Tavern: Tropical drinks, beer, wine, and cocktails are served at this restaurant lounge in Old Port Royale. Items from the restaurant are available during dinner hours.

CONTEMPORARY

California Grill Lounge: Prime 15th-story digs eye-level to the Magic Kingdom fireworks. A large selection of California wine (all available by the glass), all manner of other drinks, and items from the restaurant menu are offered in this atmospheric spot adjoining the California Grill.

Outer Rim: This lounge overlooking Bay Lake serves beer, wine, cocktails, appetizers, and desserts.

Sand Bar: A full bar and fast-food items are offered poolside, weather permitting.

CORONADO SPRINGS

Francisco's: Located in the main building, this lounge serves specialty drinks, beer, wine, and light Mexican snacks.

Siesta's: Swimmers can take time out for burgers, sandwiches, tacos, and cocktails at this spot near the pool in the Dig Site area.

DISNEY-MGM STUDIOS

Tune-In Lounge: A sitcom living room setting, with couches, chairs, and TV dinner-tray tables, characterizes this lounge next to the 50's Prime Time Cafe. Waiters in V-neck sweaters play the roles of sitcom "Dads," and old TV sets play scenes from beloved sitcoms. Appetizers, mixed drinks, beer, and wine are served.

DISNEY'S OLD KEY WEST

Gurgling Suitcase: This pocket-size lounge on the Turtle Krawl boardwalk serves an assortment of Key West specialties along with traditional cocktails, beer, and wine.

Turtle Shack: Refreshments at this poolside spot include beer, specialty drinks, and fast-food items.

DIXIE LANDINGS

Cotton Co-Op: Situated in a room designed as a cotton exchange, this lounge features specialty drinks as well as some light hors d'oeuvres. There is entertainment here five nights a week.

Muddy Rivers: The poolside bar serves beer, specialty concoctions, and selected fast-food items.

DOWNTOWN DISNEY

All clubs have bars serving specialty drinks (with and without alcohol), beer, wine, and cocktails. The excellent **Stone Crab** lounge inside **Fulton's Crab House** (located between Pleasure Island and the Marketplace) and **Bongos Cuban Cafe** (the West Side) are notable for exotic cocktails and scenic outdoor seating. Pleasure Island's **Portobello Yacht Club** also has a pleasant lounge. The **Rainforest Cafe** (the Marketplace) is the site of the whimsical Magic Mushroom bar.

Cap'n Jack's Restaurant (Downtown Disney Marketplace): Agleam with copper and right on the water, this bar's specialty is its delicious strawberry margaritas. The nibbles of garlic oysters, clam chowder, and shrimp on the appetizer menu are great for a snack, but substantial enough for a meal.

EPCOT

All restaurants, including some of the fast-food spots, serve alcoholic beverages. Restaurants such as the San Angel Inn have a small lounge at which patrons may wait for tables. And then there are a few other places that specialize in spirituous liquid refreshments:

Matsu No Ma: In addition to exotic sake-based specialty drinks, this Japan pavilion establishment offers a fine panoramic view over the whole of Epcot—including the World Showcase Lagoon, with Spaceship Earth as a backdrop—one of the best vistas of the property available. Japanese beer, green tea, and sushi are also served.

Rose & Crown Pub: This watering hole—a veritable symphony of polished woods, brass, and etched glass—adjoins the Rose & Crown Dining Room in the United Kingdom pavilion. British, Irish, and Scottish beers are available, along with a score of specialty drinks and appetizing snacks imported from the other side of the Atlantic. An entertaining pianist plays and sings just about any request well into the evening.

Sommerfest: Just outside the Biergarten restaurant in Germany, there's a small shaded terrace where soft pretzels, bratwurst, Black Forest cake, Beck's beer, and German wine are available.

FORT WILDERNESS

Crockett's Tavern: Cocktails, beer, wine, appetizers, and light sandwiches are served.

GRAND FLORIDIAN

Garden View: A lovely view of the lushly landscaped pool and garden area makes this lounge a pleasant place to meet for a drink or dessert. Traditional afternoon tea is also served here each day.

Mizner's: Named after the eccentric architect who defined much of the flavor of southeastern Florida's Gold Coast, this handsome retreat is on the second floor of the main building. Ports, brandies, and appetizers are featured.

Narcoossee's: This elegant, lagoonside bar-within-a-restaurant offers a variety of international wines.

Summerhouse: This bar between the pool and the beach stands by with beer, frozen drinks, and fast-food items.

POLYNESIAN

Barefoot Bar: This oasis next to the swimming pool lagoon serves beer, frozen tropical drinks, and fast food. Seasonal.

Tambu: Adjoining 'Ohana restaurant, this small bar offers Polynesian-style appetizers and specialty drinks in a relaxing, tropical setting. (There's a large-screen television, too.)

> **HOT TIP**
> At many Walt Disney World lounges, you can order food from a neighboring or nearby restaurant's menu.

PORT ORLEANS

Mardi Grogs: Beer, specialty drinks, popcorn, hot dogs, and hot pretzels are among the offerings at this poolside spot.

Scat Cat's Club: Traditional offerings from the bar join New Orleans specialties and hors d'oeuvres at this comfortable little lounge. Lively musical entertainment is featured here five nights a week.

SWAN & DOLPHIN

Cabana Bar & Grill: Beer, frozen drinks, and fast-food selections are the main offerings at this Dolphin poolside spot.

Copa Banana: The tabletops in this Dolphin bar resemble oversize slices of fruit, and giant pineapples and palm trees offer a fitting backdrop for tempting tropical libations. There is also a large-screen television.

Kimonos: This Swan spot, attractively decorated in Japanese style, has a full bar, as well as sushi and a variety of oriental specialties.

Lobby Court: The winding corridors of the Swan lobby have comfortable couches and chairs, punctuated by pianos where able musicians often perform. Specialty coffees, desserts, and wines by the glass are featured. A special menu with ports, cognacs, and cigars is offered seasonally.

Only's Bar & Jail: An array of margaritas, cocktails, and beers join Mexican-style appetizers on the menu here at the Dolphin. The small, atmospheric lounge, adjacent to Juan & Only's restaurant, was designed to resemble a jail.

Shula's Steak House Lounge: This cozy cigar bar adjoining Shula's Steak House features rich wood tones and leather chairs—the perfect place to sip a cocktail and puff a stogie while playing armchair quarterback.

Splash Grill: Beer, frozen drinks, and fast food are served at this Swan poolside cafe.

WILDERNESS LODGE

Territory: Located between Artist Point and Whispering Canyon Cafe, this homage to the Old West is a nice spot for a light lunch or predinner treat. Appetizers, microbrew beer, wine, and specialty drinks are served.

Trout Pass: This poolside bar serves beer, frozen drinks, and snacks.

YACHT & BEACH CLUB

Ale and Compass: The lobby watering hole proffers a specialty drink menu complete with coffee and ale.

Crew's Cup: Styled after a traditional New England waterfront pub, this lounge has a sea-faring feel to it. It's right next door to the Yachtsman Steakhouse, has almost 40 beers on hand, and is a choice spot for a drink before dinner.

Hurricane Hanna's Grill: This poolside refreshment spot, located near Stormalong Bay between the Yacht Club and Beach Club, offers specialty beverages, frozen drinks, and beer as well as a selection of fast-food items.

Martha's Vineyard: A light and airy atmosphere prevails at this cozy retreat. Wines from a real Martha's Vineyard winery, as well as selections from California, Long Island, and European vineyards, are on the extensive list. While wine is the house specialty, this is a full bar. Hors d'oeuvres and desserts are served.

Rip Tide: This lobby bar features California wines, wine coolers, and frosty drinks that are consistent with the hotel's beachside theme.

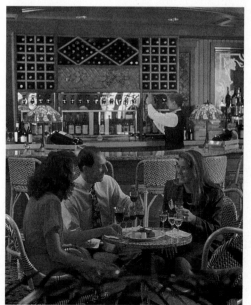

INDEX

A

accommodations, 47-88
  All-Star resorts, 51, 53, 75
  Animal Kingdom Lodge, 42, 49, 52, 76-77
  Beach Club resort, 50, 52, 64-65
  bed & breakfast inn, 85
  BoardWalk resort, 49, 52, 68-69
  Caribbean Beach resort, 51, 53, 62-63
  Celebration Hotel, 204
  check-in and check-out times, 48, 53
  Contemporary resort, 49, 52, 54-55
  Coronado Springs resort, 51, 53, 77
  deposit requirements, 48
  Disney Cruise Line, 78-79
  Disney Vacation Club, 69
  Dixie Landings resort, 21, 51, 53, 71
  Dolphin resort, 50, 52, 65-67
  for meetings and conventions, 63
  Fort Wilderness resort and
    campground, 51, 52, 53, 61
  Grand Floridian Resort & Spa,
    49, 52, 57-59
  for guests with disabilities, 35, 48
  Hotel Plaza Boulevard, resorts on,
    80-83
  ID cards, 48
  in Kissimmee, 88
  in Lake Buena Vista, 84-85
  in Orlando, 86-87
  last-minute lodging, 88
  money-saving tips, 20, 33
  Old Key West resort, 50, 52, 73-74
  payment methods, 48
  Polynesian resort, 49, 52, 55-57
  Port Orleans resort, 51, 53, 70
  rates, 52-53
  reservation guide, 23, 53
  resort finder (rating system), 49-51
  Shades of Green, 57
  special room requests, 48, 66, 67
  Swan resort, 50, 52, 65-67
  tipping, 41
  Villas at the Disney Institute, The,
    50, 53, 72-73
  Wilderness Lodge & Villas,
    42, 50, 52, 59-60
  Yacht Club resort, 50, 52, 64-65
admission prices, 17-19
  Blizzard Beach, 195
  Disney-MGM Studios, 153
  Disney's Animal Kingdom, 169
  Downtown Disney Pleasure
    Island, 187
  Epcot, 121
  Magic Kingdom, 93
  River Country, 197
  Typhoon Lagoon, 193
Adventureland, 96-97, 113, 216
Africa, 174-175, 181, 231, 232
air travel, 14

All-Star resorts, 51, 53, 75
  lounges, 75, 249
  restaurants, 75, 236
AMC Theatres, 31, 189
American Adventure, The, 142-143, 226
American Film Institute Showcase, 159
Ariel's Grotto, 105
Asia, 176-177
Astro Orbiter, 109-110
ATMs, 39
  Disney-MGM Studios, 154
  Disney's Animal Kingdom, 170
  Downtown Disney, 184
  Epcot, 122
  Magic Kingdom, 93
automobile clubs, 13, 14

B

Baby Care Centers, 32
  Disney-MGM Studios, 154
  Disney's Animal Kingdom, 170
  Epcot, 122
  Magic Kingdom, 92
Backstage Pass, 158-159
banking. see ATMs; money matters
barbers, 37
basketball, 54, 200, 214
Beach Club resort, 50, 52, 64-65
  lounges, 64, 251
  restaurants, 64, 241
beaches, 194-195, 198, 211
Bear in the Big Blue House, 157
Beauty and the Beast—Live on Stage, 156
behind-the-scenes tours, 127, 203
Best Western Lake Buena Vista, 81
Big Thunder Mountain Railroad, 100
biking, 60, 63, 69, 70, 71, 73, 74, 77,
    79, 198, 213
Birnbaum's Walt Disney World For Kids,
    By Kids, 15, 32
Birnbaum's Walt Disney World Without
    Kids, 15, 33
Blizzard Beach, 194-195
BoardWalk Inn & Villas resort,
    49, 52, 68-69
  entertainment district, 191
  lounges, 68, 249
  restaurants, 68, 236
boating, 55, 56, 59, 60, 63, 65, 67, 70,
    71, 73, 74, 77, 198, 209-210
Body Wars, 133
Boneyard, The, 178
Bonnet Creek Golf Club, 206-207
  lounge, 249
  restaurant, 240
bus travel, 14
  in WDW, 46-47, 91, 121, 153,
    169, 184
business services, 37
Buzz Lightyear's Space Ranger Spin, 109

C

cameras and films, 37
  Disney-MGM Studios, 154
  Disney's Animal Kingdom, 170
  Epcot, 122, 125, 130
  Magic Kingdom, 92, 112
campfire program, 198
Camp Minnie-Mickey, 180
campsites at Fort Wilderness, 51, 52,
    53, 61
Canada, 136, 223, 226
Caribbean Beach resort, 51, 53, 62-63
  lounges, 63, 249
  restaurants, 62, 237
Caribbean Coral Reef Ride, 126
car travel, 13, 14
  automobile clubs, 13, 14
  parking, 44, 91, 121, 153, 169
  rentals, 45
  road maps, 13, 14
  service and maintenance, 38
cash machines. see ATMs
Castaway Cay, 79
Celebration, Florida, 204
celebrations. see special events
check-in and check-out times, 48, 53
children, traveling with, 32
  Birnbaum's Walt Disney World For
    Kids, By Kids, 15, 32
  child care, 32
  half-day schedules with young
    children, 29-30
  learning programs for, 203
  lost children, 32, 93, 122, 154, 170
  restaurant dining suggestions,
    217, 244-247
  stroller rentals, 32, 93, 122, 138,
    154, 170
  See also Baby Care Centers
China, 146-147, 224, 226
Christmas festivities, 8, 12, 149, 165
Cinderella Castle, 103
Cinderella's Golden Carrousel, 103
Circle of Life, The, 127-128
Cirque du Soleil, 189
climate. see weather
clubs. see BoardWalk; Downtown Disney
    Pleasure Island; Downtown Disney
    West Side
Conservation Station, 175
Contemporary resort, 49, 52, 54-55
  lounges, 54, 249
  restaurants, 54, 237
convention and meeting facilities, 63
Coronado Springs resort, 51, 53, 77
  lounges, 77, 249
  restaurants, 77, 237
Country Bear Jamboree, 98
Country Hearth Inn, 86
Courtyard by Marriott, 81

Cranium Command, 132-133
credit cards, 39, 93, 122, 154, 170
Cretaceous Trail, 179
Crossroads of Lake Buena Vista, 188, 235
crowd patterns, 8, 9
cruises
  fireworks cruises, 202
  See also Disney Cruise Line

D

Diamond Horseshoe Saloon Revue,
  21, 98, 115, 217
dining. *see* restaurants
dinner shows, 23, 243, 245
DinoLand U.S.A., 178-179, 181, 231, 232
Dinosaur, 179
disabilities, hints for travelers with,
  35, 48, 92, 122, 154, 170
  transportation, 35
  wheelchair rental, 35, 93, 122, 138,
    154, 170
Disney characters
  at Disney-MGM Studios, 166
  at Disney's Animal Kingdom, 180
  at Epcot, 150
  at Magic Kingdom, 116
  meals with, 242, 244
Disney Club, The, 21
Disney Cruise Line, 78-79
  lounges, 79
  restaurants, 78-79
Disney Dollars, 39, 93, 170
Disney Institute
  Spa & Fitness Center at, 201
  Villas at the, 50, 53, 72-73
Disney Magic (Disney Cruise Line ship), 78
Disney-MGM Studios, 151-166
  admission prices, 153
  attractions, 155-162
  best times to visit, 8, 153, 166
  camera needs, 154
  disability information, 154
  Disney characters, where to find, 166
  early-entry days, 154
  entertainment, 165
  first aid, 154
  getting oriented, 153
  Guest Relations, 154
  holiday happenings, 11, 12, 165
  Hollywood Boulevard, 163
  hours, 10, 153, 166
  information, 154
  lockers, 154
  Lost and Found, 154
  lounges, 249-250
  map, 152
  money matters, 154
  parking, 153
  restaurants, 228-230
    priority seating, 248
  same-day re-entry, 154
  sample schedules, 27, 30
  shopping, 163-164, 166
  stroller and wheelchair rentals, 154
  Sunset Boulevard, 163-164

Tip Board, 154
tips, 166
transportation to, 153
Disney-MGM Studios Backlot Tour, 158
DisneyQuest, 31, 189
Disney's Animal Kingdom, 167-182
  admission prices, 169
  Africa, 174-175
  Asia, 176-177
  best times to visit, 8, 182
  camera needs, 170
  Camp Minnie-Mickey, 180
  DinoLand U.S.A., 178-179
  disability information, 170
  Disney characters, where to find, 180
  entertainment, 182
  first aid, 170
  getting oriented, 169
  Guest Relations, 170
  hours, 10, 169, 182
  information, 170
  Kilimanjaro Safaris, 174
  lockers, 170
  Lost and Found, 170
  lounges, 249
  map, 168
  money matters, 170
  Oasis, The, 171
  parking, 169
  resorts, 75-77
  restaurants, 231-232
    priority seating, 248
  Safari Village, 172-173, 181, 231-232
  same-day re-entry, 170
  sample schedules, 28, 30
  shopping, 181
  stroller and wheelchair rentals, 170
  Tip Board, 170
  tips, 182
  transportation to, 169
Disney's Animal Kingdom Lodge, 42, 49,
  52, 76-77
  lounges, 76, 249
  restaurants, 76
Disney's Doug Live!, 160-161
Disney's Fastpass, 19
Disney's The Hunchback of Notre Dame, 162
Disney's Magical Moments Parade, 115
Disney's Old Key West resort, 50, 52, 73-74
  lounges, 74, 250
  restaurants, 74, 237
Disney's Racquet Club, 55, 208
Disney's Wide World of Sports, 31, 212
Disney Vacation Club, 69
Disney Wonder (Disney Cruise Line ship), 78
Dixie Landings resort, 21, 51, 53, 71
  lounges, 71, 250
  restaurants, 71, 237-238
Dolphin resort, 50, 52, 65-67
  lounges, 66, 251
  restaurants, 66, 239-240
Doubletree Castle, 86-87
Doubletree Guest Suites, 81-82
Doubletree Guest Suites Orlando
  Maingate, 88

Downtown Disney, 184-190
Downtown Disney Marketplace,
  185-186
  hours, 10
  lounges, 250
  restaurants, 233, 234, 235
  shopping, 185-186
  transportation to, 184
Downtown Disney Pleasure Island, 187-188
  clubs, 187-188
  entertainment, 188
  hours, 10
  lounges, 250
  restaurants, 233, 234-235
  shopping, 188
  transportation to, 184
Downtown Disney West Side, 189-190
  hours, 10
  lounges, 250
  resorts, 70-74
  restaurants, 189, 190, 233, 234, 235
    priority seating, 248
  shopping, 190
  transportation to, 184
drinking laws, 38
Dumbo the Flying Elephant, 104-105

E

Eagle Pines golf course, 206-207
Electrical Water Pageant, 199
electric cart rentals, 199
Electric Convenience Vehicles (ECVs),
  35, 93, 122, 154, 170
Enchanted Tiki Room, 96-97
Epcot, 119-150
  admission prices, 121
  best times to visit, 8, 150
  camera needs, 122, 125, 130
  crowd size, 9, 124, 150
  disability information, 122
  Disney characters, where to find, 150
  early-entry days, 122
  entertainment, 149
  first aid, 122
  getting oriented, 121
  Guest Relations, 122, 150
  holiday happenings, 11, 12, 149
  hours, 10, 121, 150
  information, 122
  lockers, 122
  Lost and Found, 122
  lounges, 250
  map, 120
  money matters, 122
  parking, 121
  resorts, 62-69
  restaurants, 221-227
    priority seating, 248
  same-day re-entry, 122
  sample schedules, 26, 29
  stroller and wheelchair rentals, 122, 138
  Tip Board, 122
  tips, 150
  transportation to, 121
  See also Future World; World Showcase

E-Ride Nights, 17
ExtraTERRORestrial Alien Encounter, 108-109

F

Fairy Tale Garden, 103
Fantasmic!, 165
Fantasy in the Sky, 115, 202
Fantasyland, 103-105, 114, 216-217
fast food and snack spots. see restaurants
Fastpass. see Disney's Fastpass
Festival of the Lion King, 180
fireworks cruises, 202
fireworks displays, 8, 115, 165
    Fantasy in the Sky, 115, 202
    IllumiNations: Reflections of Earth, 137, 149, 202
first aid, 39, 92, 122, 154, 170, 193, 195, 197
fishing, 56, 59, 60, 65, 69, 71, 73, 199, 210-211
fitness centers. see health clubs
Flights of Wonder, 177
Food Rocks, 128
foreign currency exchange, 34, 40
Fort Wilderness, 51, 52, 53, 61, 198-200
    activities, 198-200
    campfire program, 198
    family entertainment after dark, 61
    lounge, 61, 250
    resort and campground, 51, 52, 53, 61
    restaurant, 61, 200, 238
    transportation to, 61, 200
Fountain of Nations, 149
France, 138-139, 223-224, 226
Frontierland, 98-100, 113, 217
Future World, 31, 119, 123-134
    Ice Station Cool, 125
    Imagination!, 129-130
    Innoventions, 125-126
    Land, The, 127-128
    Living Seas, The, 126-127
    map, 120
    restaurants, 221-222
    Spaceship Earth, 124-125
    Test Track, 131
    Universe of Energy, 133-134
    Wonders of Life, 131-133

G

Germany, 145-146, 223, 227
golf, 73, 206-207
    miniature, 213
    tournaments, 207
Grand Cypress, 84-85
Grand Floridian resort, 49, 52, 57-59
    lounges, 58-59, 250
    restaurants, 58, 238-239
    spa, 201
Great Movie Ride, The, 159-160
Grosvenor, 82
Guest Relations, 18, 92, 122, 150, 154, 170
    tips for international travelers, 34
guided tours, 127, 203

H

Hall of Presidents, The, 101
Haunted Mansion, The, 102
hayrides, 199
health care. see medical matters
health clubs, 55, 57, 59, 60, 65, 67, 69, 73, 74, 77, 201, 213-214
Hiking, 200
Hilton, 82
holiday happenings, 11-12, 116, 149, 165
Holiday Inn Sunspree-LBV, 84
Hollywood Boulevard, 163-164
Honey, I Shrunk the Audience, 130
Honey, I Shrunk the Kids Movie Set Adventure, 162
honeymoons, 36
Hoop-Dee-Doo Musical Revue, 61, 198, 243
horseback riding, 199, 214
Hotel Plaza Boulevard, resorts on, 80-83
hotels. see accommodations
hours, 10
    Disney-MGM Studios, 153, 166
    Disney's Animal Kingdom, 169, 182
    Epcot, 121, 150
    Magic Kingdom, 91, 118
Howard Johnson Maingate East, 88
Hyatt Regency Grand Cypress, 84-85

I

ID cards, 46, 48
IllumiNations: Reflections of Earth, 137, 149, 202
Image Works: Kodak "What If" Labs, 42, 129
Imagination!, 129-130
Impressions de France, 139
Indiana Jones Epic Stunt Spectacular, 161
information sources, 15-16
Innoventions, 125-126
International Gateway, 138
international travelers, tips for, 34
Internet address for WDW, 8, 15, 20, 23, 35
Italy, 144-145, 224
It's a Small World, 104
It's Tough to be a Bug!, 173

J

Japan, 141-142, 224, 227
Jim Henson's Muppet*Vision 3-D, 162
jogging, 56, 213
Journey Into Your Imagination, 129
Jungle Cruise, 96

K

Kali River Rapids, 176-177
Kilimanjaro Safaris 174
KinderCare, 32
Kissimmee, accommodations in, 88

L

Lake Buena Vista, accommodations in, 84-85
Lake Buena Vista golf course, 207
Land, The, 127-128
learning programs. see guided tours
Leave a Legacy program, 123
Legend of the Lion King, 103-104
Liberty Belle Riverboat, 102
Liberty Square, 101-102, 113-114, 218
Living Seas, The, 126-127
Living with the Land (boat ride), 127
lockers, 38, 92-93, 122, 154, 170, 193, 195, 197
lost adults, 33
Lost and Found, 38, 93, 122, 154, 170
lost children, 32, 93, 122, 154, 170
lounges, 249-251

M

Mad Tea Party, 105
Maelstrom, 147
Magic Carpets of Aladdin, The, 42, 97
Magic Kingdom, 89-118
    admission prices, 93
    Adventureland, 96-97, 113
    best times to visit, 8, 91, 118
    camera needs, 92,
    Caribbean Plaza, 113
    Cinderella Castle, 103
    crowd size, 9, 91, 92
    disability information, 92
    Disney characters, where to find, 116
    early-entry days, 92
    entertainment, 115-117
    E-Ride Nights, 17
    Fantasyland, 103-105, 114
    first aid, 92
    Frontierland, 98-100, 113
    getting oriented, 91
    Guest Relations, 92
    holiday happenings, 11, 12, 116
    hours, 10, 91, 118
    information, 92
    Liberty Square, 101-102, 113-114
    lockers, 92-93
    Lost and Found, 93
    Main Street, U.S.A., 94-95, 111-112
    map, 90
    Mickey's Toontown Fair, 106-107, 114
    money matters, 93
    parking, 91
    resorts, 54-61
    restaurants, 111, 118, 216-220
        mealtime tips, 220
        priority seating, 248
    same-day re-entry, 93
    sample schedules, 25, 29
    shopping, 94, 111-114
    SpectroMagic, 117
    stroller and wheelchair rentals, 93, 112
    Tip Boards, 93, 118
    tips, 118
    Tomorrowland, 108-110, 114, 220
    transportation to, 91, 92
Magic Kingdom Club. see Disney Club
Magic of Disney Animation, The, 156-157

Magnolia golf course, 206
Maharajah Jungle Trek, 177
mail, 38
Main Street, U.S.A., 94-95, 111-112, 219-220
Many Adventures of Winnie the Pooh, The, 105
map(s)
    Disney-MGM Studios, 152
    Disney's Animal Kingdom, 168
    Epcot, 120
    Hotel Plaza Boulevard area, 80
    Magic Kingdom, 90
    road maps, 13, 14
medical matters, 39
meetings and conventions, 63
Mexico, 148, 226
Mickey's Toontown Fair, 106-107, 114
miniature golf, 213
money matters, 39-40
    Disney Dollars, 39, 93, 170
    Disney-MGM Studios, 154
    Disney's Animal Kingdom, 170
    Epcot, 122
    foreign currency exchange, 34, 40
    Magic Kingdom, 93
    payment methods at WDW resorts, 48
    rates at WDW resorts, 52-53
money-saving tips, 14, 20-21, 33
    discounts, 21
    making a budget, 22
Morocco, 140, 224, 227
motels. see accommodations
movies, 31, 189
Mulan Parade, 165

N

New Year's Eve celebration, 12, 116
nightlife
    BoardWalk, 191
    dinner shows, 243, 245
    Downtown Disney Pleasure Island, 187-188
    Downtown Disney West Side, 189-190
    family entertainment, 61
    fireworks cruises, 202
    lounges, 249-251
Norway, 147-148, 222-223, 226

O

Oak Trail golf course, 206
Oasis, The, 171
O Canada!, 136
older travelers, hints for, 33
Orlando area
    accommodations, 86-87
    highways, 44
Orlando International Airport, 13
Orlando/Kissimmee Resort Hotel, 88
Osprey Ridge golf course, 206-207

P

packages (package tours), 8, 16
    tours for visitors with disabilities, 35

packing suggestions, 15
pagers, 40
Palm golf course, 206
Pangani Forest Exploration Trail, 175
parades, 115, 117, 165
parking, 44, 91, 121, 153, 169
Peabody Orlando, 87
PerriHouse Bed & Breakfast Inn, 85
Peter Pan's Flight, 104
pets, traveling with, 40
petting farm, 199
pharmacies, 39
physicians. see medical matters
picnicking, 20, 193, 195, 197, 204
Pirates of the Caribbean, 97
planning the trip, 7-42
    admission prices, 17-19
    crowd patterns, 8, 9
    getting there, 13-14
    hours, 10
    information sources, 15-16
    international travelers, 34
    itinerary time line, 23
    making a budget, 22
    money-saving tips, 14, 20-21, 33
    packages, 8, 16
    reference guide, 37-41
    reservations guide, 23, 53
    sample schedules, 24-31
    special events calendar, 11-12
    teens, tips for, 34
    telephone calls, 41
    travelers with disabilities, 35
    traveling with children, 32
    traveling without children, 33
    weather, 10, 41
    weddings and honeymoons, 36
    when to go, 8
Pocahontas and Her Forest Friends, 180
Polynesian resort, 49, 52, 55-57
    lounges, 56, 251
    restaurants, 56, 239
pontoon boats, 202, 209
Port Orleans resort, 51, 53, 70
    lounges, 70, 251
    restaurants, 70, 239
prescriptions, 39
priority seating at WDW restaurants, 216, 248

Q

Quality Inn Plaza (Orlando), 87

R

rain ponchos, 31, 112
rainy-day activities, 31
rating system for WDW resorts, 49-51
religious services, 40-41
reservations, 23, 53
    for dinner shows, 23, 243
    for golf courses, 207
    special room requests, 48, 66, 67
    for tennis courts, 208
    time line, 23

See also priority seating at WDW restaurants
restaurants, 215-248
    advance planning, 248
    All-Star resorts, 75, 236
    Beach Club resort, 64, 241
    Blizzard Beach, 195
    BoardWalk, 68, 236
    Bonnet Creek Golf Club, 240
    Caribbean Beach resort, 62, 237
    Contemporary resort, 54, 237
    Coronado Springs resort, 77, 237
    Crossroads of Lake Buena Vista, 235
    dining with children, 217, 244-245
    dining with Disney characters, 242, 244
    dinner shows, 243, 245
    Disney Cruise Line, 78-79
    Disney-MGM Studios, 228-230
    Disney's Animal Kingdom, 231-232
    Disney's Animal Kingdom Lodge, 76, 236
    Disney's Old Key West resort, 74, 237
    Disney's Wide World of Sports, 212
    Dixie Landings resort, 71, 237-238
    Dolphin resort, 66, 239-240
    Downtown Disney, 233-235
    Epcot, 221-227
    Fort Wilderness, 61, 200, 238
    Grand Floridian resort, 58, 238
    healthier options, 218
    Magic Kingdom, 111, 118, 216-220
    mealtime tips, 220, 227, 230, 232
    money-saving tips, 20
    Polynesian resort, 56, 239
    Port Orleans resort, 70, 239
    priority seating, 216, 248
    recommended restaurants, 244-247
    River Country, 197
    smoking policy, 216
    special requests, 225
    Swan resort, 66, 239-240
    tipping, 41
    Typhoon Lagoon, 193
    Villas at the Disney Institute, The, 73
    Wilderness Lodge, 60, 240
    Yacht Club resort, 64, 241
"rider switch" policy, 32
River Country, 196-197
rock climbing, 213
Rock 'n' Roller Coaster, 156
Rosen Plaza, 86
Royal Plaza, 83

S

Safari Village, 172-173, 181, 231-232
sailing, 210
salons, 37
sample schedules, 24-31
scuba diving, 127, 203
Sea Base Alpha, 127
senior citizens. see older travelers, hints for
Shades of Green, 57
shopping
    at Crossroads of Lake Buena Vista, 188

at Disney-MGM Studios, 163-164, 166
at Disney's Animal Kingdom, 181-182
at Disney's Wide World of Sports, 212
at Downtown Disney Marketplace, 185-186
at Downtown Disney Pleasure Island, 188
at Downtown Disney West Side, 190
at Magic Kingdom, 94, 111-114
mail-order shopping, 114
for necessities, 41
package pickup, 93, 122, 154, 170
See also World Showcase
single travelers, hints for, 33
smoking policies, 41
Snow White's Scary Adventures, 105
solo travelers, hints for, 33
Sounds Dangerous starring Drew Carey, 160
Space Mountain, 110
Spaceship Earth, 124-125
spas. *see* health clubs
special events
calendar of, 11-12
engagements, 36
weddings and honeymoons, 36
See also holiday happenings
SpectroMagic, 117
Splash Mountain, 99-100
sports, 205-214
basketball, 54, 200, 214
biking, 60, 63, 69, 70, 71, 73, 74, 77, 79, 198, 213
boating, 55, 56, 59, 60, 63, 65, 67, 70, 71, 73, 74, 77, 198, 209-210
Disney's Wide World of Sports, 31, 212
fishing, 56, 59, 60, 65, 69, 71, 73, 199, 210-211
golf, 73, 206-207, 213
health clubs, 55, 57 59, 60, 65, 67, 69, 73, 74, 77, 201, 213-214
hiking, 200
horseback riding, 199, 214
jogging, 56, 213
reservations guide, 23
rock climbing, 213
sailing, 210
scuba diving, 127, 203
stock car racing, 214
swimming, 55, 57, 59, 60, 63, 65, 67, 69, 70, 71, 73, 74, 75, 77, 79, 192, 193, 195, 196, 198, 211
tennis, 55, 57, 59, 65, 67, 69, 73, 74, 199, 208
volleyball, 54, 60, 66, 79, 200, 214
waterskiing, 55, 59, 210
stamps, 38
Star Tours, 161
stock car racing, 214
stroller rentals, 32, 93, 122, 138, 154, 170
Summerfield/Sierra Suites Lake Buena Vista, 85
Sunset Boulevard, 163-164

Swan resort, 50, 52, 65-67
lounges, 66, 251
restaurants, 66, 239-240
swimming, 55, 57, 59, 60, 63, 65, 67, 69, 70, 71, 73, 74, 75, 77, 79, 192, 193, 195, 196, 198, 211
Swiss Family Treehouse, 96

T

Tapestry of Nations, 149
Tarzan Rocks!, 179
taxi service, 46, 184
teenagers, tips for, 34
telephone calls, local, 41
temperature, year-round, 10
tennis, 55, 57, 59, 65, 67, 69, 73, 74, 199, 208
Test Track, 131
tickets. *see* admission prices
Timekeeper, The, 108
tipping, 41
Tomorrowland, 108-110, 114, 220
Tomorrowland Indy Speedway, 110
Tomorrowland Transit Authority, 109
Tom Sawyer Island, 98-99
tours. *see* guided tours; packages
trail rides, 199, 214
train travel, 14
transportation, 45-46
from airport to WDW, 13
to Blizzard Beach, 195
to Disney-MGM Studios, 153
to Disney's Animal Kingdom, 169
to Disney's Wide World of Sports complex, 212
to Downtown Disney, 184
to Epcot, 121
to Fort Wilderness, 61, 200
ID requirements, 46
to Magic Kingdom, 91, 92
money-saving tips, 14, 20-21
Orlando-area highways, 44
to River Country, 197
taxi service, 46, 184
travelers with disabilities, 35
traveling arrangements, 23
to Typhoon Lagoon, 193
Walt Disney World transportation system, 45-46
See also air travel; bus travel; car travel; train travel
Transportation and Ticket Center (TTC), 19, 45, 46, 55, 59, 60, 61, 70, 91, 92, 118, 121, 153
travel agents, using, 14, 16
traveler's checks, 40
Tree of Life, The, 172-173
Tri-Circle-D Ranch, 199-200
Twilight Zone Tower of Terror,The 155-156
Typhoon Lagoon, 192-193

U

United Kingdom, 136-138, 224-225
Universe of Energy, 133-134

V

Villas at the Disney Institute, The, 50, 53, 72-73
Villas of Grand Cypress, 84-85
visual disabilities, hints for guests with, 35
volleyball, 54, 60, 66, 79, 200, 214
Voyage of The Little Mermaid, 157

W

Walt Disney's Carousel of Progress, 109
Walt Disney Travel Company, 8, 16
Walt Disney World Railroad, 91, 95
water parks, 192-197
Blizzard Beach, 194-195
hours, 10
picnicking, 20, 193, 195, 197
River Country, 196-197
Typhoon Lagoon, 192-193
waterskiing, 55, 59, 210
WDW information (WDW-INFO), 15
weather, 10, 41
rainy days, 31, 112
Websites
www.disneycruise.com, 15, 78
www.disneytravel.com, 16
www.disneyworld.com, 8, 15, 20, 23, 35
weddings and honeymoons, 36
wheelchair rentals, 35, 93, 122, 138, 154, 170
Wilderness Cabins (at Fort Wilderness), 52, 61
Wilderness Lodge & Villas, 42, 50, 52, 59-60
lounges, 60, 251
restaurants, 60, 240
Wonders of China, 146-147
Wonders of Life, 131-133
World Showcase, 119, 135-148
American Adventure, The, 142-143, 226
Canada, 136, 223, 226
China, 146-147, 224, 226
entertainment, 149
France, 138-139, 223-224, 226
Germany, 145-146, 223, 227
International Gateway, 138
Italy, 144-145, 224
Japan, 141-142, 224, 227
map, 120
Mexico, 148, 226
Morocco, 140, 224, 227
Norway, 147-148, 222-223, 226
restaurants, 138, 222-227
shopping, 136, 137, 138, 139-142, 143, 144-146, 147-148
stroller and wheelchair rentals, 138
Tapestry of Nations, 149
United Kingdom, 136-138, 224-225
Wyndham Palace Resort & Spa, 83, 201
Wynfield Inn Westwood, 87

Y

Yacht Club resort, 50, 52, 64-65
lounges, 64, 251
restaurants, 64, 241